LET THE PEOPLE SEE

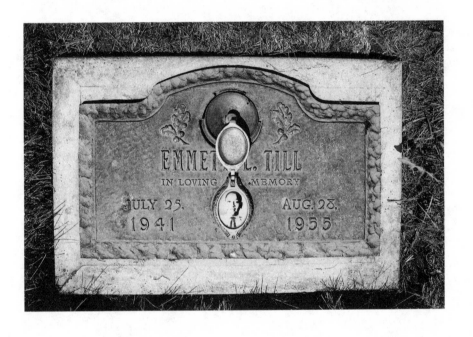

LET THE PEOPLE SEE

THE STORY OF EMMETT TILL

ELLIOTT J. GORN

OXFORD
UNIVERSITY PRESS
2018

OXFORD
UNIVERSITY PRESS

Oxford University Press is a department of the University of Oxford.
It furthers the University's objective of excellence in research, scholarship,
and education by publishing worldwide. Oxford is a registered trade mark of
Oxford University Press in the UK and certain other countries.

Published in the United States of America by Oxford University Press
198 Madison Avenue, New York, NY 10016, United States of America.

Library of Congress Cataloging-in-Publication Data
Names: Gorn, Elliott J., 1951– author.
Title: Let the people see : the story of Emmett Till / Elliott J. Gorn.
Other titles: Story of Emmett Till
Description: New York: Oxford University Press, [2018]
Identifiers: LCCN 2018001885 I ISBN 9780199325122 (hardback : alk. paper)
Subjects: LCSH: Till, Emmett, 1941–1955. I
Lynching—Mississippi—History—20th century. I African Americans—Crimes
against—Mississippi. I Racism—Mississippi—History—20th century I
Trials (Murder)—Mississippi—Sumner. I Hate crimes—Mississippi. I
Till-Mobley, Mamie, 1921–2003. I Racism—Mississippi—History—20th
century. I United States—Race relations—History—20th century. I
Mississippi—Race relations.
Classification: LCC HV6465.M7 G67 2018 I DDC 364.1/34 [B] —dc23 LC record
available at https://lccn.loc.gov/2018001885

3 5 7 9 8 6 4
Printed by Sheridan Books, Inc., United States of America

For Jade and Farid

Chinese + Bessarabian + Latvian + Iranian + Canadian = American

CONTENTS

TRIAL

69

MEMORY
233

LIST OF ILLUSTRATIONS

INTRODUCTION

WE ALL KNOW the story: In late August 1955, a fourteen-year-old Chicago kid named Emmett Till went to visit family in Mississippi. At a crossroads store in the tiny Delta town of Money, Till whistled at the white woman behind the counter. A few days later, he was kidnapped, beaten, and shot. His abductors weighted his body down and threw it in the Tallahatchie River.

A friend of mine from Chicago was also fourteen when they murdered Emmett Till. He told me recently about the photo he saw back then in the newspaper, a photo of Till's body after it had been pulled from the river, his face crushed, a cotton-gin fan tied around his neck with barbed wire as a weight.

No such photo exists. No journalists were by the riverbank to take pictures, and the police photographer who waited back at the sheriff's office in Greenwood took the official photos long after they cleaned the muck off Till's body and removed the weights tied around his neck.

Maybe my friend was thinking of the funeral pictures, taken a few days later in Chicago, and which have now become horrifically iconic. When Mamie Till Bradley saw how savagely her son had been beaten, she asked the mortician not to prettify him, and more, she insisted on a glass top over his coffin. "Let the people see what they did to my boy," she famously said.

But I am sure my friend did not see those photos either. He is white. He was not a reader of *Jet* magazine or the *Chicago Defender*, two publications that carried them. African Americans across the country saw the pictures. They passed them around, discussed them, and took grim determination from them. While mainstream newspapers and magazines devoted lots of coverage to the Till story, none published the photos of Emmett's battered face. Few white Americans saw those now-infamous images until video documentaries of the Civil Rights Movement made by African Americans began to appear late in the 1980s.

Our memories are not always reliable. Emmett Till's story has been repeated so often in recent years, the photographs so widely reproduced, that it feels as if we have always known about them. Even as I write these words, a new cover story in *Time* magazine, "The Most Influential Images of All Time," featuring the one hundred photos that "changed the world," includes two of Emmett Till. These photographs "proved a black life matters," *Time*'s editors declared; the pictures "forced the world to reckon with the brutality of American racism."[1]

Seeing had moral consequences in *Time*'s telling of the story; Americans were converted by the visceral impact of those horrifying images. But if "seeing" did not happen until decades later, then surely it could not explain that moral reckoning. Similarly, in 1995, forty years after covering the trial of Till's killers in Sumner, Mississippi, the journalist David Halberstam called it "The first great media event of the Civil Rights Movement." Yet only after all that time had passed could Halberstam understand fully the significance of what he witnessed back in 1955, only then could he put the name Emmett Till together with "media event" and "Civil Rights Movement."[2]

The Till saga is like that. Our popular version of the story, worn smooth as an ancient ballad, tells the essential truths: that an innocent boy was murdered because he violated a social code he did not understand, that his mother invited the world to look at his destroyed face, and that her courage helped propel the Civil Rights Movement. All of this is true. The implied part, however, is not. That the crucifixion in Emmett Till's face softened white peoples' hearts and put America on the road to racial justice—that, as a television report on CNN put it in 2003, "everything changed after the murder of Emmett Till"—is a pleasant untruth. Few white people saw the photographs. Radical change demanded years more struggle and far more blood.[3]

Depending on who told it, where, when, and why, Emmett Till's story was filled with ambiguity, distortions, even outright lies. Whole books have been written about the murder expressly to test and debunk some of the "facts" that have grown up around it—among them, that Emmett's cousins egged him on to whistle at the white woman at Bryant's Grocery Store; that Emmett bragged about his white girlfriends back in Chicago; that Emmett acted belligerently toward his captors. Getting the facts straight is a worthy goal for its own sake, but also because truth is a precondition of justice.

Still, to seek only the literal truth misses something larger about Emmett Till's story, which was never simple, never reducible to mere facts. Even things we know as stone-hard truth—that white men savagely beat a black boy, then executed him for reasons that seem trivial—has mystery at its core: How can we comprehend this blend of sadism and bigotry? Where does such evil come from? How could whole communities, whole states, a whole region rationalize the atrocity? As is always true of the past, the literal truth takes us only so far in exploring moral questions, the very heart of historical studies.

The Emmett Till story is an American Rashomon, for how it was told in 1955 or 1985 or 2015 depended not just on "the facts" but on what you believed they were, what they ought to be, and above all, what they meant. Of course, it is the historian's duty to get the facts as accurately as possible. Not all versions of a story are equal; some claims are demonstrably false, shamelessly prejudiced, self-serving. Some tellings are fuller, richer, and more accurate than others. That there are things we can never know for sure, however, is also a fact, and understanding how people try to fill those gaps carries its own kind of truth.

Sixty years after they killed Emmett Till, his story refuses to go away. Indeed, his memory is more alive now than at any time since 1955, invoked in many variations. I know African American parents who told their children about him in order to teach them the savage history of racism and warn them of its living perils. While doing research for this book I also met white Mississippians who told me that Till was indeed a would-be rapist with designs on Carolyn Bryant, designs that were foiled only at the last minute. Back in Chicago, I heard northerners talk about his murder with all the regional sanctimoniousness of 1955, as if racism was purely a southern phenomenon, then and now.

Today, some tell Emmett Till's story to illustrate how far we have traveled in racial relations, how America has overcome the bigotry of his killers, how our tears for this long-dead child reveal our own purity of heart. Others vehemently disagree, arguing that his lynching was a textbook case of race-based injustice, foreshadowing contemporary chapters filled with police shootings of unarmed black men. How people have told the Emmett Till story over the years depended on why they were telling it.

Like the buses of Montgomery and the neighborhoods of Chicago, memory itself was segregated. African Americans kept Emmett Till's flame alive through the years of the Civil Rights Movement, and activists born around the same time as the young martyr are sometimes referred to as "the Emmett Till generation." But white Americans whose local newspapers and television sets carried daily stories about him in September 1955 had all but forgotten him a year later, and the media did little to remind them. A generation after his death, Till's name was mostly gone from their history and memory.

That started to change beginning in the late 1980s. The PBS television history of the Civil Rights Movement *Eyes on the Prize* aired in early 1987. The first few minutes highlighted Till's murder, implicitly marking his story as the beginning of the freedom struggle. The next thirty years witnessed a rising tide of new material: books—both academic and popular—articles, anthologies, documentaries, museum exhibits, and websites. Just in the last two years came Devery Anderson's substantial work of historical sleuthing, *Emmett Till: The Murder That Shocked the World and Propelled the Civil Rights Movement*, followed by Timothy Tyson's *The Blood of Emmett Till*, which featured Carolyn Bryant's startling yet vague admission that she lied back in 1955.

I have two goals in this book: To tell the Emmett Till story well, and to take it seriously as a story. The first part means capturing what happened with fairness and accuracy. The second part is trickier. In telling the story, I am joining many others who have done so over the years. Till's murder came at a particularly fraught moment in American racial history, when the mere suggestion of anything sexual between black men and white women was social dynamite. For example, newspapers were powerful organs of opinion in 1955, and how they first reported the story—was it a lynching or a murder, an honor killing or mere bloodlust?—reflected deep racial, regional, and political assumptions. A month later, the sensational trial of Till's killers in Sumner, Mississippi, sharpened the conflicts, as attorneys and witnesses, judge and jury fought over the evidence and its interpretation. How to tell the story—and whether to tell it at all—grew more contentious, as Americans struggled with their assumptions about race, segregation, rights, and equality. Months after the trial, Americans kept relitigating the case, probing its meanings, interpreting its significance.

Let the People See tries to capture the shock that Americans felt in 1955 when suddenly their attention was riveted on the Mississippi Delta. I take readers inside the courtroom to hear the attorneys and the witnesses in order to understand what was at stake during that hot week in Sumner. On trial were not just Till's killers but Jim Crow segregation, the Southern

Way of Life. On trial, too, was how Americans thought about race and, more explosively, how they thought about race *and* sex. Above all, I explore not just history but memory: How and why have we forgotten and remembered the story over the years?

This book is arranged chronologically in four sections: "Murder," "Trial," "Verdicts," and "Memory." Till's body was no sooner pulled from the Tallahatchie River than questions began. Would the federal government intervene in the case? How should the press cover the story? Was the body really Till or someone else? By the time the killers came to trial, it had become an international story, headline news as the world struggled with decolonization and the Cold War. For six months, into early 1956, the press was filled with accusations, confessions, and new revelations. Tens of thousands of African Americans joined Emmett Till rallies across America. Then as quickly as it came, interest in Emmett Till almost vanished, among white people anyway, only to be revived decades later as America began to reassess its long racial past.

Let the People See is an African American story and a southern one too, but above all, it is an American story about race and racism. Two bookends flank this volume, the election of Barack Obama in 2008 and that of Donald Trump in 2016. I began research shortly after the former and finished writing a year after the latter. That moment in Chicago's Grant Park in 2008 when Obama took the stage as America's president-elect remains an electrifying memory. No matter the accomplishments or disappointments of the next eight years, America did something remarkable that day. Fifty-three years earlier, when Emmett Till went to Mississippi, most African Americans could neither vote nor run for office, let alone imagine a black president.

Yet America had not suddenly become "post-racial," quite the contrary. As if operating under some inexorable law of physics the reaction set in, starting with innuendo—he was an African, an Islamist, certainly not an American. A leading purveyor of these racist charges became our next president. He doubled down: Mexicans were criminals, Muslims terrorists, African countries shitholes.

I never thought we would elect a black president in my lifetime, and I never thought we would regress to the likes of Donald Trump. As a historian, I should have known better, America has done this repeatedly: Civil Rights Movement follows Jim Crow which follows emancipation; racially motivated laws slam shut the doors of immigration, followed by reopened doors, followed by dreams of impenetrable walls; we defeat a racist Japanese regime while imprisoning our own Japanese American citizens, then apologize to them decades later. Less a mountain to climb or a nightmare to wake up from, racism is more like a shape-shifting demon we must wrestle again and again.

The Emmett Till story has been like that, disappearing, then resurfacing in new guises. A friend of mine who was born in Mississippi a decade after the Till lynching, recalled a joke he heard as a boy. On any occasion when whites denigrated blacks, someone might remark that they were so ignorant they would steal a chain and a gin fan and try to escape across a river. Years later, my friend visited Botswana in southern Africa. Introduced to some local gentlemen, he told them that he was from Mississippi. "Oh yeah," one of them said? Did you hear the one about the black who stole a length of chain? He would have gotten away with it if he hadn't tried to swim a river with it." They all had heard that one, knew the joke.

Emmett Till's killers could not hold his memory down any more than his body, and it still keeps surfacing in unexpected times and places. Even as this book goes to press, the FBI once again is reopening the Till case. Conscience, like the dark Tallahatchie River, gives up its secrets in its own good time.

MURDER

CHAPTER ONE

I SEEN TWO KNEES AND FEET

SEVENTEEN-YEAR-OLD Robert Hodges walked down to the Tallahatchie River at dawn on Wednesday morning, the last day of August 1955, to check his fishing lines. A month later, Assistant District Attorney Robert Smith questioned the young man about what he saw:

Smith: Robert, did anything unusual happen while you were out there setting out the lines?
Hodges: Yes, Sir. I seen two knees and feet.
Smith: Just describe to the jury and court what you saw there.
Hodges: Well, I saw right along here, up and down, both of them (gesturing with his hands along his own lower legs).
Smith: And that would be from the top part of the legs and knees down, is that right?
Hodges: Yes, Sir....

Hodges told the court that the legs were part of a body hung up on a snag in the Tallahatchie, head, trunk and thighs below, naked knees, shins and feet floating on the surface. He checked his fishing lines, then went home to tell his father about it. Hodges Senior, a white tenant farmer, contacted his landlord, B. L. Mims, who alerted Deputy Sheriff Garland Melton, and all came back for the body in two boats. They tied a rope around the legs, dragged the corpse to shore, then laid it face down in one of the boats.[1]

Attorney Smith continued his questioning:

Smith: When you pulled it out on the bank, what if anything, was attached to the body?
Hodges: An iron weight.
Smith: What?
Hodges: A weight.
Smith: What kind of a weight was it?
Hodges: A gin fan.
Smith: Robert, how was that weight or fan, as you say, attached to the body?
Hodges: With a piece of barbed wire.
Smith: How was the barbed wire attached to the body?
Hodges: It was wrapped around his neck....

The prosecutor asked Hodges to examine a seventy-four-pound gin fan and a length of barbed wire resting on the floor in front of the witness stand. Hodges identified them as the very ones wrapped around the body they'd fished out of the Tallahatchie that hot summer morning.[2]

Next, Attorney Smith asked young Hodges about the corpse.

Smith: Did you have a chance to observe the body there relative to any blows or wounds of any kind?
Hodges: It was beaten pretty bad in the back.
Smith: On the back?
Hodges: Yes, Sir, and hips.
Smith: What about the head?
Hodges: It was also gashed in on the side....

The attorney for the defense, J. J. Breland, rose and objected to the witness's statement that the body had been beaten. Judge Curtis Swango agreed and instructed young Hodges to limit his testimony to descriptions of the body itself, to make no inferences as to the causes of any marks or wounds. Judge Swango added, addressing the jury, "And you gentlemen will, of course, disregard that statement made by the witness."[3]

Landlord Mims followed Hodges on the witness stand, and in his brief remarks he confirmed how he, Deputy Melton and the others found the body, dragged it ashore, and put it in the boat. He added one important detail: "We could tell by looking at it that it was a colored person."[4]

CHAPTER TWO

ARGO, ILLINOIS

EMMETT TILL'S KIN WERE part of the Great Migration. After the Civil War, black freedom meant movement. People who previously could not leave the plantation without risking a whipping or worse now exercised their newfound liberty. For the first fifty years after emancipation, most of them moved within the South to nearby towns or across county lines, or maybe to the next state. They went searching for family members sold away in the slave trade or for better terms as farmers or for jobs in the cities. Others simply enjoyed getting around, an exhilarating new feeling.[1]

Early in the twentieth century, however, the flow of people on the road changed, deepened, increasingly ran to the North out of the old Confederate states, to New York City, and to the booming industrial towns along the Great Lakes like Cleveland, Detroit, and above all, Chicago. The First World War gave a big boost to this trend, as many African Americans went north to take advantage of job opportunities created by the crisis. Illinois Central Railroad trains, running straight from New Orleans through the Mississippi Delta to the Windy City, grew ever more crowded.[2]

In the fifty years after 1900, half of Emmett Till's extended family remained in the South, half headed north. His great uncle Moses Wright, born in 1892, was committed to farming in Mississippi, but he moved repeatedly within the state, always in search of a landlord who would not cheat him, first to Durant in Holmes County, then over to Schlater in Leflore County, then north to Money, also in Leflore County—all within a thirty-mile radius. Moses' wife, Elizabeth Smith—granddaughter of a white slave owner—traveled further, from Hazelhurst south of Jackson to Webb in the Delta, then to Memphis to teach school, 250 miles from where she started, before settling down in nearby Money with Moses. But her younger sister Alma was much more footloose. She married a man named Wiley Nash Carthan, "John," friends called him, and they followed the human stream north toward Chicago.[3]

Southern migrants like the Carthans certainly did not find paradise, but they were not so naïve as to expect it. The North had its own patterns of racism and inequality, of neighborhood and workplace segregation, and of violence for those who "got out of line." Residentially, Chicago was rigidly divided. Much of the South Side was jammed with black migrants from Mississippi and neighboring states, forbidden to buy or rent property elsewhere in the city. Urban density only grew over the decades as more and more people crammed inside segregated boundaries that expanded only slowly. The borderlands between black and white neighborhoods were always tense, and sometimes violence exploded, as it did during the summer of 1919 in a terrible race riot that claimed thirty-eight lives, or in later years with frequent bombings and assaults when black families tried to move to homes on white streets.[4]

Still, life in Chicago, like most of the industrial North, was better than life in the Deep South. African Americans could vote, giving them a little political clout. Some acquired property, a few owned their own businesses, industry offered more ways to earn a decent living. And for their children, school terms were longer and teachers better. Far from perfect, Chicago still remained "the land of hope."[5]

But the Carthans did not move to Chicago, not exactly; they would not live within the city limits until the 1950s. In 1923, Wiley Carthan found steady work in Argo, Illinois, an adjoining town still in Cook County, about twelve miles south and west of downtown Chicago. Carthan sent for his wife and two-year-old daughter Mamie in January 1924, and the family made Argo its home for most of the next three decades. Though born in Cook County Hospital, July 25, 1941, Emmett grew up in Argo.[6]

The town's official name was Summit, and it was there, almost three hundred years earlier, that native peoples showed Father Jacques Marquette and the French explorer Louis Joliet the portage that connected the Mississippi River—via the Chicago, Des Plaines, and Illinois Rivers—to Lake Michigan. Roughly a mile north of where Emmett Till grew up was the very spot—

the summit, the tiny continental divide just a few feet higher than the land to the east or west—that separated the two great North American watersheds.[7]

Follow the St. Lawrence River inland from the Atlantic Ocean to Lake Ontario, and from there along those fresh water seas to the southwest corner of Lake Michigan at its confluence with the Chicago River; now follow that little river just a dozen miles west then south, to where it comes within a few thousand feet of the Des Plaines River. Cross that portage—that summit separating the two rivers, frozen in winter, muddy in spring and fall, dry in summer—and the whole Mississippi basin beckons, all the way west to the foothills of the Rocky Mountains and south to the Gulf of Mexico. Once across that little patch of land, the eastern two-thirds of what became the continental United States opened up to markets via water transport.[8]

Centuries after Indians as well as French trappers and traders carried their canoes across the portage, Americans built the Illinois and Michigan Canal in 1848, then finally in 1900 the Chicago Ship and Sanitary Canal. Railroads followed these water routes, and the pattern was set: growing up right alongside the summit, Chicago made itself the gatekeeper, the fulcrum for commercial and industrial development in the heartland. Emmett Till was raised right beside the very place that opened Chicago to the Great West and to the Deep South.[9]

The lower part of Summit was called Argo in honor of the world's largest corn processing plant, built in 1906 on a plot of land more than one hundred acres in size, south of Sixty-Third street and west of Archer Avenue, alongside the canal. The Corn Products Refining Company manufactured things like corn syrup, cooking oil, processed foods, and laundry starch under trade names such as Mazola, Karo, Bosco, and of course, Argo—household words in a burgeoning consumer society. In the 1920s and '30s, the company expanded its refining operations into Korea, Japan, Argentina, Columbia, Brazil, and Mexico. This was big business, a multinational corporation. The enormous plant in Argo, Illinois, employed thousands, and in the 1920s, the company even built housing for its workers. The Carthan family arrived in boom times, and the burgeoning population strained the town's schools and services.[10]

Though it was just beyond the metropolis, the town of Argo replicated in miniature Chicago's blue-collar character; it was less a bedroom community than an industrial satellite town. With the canal just to the west and multiple railroad spurs, Argo attracted midsized factories where thousands of European immigrants and their sons found steady labor. So did hundreds of African Americans, migrating up from the South, especially in the 1920s, when Argo and Summit boomed with post–World War I demand. Men like Wiley Carthan took their place on Corn Product's floor, as did his future son-in-law, Louis Till, Emmett's father.[11]

It was dirty, dangerous work. African Americans got the least-skilled, lowest-paid jobs; rarely were they offered the more desirable positions. But when a Congress of Industrial Organizations union came to Corn Products late in the 1930s, all workers began to receive better pay, overtime, and benefits. The Argo local of the Oil, Chemical, and Atomic Workers Union brought to the men in the plant, black and white, a measure of dignity and security that translated into a decent material life for their families. Once again, it was never equality for African Americans, but it was fairer than Mississippi. Argo was not pretty, it smelled of factory waste and sewage overflows, but all of that was part of the bargain for jobs, homes, and a livelihood.[12]

So when the Carthans arrived, Argo-Summit was a semi-self-contained community of roughly twelve thousand people—stable, growing, with its own schools, churches, mayor's office, police department, and a newspaper serving the local area. It was long a remarkably diverse community. In the mid-1920s, three out of five residents were either immigrants or the children of immigrants, Poles, Slovaks, Russians, and Italians. Nearly 10 percent of the population was African American, and by the time Emmett Till grew up, that figure was between 15 and 20 percent.[13]

People kept to themselves, but Argo felt safe, safer than Mississippi or Chicago. Doors went unlocked, or keys were conveniently placed under front-porch mats. Black people came as tendrils of extended families, chain migrations from Delta towns. Emmett's mother called Argo "Little Mississippi." Some of the warmth and security of rural and small-town life made its way north: "Our whole neighborhood was like an extended family," she wrote fifty years later in her memoirs. "Aunt Marie and Uncle Kid and June Bug lived west of us. Uncle Crosby and his family lived to the east of us. In back of us were Aunt Babe and Uncle Emmett, and in front of us was Bo's great-uncle, Lee Green." "Bo" was young Emmett: everyone called him "Bobo," or "Bo" for short.[14]

African Americans lived mostly in modest single- and two-family homes at the southern edge of town below Sixty-Third Street and to the west along the fringe between Archer Avenue and the canal, all just a few minutes' walk to the Corn Products plant. Argo was segregated, though not rigidly so. The 1930 census, for example, shows one race or the other predominating on each block but not strict segregation door to door. Ten years later, the census reveals that residential segregation had intensified but not with the rigidity of, say, Chicago's South Side.[15]

Black-owned small businesses catered mostly to black patrons. The stores clustered around Sixty-Third and Archer were the center of African American commercial life, a handful of taverns and restaurants, a barbershop, and so on. The local bank made home loans to blacks, but generally not on predominantly white blocks. Schools were integrated, as were the athletic teams and leagues. Mamie Carthan graduated with honors from Argo High, the town's only upper school. Still, whites mostly called blacks by their first names, rarely the reverse.[16]

It was far from perfect, but so much better than what they had left behind. African Americans did not talk a lot about what they had endured down south, Emmett's mother recalled years later, but the memories—of lynchings, beatings, poverty, humiliation—were alive, invoked just often enough to keep Argo feeling like a haven. She recalled of the 1940s and '50s, "it really seemed like almost everybody from Mississippi was coming through our house—the Ellis Island of Chicago. Actually, it was more like a terminal on the Underground Railroad."[17]

And she remembered her own mother, Alma, as a Harriet Tubman figure, taking in relatives and friends, helping them find jobs at Corn Products and homes in the neighborhood, making her own Sunday dinner table the communal center: "Our house was the meetinghouse, the gathering place, the center of the community. It was the place where Mama had helped to found the Argo Temple Church of God in Christ, and where she recruited new church members with practically each new Mississippi migrant." There was a sense of promise here, of hope, of a better life for one's children, a version of the American Dream.[18]

Of course, all was not sweetness and light. Mamie had painful memories of her parents' marriage falling apart when she was eleven years old, during the Great Depression. Wiley Carthan used to disappear on weekends, and only later did his daughter learn that to earn extra money, he played piano for tips and drinks at clubs in Chicago. Alma, with her strict rules and strong attachment to the church, disapproved. One day Carthan gave his daughter a nickel and then drove away, just like any other Friday, except this time he never came back. He found work in Detroit, and father and daughter were estranged for nearly twenty years. More than ever, Alma was Mamie's rock. Socially and spiritually centered, Alma gave Mamie a stable if highly sheltered home life. And Mamie thrived, first in school, and then with a series of solid white-collar civil service jobs. It was certainly not all that one of her ability might aspire to, but it was far better than what seemed possible in her family just a generation earlier.[19]

Freshly graduated with honors from high school in 1940, Mamie fell in love with a young man named Louis Till. Till was five feet ten inches tall, good-looking, a boxer. He was new in town when they met, having recently come north from New Madrid, Missouri. He left school after eighth grade, knocked around, and now worked as a laborer at Corn Products. Mamie still lived at home, and Louis Till was the first man she ever dated. When Alma Carthan finally let her daughter get beyond chatting on the front porch with him, the couple walked down to Berg's Drugstore for banana splits. Berg served African Americans, but only on a take-out basis. Louis Till was either unaware of that fact or had no intention of respecting it. He paid for their sundaes and they walked from the counter to a booth by the window. Mr. Berg came out to protest, but before he could say much, Till simply stood up slowly and stared at him. Berg retreated. Seeing the young couple in the window, other blacks came in, ordered ice cream, and ate it right there in the store. Mamie Carthan was deeply impressed.[20]

That initial good impression lasted long enough for the couple to get married in Alma's front room a few months later, conceive a child, and move into their own apartment. However, it became increasingly clear while Mamie was pregnant and then, in the months after Emmett was born, that Louis Till was not the husband she had hoped for. He gambled away the rent money, drank too much, and considered sexual fidelity optional. And he was physically abusive. One night when Emmett was just a few months old, staying with his grandmother, Louis came home drunk and angry about his gambling losses; the next thing Mamie knew he was beating and choking her. When she came to, he was gone. Knowing he would soon be back, she turned out the lights, boiled a pot of water, and when he walked through the door she flung it at him, burning him so badly that some of the skin peeled away.[21]

Over the next few weeks, Till stalked his wife, alternately sweet-talking, threatening, and browbeating her. She refused to reconcile and got a court order to keep him away, which he violated once too often. The judge gave him a choice, jail or the army. He was inducted on July 9, 1942, seven months after the Japanese attack on Pearl Harbor and America's entry into World War II. He came back once from basic training to see his son and try to persuade his wife to get back together. As they chatted, military police knocked on her apartment door. When she answered, they came in and arrested Louis Till. He was AWOL.[22]

After the army shipped him out to Europe, a small military pension came for Emmett and Mamie each month. Louis also occasionally sent home his winnings from boxing matches and gambling. Then in July 1945, two months after the war in Europe ended, the money stopped coming, and Mamie Till received a telegram that her husband had died in Italy. There was no explanation as to the circumstances of his death, she later said, just the words "willful misconduct." The army returned a few of Louis Till's effects, including a ring he bought in Casablanca, inscribed with the initials "L.T." and the date May 25, 1943.[23]

So Emmett Till never really knew his father, and given the circumstances of their estrangement, Mamie probably spoke of Louis infrequently. Emmett's young life held other hardships too. At age six, he contracted infantile paralysis, polio, a disease that killed and maimed children until just after midcentury when Jonas Salk and others finally developed an effective inoculation. Emmett was lucky; he had a mild case of the disease. It left him with a slight limp and a speech impediment, a stutter, nothing terrible, though occasionally he struggled to get words out. Mamie taught him to whistle when he started to stammer, a trick that usually got the flow of words going again.[24]

Despite these troubles, Emmett Till had a mostly happy childhood. His mother held steady clerical jobs, first at the Coffee School of Aeronautics—which trained African American pilots, including several cadets who joined the Tuskegee Airmen during the war—and at the Social Security Administration, so the family's material life was stable, though far from lavish. He never lacked for a bicycle or baseball equipment. The family had a radio and a television, and Emmett especially liked comedy—Abbott and Costello, Dean Martin and Jerry Lewis, and his favorite, "Lonesome" George Gobel. Emmett also was a bit of a clotheshorse, a passion his mother indulged.[25]

And it was not just material things. Mamie and Alma and the whole extended family made sure Bo got plenty of love and attention. His cousin Thelma, twelve years old when Emmett was born, came up from Money, Mississippi, to go to school, and she helped take care of him. Another cousin, Loretha, also helped raise Bobo. When he was just three, his five-year-old cousin Wheeler Parker moved next door, and they became fast friends. In the coming years, they wandered all over town, played games and sports together, explored Argo's industrial landscape, biked everywhere.[26]

Beyond Argo, there were family trips to the Brookfield Zoo and Riverview Amusement Park in Chicago. As a student, Emmett was solid and conscientious, but he was more interested in making his classmates laugh than earning As. He talked about being a fireman or policeman someday, or maybe a Major League baseball player, manly, heroic jobs, and not unreasonable for an African American kid living near Chicago—Argo's tiny police force had a black cop, Chicago long had hired black civil servants, and Emmett even got to watch Minnie Minoso, the White

Sox star third-baseman, play ball in Comiskey Park, just a few miles east of Argo.[27]

Of course, theirs was not a perfect world. Mamie subscribed to the *Chicago Defender*, the crusading black newspaper that circulated every week far beyond the metropolis and into African America. The *Defender*, and other papers like New York's *Amsterdam News*, the Pittsburgh *Courier*, the *Baltimore Afro-American*, and the St. Louis *Argus* made sure readers understood how formal and informal codes of segregation operated in the North. The *Defender*, for example, inveighed against the customs and policies segregating Chicago's South and West Sides, the "redlining" of neighborhoods by government agencies, the refusal of banks to grant loans to African American customers, the "block-busting" real estate brokers who manipulated the housing market, not to mention the bombings and riots fomented by vigilantes against blacks who dared move into white neighborhoods.[28]

But Argo was less harsh, and Emmett's early life seemed far away from Chicago's turmoil. He was funny and mischievous, a bit of a prankster. He and his friends memorized humorous routines they'd picked up from radio and television and entertained anyone who would listen to their versions. Bo was not a troubled kid and never attracted the attention of juvenile authorities, but he was high-spirited. "I know him...I lived next door to him," Wheeler Parker remembered of his younger cousin decades later. Parker called Emmett "Leo the Lion." He meant that like others born in July, Emmett loved being the center of attention, making others laugh, acting a little outrageous. Bo's Mississippi cousin, Simeon Wright, recalled how Emmett was a great storyteller, how he could talk endlessly about the excitements of Chicago, and keep his Mississippi kin enthralled. Never a gifted athlete—at age fourteen Emmett was about five feet four, and pudgy at 150 pounds—he nonetheless loved baseball and basketball and played both with passion. He had an ability to joke with people and keep them smiling, laughing.[29]

Sometimes Emmett took things a little far. Wheeler Parker remembered walking with Emmett and their cousin Sonny Crosby on a South Side street in Chicago in 1953. Emmett was twelve, his companions a couple of years older, and when they passed some other teens, Emmett blurted out, "I've got my two big cousins here from Argo, Illinois, and can't n-n-nobody beat them up." By the midfifties, most Chicagoans had heard about gangs on South Side streets and how violent they could be. "We looked at him," Parker told an interviewer fifty years later, "'Have you lost your mind?' We grabbed him up real quick!...Those are the kinds of things he would do, and it was funny to him. It wasn't funny to us at all, because, as far as we were concerned, he could have got us killed." But Emmett was not hard-edged or mean, Parker added, emphatically; "I never saw him angry or bitter at anybody. Never! Never!"[30]

A few stories intimated that Emmett could be tougher than Parker let on. Argo had become a bit claustrophobic for Mamie, and in 1951 she took the opportunity to reconnect her son with her father in Detroit, and to date a man there she called "Pink." She found work at the army induction center in Fort Wayne, Indiana, and had Bo stay with friends and family in Detroit, while she commuted. Emmett was very unhappy, and he eventually persuaded her to let him return to Argo and live with his grandmother and other relatives. Mamie married Pink, but once they were wed he lost all interest in working and became increasingly abusive. The couple moved back to Argo, where their troubles deepened. Finally, one day Mamie asked Pink to leave. He threatened her, then Emmett appeared in the doorway. "Pink," she recalled her son's words, "Mama wants you to go and I think you should go." Mamie noticed that Emmett held a butcher knife from the kitchen, and he added, "If you put your hands on her…I *will* cut you." Mamie managed to hustle Pink out of her home before it went any farther; soon he was out of her life for good.[31]

Mamie took a civil service job as a clerk working for the air force in an office just south of the Loop, making $3,600 per year. She and Emmett settled into the South Side of Chicago, in a home on St. Lawrence Street, just below Sixty-Third, a two-flat on a block of mostly family-owned homes. Emmett was an eighth grader at the McCosh School, located just around the corner, with its 1,600 students, all black, enrolled in kindergarten through grade eight. McCosh's principal, Curtis Melnick, remembered Emmett as an average student, quiet in school, but never in any trouble. He made friends, and once again, there was extended family in the neighborhood.[32]

Still, Mamie worked long days, sometimes into the weekends, so Emmett carried much of the load around the house. When he was not in school, he swept, cleaned, did the laundry, paid bills, and made dinner. One neighbor recalled that Emmett "kept that house a-shining," and described how torn he was one day between painting the garage and playing baseball with his friends, running back and forth from one to the other. Everyone on St. Lawrence Street described Emmett as a good kid, close to his mother, lively, and a regular churchgoer. One final change came to the Till household in 1954; Mamie met, dated, and married Gene Mobley, an autoworker and part-time barber. Bo quickly grew close to his stepfather, who had two daughters of his own.[33]

But Emmett Till was the sort of youth who needed a close circle of friends, and he did not really have that in Chicago. He missed Argo and all of his chums, so he took the streetcar back to his old haunts (about an hour's ride) and spent most weekends with family and friends. "I never worried about him when he was there," Mamie recalled:

> I knew he was in good hands. I knew the entire community was looking out for him. It had always been that way. Kids in Argo couldn't walk to the corner without speaking to every adult they saw, by name. They'd have to do the same thing on the way back. Argo was a good fit for Emmett....He would hang out with his friends all day on Saturdays and spend a good part of Sundays in Church, where, of course, he'd find his friends again. He lived for the fellowship. He lived for the fun. That most of all.

Her son and the other boys singing doo-wop under the streetlamps, and all of them home by 8:59 p.m., just ahead of their 9:00 p.m. curfew, was how Mamie remembered Emmett in Argo. Even his first and only date was with an Argo girl. Chicago never quite seemed like home to him. The South Side extended miles in every direction, an impersonal ghetto for a newcomer from the village. Mamie later described her son as "so hungry for laughter," for the joy of life, and Argo, small and familiar, fed his hunger in a way Chicago never did. No doubt in retrospect she romanticized it all, but Argo gave her son a good measure of freedom, stability, and security.[34]

In August 1955, a month after Emmett turned fourteen, his great-uncle, Moses Wright, came up to visit from the Mississippi Delta. Wright had been a cotton farmer all his life. He was known as "Preacher" because until just a few years earlier, he was a pastor in the Church of God in Christ, a denomination founded by the sons and daughters of slaves in rural Mississippi in the late 1800s. With the twentieth century, new congregations arose out of the Great Migration, first in Memphis, then in cities in the urban North. One of Wright's old congregants had passed away, and Mose, as his family called him, had come to Chicago for the funeral. Before returning home, he offered to take his nephews Wheeler Parker and Emmett Till back to Mississippi for two weeks. They could help with the cotton harvest and enjoy the country pleasures of a Mississippi summer, swimming and fishing and hanging out with their cousins.[35]

Emmett had been back to Mississippi a couple of times as a child with his grandmother Alma, and he was eager to go again. A summer trip south was something of a pilgrimage for extended families, black and white alike, and the roads and trains were always busy. Mamie hesitated. She had time off coming from her job, and thought about going with Emmett to Detroit, or maybe Nebraska, where she also had family. Besides, she worried about Mississippi; Emmett was a child the last time he visited, too young to understand the deadly serious rules African Americans must follow there. But Emmett very much wanted to go south, and his cousins were eager to see him too. As Mose Wright's youngest son, Simeon, recalled, "We'd just get so much joy to see someone from the North to come down to visit and tell us about...life in Chicago and the North. And, oh, we were just full of excitement. We wanted to show them, you know, the things that we did in Mississippi to have fun."[36]

Finally Mamie said yes. She and Emmett got to the Englewood Station at Sixty-Third and Woodlawn just in the nick of time. He almost missed his train, tarrying to hug his mother and kiss her goodbye. But he made it, found his uncle and cousin who had boarded at the Twelfth Street Station, and the three of them, Emmett Till, Wheeler Parker, and Moses Wright, rode the Illinois Central—on the train they called the City of New Orleans—through downstate Illinois, past Memphis, and into the Mississippi Delta.[37]

CHAPTER THREE

MONEY, MISSISSIPPI

MOSES WRIGHT STOOD a little over five feet tall on a slender frame, yet he was a big man in his community. Sixty-three Mississippi summers lined his face, and still he loved the life of a farmer, took pride in his substantial cotton harvests and his ability to pick two hundred pounds a day. He was a sharecropper, like many African American farmers in Mississippi, few of whom ever managed to buy their own land. Saving that kind of money, getting credit, finding an honest white man willing to sell, made it all but impossible for most southern blacks to own their own farms.[1]

A man like Mose Wright had two alternatives: rent land or sharecrop. The former meant paying whatever the white landlord asked. The latter was more complex, with the owner "furnishing" the acreage, a house, seed, fertilizer, and so forth, and the family living on the property adding their labor. At the end of the harvest, landlord and farmer shared the profits. Each system had problems. Most black farmers who rented still depended on whites to buy seed and fertilizer in the spring, and to sell their crops at the end of summer. Finding someone who gave a fair market price was not easy, but sharecropping was no better; white owners routinely manipulated the books so that black farmers ended up with nothing—or deep in debt, which they were bound by law to work off—at the end of the year.[2]

Mose Wright believed that whichever system he chose mattered less than the honesty of the white man to whom he tied his fate. Good ones were hard to find. Wright rented successfully for ten years from a planter in Schlater, Mississippi, but when the owner sold the land, Wright moved on. He decided to switch from renting to cropping when he met a German émigré near Money, Mississippi, a born-again Christian named Grover Frederick, who, by the standards of cotton farming, was quite fair with the Wright family. For ten years Mose Wright share-cropped forty acres of cotton and tended two big gardens under Frederick. Chickens, hogs, fish, and game kept the family in meat, and produce from the gardens fed them all year. It was good land, produced big cotton crops, and there was always a relatively fair settlement after the harvest; some years Wright cleared $2,000, more commonly half that figure. And the house that came with the land was no "shack" as some later called it. The Wrights were proud of their home, with its six rooms and big screened-in porch; Mr. Frederick himself had lived in it for years.[3]

"Papa" Mose sired a dozen children and was the father figure for an extended family. "No nonsense," Wheeler Parker remembered of his grandfather. "He carried himself with dignity... and he got great respect from people. Gentle man, always willing to help, but he carried himself in that kind of way that people really respected. They looked up to him." Parker concluded, "He was a man of means: Said what he meant, meant what he said." Mose Wright expected his children to work hard and treat others with respect, and they risked a good whipping if they failed. He was a tough man, yet even for him Mississippi could be terrifying. His son Simeon Wright recalled that the May 1955 murder in Belzoni of George Wesley Lee—a preacher who owned his own small business, but whom local whites warned to quit registering black voters—deeply disturbed Mose Wright. If a man of God was so cavalierly assassinated without any semblance of justice, then no one was safe.[4]

Like George Lee, Mose Wright was nothing if not a man of God. A bit of a hellion as a young man, his first wife, Lucinda, converted him by her example to the Church of God in Christ. The church demanded upright behavior from its members and was less concerned with racial uplift and advancement through organizations like the National Association for the Advancement of Colored People than promoting the "sanctified life." Not this world but God's kingdom was the ultimate focus, yet a respectable earthly life was surely a sign of a sanctified one, and affairs of the world often meshed with God's ways. Preacher Moses Wright was a living example of the sort of person the church cultivated—a sinner turned solid family man, a hard worker, honest and punctual, one who could build a life for himself and his kin even in Mississippi.[5]

Wright became a locally renowned circuit preacher, a man who traveled to tiny all-black congregations each Sunday, propounding the Word of God. When World War I came, he followed the example of Bishop Charles Harrison Mason, founder of the Church of God in Christ, and refused to be drafted into the army, believing that men were brothers and must not take up arms against each other. Wright served a month in jail, and only his status as a minister saved him from a longer sentence. He kept preaching and farming, but in the early 1920s Lucinda died suddenly, leaving him with four children to raise.[6]

Preaching was how Wright met his second wife, Elizabeth Smith, a schoolteacher in Memphis, where Wright had been a guest in the pulpit. "Lizzy" soon followed him back to Mississippi. She was a small woman, under five feet tall, light-skinned because her grandfather was a white man, a former slave owner. Mose and Lizzy married in 1925 in Sumner, Tallahatchie County, where she had family, including a brother, Crosby Smith. The couple had eight children together, and they eventually settled down near Money, Mississippi, on the Frederick place. Her children later remembered her as a very sweet and generous woman ("Mama, when are you going to whip us," her sons prodded when they had been bad). Sometimes, though, she argued with Mose about leaving Mississippi and going north, about following most of her kin to Chicago where her own children would have more opportunity. But Mose Wright was a farmer, the kind of man who got excited at the sight of new cotton seedlings. He declared that he was born and bred in Mississippi, and that was where he would die.[7]

So Mose Wright arrived home with his nephews Emmett and Wheeler on Saturday, August 20. For kids from Chicago, Mississippi was both scary and exotic. There were poisonous snakes in the nearby lake, the summer sun was unrelenting, and the county road beside which the Wright home stood, "The Dark Ferry Road," was known to local blacks as "The Dark Fear Road," with stories of lynched bodies dangling from trees. The Wrights hauled water for drinking, cleaning, and bathing from a nearby pump, and Lizzy cooked the morning biscuits and every other meal on a woodstove. There was no indoor plumbing, but electrification had come to the Delta, and the Wrights owned a new refrigerator and washing machine, as well as a radio and record player.[8]

Lizzy considered the Victrola hers, and she insisted that it play only gospel music, no jazz or blues. But the radio belonged to the whole family and sounds from Nashville poured into the Wright home at night, country music from the Grand Ole Opry and rhythm and blues on Ernie's Record Parade. Three sons still lived at home—sixteen-year-old Maurice, fourteen-year-old Robert, and twelve-year-old Simeon—and they and their father also listened to baseball games and boxing matches, cheering the St. Louis Cardinals' first black player Tom Alston, the light-heavyweight boxing champion Archie Moore, and the great middleweight champ Sugar Ray Robinson. Close by the Wright's farmhouse was a tiny settlement with a sawmill, a small fruit orchard, a little church, and a one-room schoolhouse. There were country pleasures here for kids—"telling lies" and playing games with friends, "borrowing" watermelons from a neighbor's patch, swimming and fishing and driving country roads.[9]

The Wright household was lively but strict. Swearing was forbidden, even whistling was considered rude. Above all, there was work. Given life's limits for African Americans in the segregated South, Mose and Lizzy were proud of what their family accomplished through hard work. Cotton harvests gave them money for consumer goods, including a car. Work put food on the table. They butchered and salted a hog each November, planted vegetables in the garden in spring and harvested them through the summer and fall. The children, their parents insisted, must finish high school, even as they worked at home and in the fields. The Wrights were literate people; the *Memphis Commercial Appeal,* a little more progressive on race matters than the local newspapers, was delivered every day. Family members also went into the world well dressed; most newspaper photos later show Mose in his farm clothes, but he owned several good suits and always had his shirts cleaned and pressed in nearby Greenwood.[10]

If Mississippi seemed exotic to Emmett, he must also have appeared so to his kin. When the Illinois Central train pulled into the station, he emerged in his Sunday best: fedora, khaki slacks, a short-sleeve cotton shirt, and a big silver ring on his finger with the initials "L.T." engraved on it. Simeon recalled how Emmett's clothes stuck out, how they shouted "city kid" and "money." While his cousins did their chores or picked cotton in overalls or jeans, Emmett was, "a sight to see in the cotton fields, dressed like he was on his way to a party." He even wore a pair of penny loafers. But Emmett's efforts at farm work did not last long. He wilted in the Delta sun, and after his first day in the field, he stayed at home with his Aunt Lizzy and did inside chores.[11]

Emmett stood out in other ways as well: he was a great talker, regaling his cousins with stories of Chicago, the zoo, the lake, and the amusement parks. Simeon remembered how funny he could be, cracking jokes, just like the comics on the radio. But there was something else too. Simeon described a moment on Emmett's second day in Mississippi, when ten or so friends gathered to horse around about a mile from the Wright house, near a local church. One young man grew threatening, bullying another, and everyone reacted with embarrassed silence. After the incident passed, Simeon recalled decades later, Emmett said they should have confronted the bully, adding, "You can't allow anyone to come around and disrespect you like that. We would never tolerate this in Chicago. What are you, a bunch of chickens?"[12]

Cooped up around home all day, Emmett was eager to spend time with his cousins after they finished the day's work. And that is what they did on a Wednesday night, August 24, while Mose and Lizzy were in church. Maurice Wright borrowed his father's 1946 Ford sedan and drove Wheeler, Simeon, Emmett, and a neighbor, Roosevelt Crawford, three miles west, down the Dark Fear Road into Money, Mississippi.[13]

The town was named for Hernando DeSoto Money, a Confederate Army veteran, attorney, farmer, and newspaper editor. As a young man after the Civil War, Money lived in this northeast corner of Leflore County just long enough to establish himself as a substantial cotton planter. He moved away and become a congressman, then a US senator, and decades after he left the area, the tiny town of Woodstock renamed itself in his honor. But now the name was all that remained of him; his old mansion burned to the ground in 1909. Half a century later, the town of Money had a post office, a gas station, a cotton gin, and Bryant's Grocery Store. You could pass by on the road from Greenwood and not even know you had been through a town.[14]

The boys stopped at Bryant's, which served a mostly black clientele of two or three hundred sharecropper families in the area. On a bench outside the store, several young black boys and men played checkers. Inside, Carolyn Bryant, a twenty-one-year-old white woman, the mother of two, waited for the evening's last business before closing up shop. Her husband, Roy, was away, trucking shrimp from the Gulf Coast. In the living quarters in back of the store were Carolyn's two boys, and her sister-in-law, Juanita Milam, with her own small sons.[15]

Countless stories circulated over the years about those moments at Bryant's, as people have tried to fill in gaps that cannot be filled. For a few moments, Emmett and his cousins stayed on the porch, talking and bantering. Then Wheeler went in and bought some sweets. As he was leaving, Till walked in, alone. "And when Emmett came in," Parker recalled fifty years later, "I felt, you know, this apprehension, because I knew how he was and I knew where we were."[16]

Was Emmett bragging about his white girlfriend up in Chicago before he entered Bryant's, showing her photo from his wallet? Did he even have a white girlfriend or her picture in his wallet? Were his friends egging him on, telling him to proposition the pretty white lady in the store? What racial taboos, if any, did he violate? Did he fail to call Carolyn Bryant "ma'am?" Did he put change directly in her hand rather than on the counter? Did he utter an inappropriately familiar, "good-bye" to her on his way out, or an even less appropriate, "bye baby?" Did he take a dare from his friends and ask her for a date? Did he touch her? Did he assault her? Emmett's cousins who stood outside, not twenty feet from where it all allegedly occurred, consistently maintained over the years that none of those things happened.[17]

Emmett was not inside for long, maybe a minute, when Maurice sent in his younger brother, Simeon. "Maurice sent me in behind Emmett to make sure that he didn't say anything that he shouldn't, because he just didn't know the ways of the South," Simeon remembered. A couple of days earlier, they had all gone to a different store to buy some fireworks, and Emmett started setting them off outside, not knowing it was illegal within town limits. In any event, Emmett was briefly in the store alone with Carolyn Bryant. Simeon later said he did not hear anything odd or inappropriate when he walked in, that everything appeared normal, that Bryant remained behind her counter, did not seem upset, while Emmett made his selection, paid her, then left. Did something untoward happen in that minute before Simeon entered the store? "I don't have no idea," Simeon wrote years later in his memoirs; "only Carolyn Bryant can correct that."[18]

But there was one racial taboo Emmett certainly did violate. As the two cousins walked out of the store, Carolyn Bryant trailed behind them. She headed to her car to retrieve something—a gun, she said later. At that moment, Wheeler Parker said in an oral history recorded fifty years later, Emmett whistled at Carolyn Bryant. "And we just could not believe, I mean, this—this is like something out of the sky blue, you know. Where did this come from? What's wrong with him, and even now we don't know what possessed him. He had no idea. He had no idea, didn't have any idea the danger." Simeon Wright too recalled the fateful moment:

We had been outside the store only a few seconds when Mrs. Bryant came out behind us, heading straight for her car. As she walked, Bobo whistled at her. I think he wanted to get a laugh out of us or something. He was always joking around, and it was hard to tell when he was serious. It was a loud wolf whistle, a big-city "whee wheeeee!" and it caught us all by surprise. We all looked at each other, realizing that Bobo had violated a long-standing unwritten law, a social taboo about conduct between blacks and whites in the South. Suddenly we felt we were in danger, and we stared at each other, all with the same expression of fear and panic. Like a group of boys who had thrown a rock through somebody's window, we ran to the car.[19]

They dove into the Ford, Maurice fired it up, and flew out of Money and onto the Dark Fear Road, kicking up dust and gravel. Headlights approached from behind. Terrified that it was Carolyn Bryant's husband, Maurice pulled over to the side of the road, and they all ran into the cotton fields to hide. But the car just drove past them; it was only a neighbor. Relieved, they piled back into the Ford. Emmett made them all promise to say nothing to Mose or Lizzie Wright; he was having too much fun to be sent back to Chicago early. Roosevelt Crawford's sister, Rutha Mae, told the Wright boys the next day, "we know these people, and ya'all are going to hear some more about this." But three more long hot days of picking cotton passed without incident and with them disappeared fears of retribution.[20]

Here, once again, hearsay and speculation braid themselves into the story. Supposedly Carolyn Bryant had no intention of telling her husband about the incident, fearing his reaction, fearing even more what Roy's half-brother, J. W. "Big" Milam, might do. By Friday, when Roy returned from the Gulf Coast, rumors of the event were rife in the community. The story that circulated among African Americans was that a "Judas nigger," a man who would rather curry favor with whites than stay loyal to his own people, told Bryant about it. Fearing his neighbors ridicule, imagining both whites and blacks laughing at him, Roy told his older brother, and they made a plan.[21]

On Saturday night, after the week's labors ended and before church on Sunday, people for miles around went to Greenwood. It was the night to do some shopping, to kick back, to see and be seen. Mose Wright went with the boys, but Lizzy stayed home. "Man, we went to Greenwood," Wheeler Parker remembered years later of the weekly ritual, "and people from everywhere, all the girls and the guys, and they're walking down Johnson Street, man, just—it was just entertainment to see all these people coming." The older boys, Emmett included, checked out the action and ended up at a juke joint called the "Four Fifths Plantation," where music and dancing, gambling, and white lightning were the order of the evening.[22]

Younger lads like Simeon Wright recalled more innocent pleasures after the grueling workweek: "Man it was something! I mean, you have a joy—it's Christmas morning in August to go to Greenwood and enjoy the foot-long hotdog, the malt, and go to the movies." From 6:00 p.m. until midnight, Greenwood's Johnson Street belonged to black folks, literally thousands of people from all over Leflore County. The Wright boys drove home happy but exhausted, arrived just as the Sabbath day began, and went to bed.[23]

Someone pounding on the door awakened Mose Wright at 2:00 a.m. "Preacher, Preacher.... This is Mr. Bryant. I want to talk to you and that boy."

CHAPTER FOUR

I'M KINDA SCARED THERE'S BEEN FOUL PLAY

EMMETT TILL ARRIVED in Mississippi on Saturday, August 20. The incident with Carolyn Bryant in Money happened four days later. The door-pounding in the night came after three more days had passed, and Robert Hodges found the body in the Tallahatchie River four days after that, on Wednesday, August 31. During that week-and-a-half, the Till story moved from local to national news coverage, and soon it was grabbing front-page headlines across the country, and, eventually, international attention. (The African American press would become a crucial voice in the Till story, but because papers like the *Chicago Defender* were weeklies, their coverage and commentary only began to appear several days after Emmett's body surfaced.)

Till's disappearance did not even get much local attention at first. Greenwood, the seat of Leflore County, located about twelve miles south of Money, was the largest city in the southeastern part of the Mississippi Delta—twenty thousand people, larger than any town for fifty miles. The daily paper, the *Commonwealth*, brought news stories to the whole county, and on Monday, August 29, they were all pretty dull: the never-ending negotiations two years after the fighting in Korea ended; the inconclusive nuclear disarmament talks at the United Nations; Hurricane Edith missing land entirely and sweeping out to the Atlantic. The society page noted wedding rehearsals for couples on the verge of marriage and dinner parties for Greenwood High School seniors. The sports page was more interesting, with the Brooklyn Dodgers—the first and most integrated team in baseball, starring Jackie Robinson, Roy Campanella, and Don Newcombe—running away with the National League Pennant. Most significant to local folks in these dog days of summer were predictions for the impending cotton harvest, which promised to be a good one.[1]

Monday's *Commonwealth* put the Till story on the front page but did not give it much space. "Chicago Negro Youth Abducted by Three White Men at Money" reported that Leflore County Sheriff George Smith received a complaint on Sunday and picked up Roy Bryant at his store that afternoon. The news story described how two white men entered the home of the black farmer Mose Wright and took his nephew, a boy from Chicago, at gunpoint. Wright had asked them where they were taking him, and one of the kidnappers replied, "'nowhere if he's not the right one.'" Three days before the abduction, the *Commonwealth* story said, a group of black youths had driven to Bryant's Grocery Store in Money where one of them made some "ugly remarks" to Bryant's wife and also wolf-whistled at her. Roy Bryant admitted to Sheriff Smith that he took the boy but claimed to have released him since he turned out to be the wrong kid. No one had seen the lad since the abduction, and already there were rumors that the whole thing was some sort of hoax or misunderstanding. Sheriff Smith, though, said his office was taking the case very seriously.[2]

Small wire service stories appeared in other Mississippi papers on Monday and Tuesday. The *Delta Democrat-Times* in Greenville now reported that the two white men, brothers, were in custody, but both suspects insisted that they released Till when they discovered he was not the one who "insulted" Mrs. Bryant. The story added that the Negro youths who were with young Till at Bryant's store forced him to leave for being rowdy. The *Jackson Daily News* quoted Sheriff Smith on Tuesday that there was nothing new to report regarding Till's whereabouts, that it was possible his relatives were hiding him or had sent him back to Chicago. But Smith added, "I'm kinda scared there's been foul play." At this point, it was still a local story, muffled and unclear, like a voice coming from a distant room.[3]

Then on Wednesday, August 31, the *Jackson State Times* reported young Robert Hodges's grizzly find: "A 15-year-old Chicago negro, who mysteriously disappeared from the home of a relative during the weekend, today was found floating in a river near here, a bullet wound in his head." There was no question that the boy kidnapped on Sunday and the body found in the Tallahatchie on Wednesday were one and the same. The *Greenwood Commonwealth* managed to get Emmett Till's age right, fourteen, and added that two deputy sheriffs brought Moses Wright to the body to make the identification. The report also noted that Till's corpse floated to the surface despite being weighed down with a cotton-gin pulley and barbed wire. The body was found in Tallahatchie County, about twenty-five miles north of Greenwood—where brothers J. W. Milam and Roy Bryant waited in jail—and about twelve miles north of Money, where they abducted Till.[4]

This local story grew exponentially during the next month, headlining the national news, and finally spilling into the international media. The first big report came from the Associated Press the day after the body surfaced, and while local editors modified some of the details, the same basic story appeared in newspapers across America. It reprised the original Mississippi coverage but added some new details. The Tallahatchie County Sheriff, H. C. Strider, made his first appearance, declaring that Till had been badly brutalized: "We found a bullet hole one inch above his right ear. The left side of his face had been cut up or beat up—plumb into the skull." Strider suggested that an ax might have been used.[5]

Other details emerged. The AP now reported that a woman was also in the car that first drove out to Mose Wright's home. The story noted that the FBI in Washington was following the case closely, though as yet they had found no civil rights violations or crossing of interstate borders to make it a federal crime. Some reports claimed incorrectly that Till's body was buried immediately in Money, Mississippi. Most dramatically, many newspapers reprinted the story with a photo of a grim-faced Leflore County deputy sheriff named John Ed Cothran kneeling in front of the blocky, muddy, seventy-five-pound industrial fan.[6]

Early reports noted that the sheriffs continued to search for Till's clothes since his body came out of the river naked. They also looked for a cotton gin missing a fan, assuming that the murderers stole the one tied around Till's neck. Officers hoped that the fan might connect the suspects more closely to the crime or lead them to the scene of the murder itself (the body turned up just over the Tallahatchie line, but if authorities determined that the murder took place in Leflore, the case would be tried there).[7]

Newspapers also reported that county sheriffs were unable to find Carolyn Bryant, the woman whom young Till allegedly insulted and the wife of one of the accused murderers. Since some reports had her accompanying the brothers on their kidnapping mission, her testimony would be vital. There were other problems. Even though the science of ballistics was well advanced by the mid-1950s, there seems to have been little thought about finding the bullet or the gun that killed Till, doubly strange since the body did not appear to have an exit wound. Nor was there talk of an autopsy, just a quick burial. In the world of Mississippi county sheriffs, forensic work remained cursory, and if the victims were African American, all but nonexistent. Black bodies were best disposed of before anyone asked too many questions.[8]

In the days immediately after the corpse appeared, in an attempt to give a human face to the story, reporters sought out the families of the victim and the accused. In so doing, newsmen exposed, perhaps inadvertently, what was simmering just below the surface. Seemingly innocent tidbits carried emotional charges. For example, Emmett Till's bout with childhood polio left him with a speech impediment. Mamie Till Bradley had taught him how to break his stammer by whistling. For years after her son's murder, she referred to the fact that Emmett whistled whenever words failed him. It was not a long leap to the conclusion that his killers butchered not just a child but one who suffered a disability, and worse, maybe Emmett's "wolf whistle" was merely the sound of a frightened kid struggling for words.[9]

Mamie Till Bradley's statement to reporters that she had warned her son to be careful in Mississippi, telling him "even if you have to get on your knees and bow when they [whites] pass, do it willingly," raised more questions. What was she so worried about, a few southern editorialists asked? Was Emmett some sort of troublemaker, the kind of kid who needed such warnings? Why did she fill him with ideas about white Mississippians being so threatening? Why did she immediately hire an attorney, William Henry Huff, who did legal work for the NAACP and who said he intended to sue the state of Mississippi if Milam and Bryant failed to receive the death penalty? And what about her joining with Chicago's new mayor, Richard J. Daley, in calling for a federal investigation before indictments had even been handed down? Was this not a slur against Mississippi, as if the state's justice system was incapable of, well, justice?[10]

The news media also gave the public glimpses of Milam, Bryant, and their families. A writer for the *Memphis Commercial Appeal* interviewed their "graying, worried mother," Eula Lee Bryant, in her grocery store in Sharkey, Mississippi. Grocery stores serving mostly blacks in tiny Delta towns were the family business, Roy in Money, J. W. in Glendora, their mother in Sharkey; even Roy Bryant's father, divorced from Eula Lee, ran a rural store in Curtis, Mississippi. "They were never into meanness," she said of her boys in this widely syndicated story just two days after Emmett's body surfaced; "I raised them and I'll stand by them." She showed photographs of her eleven children—including eight sons, seven of whom had served in the military—and she gave reporters photos of Roy and J. W. in uniform. Young Roy spent three years as a paratrooper, she said, while J. W. fought in Germany during World War II, getting his commission "the hard way," rising from private to lieutenant in combat, winning a Purple

Heart, and bearing enormous scars on his chest and back where army medics took out twenty-seven pieces of shrapnel.[11]

They were just one big Mississippi family, Eula Lee said, getting together regularly for supper and fellowship and church services. The boys liked to hunt, fish, and play cards; they were always well liked, wherever they lived, though they moved around a lot, from Charleston to Tutwiler to other nearby towns. She spoke especially warmly about J. W. Not only was he worshipped by his two sons, she added that "all the Negroes at Glendora...liked him like a father. They always came to him for help." There was no "racial feeling" among the men in her family, and just months before Till's body floated up in the Tallahatchie, J. W. Milam dove into that very river to save a drowning black girl.[12]

The Till family did not get such good press. On the day Emmett's body emerged, an interview—a purported interview—with Mamie Till Bradley, appeared in the Jackson, Mississippi, *Daily News*, and the story was quoted all over the country the next day. It is hard to imagine how the *Daily News* pulled off an interview at all, assuming it was not completely made up. Till's body was brought into Greenwood in late morning, so a reporter in Jackson would first have had to be tipped off to that fact by someone in the Delta, obtain phone numbers for Mrs. Bradley in Argo and Chicago, get through to her, have her agree to speak on the record, then write up the interview in time for the afternoon paper—possible, but given the circumstances, unlikely.[13]

The headline from the original *Daily News* story was highly incendiary: "'Mississippi to Pay for This,' Stunned Mother of Slain Negro Boy Sobs after Body is Found." The report did not carry a byline, and it consisted mostly of Mamie Bradley's words—her alleged words: "I can't think, I just can't think. I'm frozen. He didn't do anything to deserve that. Somebody is going to pay for this. The entire state of Mississippi is going to pay for this."[14]

She went on to say that she had nothing left to live for, that her life was ruined, that all she wanted was to give her son a decent burial, that then she would fight to see that justice was done. Then she continued her rant against Mississippi: "The state of Illinois doesn't allow these things to happen. But down there it's an everyday occurance [sic]....It's like walking into a den of snakes....They will do these things with hardly any provocation—they don't even need provocation." What could a fourteen-year-old boy like her son do to a grown woman like Carolyn Bryant, Emmett's mother asked, and she answered her own question—no matter what he did, he did not deserve to die.[15]

The difficulty of obtaining such an interview is not the only reason to doubt its veracity. The *Jackson Daily News* figured prominently in the Emmett

Till story, as did the *Jackson Clarion-Ledger*. Other newspapers borrowed freely from them. Both were owned by a prominent Jackson family, the Hedermans, and both papers were highly suspect. Two veteran journalists, Gene Roberts and Hank Klibanoff, who chronicled how newsmen covered the unfolding civil rights struggle during this era in their Pulitzer Prize–winning book *The Race Beat,* wrote of the two Jackson papers, "They were journalistically the worst major-city newspapers in the South, not because the owners, top editors, and columnists were fervently segregationist—which they were—but because they allowed their zealotry to dictate the scope, depth, tone and tilt of their coverage." Roberts and Klibanoff conclude that the *Daily News* and the *Clarion-Ledger* "were vindictive, poorly written, and error-ridden," and that they helped to make Mississippi the most reactionary state in the South.[16]

In contrast, the *Chicago Tribune* quoted Mamie Till Bradley a day later, on September 1. The *Tribune's* reporter gave details of how he'd actually spoken to her face-to-face at her home on the South Side. She described how she learned of her son's death, and her words were measured, more like how she sounded in dozens of subsequent interviews. "Emmett," she told the *Tribune*, "was a good boy. I know he didn't do anything wrong....Emmett was mischievous, but he was not a bad boy....He's never been in any trouble. He's been my life saver—did the washing, ironing and housework so I could work. He has stood by me like a man. How could anyone do this terrible thing to him?" Nevertheless, it was the *Jackson Daily News*, not the *Chicago Tribune,* that was quoted over and over again by other American newspapers.[17]

Conflicting points of view, factual lacunae, misinformation, slanted and confusing accounts, all were just beginning in the press coverage, and they would reveal deep conflicts about race and region, sex and gender, policy and ideology. For the next several months, the Emmett Till story became an American Rorschach.

CHAPTER FIVE

LYNCHING

THE CASE SEEMED simple at first: a kid violated customs he little understood and paid with his life. Most people in the South were horrified by the murder. They had little doubt that J. W. Milam and Roy Bryant committed the crime and that the body in the river was Till's.

But race was involved—race *and* sex—so nothing remained simple for long, especially not at that moment in history. The drama playing out in the Mississippi Delta took place as old ideas, policies, and traditions were becoming unstuck. In the decades following Reconstruction, the southern states installed a regime of white supremacy that despite some challenges and variations remained quite stable for more than half a century. Backed by federal law, secured by a southern stranglehold on Congress, affirmed by the Supreme Court, underscored in popular culture, southern apartheid stood rock solid from the late nineteenth century until World War II.[1]

Then fissures began to appear in the wall separating white and black. Deeply American institutions—the army, for example, and major league baseball—had integrated, at least nominally, by the end of the 1940s. Even World War II itself, the war against fascism and Nazism, raised questions in many minds about racial hierarchies and about the appropriateness of doctrines based on the superiority of some ethnic groups over others. The United States, after all, had just battled racist regimes, and our own wartime propaganda celebrated that fact, exulting in the triumph of democracy and inclusiveness over bigotry.[2]

Yet by midcentury, in the context of a rapidly escalating Cold War, a number of African, Asian, and Latin American leaders spearheaded homegrown nationalist movements, anticolonialist and anti-imperialist to their core. Newly liberated peoples in the "Third World" cast a skeptical eye on America. Could it really be a beacon for freedom overseas while oppressing people of color at home? Didn't Jim Crow segregation and white supremacy give the lie to America's democratic pretentions?[3]

All these issues were not far in the background when a simple question arose just a day or two after they found Emmett Till's body: Was it a lynching? The label had enormous implications. The struggle over lynching had been one of the oldest battles for civil rights, a weak spot in Jim Crow's armor, a place where activists found mainstream converts. Extrajudicial killing by private citizens of alleged criminals was neither purely a southern phenomenon nor always racial in nature. Yet from the time Ida B. Wells published her *Southern Horrors* in 1892, lynching was associated indelibly with the South. Roughly five thousand racially based lynchings occurred between the publication of Wells's book and the civil rights era, most of them from the 1890s through the 1920s, and more of them in Mississippi than any other state. The numbers started to decline throughout the region during the Great Depression to the point where few were recorded in the years after World War II. The federal government never enacted a ban on lynching; southern congressmen repeatedly blocked such legislation, and although Franklin Roosevelt expressed sympathy for the cause, he refused to antagonize southern Democrats by pushing for anti-lynching laws.[4]

In its heyday, lynching buttressed white supremacy through terror. It was not just the hangings and shootings and immolations themselves, it was all of the news stories and photos of white men looking on with satisfaction at a black corpse swinging from a tree. Lynching was not intended merely to punish those who allegedly committed crimes, the most heinous, southern whites said, being sexual assaults on white women. It was terror, pure and simple, a message to the living: don't even think of getting out of line. While many white southerners were embarrassed by the practice, they nonetheless justified it as a necessary evil or just shrugged their shoulders, helpless to do anything about it. Above all, lynching was not just killing, it was torture turned into spectacle—mutilation, use of blow torches, cutting off body parts, burning victims alive—all elements of vigilante justice.[5]

By the 1950s, most southern whites considered lynching part of a benighted past, best forgotten. Had not the numbers fallen to the vanishing point? Even defenders of the practice argued that the decline in extrajudicial killings was evidence of interracial harmony and of the improving morality of black people. Could anyone even remember the last time men (and a few women) gathered openly, publicly, to burn, hang, and shoot some poor black soul? Those days were long gone now, most southern whites insisted, replaced by genuinely cordial feelings between the races.[6]

To label Till's death a "lynching" seemed anachronistic because the very word implied that such killings were part of an ongoing and pervasive pattern of racism, terror, white supremacy. Calling Till's killing "murder," on the other hand, meant that it was a random crime by evil men, having nothing to do with larger questions of race. "Murder" was a matter of individual depravity; "lynching" invoked societal guilt. For many white southerners, the very word was a provocation.[7]

While whites insisted that segregation should endure, that everyone preferred things that way, many were also fond of pointing out how the barriers between the races had come down a bit, especially in the border states, such as Kentucky, Virginia, and Maryland. A few schools were nominally integrated, some districts tried to spend more equally on black facilities as on white, a handful of African American students now attended southern universities. Lynching's demise was part of the southern enlightenment reported by the national media.[8]

For example, *Time* ran a long story titled "The U.S. Negro, 1953." It began by noting the rising numbers of black golfers, then outlined a series of improvements in African American life—a fourfold increase in wages since 1940 (although average black pay was half that of whites); a tripling of African American voters in the South (although the numbers remained a tiny fraction of the voting age population); greater access to the courts (although cases were almost always argued before white judges and segregated juries); a growing percentage of black college students (although the absolute numbers remained miniscule). Steady progress was the order of the day, maybe not as fast or as sure as some would like, but constant improvement nonetheless. Lynching's decline was part of this sunny narrative.[9]

A year later, *Collier's* published a two-part story by the South African writer Alan Paton, author of the celebrated novel *Cry the Beloved Country*. After touring America, Paton ticked off a list of improvements—more black voters, college students, army officers—and added, "One gets a vivid impression that the Deep South, the Deep South of the grossest inequality, the worst discrimination, of murder and violence, is slowly retreating. Its theories of white supremacy and segregation are slowly being forced into the Gulf of Mexico, where they will be drowned...." Things were far from perfect, Paton concluded, but getting better: "World Opinion, the

Constitution and the courts, the determination of Negroes to be Americans, the conviction in the conscience of America that Negroes should be Americans—all these are forcing the white supremacy advocates of the Deep South back on their heels."[10]

Such talk must have seemed insane to most black Mississippians. Emmett Till's murder was the state's third racial killing in just a few months (more precisely, the third *known* killing, for mysterious deaths and disappearances of blacks remained realities). Before Till there had been the Reverend George Lee in Belzoni in early May, then Lamar Smith in Brookhaven in mid-August. Both men were outspoken about inequality, and both worked to register black voters. Their killers never stood trial.[11]

Dr. T. R. M. Howard, the state's leading black activist and president of the Mississippi Council of Negro Leadership, linked the Till murder with these other two and demanded a federal investigation, adding: "If this slaughtering of Negroes is allowed to continue, Mississippi will have a civil war. Negroes are going to take only so much." Roy Wilkins, newly appointed executive secretary of the New York–based National Association for the Advancement of Colored People (NAACP) immediately called Till's murder a lynching and added, "It would appear that the State of Mississippi has decided to maintain white supremacy by murdering children." Wilkins accused the state's institutions—government, newspapers, churches—of abetting its citizens' worst impulses. Based on Governor Hugh White's refusal to order a special investigation of the Lee and Smith murders, Wilkins added he expected no state intervention in the Till case.[12]

Governor White was indeed dismissive of Wilkins and the NAACP, telling reporters, "They're in the press all the time, that gang." He wondered aloud why dozens of murders in New York City and Chicago escaped the glare of publicity garnered by the Till case. But he soon moderated his tone, publicly sending a telegram to NAACP headquarters pledging that justice would be served: "Parties charged with the murder are in jail. I have every reason to believe the courts will do their duty in prosecution. Mississippi does not condone such conduct." Nonetheless, White insisted that the slaying was a murder, not a lynching, and that it had nothing to do with issues like desegregation of the schools or voting rights. This was a homicide, and the courts would treat it as such.[13]

Till's body was found on Wednesday; on Thursday, Mississippi editors expressed shock at the murder's barbarity. By Friday, however, their horror began to morph into anger directed to the likes of Howard and Wilkins. The *Jackson Clarion-Ledger* ran an editorial castigating the killers as "hoodlum white trash," the "sick" and "depraved" men who committed such a brutal, senseless, stupid crime, and the craven politicians who ran for office on a "platform of hatred." But the paper gave equal space to condemning the NAACP for turning the rest of America against Mississippi. Till's murder "was not a lynching and when NAACP so says, it proves its cynical purpose of inflaming the Negro people of this state against the whites."[14]

Hodding Carter's *Delta Democrat-Times*, published in Greenville, Mississippi, and considered one of the most liberal newspapers in the region, declared in an editorial, "We have met no Mississippian who was other than revolted by the senseless brutality of the kidnap-slaying of the 15-year-old Negro youth near Greenwood this past weekend." Carter called for the swift prosecution of whoever committed this savage crime but insisted that Roy Wilkins's blaming Mississippi for the violence of a few of its citizens made no sense. The best way to answer such a charge was for the state to seek justice against the murderers, a fate that almost never befell lynch mobs. "We feel confident that this will be done," he concluded.[15]

Southern papers outside Mississippi agreed. The liberal *Raleigh News and Observer* editorialized, "For a Negro leader publicly to put into the company of brutal killers all the best people of Mississippi neatly conforms with the most prejudiced statements of those who would put the best, most respectable Negroes on the level with the worst." The *Atlanta Journal*, went out of its way to reject any notion of special regional shame. How could this be called a lynching? There was no mob violence. "The South is having a hard-enough time, trying to struggle out of the racial bog, without a murder being warped into a lynching and added to the Southern burden." How dare the mayor of Chicago criticize Mississippi, the *Journal* added, when his city witnessed twenty-seven bombings in a sixteen-month period, vigilante acts by Chicago whites to keep blacks out of their neighborhoods? Lynching implied some special regional depravity, and it was this singling out of the South that most rankled editorialists.[16]

Within days of Emmett Till's murder then, southern liberals and conservatives rejected the lynching label. To believe otherwise gave in to the old stereotype of the South as gothic, benighted, primitive, a throwback in an age of postwar enlightenment. Theirs was a New South, racially progressive yet segregated, where blacks and whites coexisted in harmony. Emmett's death was no warrant to tamper with Jim Crow. Blacks and whites understood each other, and leaders on both sides were committed to fairness and progress. Lynching was over, and for the sake of racial harmony, it was best not talked about. Just on the other side of this happy mythology, however, was the same old guard of wealthy men and conservative politicians who, in John Egerton's words, "provided their faithful followers with a stone tablet of sacrosanct beliefs: the Lost Cause, the common Yankee enemy, Jim Crow segregation, states' rights, the solid South, and the undefiled purity of the white female." White racial violence too remained part of this mix.[17]

For decades the Department of Records and Research at Tuskegee Institute, Alabama's historically black college, kept files and clippings on lynchings and was considered the national authority on the subject. According to Jessie Guzman, director of that office, Tuskegee's definition of lynching—an extralegal killing committed by at least three people—fit Emmett Till's case. Only two men were under arrest, but it was becoming clear there were others involved. Their motive was explicitly racial: a young black male had insulted a white female. So now Tuskegee joined the conversation, adding Emmett Till's name to its long list of lynching victims. The National Urban League agreed with Tuskegee, noting that the Till lynching was an atrocity borne of contempt for human dignity.[18]

Soon northern editors picked up the thread. The *New York Herald Tribune*, for example, acknowledged that the subject had grown murkier in recent years: "Lynching has sort of moved into the haze of maybe and maybe not.... Bodies are found, Negroes are found shot. But now it's usually by persons unknown, and not by mobs." But the newspaper rejected southern editors' parsing of the word. In an editorial titled "Disgrace in Mississippi," the *Herald Tribune* noted that before Till, Tuskegee's last officially recorded lynching took place in 1951, so "the country congratulated itself thereafter that this particular outrage against law and order, especially directed against the Negro minority, had been stamped out by growing enlightenment." That celebration was premature, the editor declared; whether or not the crime met some technical definition, Emmett Till "was murdered by lynchers in spirit."[19]

The controversy grew more heated, southern defensiveness more strident. In Friday afternoon's *Greenwood Commonwealth*, an editorial "A Just Appraisal" appeared on page one in lieu of a lead story. Till's brutal murder, the editor declared, made Leflore and Tallahatchie Counties "the target of unjustifiable criticism, thoughtless accusations, and avenging threats." Individuals murdered Emmett Till, not the state of Mississippi, and incendiary newspaper columns were "evidence of the poison selfish men have planted in the minds of people outside the South." In response to Roy Wilkins's statement that "Mississippi has decided to maintain white supremacy by murdering children," the *Commonwealth* pointed out that a white girl had risked her life just a few months earlier to save a drowning black woman from the Tallahatchie. The real enemies of justice are those who deflect anger from crimes like the Till murder by their "wholesale and indiscriminate accusations against the law-abiding and justice-loving people of our state." Groups like the NAACP must stop throwing bricks—"cease using the case as manufactured evidence to wage war against segregation"—and let justice do its work. Mississippians, the editor concluded, were not to blame for Emmett Till's murder, but they would take responsibility "for seeing that justice is administered through the courts of law and that the guilty parties shall pay for their crimes."[20]

Yet just to the side of the *Commonwealth*'s indignant editorial upholding the majesty of the law was an AP story about Herbert Brownell, the Eisenhower administration's attorney general, and his investigation into charges that duly registered African Americans in Mississippi were barred from voting and, in some cases, had their ballots thrown away in the just-concluded gubernatorial primary. In fact, the number of registered African Americans had declined in recent years, as black voters were threatened with loss of their jobs and their homes, while local registrars used every legal subterfuge to reject new voters. All five Democratic candidates in the primary—and winning the Democratic primary was tantamount to being elected governor in Mississippi—had vowed to maintain segregation. Governor White pledged to resist federal interference, and the winner of the primary, J. P. Coleman, the state attorney general, declared, "we can run our elections without the help of the National Association for the Advancement of Colored People and we don't appreciate Mr. Brownell's interference."[21]

In Tallahatchie County, where the trial of Till's killers would take place, no one had to worry about African American ballots being thrown away. A black majority county in 1955—indeed almost two to one, black to white—not a single African American was allowed to register, so none could vote, serve on a jury, or run for office. And if denying blacks their civil liberties was not enough, there was always the threat of violence. The day after Till's body was found, alongside the *Commonwealth*'s front-page coverage, a small headline declared, "Fiery Cross Is Burned in Jackson." The KKK itself had faded in recent years but had not disappeared entirely, and sharp memories of Klan terror lingered among the black population. Roy Wilkins and the NAACP may have engaged in some hyperbolic rhetoric about Emmett Till, but they were right, the murder was not merely the act of two depraved individuals. It took willful myopia not to see that Till's death was embedded in a culture of white violence, a social structure of white privilege, and a deepening campaign to resist any movement toward change. This was a racial killing in a racially fraught state.[22]

Civil rights groups, especially the NAACP, had long pushed for anti-lynching legislation that would give the federal government an opening to intervene. Denying that Till's murder was a lynching highlighted why southern congressmen had stifled federal legislation for decades. Days after he went missing, telegrams and letters came into the White House from Mamie Till Bradley, her attorney William Henry Huff, the *Chicago Defender* publisher John Sengstacke, the Illinois governor William Stratton, a dozen US congressmen and senators, and countless citizens, all of them asking for federal intervention in the case. "I strongly urge," Chicago's young mayor Richard J. Daley wrote to President Eisenhower, "that all the facilities of the federal government be immediately utilized so that the ends of justice may be served."[23]

A federal anti-lynching law would have made such intervention automatic, but lacking that, the response from presidential staffers was always the same: no one violated federal law and the perpetrators never crossed state lines, so the US government's hands were tied. Over at the Justice Department, attorneys sent out hundreds of replies to congressmen, senators, and citizens explaining there was nothing to be done. And although "Negro newspapers and colored organizations" generated, "considerable pressure," the Federal Bureau of Investigation insisted that the government had no cause to intervene.[24]

But this did not mean the FBI was uninvolved in the Till case. What worried Director J. Edgar Hoover were Communists using it for their own purposes. Less than a week after Emmett Till's body emerged, on the very day they buried him, Hoover wrote a memo to Dillon Anderson, special assistant to Eisenhower. Intelligence had just come in from a confidential informant in Chicago that the chairman of the Illinois/Indiana Communist Party—a man named Claude Lightfoot, an African American recently indicted under the Smith Act for belonging to an organization dedicated to the overthrow of the US government—planned with his comrades to launch a protest campaign. Radical leaflets, speeches, mass meetings, and petitions would all be designed "to show that full equality for all races does not exist in the United States." Hoover noted that the Communists hoped to work through Chicago ministers, South Side churches, and the NAACP. "This campaign is designed by the Communist Party for the purpose of rabble rousing," Hoover wrote; "Indications are that the Negro people on the South Side of Chicago are already aroused to a fever pitch over this incident."[25]

A week later, Hoover wrote to the White House again. The Communist newspaper, the *Daily Worker,* was filled with Till stories, Hoover reported, and the Reds were making common cause now with labor unions, including the United Steelworkers, and party delegations would soon head to Washington to lobby the president, the attorney general, and the Senate Judiciary Committee for anti-lynching and anti-poll-tax legislation. In other words, when it came to prosecuting Emmett Till's killers, the FBI's hands were tied, but no restrictions applied to spying on those who sought justice.[26]

CHAPTER SIX

WE WILL NOT BE INTEGRATED

WITHIN JUST a few days of Emmett Till's disappearance, the story braided itself around old hostilities, North and South. It became a new battleground in the war over integration, white supremacy, The Southern Way of Life, and over fears of "outside agitators" like the Communists and the NAACP. Almost from the moment that Till's body surfaced, the case had been politicized. The racial killing of a fourteen-year-old—a black male who "talked ugly" to a white woman—was emotional dynamite. A generation earlier, Milam and Bryant might have, with impunity, led a mob, captured Till, cut off his genitals, roasted him alive or shot or hanged him, cut off body parts for trophies, then surrounded by blood-sated accomplices, smiled for the cameras. The decline of such horrific public performances, however, did not signal placid times in the South—quite the contrary.[1]

The day after the body rose, before it was even shipped back to Chicago, Robert Patterson, the executive director of the Citizens' Councils—a group essential to understanding the South at this historical moment—spoke out. Patterson called the Till murder regrettable but said his organization had nothing to do with it. One of the primary purposes of the Citizens' Councils, he noted in an interview, was to prevent violence by maintaining good relations between the races through segregation. "Keeping segregation in all walks of life," was the Councils' goal, Patterson said, despite, "constant agitation and inflammatory statements by the NAACP and outside agitators." And he added that any weakening of Jim Crow barriers opened the door to tragedies like the Till murder. He was right, for one of those barriers had fallen a little more than a year before Emmett Till died.[2]

On May 17, 1954, the United States Supreme Court handed down its unanimous *Brown v. Board of Education* decision, which declared that segregated public schools were inherently unequal. In doing so, the Court overturned its own 1896 *Plessy v. Ferguson* ruling. *Plessy* along with other decisions had given federal blessings to state policies and customs that rigidly divided the South into "White" and "Colored" spaces, while politically disenfranchising and economically disempowering African Americans. The Fourteenth Amendment might guarantee equal citizenship, but *Plessy* allowed states enormous leeway to define what that meant and how it would be enforced. Rigid legal segregation was always a little unstable—the messiness of commerce, love, and desire often muddied racial divisions. But now, in 1954, the Supreme Court assaulted a bulwark of segregation, the schools, and potentially the entire Jim Crow regime.[3]

When the *Brown* decision first came down, some southerners spoke of compromise to salvage Jim Crow, but most were more defiant. One voice rose with special clarity. In late May, a circuit court judge, Tom P. Brady, a graduate of Yale College and the University of Mississippi Law School—gave a speech titled "Black Monday" in Greenwood to the Leflore County Sons of the American Revolution. His talk was so well received that a month later he expanded it into an eponymous little book, which became the Magna Carta of the Citizens' Councils Movement. *Black Monday* was far from original. Rather, it took common racist tropes along with discredited "science" and fashioned them into powerful and compelling propaganda.[4]

Racially based ideas about "inferior" peoples buttressed 1920s immigration laws that blocked most Jews, Poles, Italians, Slavs, Greeks, Chinese, Mexicans, and other "undesirables" from coming to the United States. Immigration restriction was part of a larger assault on those who failed to be white, native-born, or middle class. Eugenic science held that genetics sorted success and failure and justified sterilizing thousands of poor and "feeble-minded" Americans thirty years before Brady wrote "Black Monday." Brady's intellectual fathers were men like Lathrop Stoddard, William Graham Sumner, and Madison Grant—East Coast elites, Harvard and Yale educated, men from Boston and New York, not Alabama and Mississippi.[5]

At the same time the Ku Klux Klan rose again in the 1920s, now taking aim at Catholics and Jews as well as African Americans, "scientific" studies divided the so-called superior Nordic whites from inferior Balkan and Mediterranean peoples. Brady's intellectual ancestors devised a long typology of race, with the whitest whites coming from northern and western Europe, their descendants threatened in America by teeming hoards from eastern and southern parts of the Continent, not to mention the descendants of Africa, Asia, and Latin America. Such ideas from America flowed into deadly currents of European fascism and Nazism in the 1930s and '40s.[6]

Black Monday adapted and applied all this to contemporary southern society. Of course, Judge Brady ignored the new anthropology emergent at that time, which in effect demolished the concept of racial hierarchy altogether. He ignored, too, his predecessors' gradations of racialist thinking for a streamlined version that focused mainly on the binary of white and black. "White civilization" for Brady had once occupied all of Europe and the Levant, from the Atlantic to the Urals, from the Barents Sea to the Sahara. Brady posited "Three Species of Man," Homo Caucasius [*sic*], Homo Mongoloideus, and Homo Africanus. The white race, "through evolutionary development and great labor," spawned geniuses, from William Shakespeare to Thomas Edison. The danger now was "mongrelization." The once great civilizations of India and Egypt, Greece and Rome, all fell because of this curse, the encroachment of "negroid blood" which, like the jungle, steadily and completely swallowed up everything.[7]

So would it be for the South with integration: "Water does not rise above its source, and the negro could not by his inherent qualities rise above his environment as had the other races. His inheritance was wanting. The potential did not exist. This is neither right nor wrong; it is simply a stubborn biological fact." Heredity shackled Africans:

> Clothed only in a loin cloth, . . . his teeth sharpened by rough rocks so that they can more easily tear human flesh, he squats and utilizes the great discovery he has made, namely, that the point of his green spear can be hardened by a flame of fire. Here we find the negro only one-half step from the primordial brute. . . . You can dress a chimpanzee, house break him, and teach him to use a knife and fork, but it will take countless generations of evolutionary development, if ever, before you can convince him that a caterpillar or a cockroach is not a delicacy.

Under the imprimatur of "science," Brady concluded that the social, political and religious preferences of African Americans "remain close to the caterpillar and the cockroach."[8]

Now His Honor got down to what was truly at stake in Mississippi: "The loveliest and the purest of God's creatures, the nearest thing to an angelic being that treads this terrestrial ball is a well-bred, cultured Southern white woman or her blue-eyed, golden-haired little girl. . . . The maintenance of peaceful and harmonious relationships, which have been conducive to the well-being of both the white and negro races in the South, has been possible because of the inviolability of Southern Womanhood." The most fevered nightmare for Brady and his followers was white men losing control of white women. Maintaining purity of blood, his single greatest concern, meant regulating intimacy. The "inviolability of Southern Womanhood" was key to policing bloodlines. That was the danger in the *Brown* decision— open the schools and you open the gates to social intimacy and from there to miscegenation. It was as if *Brown* would overthrow three hundred years of southern chasteness (Brady failed to mention the centuries of forced race mixing—rape—of white men with African American women).[9]

The logic was self-reinforcing, racial segregation kept white women pure, and the purity of white women proved the efficacy of segregation. The hierarchy of race and gender placed white men atop subject peoples, whether dark skinned or female, or both. Sociologists of the South, Brady's contemporaries like Gunnar Myrdal, John Dollard, and Wilbur J. Cash, observed that this combination of race and sex was at the core of white male identity and, tragically often, the font of racial violence.[10]

There was much more in *Black Monday*. Brady discussed how Yankee slave traders made their piles of money then, hypocritically, condemned the south for holding slaves; he spent many pages on court decisions and laws and precedents that *Brown* foolishly swept away. Then he borrowed from William Graham Sumner, the Yale sociologist who argued more than fifty years earlier that customs and mores were far deeper and more intractable than laws. From this, Brady asserted that white southerners understood Negroes, took care of them, unlike those who criticized segregation from afar. Brady also went out of his way to quote liberals who questioned the wisdom of integration, including the *Delta Democrat-Times* editor Hodding Carter: "'The southern negro, by and large, does not want an end to segregation in itself any more than does the southern white man. The negro in the South knows that . . . those things which he does want— the vote, educational opportunities and the rest—are more readily attainable in the South that is not aroused against Federal intervention in the field of segregation.'"[11]

Finally, there was Communism. Brady wrote in the shadow of the McCarthy era and the hearings of the House Committee on Un-American Activities. He dedicated *Black Monday* to anti-Communists and praised the defenders of state's rights against the growing power of the federal government. American schools and churches were infected with Communist ideas, Brady argued, easing citizen's acceptance of the unconstitutional *Brown* decision. Overseas, he added, "the Communist masses of Russia and Red China must have howled with glee on 'Black Monday,'" for they realized that racial intermarriage would fatally weaken America.[12]

It all circled back to genetics. Both the NAACP and the Communists wanted "amalgamation." Radical blacks believed they could fix their own biological inferiority through intermarriage, "just as the strain of a long horn can be improved by being bred with a white-faced Hereford." Communists wanted nothing more than for America to become "a race of long horns," of inferior cattle, so the Reds were happy to encourage intermarriage. The solution for Brady was to root out those who sought the dilution of America's racial stock, domestic Communists (who were mostly immigrants anyway), and NAACP agitators.[13]

Black Monday's ideology was stale and derivative, but Brady freshened old ideas with his prose. His timing was perfect. The thousands of copies that came off the presses in Winona, Mississippi, along with Brady's peripatetic speech giving, ignited the Citizens' Council brushfire. By the end of summer, 1954, Robert Patterson and half a dozen others founded the very first chapter in Indianola, thirty miles from Greenwood, in Sunflower County. In just one year there were hundreds of Citizens' Council chapters and tens of thousands of members—estimates ran as high as a quarter million—throughout the South.[14]

The Citizens' Councils were not to be confused with the Ku Klux Klan. As Brady himself said, Klansmen wore masks, members of the Citizens' Councils were proud to show their faces. There was no shame, and nothing illegal. The Councils were filled with the cream of southern society. "Delta aristocrats," Will Campbell, a white Mississippi Baptist preacher who devoted his life to the freedom struggle, called them. Campbell described the founders at Indianola: "A Harvard-educated attorney, a prominent banker, and the manager of the well-known Indianola Cotton Compress were among those present." Before the year was up, the group included many "of the most substantial civic and business leaders in the area, none of whom could be called ignorant rednecks or any of the other names which have so often been used to identify southern racists."[15]

Brady's words inspired these men because he was one of them, their kinsman in social rank. "They were not only leaders in business and commerce, they were leaders in culture and learning," Campbell wrote; "They would spread from there to every part of the South and would develop a method and expertise of community organizing seldom rivaled in America." Even J. Edgar Hoover confirmed Campbell's assessment, telling President Eisenhower's cabinet, not unapprovingly, that the Citizens' Councils featured bankers, lawyers, doctors, legislators, industrialists, in a word, "some of the leading citizens of the South."[16]

The Citizens' Councils employed a variety of tactics: outing local NAACP members, proselytizing whites, courting favors from local politicians who themselves sometimes were members, pressuring other politicians to toe the line, Red baiting alleged Communists, leaning on local justice officials and juries. In particular, the Councils applied economic pressure to activist African Americans, including calling in mortgages, refusing to grant loans to farmers, and getting people fired from their jobs for such activities as voter registration. A black gas station owner who refused to put up a "Colored Only" sign had his mortgage called in. A black dentist had his credit cut off. An African American medical doctor who joined the NAACP was told by his patients that their employers would not pay their bills anymore. The Yazoo City Citizens' Council advertised the names of fifty-three blacks who petitioned in the local paper for integrated schools, and they suddenly started losing their jobs, credit, and access to stores until all but two of them withdrew their names. In the town of Isola, two African American farmers were forced to remove themselves from the voting rolls before the local cotton gin would process their cotton.[17]

Leaders in the Citizens' Councils disavowed the use of violence and even claimed they exerted no economic pressure. In a narrow sense, this was true—the Councils were clearinghouses of information, the mimeograph machine their weapon of choice. For example, the Jackson chapter issued "Confidential Communique No. 14" to members, notifying them that a local man was publishing a newspaper advocating integration. The bank soon closed his accounts, and someone smashed his windows. His newspaper ceased publication, but the Jackson Council claimed no credit; it just quietly spread the word, and Mississippi's climate of fear and intimidation did the rest.[18]

The Councils billed themselves as modern versions of old-time town meetings, expressing the will of the people while upholding their Constitutional rights to free speech and assembly. Above all, they raised awareness that whites were in a fight to preserve The Southern Way of Life. They distributed thousands of pamphlets with titles like "A Christian View on Segregation," "A Jewish View on Segregation," and "The Ugly Truth About the NAACP." Asked by librarians at the University of Mississippi to suggest some books that expressed the "southern viewpoint" on race relations, Robert Patterson sent a list that included Madison Grant's *The Passing of the Great Race*, Lothrop Stoddard's *The Rising Tide of Color Against White World Supremacy*, and Claude Bowers's history of Reconstruction, *The Tragic Era*, all well-worn racist texts, popular in the 1920s.[19]

The goal? "The Citizens' Council is the South's answer to the mongrelizers," explained one of their popular pamphlets: "*We will not be integrated. We are proud of our white blood and our white heritage of sixty centuries.*" If white southerners were bigoted, then so were George Washington,

Thomas Jefferson and Abraham Lincoln. The stakes were high and the fight would be long: "Eighty years ago our unconquerable ancestors were beaten, in poverty and degradation, unable to vote and under the heel of negro occupation troops. All they had was their underlying courage and faith that the Almighty helps those who help themselves." White southerners would prevail again, just like their Reconstruction-era ancestors: "Are we less than they? We are the same blood; white blood that was kept pure for you for 6,000 years by white men."[20]

Jim Crow had gone upscale. Citizens' Councils' members were mostly middle class and higher, and each chapter cultivated an image of respectability. They were at pains to avoid the Klan's reputation for "red-neck" crudity and violence. The better sort of people would maintain apartheid without cross-burnings and white robes, whippings and beatings. But violence certainly had not disappeared, and it often followed in the Citizens' Councils' wake.[21]

Segregation meant racially separate schools, restrooms, water fountains, cafes, and hotels. Less formally, white supremacy required those subtle markers of superior and inferior status, of caste: blacks doffing their hats to whites; always using honorifics like Mr. and Mrs., Sir and Ma'am; stepping off the sidewalk as white people approached; avoiding eye contact; never offering to shake hands with a white person, as if black touch might contaminate. While in theory, African Americans could acquire property and power, for the most part they could not vote or run for office, and they remained an impoverished rural peasantry by law and custom. Needless to say, segregated black schools were inferior ones, with short semesters designed to get kids into the cotton fields to sow and tend and harvest. Above all, school segregation meant keeping black boys away from white girls: the most emotionally charged issue that Jim Crow segregation sought to address was black men becoming intimate with white women, and worse, white women reciprocating the attraction. Segregated lunch counters mattered; segregated bedrooms mattered more.[22]

The Citizen's Council's bête noire was the NAACP. Judge Brady accused the organization of taking over the executive and judicial branches of the federal government and attempting to do the same to the states. Referring to NAACP "aggression," Robert Patterson declared, "Southerners will not be intimidated, and the character and integrity of the South will preserve itself just as it did 80 years ago.... There won't be any integration in Mississippi. Not now, not 100 years from now, maybe not 6,000 years from now—maybe never."[23]

Though bigoted and paranoid, men like Brady and Patterson had reason to be fearful. The fact is the NAACP legal defense team, headed by Thurgood

Marshall, was very formidable, steadily chipping away at Jim Crow, culminating with the *Brown* decision. If not the subversive juggernaut of southern whites' nightmares, the NAACP was indeed determined to end segregation by undercutting white supremacist laws. That assault was gathering steam, and worst of all, it was not entirely the work of northern meddlers, far from it. At the core of white southern mythology was the belief that black folks were content with their lot, that left alone by outsiders, they remained loyal to The Southern Way of Life. But growing evidence contradicted that faith. Indeed, what necessitated the Councils was the fact that local black leaders in the South were not backing down.[24]

On the eve of Emmett Till's death, both movements—to preserve Jim Crow and to extend black freedom, exemplified by the Citizens' Councils and the NAACP respectively—were growing, not just in the Delta but also across the entire South. Two weeks before the lynching of Emmett Till, two thousand white Mississippians gathered in Senatobia to hear Senator James O. Eastland and Judge Brady rail against the Supreme Court's new directive to desegregate the schools "with all deliberate speed." The court had destroyed the Constitution with the *Brown* decision, Eastland thundered: "You are not required to obey any court which passes out such a ruling. In fact, you are obligated to defy it." Just a few days after the Senatobia meeting, more than a thousand citizens in nearby Clarksdale organized that town's own chapter of the Citizens' Council.[25]

In a stump speech given to Councils across the South in late 1955 and early 1956, Eastland accused the Supreme Court of doing the bidding of "a pro-Communist political movement." The NAACP was a front, and other "large organizations with tremendous power" now openly tried "to brainwash and indoctrinate the American people to accept racial integration and mongrelization." All based in the northeast, these liberal groups included "the blood red Communist party," the "almost equally Red" National Council of Churches of Christ, the Ford Foundation, the Carnegie Foundation, the Marshall Field, Rosenwald, and Rockefeller Foundations. All campaigned for integration, and together created "a continual rain of propaganda" through their control of newspapers, magazines, radio and television.[26]

The *Brown* decision, Eastland argued, constituted "the most dangerous abrogation of the sovereign rights of the states" ever perpetrated by a branch of the federal government, and it was the state legislatures' obligation to pass acts of nullification—laws contravening the court's decision. "We are about to embark on a great crusade," Eastland repeatedly emphasized in the weeks before and after Emmett Till came to Mississippi, "a crusade to restore Americanism, and return the control of our government to the people." The senator concluded, "Generations of Southerners yet unborn will cherish our memory because they will realize that the fight we now wage will have preserved for them their untainted racial heritage, their culture, and the institutions of the Anglo-Saxon race."[27]

Such talk did not sit well with Hodding Carter, the editor of the liberal *Delta Democrat-Times*, who expressed his feelings in an article in *Look* magazine. Early in 1955, the Councils helped secure two constitutional amendments in Mississippi, one further restricting black voting rights and another abolishing public schools should enforcement of the *Brown* decision appear imminent. For opposing these amendments, Carter received threatening letters. The intimidation rankled him. Even though he opposed school integration, Carter believed that compromise—"the genius of democracy"—was still possible. It was not American, he wrote, to bully people out of their rights or to believe in a master race. Worst of all was the deepening feeling of white against black and the specter of violence: "The threat has always lurked in rural Mississippi," Carter wrote, "in the courthouse corridors every time a Negro seeks to register, every time he is suspected of believing in or advocating integration or support of the NAACP; every time he appears to step out of line in any way." The community leaders who organized the Councils might not bloody their hands, Carter warned, but they all knew plenty of men who would.[28]

Hodding Carter was right about the dangers posed by the Citizens' Councils, but the bullying and intimidation he described were not irrational. The attack on Jim Crow was no figment of racist imaginations: it was real, and a growing number of African Americans joined the battle. Blacks resisted the assaults that came from the likes of Brady, Patterson, and Eastland in countless ways, everything from the dozen children in Jackson who signed a petition asking that their schools be desegregated just a month before Emmett Till's death, to a St. Louis youth council boycott of White Castle's segregated lunch counters—"Boycott Bigot Burgers," their signs read as they marched. This was happening even as officials searched for his body.[29]

But the most dramatic moment of black opposition to the white power structure came just a few months before Emmett Till's murder. The journalist Simeon Booker had never set foot in Mississippi before April 1955. Booker was thirty-seven years old, the Washington Bureau chief for *Jet* magazine, which was founded in 1951 by Chicago's John H. Johnson Publishing Company and was the first national magazine devoted to African American society and culture. Every week the cover of the pocket-sized periodical featured a black starlet or celebrity. *Jet* was an aspirational publication, highlighting success stories, folks who had made it and whose examples might point the way for others. It was more about lifestyle than politics yet dispatches from the developing freedom struggle often found their way onto its pages.[30]

Booker, along with a photographer, David Jackson, flew from Chicago to Memphis in April 1955 to cover an organizing drive for black voting rights. They changed into work clothes, rented a beat-up car, and, hoping to pass as field workers, drove into the Delta. Mississippi scared them, especially the thought of being on the road after nightfall. Booker recalled the old joke about a black preacher from Chicago who asked God to be with him on his first trip to the Deep South. Yes, I'll stay with you, the Lord told the preacher, but only as far as Memphis.[31]

Booker and Jackson made it safely to Mound Bayou, where they met Dr. T. R. M. Howard, who organized the upcoming event for the Regional Council of Negro Leadership, a growing southern civil rights organization, led by a rising black middle class. Howard himself was a successful medical doctor and owner of an insurance company—Medgar Evers, a local leader of the NAACP, made his living selling policies for Howard's company—and he used his money to build a secure, armed compound, a safe space for organizing. In the middle of the Mississippi Delta, Mound Bayou was a heavily guarded, all-black town.[32]

Ten thousand Afro-Mississippians descended on Mound Bayou, where they heard speaker after speaker discuss the movement for civil liberties and strategies to register voters. This was not the first such gathering, but it was the largest, and it got little coverage outside the black press. Booker later called the meeting the beginning of the Civil Rights Movement and the fore-runner of events like the Mississippi Freedom Summer ten years later.[33]

After speaking to the crowd at Mound Bayou, a local activist, the Reverend George Lee returned to his hometown of Belzoni in Humphries County. He was assassinated just days later, when a car pulled alongside his vehicle and shotgun blasts tore through his face and body. The local sheriff's office never seriously investigated the case, and Governor Hugh White refused to intervene. African American newspapers like the *Chicago Defender* gave his murder extensive coverage and, honoring his wife's request, carried photos of Rev. Lee's funeral, his coffin open, his facial wounds unmasked. Three months later, another voting rights activist who attended the Mound Bayou meetings, a sixty-one-year-old farmer and World War I veteran by the name of Lamar Smith was shot to death just outside the Lincoln County courthouse in Brookhaven, hometown of Judge Tom Brady. The sheriff's office never brought charges, never identified the killers, but suggested, absurdly, that Smith died at the hands of a jealous rival. The white press, North and South, ignored Smith's murder too.[34]

As northerners and newsmen, Booker and Jackson took a serious risk by going south to cover those early days of ferment. But they knew that the danger they courted was nothing compared to what thousands of southern black citizens faced standing up for their rights. The freedom struggle began long before Greensboro, Selma, and Birmingham. The Citizens' Councils represented a backlash against a rising assault on white supremacy. Blacks attempting to vote, the threat of school integration, politicians fanning the flames against desegregation, all grew more intense during the summer of 1955. And Emmett Till's murder was about to become part of that story.[35]

CHAPTER SEVEN

LET THE PEOPLE SEE WHAT THEY DID TO MY BOY

ONE OF EMMETT TILL'S COUSINS, Curtis Jones, called his mother in Chicago from Mississippi early Sunday morning, August 28; Willie Mae Jones in turn called her cousin Mamie with the news that some white men had come in the night and taken Bo. There was so little to go on—who were they, what did they want, why Emmett, where was he now? In a fog of shock and fear, she and her husband, Gene, drove to Argo to be with family, especially Mamie's mother, Alma. Friends and relatives gathered at Alma's home, and they tried to learn more but could not reach Mose Wright by phone. They called Alma's brother Crosby Smith in Sumner, Mississippi, who reported that Aunt Lizzy and the boys were staying at his home, and that he and Papa Mose were going to the sheriff's office in Greenwood, so everyone was safe for now—except Emmett. Family and friends all walked over to Argo's Church of God in Christ, where the congregation prayed for them.[1]

Later, Alma's husband suggested that Mamie speak with his nephew, Rayfield Mooty. Mooty worked for Inland Steel and was head of his union local. He seemed to know everyone in Chicago: politicians, civil rights officials, and leaders of the auto, packinghouse, and sleeping car porters unions. By Monday morning, August 29, Mooty had arranged for Mrs. Bradley to meet with Chicago NAACP leaders, including an attorney, William Henry Huff. Huff was long involved with Mississippi issues, and between him, Mooty, and their friends, stories started showing up in the Chicago newspapers. Statements of support came from Mayor Richard J. Daley and the Illinois governor William Stratton; the South Side congressman William Dawson also quietly got involved. But mostly the Till Family, North and South, waited hour by hour, fearing for Emmett's fate.[2]

The call came Wednesday morning, August 31, not long after Robert Hodges found two legs dangling on top of the water.

Since the body floated up a few hundred feet within his jurisdiction, the Tallahatchie County Sheriff Clarence Strider came out to the river, but so did deputies from Leflore County, who stopped at Mose Wright's home, picked him up, and drove him out to identify the body. They sent the corpse back to Greenwood with an undertaker who had been called to the scene, and arranged for a quick burial later that day in in a Money churchyard.[3]

Mamie Till Bradley and her family must have expected this because as soon as they heard about the internment plans, they started making calls. Mamie's uncle, Crosby Smith, promised that Emmett would not rest in Mississippi soil. Three hours after they dragged the body from the river, Smith drove down to Money, where he found a shallow grave. "They were getting ready to spill the boy into that," Smith later told reporters; "He hadn't even been embalmed." Smith swore that Emmett's body would get to Chicago, "if I had to take it in my own truck." Later that day, Sheriff Strider signed the death certificate: Emmett Till, Negro, Male, homicide by gunshot or a blow with an ax, body removed to Chicago Illinois for burial.[4]

Mrs. Bradley contacted A. A. Rayner, who owned one of the largest African American mortuaries in Chicago, and Rayner secured her son's transfer back home for $3,300 and a pledge to bury him immediately. First, the body was taken from Greenwood to Tutwiler for embalming. Then on Thursday, September 1, little more than a day after they found him, he was on an Illinois Central train, heading back to Chicago. Later it was revealed that Congressman William L. Dawson intervened on Mrs. behalf, contacting the governor of Mississippi to stop the burial in Money and bring Emmett home. Dawson was the consummate political insider, a cog in Chicago's political machine, certainly not an outspoken "race man." Yet he worked quietly for his constituents, gaining patronage and contracts, chiseling at the edges of racial discrimination. Mrs. Bradley later credited Dawson with being a secret benefactor during and long after the summer of 1955.[5]

The train arrived early Friday morning at the Twelfth Street Station, on the very platform where tens of thousands of black southern migrants had disembarked for a new life in Chicago. Mamie's family in Mississippi tried to let her know by phone what to expect, but there really was no preparing for what came next.[6]

Newspapers carried notices of the train's arrival, so hundreds of South Siders milled around the station as the train pulled in, and a crew began to unload an enormous crate. "A morbid silence engulfed the station," reported the *Chicago Defender*. "Veteran newspaper men and photographers, whose daily schedules include murders and fatal accidents, were grim-faced as they watched the procedure." Workers hoisted the crate off the train and opened it, releasing a terrible smell. They lifted out a smaller box and placed it in a hearse, which then headed to the Rainer Funeral Home on Cottage Grove Avenue.[7]

Mamie Till Bradley watched it all from a wheelchair at train side—she did not trust her legs to bear the weight of the day. "Oh, God, Oh God. My only boy," she cried out when they opened the crate. *Life* immortalized the moment with a photo and caption, "Homecoming of a Lynch Victim." She stood, then collapsed, finally helped to her feet by her husband, her father, Rayfield Mooty, and other kin, as well as Bishop Louis Ford and the Reverend Isaiah Roberts, both of the Church of God in Christ. There, too, stood her Uncle Crosby, who, good as his word, had accompanied Emmett's body back home. All prayed together and then followed the hearse to Rayner's.[8]

Mr. Rayner promised Mississippi officials that he would not open the box when it arrived in Chicago, but Mrs. Bradley insisted. She must know for sure that it was her son, she must see him. Rayner explained that he had signed papers agreeing not to break an official Mississippi seal on the casket; Mamie's own family in Mississippi signed similar documents. She would not be denied. Rayner told her to wait for a few minutes, then he brought her to view Emmett.[9]

She had been on the verge of collapse that whole morning, but now she steeled herself, knowing that she had to make the identification and be certain. "I couldn't allow myself to get emotional, to lose control now. I had to get through this," she recalled years later. She surveyed Emmett's body, beginning with his feet, noting things that never registered before, his graceful ankles and chubby knees. Finally she got to his neck, then his face: "I had started out doing this item analysis with the kind of detachment a forensic doctor might have, but I wasn't a forensic doctor. I was Emmett's mother and I was overwhelmed by a mother's anguish as I continued tracking Emmett through his night of torture." She looked at his tongue swollen and choked out of his mouth, his own right eye, hanging by the optic nerve out of its socket, the back of his skull crushed, a bullet hole over his ear. "I thought about what it must have been like for him that night. I studied every detail of what those monsters had done to destroy his beautiful young life. I thought about how afraid he must have been, how at some point that early Sunday morning he must have known he was going to die. I thought about how all alone he must have felt, and I found myself hoping only that he died quickly."[10]

Viewing her beloved son lying on a slab, she made a decision: "Let the people see what they did to my boy."[11]

Mamie Till Bradley was not the first to do this. George Lee's widow insisted on an open coffin after his assassination in Belzoni the previous May, and Mrs. Bradley probably read about it in the *Chicago Defender*. The funeral directors knew they could not do much more with Emmett's appearance, that the smell too would never fully go away—an embalmer had worked on the body in Tutwiler, Mississippi, then packed it in lime before shipping it on to Chicago—another reason why A. A. Rayner tried to persuade his client to keep the coffin lid closed. His job was to clear mourners' paths, to blur the line a bit between the living and the dead, to make funerals more palatable, not less. But she stood by her decision.[12]

The morticians made a few cosmetic changes, sewed Emmett's tongue back into his mouth and his eye into its socket, stitched up the back of his skull, closed his eyelids, dressed him in the suit that Mamie brought in, the suit she gave him for that happy Christmas in 1954. Rayner placed the coffin in the front room, with only a pane of glass over it separating Emmett from his viewers. Mamie attached a few Christmas photos of her son to the satin on the open casket lid—happy pictures, Emmett in his holiday best, mother and son smiling for the camera—a vivid contrast to the human ruin in the coffin.[13]

Friday evening, September 2, the Rayner Funeral Home at 4141 Cottage Grove Avenue, opened its doors.[14]

Over the next two days as many as fifty thousand people came to the viewing, as squads of Chicago policemen kept order. Most of those who filed past Emmett's coffin were residents of the South Side, children of the early twentieth century's Great Migration, and even more new Chicagoans who came in the flood tide of the 1940s and early '50s from vast plantations and tiny towns. They were southerners and the descendants of southerners, sharecroppers and tenant farmers, maids and cooks, all of whom fled poverty and violence, bigotry and indignity.[15]

For a moment, staring down at young Emmett, they were back in the grip of their old southern nightmare.

The crowd was beyond the capacity of the Rayner Funeral Home, so the police roped off a three-block area around the mortuary. Some news reports referred to the funeral as a "mass demonstration," with people outside handing out radical literature, windows broken, the funeral home left in shambles. But it was the sheer crush of tens of thousands of people that did the damage. The Chicago police reported that the crowds were orderly. People were not violent but angry, very angry, according to the *Chicago Defender*. They had never heard of Emmett Till before this week, but they thought to themselves, "It was no crime for a boy to whistle at a pretty woman....My son might do it—or yours." And with that realization, the reporter wrote, "Bobo Till belonged to them. They came to see him, to talk to him, all swore they never would forget him. All day on Saturday the mourners came, and the police finally sent them home at 2 a.m."[16]

On Sunday, the staff at Rayner's took Emmett's body to the Roberts Temple of the Church of God in Christ on State Street, the "Mother Church" in Chicago. Long the spiritual home for the Till family in Mississippi and in Argo, the Church of God in Christ was a holiness denomination, Pentecostal in faith and practice; COGIC, as it was sometimes called, traced its origins to the Mississippi Delta in the late nineteenth century. The holiness churches were part of the culture of field hands and domestic workers, hard-working people freed from slavery only to fall victim to the American apartheid known as Jim Crow. In a white world that constantly preached black inferiority, the holiness churches taught that sanctification cleansed away sin, and Pentecostalism emphasized the personal experience of God through baptism. Ecstatic worship, the immediate presence of Jesus's saving grace, gospel music, and personal testimony, shouting and speaking in tongues, all were antidotes to segregation's poison.[17]

The Church of God in Christ was as much a hallmark of Delta cotton culture as the blues, and like the blues, integral now to northern black communities too. From tiny churches scattered in the countryside, the Church of God in Christ headed northward, first to Memphis in the early twentieth century, where tent revivals eventually blossomed into the thirty-thousand-square-foot Mason Temple, and finally up to Chicago, where a hundred storefront churches sprang up on the South Side, and the Mother Church, the stately Roberts Temple, presided at State and Fortieth Streets.[18]

The church held two thousand worshippers, nowhere near the capacity needed to accommodate the crowds that began to gather on the sidewalks early in the morning on September 4. They were well dressed and subdued but once inside the church, their emotions poured forth. "Loud screams pierced the air...as mourners caught sight of the body," the United Press reported. One woman fainted, then sobbed and screamed as she regained consciousness. Dozens of Emmett's friends and relatives came from Argo, and their presence also brought a wave of emotion.[19]

For an hour and a half, Bishop Isaiah Roberts, pastor and founder of the Roberts Temple, presided at the interdenominational service, as speaker after speaker came to the pulpit. Outside the church, thousands more listened over loudspeakers. The Reverend Cornelius Adams of the Greater Harvest Baptist Church urged mourners to contribute to a fund set up by the NAACP. The money, Adams said, went to pay legal expenses to end southern lynching, "fighting dollars" for Negro America. Adams also urged mourners to ignore the Communists distributing leaflets outside: "Pay them no heed. . . . We don't need communists." The Illinois state senator, Marshall Korshak, representing Governor Stratton, called Emmett, "a young martyr in the fight for democracy and freedom." Archibald Carey, another minister and former Chicago alderman, who sensed the anger in the pews, told the congregants that mob rule was no better in Chicago than in Mississippi, declaring, "revenge is not for us to seek and will not correct the thing that has happened."[20]

Bishop Louis Ford preached the funeral sermon, and congregants gave him loud and long approbation when he quoted from the New Testament Book of Matthew: "For as much as ye have done onto these, my little ones, ye have also done onto me." And again, "But whosoever shall offend one of these little ones which believe in me, it is better for him that a millstone was hung about his neck and that he drowned in the depths of the sea." What the killers did to poor Emmett would pale compared to what awaited them.[21]

While revenge belonged to God, change need not wait on divine intervention. Bishop Ford noted that "Secretary of State Dulles, Vice President Nixon, and our beloved President Eisenhower [who suffered a heart attack days earlier] are traveling throughout the world trying to buy good will for democracy." America's Cold War against Communism meant convincing others—especially people of color in Europe's old colonial empires in Asia and Africa and Latin America—that the United States was a beacon of liberty, a bulwark against tyranny. If that was true, Bishop Ford declared, then America's leaders should "go into the Southern states and tell the people there...that unless the Negro gets full freedom in America, it is impossible for us to be leaders in the rest of the world."[22]

Bishop Roberts closed the services by saying that Emmett Till's lynching was a black mark against the whole country, and only swift justice could erase it. And then he announced that the funeral would be postponed until Tuesday in accordance with the wishes of Mrs. Bradley, and Emmett's body would lie in state until then—his coffin lid up, the church doors open to all who wished to pay their respects. All through Sunday and Monday—Labor Day, September 5—people continued to come, the line on the street always at least a block or two long; still the Roberts Temple remained open day and night. Mamie Till Bradley had dared the world to come look at what the killers did to Emmett, and come they did. Captain Albert Anderson of the Chicago police, the man in charge of the funeral detail, estimated that one hundred thousand people viewed Emmett's body between Friday afternoon and Tuesday morning.[23]

Finally, on Tuesday, two thousand people jammed the temple one last time, as Bishops Ford and Roberts offered brief prayers. Mamie broke down as she peered into the coffin for a final look; her family helped her back to her seat. Then two hundred mourners in fifty cars drove down to the town of Alsip at the southern edge of Cook County, then into Burr Oak cemetery, where they laid young Emmett Till to rest. That same Tuesday, September 6, the grand jury sitting in Tallahatchie County indicted Roy Bryant and J. W. Milam for murder.[24]

Before the funeral service, shortly after the body arrived in Chicago, Mrs. Bradley had allowed *Jet* magazine's staff photographer David Jackson to photograph her son at the Rayner Funeral Home. He took more photos two days later at the Roberts Temple. The images were published in the September 15 issue of *Jet*, which sold out its initial edition and was reprinted many, many times. The magazine's parent company, Johnson Publications, authorized a few African American newspapers, including the *Chicago Defender*, to reprint them. These are the photos remembered today as icons of their era, a wake-up call to Americans that something was deeply amiss.[25]

This is only partly true. The pictures circulated widely among African Americans, North and South, stirred them deeply, saddened and outraged them, strengthened their sense of identity with each other, evoked countless conversations about what was to be done. It is hard to imagine that many black people failed to stare at Emmett Till's battered visage in the mid-1950s. However, the photographs were hardly seen by white people. The wire services never distributed them, the mainstream press did not reprint them, and they were far too graphic for television. Even the news was segregated. Years later, many white Americans remembered—falsely remembered—the epiphany of seeing Till's ruined face in 1955. Few white people saw the photos until thirty years later when the documentary *Eyes on the Prize* opened with the Emmett Till story. Only then did Mamie Till Bradley's words, "Let the people see what they did to my boy" begin to be fully realized.[26]

But for African Americans—for the tens of thousands who peered down at Emmett's body, and the hundreds of thousands moved by his death photographs—the Till funeral was revelatory. The historian Adam

Green calls it a "moment of simultaneity," of "black national feeling," of "collective racial will." There had been earlier moments of heightened racial consciousness, and there would be many more in years to come. But the death of the Chicago lad and the courage of his mother had touched a nerve. African Americans came together here in horror and outrage. All were represented—North and South, Chicago and Mississippi, leaders like Dr. Howard and Bishop Ford, mothers like Mamie Till Bradley, workers and the poor in the streets for the funeral, organizations like the NAACP, the churches, and the black press. For a moment, they saw themselves together, intensely, collectively, as one. [27]

CHAPTER EIGHT

MISSISSIPPI'S INFAMY

VIRTUALLY EVERY NEWSPAPER in America covered Emmett Till's funeral, many of them on their front pages, under banner headlines. By the time Till was buried in Burr Oak Cemetery, just six days after his body was discovered in the Tallahatchie River, interpretations of his death had gelled. Because the African American press published weekly rather than daily, it took time for coverage of the murder and funeral to appear, but when it did, fury flowed with printer's ink.

Under the headline "Mississippi's Infamy," the *Chicago Defender* described how racial killings like Till's dishonored the United States in the eyes of the world. Noting that Louis Till died overseas as a soldier during World War II, the *Defender* declared that the son "was a victim of the very thing his father fought to extirpate—racial violence." The *Defender* criticized Mamie Till Bradley's advice to Emmett, before he went to Mississippi, that he should get down on his hands and knees and beg forgiveness should a white person take offense at anything he said. No, the lesson of Money, Mississippi, was that "there is no way to avoid trouble in the South, when 'peckerwoods' are bent on creating trouble for Negroes.... The Negro who genuflects to prejudice will never gain the white man's respect—instead he invites violence."[1]

In a companion piece, the *Defender* asked what caused white men to commit such a bloody act of terror against a child? The answer was the "southern tradition," of looking at blacks as less than human, "much as one feels toward a mongrel dog." No matter how innocent his motives, by violating the taboo about black men and white women, young Till signed his own death warrant. The article echoed the dominant social-psychology of racism going back to the famous work of Gunnar Myrdal in *An American Dilemma*: "The fact is, the white men involved in Emmett's lynching are sick—sick with racial prejudice, a disease that plagues the South today." Emmett's blood, the *Defender* concluded, was on the hands of every southern legislator, teacher, and minister who accepted the diseased logic of white supremacy and failed to condemn such criminal acts.[2]

Other African American weeklies echoed the *Defender*'s critique, but not all. Southern black newspapers found themselves in a delicate position. The moderate *Jackson Advocate*, for example, published by the Mississippian Percy Greene, was ever the soul of accommodation, castigating outsiders who failed to understand local conditions, and calling for the same modest reforms as white southern liberals. Greene advocated voting rights and equal opportunities but argued these were best achieved on a separate—segregated—black track, with the cooperation of white moderates. Integration would only generate more "friction producing contacts," like Emmett Till's moment with Carolyn Bryant. The *Advocate* castigated Roy Wilkins for his blanket indictment of white Mississippians and rejected T. R. M. Howard's remarks in *Jet* magazine that any more killings like Till's could lead to a racial civil war. "The Negro who lives in Mississippi knows that there are thousands of fine white people in the state who wholeheartedly condemn the slaying of the Till boy," the *Advocate* concluded. Moderation, not integration, was the answer; black and white leaders, working in the spirit of interracial goodwill understood that "the Negroes desire and right to equality under the law" was the true path forward.[3]

One had to ignore the Citizens' Councils, massive resistance to *Brown v. Board of Education*, and the murders of voting rights activists to believe equality under the law was on its way to Mississippi. Still, Hodding Carter's *Delta Democrat-Times*, the leading liberal mouthpiece in the region, offered a pale version of such high-minded moderation. Like virtually every other southern editor, the progressive Carter was appalled by Emmett Till's funeral. It had to be a plot by the NAACP to "apply the torch of world-wide scorn to Mississippi." Carter declared, "All the macabre exhibitionism, the wild statements and hysterical overtones at the Chicago funeral of the Till child seemed too well staged not to have been premeditated." Northerners and militants were to blame if Mississippi hardened its heart to the Till family. Carter warned that the attacks on the South might make it impossible to empanel an impartial jury to convict the killers, and it would be on the conscience of the NAACP and their ilk if Milam and Bryant went free.[4]

Most Mississippi newspapers took an even harder line. Everyone knew, the *Greenwood Morning Star* declared, that the case wasn't about race at all, it was about meddlers, like Mayor Daley of Chicago, who very publicly called for a federal investigation, and the NAACP, which organized rallies and demonstrations. "Justice in the Till case appeared certain of being carried out by the court, had the outsiders not interfered," stated a *Morning Star* editorial. Fears of northern blacks coming south further poisoned the atmosphere, leading to a spike in gun sales. The media distorted the news, giving lavish coverage to Till's funeral while failing to cover stories like that of the Kearney children saving their Negro nurse who had fallen in the Tallahatchie River, stories that were "much more typical of the actual pleasant relations between the races." The *Morning Star* editors concluded, "We sum up the whole thing by giving the warning that the agitation is inspired by Communists or by persons who have become unwitting victims of the Communist plan to stir up trouble where possible."[5]

The *Greenwood Commonwealth* blasted northern editors for impugning the integrity, honor, and mercy of white people in Mississippi by assuming that a jury would set the brothers free. "The real victim here," the *Commonwealth* concluded, "was not the colored boy from Chicago but the South." Over and over, editorialists repeated the theme that critics slandered the whole state, the whole region, and that victimization was white, not black. The *Tupelo-Lee County Tribune* went further: a "smart-aleck" negro boy without the good sense to not insult a married woman got in trouble with her husband. But now a body floats up, obviously too decomposed to be that of the kid from Chicago, and every "pink-tainted" newspaper and "loud-mouth rabble-rouser" in America seizes the story. Mississippi had nothing to apologize for. Tallahatchie County would handle the Till case like any other—fairly.[6]

And on it went, condemn the killing and condemn those who made it a story about race. The *Jackson Daily News* called it a "stupid and horrible crime," the *Hattiesburg American* described its readers as "sorely distressed and severely shocked" by the killing, the *Laurel Leader-Call* labeled the murder a "brutal and devilish" act, and the *Vicksburg Post* declared that all Mississippians were "revolted by the senseless brutality." Editors reassured their readers that the rule of law would prevail. But their indignation at the murder and guarantees of swift justice also acted as a buffer against the thought that anything was fundamentally amiss, or that this was a racial crime. Being horrified by murder confirmed one's humanity; individuals could deny that Emmett Till's death was about race or white supremacy and still see themselves as sensitive, compassionate. Quite uniformly, newspapers inveighed against accusations that the murder was rooted deep in southern soil. This killing was the work of a couple of thugs whom the courts would punish—Mamie Till Bradley, the NAACP, and slanderous northern editors be damned.[7]

Milam and Bryant would go to trial in just two weeks, and that very fact looked like progress to many observers, northern and southern alike. The *New York Times* saw a great leap forward when "the Tallahatchie County grand jury, entirely made up of white men, took this step against other white men for a crime against a Negro." In the state with the largest black population in the nation, where lynching had always gone unpunished, these prompt indictments revealed, "that the people of contemporary Mississippi are against this form of murder." It was a harbinger of racial justice, according to America's "newspaper of record."[8]

Claude Barnett was having none of it. As founder of the Associated Negro Press—the AP for more than two-hundred African American newspapers—Barnett viewed the grand jury's actions with far less optimism. Yes, the indictments were the first time in Mississippi that white men stood charged with murder in the death of a black man. But it was only after the "saddest funeral" in Chicago's history that the all-white grand jury acted. Only the butchering of a child shamed the jurors into handing down the indictments. The whole sordid case, Barnett concluded, measured how far Mississippi had fallen, not how high she had risen.[9]

In a scathing editorial, the *Chicago Defender* excoriated both the Democratic and Republican parties for harboring bigots. Convicting Milam and Bryant was not enough, for they were merely the shock troops, white supremacy's henchmen who acted within a larger racist context. Mississippi's political leaders—the *Defender* singled out the Democratic candidates for governor, five "racist rabble-rousers"—routinely "campaigned on an anti-Negro platform" and "charged the atmosphere of the state for acts of violence." The lynching of Emmett Till was on their heads, and the trial and even conviction of the triggermen could not wash the blood from the hands of Mississippi politicians.[10]

Though it had just begun, the Emmett Till story already stirred age-old emotions about interracial sex, violence, white supremacy, and black freedom. The battle of images—of how to portray Till, his mother, Milam, Bryant, Mississippi, Jim Crow, black and white folks both North and South—became inseparable from the story. Southerners fingered subversives, outside agitators, naïve northerners. But resistance to segregation had troubled the South for a long time. The *Brown* decision—brought before the Supreme Court by the NAACP, backed by its Legal Defense

Fund and argued by its lead attorney, Thurgood Marshall—was only the most recent blow against Jim Crow. And much of the resistance came from inside the South, especially as young African American leaders like Medgar Evers, T. R. M. Howard, Ruby Hurley, Amzie Moore, Aaron Henry, and others emerged after World War II. A growing number of organizations, northern and southern, black and white, secular and religious, radical and moderate battled southern apartheid, attacked its moral and legal foundations, held it up to ridicule in the light of America's professed ideals of equality. With Emmett Till's murder, old conflicts suddenly snapped into sharp focus.[11]

Then the trial began.

TRIAL

CHAPTER NINE

A GOOD PLACE TO RAISE A BOY

ONLY A QUIRK of geography placed the trial in Sumner, Mississippi. Had Emmett Till's body turned up just a few yards downriver in Leflore County, the trial would have been staged in Greenwood, a city of more than twenty thousand, the "World's Largest Inland Long Staple Cotton Market," as the sign outside the courthouse read. Those covering the trial from Greenwood would have written their dispatches from a real Delta hub, with hotels and shops, movie theaters and restaurants. More important, the trial would have featured an entirely different cast—judge, sheriff, attorneys, jury.[1]

The same would have been true had the murderers dumped Emmett Till's body farther east. Tallahatchie has two county seats, Sumner to the west in the Delta, and Charleston to the east in the hill country. The two sides of the county feature vastly different landscapes, topography, and agriculture. In fact, torrential floods used to cut them off from one another before proper drainage was installed by the WPA during the Depression. In the 1950s the Delta side was a flat sea of white cotton each summer, bolls just waiting to be picked by a mostly black labor force. The hill country had smaller farms, more varied crops, substantial forests, timber production, and fewer African Americans. It also had Charleston, by far the larger of the two towns.[2]

But Till's body emerged nearer tiny Sumner, so the trial took place there.

Sumner's population was a little over five hundred, with one rooming house at the edge of town, and a classic turn-of-the century courthouse on the square with a Confederate monument in front. At the turnoff on Highway 49E, a sign announced, "Sumner: A Good Place to Raise a Boy." That, of course, depended on his color; Tallahatchie County was known as a hard case when it came to racial matters. The sign said nothing about raising girls.[3]

Sheriff's deputies moved defendants J. W. Milam and Roy Bryant from Leflore to Tallahatchie County just before the grand jury convened, but the suspects were housed in the Charleston jail because it was more secure than Sumner's. Officials were not worried about the brothers breaking out. It was the growing rumors of vigilante action against the accused that caused them concern. Greenwood's sheriff, George Smith, told the press that he had received threatening calls against Milam and Bryant after their initial arrests. And now, in Tallahatchie County, Sheriff Clarence Strider had dozens of letters coming into his office, which he described as "filthy and vicious," postmarked Chicago, swearing vengeance, especially if the brothers were acquitted. Strider showed one letter to reporters that included a photo of the defendants with their eyes poked out and bloodlike stains on their bodies.[4]

It quickly became clear, however, that Strider was bending the story. The sheriff claimed that members of the Bryant family "had their cars forced off the road over the weekend by automobiles bearing Illinois license plates." He repeated the rumor that a thousand African Americans were driving south from Chicago to the Delta with retribution on their minds. He offered no evidence, and if there was any real danger, it failed to materialize. Rumors aside, the only hard news was of Labor Day arrests near Clarksdale of thirteen people driving cars with Illinois license plates. They were speeding. Early September, of course, was still vacation season, with hundreds of families—black and white, northern and southern—on the road, visiting their families. Sunday and Monday nights remained quiet. Rumors notwithstanding, no throngs of angry northern blacks showed up in Greenwood, Charleston, or Sumner.[5]

District Attorney Gerald Chatham of Tallahatchie County sought indictments for murder and kidnapping. The eighteen-member grand jury—white men all, mostly farmers—began its work on Monday, September 6, as Emmett Till's body lay in state at the Roberts Temple, and it handed down those indictments on Tuesday, the very day Emmett's family buried him. Grand jury proceedings are secret and sealed, so we have little sense of the jurors' thinking aside from bits of information leaked to the press. Sheriffs Smith and Strider testified, as did Moses Wright, his son Simeon Wright, and deputies from Leflore and Tallahatchie Counties.[6]

Sheriff Strider changed his tune about the body he first saw just a few days earlier. "He didn't look like the picture that was run in a Jackson, Mississippi, newspaper of Till," Strider told reporters after he testified, adding that the corpse appeared to be that of a grown man, and that it was far too decomposed to have been submerged for just three days. Strider said he did not believe Milam and Bryant could be indicted on evidence "that just keeps getting slimmer and slimmer," and he suggested an alternative scenario: "I'm chasing down some evidence now that looks like the killing might have been planned and plotted by the NAACP." The corpse, Strider speculated, was not Till's but one planted by the real perpetrators to make it look like him.[7]

A grand jury decision hinged on the wishes of the prosecutor. If he (prosecutors were always men) made it clear that he had good evidence and wanted an indictment, the jurors usually delivered. Chatham must have argued hard for this one, as the grand jury disregarded Sheriff Strider's testimony. The brothers were brought to the Sumner Courthouse to appear before Tallahatchie County Circuit Court Judge Curtis Swango Jr. Standing without handcuffs, in fresh sport shirts, clean-shaven with neatly trimmed hair—their jailers had thought to stop at a barbershop—the two were arraigned, with District Attorney Chatham reading the charge that they "did unlawfully, willfully and feloniously and of their malice aforethought kill and murder Emmett Till, a human being."

"How do you plead?" Judge Swango asked.

"Not guilty," they each replied.

The murder charge carried a maximum penalty of death in the state's gas chamber, life in prison at minimum. Milam and Bryant were also charged with kidnapping, which meant at least a ten-year term. With the assent of both prosecution and defense attorneys, Judge Swango set a trial date just two weeks hence, rather than wait for the court's March session. Given the short time to trial, the accused did not post bond. Meanwhile, the Justice Department affirmed once again that no federal laws had been broken, that this would remain a Mississippi case.[8]

Shortly after the arraignments, District Attorney Chatham asked Mississippi Attorney General Coleman for an assistant. Although the trial was only expected to last a few days, the stakes were high, the publicity growing, and there was much preparation to be done in a mere two weeks. Besides, Chatham was in poor health; he planned to retire at the end of the year. Coleman consulted with Governor White and then appointed Robert B. Smith III, a former FBI agent from Ripley, Mississippi, to aid the prosecution. The governor used the occasion to emphasize his state's commitment to fair play: "The people of Mississippi are anxious to see justice done in this case according to the law and the evidence, and as governor I am glad to provide special counsel as evidence of our good faith in this prosecution." In addition, Tallahatchie County attorney Hamilton Caldwell served as the third prosecutor, though he would play a very limited role.[9]

The brutality of the murder and less-than-stellar reputation of the accused gave local residents pause, but very soon the case became a matter of defending state honor. Mamie Till Bradley's statement about Mississippi having to pay, and Roy Wilkins's remarks about lynching children to maintain white supremacy, and the spectacle of Emmett Till's funeral, and Sheriff Strider's alarm at threatening letters coming in from the North caused local elites to come together. After initially showing little interest in the case, all of Sumner's five attorneys coalesced into a defense team. J. J. Breland and John W. Whitten Jr. ran a two-man firm on the town square—Breland was Tallahatchie County Republican Party chairman, and Whitten chaired the Democratic Party and was attorney for the County Board of Supervisors. Harvey Henderson and Sidney Carlton also had their own shop; in a few years, the latter would be elected president of the Mississippi State Bar. They were joined by J. W. Kellum, another politically ambitious local light. Citizens' Council members encouraged them all to take the case.[10]

Milam and Bryant were not rich men, but in Delta towns, merchants put jars by their cash registers where patrons could donate spare change. There is no way to determine with precision how many people contributed or how much money they put up; the AP reported on the eve of the trial that the defense fund totaled $6,000, a reasonable guess. One contribution came in just three days after the arraignments. It was from Belzoni, where the Reverend George W. Lee had been murdered the previous May for encouraging African Americans to register to vote. Several dozen Belzoni citizens, almost all men, scraped up a dollar or two each and proudly sent the defense attorneys a total of $300. After the trial ended, it became clear that bigger men—wealthy Mississippi farmers and owners of agricultural equipment companies—contributed much more.[11]

The brothers' attorneys were not shy about asking for money. As enquiries came by phone and letter, Breland responded with encouragement and detailed instructions. Thomas Miller of the Miller and Arthur Insurance Company of Florence, South Carolina, for example, asked how he and like-minded locals might help the two men indicted "for defending their home and the purity of their white womanhood against the insult of an arrogant negro." Breland wrote back that the brothers' families possessed only about half the "very reasonable" attorneys' fees, and that they, "certainly could use some financial help." Breland emphasized the injustice of the kidnap and murder charges and described Emmett Till as "the negro who committed an assault and battery upon the wife of Roy Bryant and who in addition thereto, insulted her."[12]

Already the defense strategy was taking shape: attorney Sidney Carlton, their de facto spokesman, told reporters that Emmett Till did not just whistle at Carolyn Bryant, but, egged on by his companions, he entered the store, propositioned Bryant, grabbed and assaulted her, and finally had to be pulled out by one of his friends.[13]

In cases involving violent crime, a quick trial usually favors the prosecution, since feelings for the injured party run high. But who was the injured party here? The defense attorneys planned to make Carolyn and Roy Bryant the victims, hoping that they would benefit most from the emotionally charged atmosphere and a speedy trial. Besides, Carlton told the press, the publicity from Till's funeral made the prosecution's job harder because, "people here don't condone this kind of thing." Ordinarily, he pointed out, the defense would ask for a continuance to let emotions die down, "but the furor aroused by this case has served that purpose and we didn't want a delay." Then, too, the elected terms of office for both Chatham and Strider would end in 1955. The defense made no objections to an early trial, so Judge Swango, having set the date for September 19, ordered a special list of 120 jurymen to be drawn up, from whom a dozen would be selected. Women did not serve on Mississippi juries, and since no African Americans were allowed to register to vote in Tallahatchie County, none were available for jury duty.[14]

What exactly was the jury to decide? Milam and Bryant were accused of kidnapping and murder. The actual kidnapping clearly took place in Leflore County, where officials said they had an "air-tight case" against the brothers, including motives, eyewitnesses, and confessions. However, when the Tallahatchie County indictments came down, the grand jury sitting in Leflore County postponed its decision on the kidnapping charges. Kidnapping would be much harder to prove in Tallahatchie because the prosecution had to show that Milam and Bryant dragged Till into the county against his will. Since they had no such evidence, Chatham chose to let the kidnapping charges slide. He reasoned that if the Tallahatchie jury acquitted the brothers of murder, Leflore County could still indict them for kidnapping. As murder cases went, the evidence for the prosecution was not bad. True, no one came forward who had witnessed the crime or overheard a confession or produced the murder weapon. But the circumstantial evidence was reasonably strong, good enough for a conviction, all things being equal. Sheriff Smith, by the way, had drawn up papers against Carolyn Bryant but apparently thought better of it, and never arrested her. "We aren't going to bother the woman," Smith said; "She's got two small boys to take care of."[15]

Both sides rushed through their research, spoke with potential witnesses, and pondered whom to call to the witness stand. Subpoenas went out to law enforcement officers, forensic "experts," and kin of both the defendants and young Till. Prosecutor Chatham dropped the first bombshell when he announced to the press that he would ask Emmett Till's mother, Mamie Till Bradley, to come to Mississippi, adding that he extended to her his personal regret and the regret of the state of Mississippi for her son's death. She responded with equal graciousness that she was "not bitter against the white people, because you can't judge a whole race by one or two persons," and she added, "the color of a person's skin has never made any difference to me, and it never will.... Some of my best friends are among the white race." Her attorney, William Henry Huff, made it clear that she must have adequate protection in Mississippi, but he also took a conciliatory tone: "Mamie Bradley assures me that she has no ill will against the citizens of the state of Mississippi, that she knows, as we all know, that the majority of people in that state are bitterly opposed to brutalities perpetrated upon her son." Huff added, however, that he would file a $100,000 civil suit on behalf of Mrs. Bradley should the state fail to convict Milam and Bryant.[16]

CHAPTER TEN

THE NEWS CAPITOL OF THE UNITED STATES

THE DAY BEFORE Judge Swango called his court into session, Sumner residents mourned Kid Townsend, aged sixty, a "Negro man who was a town favorite" and who died of a heart attack just two days earlier. According to the *Jackson Clarion-Ledger*, many whites attended services in a special section reserved for them in a local black church. They helped raise food and money for Townsend's widow who "shed tears of gratitude" when the collection was given to her. Recalled one townsman, "Why ole Kid Townsend was just as much a part of Sumner as that Courthouse," pointing to the building where the Till trial would begin the next day.[1]

It was a cherished white view of race relations in Delta towns like Sumner, and not entirely inaccurate. Black and white worked side by side to clear the swamps, till the land, and make it bloom. One woman put it this way: "People of both races have always trusted each other. Why, there are only a few white people in Sumner who would hesitate to leave their children with a trusted Negro woman." White folks liked to think of their town as friendly, welcoming to strangers, a place where everyone knew everyone else. Blacks and whites lounged around the courthouse lawn at lunchtime, and "if any tension was felt by either race," one reporter concluded, "it wasn't evident." Locals feared, however, that the upcoming trial might spoil all of that. At the very least, Sumner would now be forever associated with Emmett Till's kidnapping and murder, though those events happened many miles away from the Tallahatchie County seat. Above all, townsfolk were bitter "against what they feel is an attempt by outside agitators to stir up trouble between Negroes and whites."[2]

These before-the-snake-slithered-into-the-garden stories—for the snake, read Chicago Negroes or the NAACP or Communists or just northerners in general—were both ubiquitous and highly selective. The African American reporter James L. Hicks attended Kid Townsend's funeral and reported that the congregation consisted of about 175 blacks but only a dozen whites. Yes, white parents left their children with "trusted" black women, but no white woman would ever demean herself to serve as a domestic worker for an African American family, assuming one so prosperous could be found in Sumner. And yes, too, both races lounged in front of the courthouse, but they rarely intermingled, for the unwritten rules of segregation gave whites the space near the courthouse entrance, while blacks congregated at the edge of the square, by the Confederate monument.[3]

Hicks found it difficult to judge how black people felt about the upcoming trial. Most were preoccupied with work, and some said they were not even aware when the proceedings would begin. Hicks did not find his interviewees to be outwardly fearful, "but when you mention the trial to them they speak of it in hushed and whispered tones and cast furtive glances about them as they speak." Fears that African Americans might storm the Delta to protest or even to kidnap Milam and Bryant proved to be a figment of Sheriff Strider's imagination.[4]

Other than Kid Townsend's send-off, Sumner was quiet on Sunday, September 18, its businesses closed for the Sabbath. Saturday, too, had been slow. African Americans normally crowded the streets for shopping, but this weekend they mostly stayed home. "It is always like that in time of trouble," a Sumner resident told one reporter. There was just a single small rooming house on the edge of town, the Delta Inn, whites only, reserved for the jury, so the newsmen, photographers, and camera crews who poured into Mississippi over the weekend stayed in the much larger town of Clarksdale—which even had three small hotels for blacks—twenty miles up U.S. Highway 49E. Many of the African American reporters roomed in nearby Mound Bayou, a town of two thousand, wholly populated and run by blacks.[5]

One visiting journalist described Sumner as "by cotton surrounded and by cotton sustained." Its namesake, Joseph Burton Sumner, moved west from Alabama with his family in 1872, part of a stream of settlers to the lands earlier seized by force from the Choctaws in the Mississippi Delta.

By early in the twentieth century the newcomers had hacked down trees, burned the underbrush, drained the swamps, killed the snakes, laid the railroad tracks, and more or less controlled the frequent flooding of this flat alluvial plain. Sumner did not trace a long, continuous history from the first cotton bolls picked by slave labor in Mississippi early in the nineteenth century, through the fall of Vicksburg in the Civil War, to the Till trial in 1955. This was the New South. Sumner was incorporated in 1900, became one of two county seats for Tallahatchie County in 1902, and acquired the courthouse in 1909. Barely two generations separated the laying of the building's cornerstone from the trial of Milam and Bryant, making it equidistant, timewise, between Appomattox and that fateful August day in Money. Sumner was part of a Delta cotton empire built mostly after slavery had ended.[6]

Ginning cotton, and then shipping it, was Sumner's main business. Cotton gave a living, though a meager one, to African American share-croppers and tenant farmers who worked the surrounding plantations or cleaned and cooked for white families. That same cotton provided wealth to build homes for white planters, professionals, and merchants, lovely homes on the banks of Cassidy Bayou, with big cypress trees growing out of its depths, located just a block east of the red brick courthouse, which was described by one Memphis journalist on the eve of the trial as "a small but stately temple of justice with businesses all around the square." Cotton wealth sustained these small businesses—bank, drugstore, doctor's office, mechanic shop, farming supply store. Local government kept it all running smoothly.[7]

The courthouse contained the sheriff's office, court clerk, county supervisor, tax assessor, and, on the second floor, the courtroom. Out front stood the obligatory monument to the county's Confederate dead, erected in 1913 by the United Daughters of the Confederacy, almost fifty years after the canons had gone silent and during the high tide of Civil War nostalgia in both the North and the South. The apex of reconciliation came just two years later, when D. W. Griffith's spectacularly popular film *Birth of a Nation* celebrated how the Ku Klux Klan saved the South from the depredations of freed slaves in their lust for white women, and saved America from the nightmare of Reconstruction. The town's five attorneys worked in the shadow of the courthouse tower, kept busy with cotton contracts, wills, and foreclosures, and now in September 1955, with defending the brothers Milam and Bryant against the charge of murder.[8]

The trial would provide high drama, a bigger news event than even the terrible floods of the 1920s and '30s. But Sumner was no static backwater. In fact, many sharecroppers' shacks sported television aerials; they also had cars parked in front, though usually of pre–World War II vintage. In fact, Little Sumner was built on trade and mobility. Just west of town were railroad tracks that carried goods and people throughout the region and out to the larger world. More importantly, just beyond the tracks was US Highway 49E, heading south toward Jackson and north to Memphis, the de facto capitol of the Delta. "The highway is life for Sumner," the journalist Robert H. Denley wrote. In summer, stray puffs of cotton, fallen from thousands of trucks and train cars, whitened the berms and roadbeds. Timber, too, had been a key commodity in the early twentieth century, as nearly all the old hardwood forests were finally cut down, shipped out, and the land put under cultivation.[9]

It was a highly mobile culture. "Delta Residents," Denley wrote, were "proud of their reputation for 'going'—thirty miles to a movie, fifty miles to a restaurant or one hundred miles to shop in Memphis to the north." Many never came back, he noted, black folks and whites too, who took the trains and buses and kept heading north, all the way to Chicago, just like the Till family of Webb, Mississippi, a town three miles south of Sumner. The flight north accelerated after World War II, spurred by the mechanization of agriculture, including cotton-picking machines. Steady depopulation was the biggest change of all in the Delta.[10]

White Sumner residents were ambivalent about the trial; most were horrified by the crime itself. Several pointed out that neither their town nor its residents had anything to do with the case, that the mere happenstance of where the body turned up sent the trial to Sumner. "We don't like notoriety being brought to our town by this trial," one citizen told a reporter. It was not just that a heinous crime was now attached forever to Sumner; there was something deeper going on. The trial could only stir things up locally, poison the good feelings between the races, especially with the northern press and the NAACP "rabble rousing" the case. "Justice should be done," a local grocer told a *Chicago Defender* reporter, "but we resent outside interference from northern Negroes who don't know the facts." A Sumner poolroom operator agreed, charging that the NAACP "commercialized on this case," even though he felt the indictments were justified. An auto mechanic told the *Defender*'s reporter, "I doubt that there is enough evidence to convict the pair of murder," but the local druggist was not so sure, and he especially thought that kidnapping charges might stick.[11]

In his first dispatch from Sumner, just before the trial began, John Popham wrote in the *New York Times* that the Till murder, "focused the glare of national attention on the intricate system of race relations which the dominant white group enforces in the name of stability." Popham was the

Times's main man on the civil rights beat, and he covered the Till case from beginning to end. A southern liberal, Popham had a keen understanding of his region's dark past but also harbored hopes for change. The real drama, Popham said, was not the guilt or innocence of the two brothers but rather Mississippi's "role as a militant defender of racial segregation practices." Popham argued that the overwhelming majority of white Mississippians reacted to the murder, "with sincere and vehement expressions of outrage." They believed that a fair trial was possible because to believe otherwise meant that a system they regarded as just was, in reality, not, that the equality African Americans allegedly found on their separate Jim Crow path was a fraud. People demanded swift, retributive action, Popham wrote, because only the "but equal" in "separate but equal" made segregation morally defensible. "The reaction to Till's murder," Popham concluded, "reveals the wrenched feelings of Mississippi. The picture is one of white supremacy that skates the thin ice separating it from white tyranny."[12]

At this point, the *Brown* decision had roiled Mississippi politics for more than a year. Letters to editors and public speeches vilified northern Communists, Supreme Court shysters, and NAACP mongrelizers who willfully misunderstood the state. The Till case became one more chapter in that story, Popham told *New York Times* readers: "N.A.A.C.P. opponents were angered at having the Till slaying labeled a 'lynching,' at the demand of public officials in Illinois for Federal Government Action in the case and at reports that Till's body was put on public view in Chicago while donations were solicited for the work of the N.A.A.C.P." The "us versus them" mentality, Popham noted, always stood ready to spring to the southern surface, beginning with the Civil War and lasting through the Jim Crow era. The *Brown* decision merely intensified old fears of an overbearing and judgmental North imposing unwarranted conditions on a victimized South, and the Till case was yet another episode in that long drama. From below the Mason-Dixon line, it was northern hypocrisy versus southern innocence, but from above, it was willful obtuseness and the denial of moral horror. Popham concluded with the hope that Mississippi's "swift sense of outrage" in the first hours after Till's body surfaced would carry the day in Sumner.[13]

Paul Holmes, writing in the *Chicago Tribune* the day before the trial began, came to similar conclusions but with less sympathy for the Delta. Not a single one of Tallahatchie County's nineteen thousand blacks was registered to vote, yet "opulent planters live a gracious, luxurious life in their feudal baronies." The planters worried, Holmes wrote, that the spotlight thrown by the trial would give the rest of America a bad impression of Mississippi. Milam and Bryant were "pawns in a wider, deeper game than a mere murder trial." They symbolized the "Delta region's tenacious grasp on things as they are." Holmes argued that their fate was a "trial balloon in the region's resistance to social change," and he expected that resistance to triumph, since no one he spoke to in the county predicted a murder conviction.[14]

The African American press was even less interested in the good intentions of liberals and the divided mind of the white South. Writing for the *Pittsburgh Courier*, James Boyack described how the local NAACP president and Greenwood businessman Edward Cochran was warned against attending the trial. "We've had enough of tyranny," Cochran told Boyack. None of the local black leaders Boyack spoke with believed that a "Mississippi jury is going to convict two white men for killing a colored." One declared, "Our backs are to the wall...politically and economically....We have patiently waited too long for our legal rights." Even newsmen, black and white, were not safe. Boyack reported that a crowd surrounded an ABC film crew—reporter, cameraman, soundman—who were set up on the courthouse square in Charleston to interview average citizens about their views of the upcoming trial, and that crowd gave them five minutes to get out of town.[15]

Pretrial coverage emphasized the chasm separating North from South. Even as innocuous a mark of regional difference as the southern accent became part of the story. Local pronunciations gave big-city newsmen fits: "[W]hen a witness mentioned 'an arn weight' there was a flurry at press tables to uncover the fact that he was talking about...'iron.' That sort of thing went on all day." But there was something more here. Modern media—movies, radio, and especially television, although it was only just now becoming ubiquitous—eroded distinct regional accents, or so it was said. It was a small but important part of why southerners felt defensive when northerners wrote about the backwardness of Tallahatchie County, its refusal to become modern. The Till story was about race and segregation, of course, but also about big cities and small towns, and about the victors of a long-ago war looking down their noses at the losers. The distinct regional accent was a stand-in for many other differences.[16]

More immediate problems pressed, however. Sumner was now about to double in size. The town drugstore saw an opportunity and advertised sandwiches for sale. A Clarksdale café opened a concession stand in the courthouse lobby and sold half-fried chicken lunches throughout the coming week. Soft drinks doubled in price; one boy sold bottled drinks in the courthouse as fast as he could open them. Being "the news capitol of the United States," as the *Greenwood Morning Star* put it, was exciting, even lucrative, but not everyone was happy. As a local grocer put it, "I hope in years to come when people pass by Sumner they won't point at us and say, 'That's the place.'"[17]

CHAPTER ELEVEN

FAIR AND IMPARTIAL MEN

THE ATTENTION to all of these details in the national press revealed one more thing: The case was getting bigger every day. By Monday, September 19, the trial scene itself was news. Sumner's courtroom snugly accommodated about 250 people; at midmorning more than four hundred—some reports said five hundred, mostly men, mostly white—packed the room. The threats continued Sheriff Strider reported, more ugly letters "in the most vile language," and menacing phone calls to his home in the middle of the night. Deputies frisked everyone before allowing them to ascend the stairs to the second-floor courtroom. Heightening the sense of danger, Strider told newsmen that two suspicious-looking black men were seen lingering around the courthouse before taking off in a Pontiac with Illinois plates. The sheriff assured the public that he and his men would be the only ones with guns at the trial, and that a staff of two dozen regular and specially appointed deputies were keeping watch. Reporter James Kilgallen wrote that in forty years of covering crime stories, he had been frisked only twice before—at the 1933 trial of Machine Gun Kelly in Oklahoma, and at the 1936 execution of Bruno Hauptmann, the kidnapper of Charles Lindbergh's son.[1]

Adding to the intensity, it was hot, well into the nineties, with barely a breeze from the windows, and of course, no air conditioning.[2]

Decades after he covered the Till trial, David Halberstam called it the Civil Rights Movement's first great media event. The whole courthouse was turned into a hub for news-gathering. Telephones and teletype machines, freshly opened in the lobby, rang and banged throughout the week. Western Union installed a booth on the ground floor and moved their Greenville office manager to Sumner for the duration of the trial. He spent the next week transmitting more than one hundred thousand words to newspaper offices across the country. Down the street, the tiny Sumner *Sentinel* opened its offices to out-of-town newsmen; many of them wrote their stories in the *Sentinel's* "back shop," as its editor William Simpson regaled them with tales of the Delta. Out on the courthouse square, radio and television crews conducted interviews, their bulky cameras and sound equipment whirring away, electrical cables as thick as a man's forearm crossed the sidewalks and the courthouse lawn. NBC announced daily film runs from an airstrip in nearby Tutwiler to New York City, and soon the other networks followed suit.[3]

Nearly one hundred newsmen came to Sumner from all over the country, a Who's Who of journalistic prominence. There was James Kilgallen of the International News Service, white-haired, over seventy, the "dean" of the scribes. Crowds gathered just to listen to him dictate his stories by phone to New York. Younger but no less notable were Murray Kempton, a future Pulitzer Prize–winning columnist for the *New York Post*; John N. Popham of the *New York Times*, a southern gentleman deeply respected by his colleagues; and, of course, Halberstam, another future Pulitzer Prize winner. Many of the South's most distinguished writers were also on hand, Clark Porteous of the *Memphis Press-Scimitar*, Bill Minor from the *New Orleans Times-Picayune*, John Herbers for the United Press, and James Featherston from the staunchly segregationist *Jackson State Times*. And there was Rob Hall, son of a Pascagoula banker, grandson of a prominent Baptist minister, reporter for the Communist *Daily Worker*. In addition to print reporters, all three television networks sent newsmen, including the future NBC anchorman John Chancellor. Major magazines too—*Life, Time, Newsweek*, and the *Nation*—sent writers, photographers, and sketch artists to capture the scene.[4]

Then too came a corps of ten reporters and editors from the "Negro Press," including James Hicks of the Baltimore *Afro-American*, Simeon Booker for *Jet*, Clotye Murdock from *Ebony*, Nannie Mitchell-Turner for the *St. Louis Argus*, Robert Ratcliffe from the *Pittsburgh Courier*, Moses Newsome of the *Chicago Defender*, and Alex Wilson for its Memphis-based sister paper, the *Tri-State Defender*. Many had never been in the Delta before, but they produced some of the best journalism on the trial, and they helped shape the Till case. Their unique perspective often led them to stories that colleagues from the mainstream press missed, and the black journalists continued to file thoughtful reports long after their white counterparts forgot about Sumner.[5]

There was plenty to report, because the Till trial featured many outsized individuals, Sheriff Strider literally so. At six feet two, two hundred seventy-five pounds, with his thick Delta accent and bluff talk about maintaining segregation, Strider seemed straight out of central casting. Tieless and coatless, he kept an unlit cigar in his mouth through much of the proceedings. Strider "walked heavy," Mamie Till Bradley's uncle Crosby Smith later said, by which he meant not just the sheriff's gait but his ability to throw his weight around as a politician and farmer. Strider owned one of the largest plantations in Tallahatchie County, fifteen hundred acres worked by thirty-five black tenant families, with the block letters S-T-R-I-D-E-R painted one each on the roofs of seven side-by-side shacks, a reminder of who was boss to passing motorists. In fact, Tallahatchie County long had a reputation for political corruption, which reformers tried to clean up by limiting office-holders to one-year terms. For a generation, Strider and his brother took turns as Tallahatchie's sheriff, effectively keeping the most powerful position in a single family, preserving, reporters said, the dry county's liquor and gambling rackets. J. W. Milam allegedly sold bootleg whiskey out of his Glendora grocery store.[6]

Judge Curtis Swango equally looked his part—tall, well built, graying at the temples but dapper. Everyone agreed he carried himself with easy grace and dignity but with great thoughtfulness too. Forty-eight years old, Swango came from the tiny town of Sardis at the eastern edge of the Delta. He had attended Rhodes College in Memphis, the University of Mississippi Law School, then devoted his life to public service. He represented his corner of Mississippi in the state legislature from 1936 until 1950, then assumed his current position, judge of the seventeenth Judicial District, appointed by Governor Fielding Wright. Reporters described his courtroom voice as soft but firm, and his photos revealed a serious man with deep, dark-rimmed eyes. Wrote one reporter, marveling at Swango's composure in the heat, "The judge kept his blue serge coat on until midafternoon but finally took it off. He kept his dignity in shirtsleeves." Another concluded that Judge Swango's handling of the case gave the South its best publicity since the invention of the southern accent.[7]

The lead prosecutor, Gerald Chatham, was a model southern lawyer—articulate, earnest, devoted to the law. He served as the district attorney of five Delta counties for fourteen years, but heart disease would force him to step down at the end of his term. In fact, he might have absented himself from the Till case, but he believed that it was his duty to stay on and do his best. Some have argued that Chatham provided a model for

Harper Lee's noble attorney Atticus Finch in *To Kill a Mockingbird*, which was published five years after the Till trial.[8]

Defense counselors too became media stars. By retaining all of Sumner's attorneys, the defendants preempted local lawyers being assigned to the prosecution side, which would have been professionally embarrassing for any of them. J. J. Breland, sixty-three years old, balding, with owl-eye glasses, was the lead attorney on the case. Described by one observer as "suave and persuasive," Breland had practiced law in Sumner since he graduated from Princeton University and the University of Mississippi Law School. His young partner, John W. Whitten, was first cousin to Congressman Jamie Whitten, a staunch segregationist. Sidney Carlton took charge of publicity; more than the other attorneys, Carlton spent time with newsmen covering the trial, pointing out weaknesses in the prosecution's case, making sure that his clients were seen as solid members of the community and good family men. His partner, Harvey Henderson, kept a lower profile throughout the proceedings, as did J. W. Kellum, who ran a one-man firm.[9]

The accused and their families also became nationally recognized. "The defendants made a dramatic entrance with their attractive wives and children," wrote one reporter; just walking into court on Monday morning, they "set off a buzz of interest and lightening like flashes from the combined action of 30 cameramen." Their confident smiles gave way in the grind of pretrial procedures: Carolyn Bryant fidgeting, Juanita Milam looking stern, all of them smoking. "Between puffs on cigarettes," James Kilgallen observed, "Bryant nestled close to his wife, Carolyn, and whispered to her. Next to Milam sat his attractive 27-year-old wife, Juanita, who watched the courtroom proceedings with unconcealed interest."[10]

Appearances matter at a media event, especially one inflamed by accusations of black male lust for white women. It was, of course, Carolyn Bryant who attracted the most attention. The local beauty queen was a "beautiful 21-year-old-brunette," Kilgallen told his readers, "five feet two, petite and slim-wasted." Indeed, reporters could barely mention Carolyn Bryant's name without adjectives like "attractive," "young," and "slender."[11]

"Big" Milam's physique also drew notice, mainly for his masculine bulk and power, with his six foot two, 225-pound frame. Milam's attorneys made sure that the press and the public noted his heroics during World War II, particularly his service in Patton's army during the Battle of the Bulge, his Silver Star, Purple Heart, and battlefield commission as lieutenant. Much noted was Milam's recent bravery when he "dived into the Tallahatchie River and saved a little Negro girl from drowning" (quite amazing in the Till case was the frequency of interracial interventions in water-related accidents). Milam's sister told reporters that once her brother "saved the life of a little negro polio victim by rushing him to the hospital in Memphis in the nick of time." Milam, his family said, got along well with Negroes, knew how to manage them because he ran two big cotton harvesting machines using black labor and hiring their services to plantation owners.[12]

Roy Bryant was less colorful. Still, one reporter wrote that he had the dark good looks of Marlon Brando; another agreed about Bryant's movie-star face but declared he more resembled Dana Andrews or William Holden. Bryant, like his brother, had worn an army uniform, serving as a paratrooper with the Eighty-Second Airborne Division during the Korean War. A friend described how Roy saw duty under a black noncommissioned officer but didn't seem to mind; "Roy told us the Negro was a good soldier and that they understood each other."[13]

During jury selection, the defendants played with their high-spirited, good-looking young sons—two boys on each father's lap, squealing and giggling. The children also wandered around the courtroom, played cowboys and Indians, pretended to shoot at people, and sometimes made it hard to hear anything. Spectators plied the kids with candy and bubble gum. "You bet they'll be there," Carlton told reporters; "we wouldn't miss a bet like that." And behind the nuclear families sat the extended one, Roy and J. W.'s mother, siblings, and other kin. The whole tableau was an alternative family drama—not the tragedy of the bereft black mother, her only son brutally murdered by thugs, but the uplifting story of faithful white families, defending themselves against groundless criminal charges, and more, against those who slandered The Southern Way of Life.[14]

The attorneys subpoenaed their witnesses and submitted their lists, nine for the defense, thirteen for the prosecution, five of them Negroes, the Associated Press noted. Would they all be called? Even Milam and Bryant? What about Carolyn, the local beauty queen; her words about what actually happened that night in Money would be critical. And Mose Wright, would he really testify, a black farmer all his life, giving evidence about a black murder victim against two white men? All were on the witness lists.[15]

But the person who got the most press, once she arrived, was Mamie Till Bradley. Prosecutor Chatham invited her to Mississippi, promised protection, had a subpoena drawn up, then expressed his impatience to reporters when she failed to show up on Monday morning during jury selection. Mrs. Bradley let Chatham know that she was worried about security, though she knew in her heart that she had to testify because someone must speak for Emmett. A young NAACP leader from Clarksdale,

Aaron Henry, came forward to assure the court that she would arrive on Tuesday. In fact, a trip to Cleveland, Ohio, had delayed Mamie Bradley's appearance in Sumner. In that working-class industrial town with its burgeoning African American population, she spoke at an NAACP rally in the Antioch Baptist Church before two thousand people, telling them that Emmett was a martyr, that she would work to bring meaning to his death, and that they should all write their congressman and support the NAACP. Then she flew south.[16]

Here was something to behold: A black woman from Chicago, fresh from addressing an NAACP rally, returned to her birthplace in Mississippi to testify at the trial of her son's murderers. She flew into Memphis overnight from Chicago, arrived at dawn, accompanied by Wiley Carthan, her father, and Rayfield Mooty, the Chicago steelworker and local union leader who helped her through the first days of Emmett's disappearance. Once in the South, they moved within a sheltering community of African American activists. A local minister brought them to the home of Dr. R. Q. Venson, where they freshened up, ate breakfast, and were then driven to Sumner by Taylor Hayes, owner of a Memphis funeral parlor. Later that day, they received the warmth of local black community leaders in Mound Bayou, where they stayed in the compound of Dr. T. R. M. Howard. For the remainder of the trial, Howard escorted his guests to the courthouse in an armed caravan.[17]

Mooty and Carthan clearly saw themselves as bodyguards for Mamie Bradley. The men surveyed the white crowds nervously as they entered the courtroom on Tuesday morning. Reporters and cameramen, white and black, surrounded her. One observer described her as "small, plump, and appearing very neat"; she was "dressed in a black shantung dress, a black velvet hat studded with rhinestones, and a considerable amount of costume jewelry." Another added that the sensation created by her appearance did not please everyone: "Attention received by the fashionably dressed Negro Woman swept an expression of almost painful dislike across the faces of the local spectators."[18]

For twenty minutes jury selection paused as Mrs. Bradley answered reporters' questions. Yes, she was pleased to be in Mississippi; yes, she felt perfectly safe; yes, she would do her best if called to testify; yes, she had received hundreds of letters over the past weeks, almost all of them from well-wishers. And yes, she was sure the body was Emmett's, otherwise she would be out searching for him. Finally Judge Swango called the court to order once again, and Mamie Till Bradley moved toward the back. Sheriff Strider followed, pushed his bulk toward her through the crowd, handed her a subpoena as she took her seat, and told her she was obliged to abide by the laws of Mississippi. For a few minutes, Carthan and Mooty stood watching over her, then they too sat down. Sitting down for them all, incidentally, meant at the small segregated table in the far corner of the back of the room, with the reporters from the African American press two dozen feet behind the accused and their families.[19]

Another celebrity of sorts also arrived on Tuesday morning, Congressman Charles Diggs of Detroit, Michigan. One of a mere handful of African American congressmen, Diggs told newsmen he came as a private citizen and observer, but that he would report back to Washington what he saw in Sumner. Unlike Mamie Till Bradley's congressman, William Dawson from Chicago's South Side—a reliable cog in the city's Democratic machine, a man not without ideals of racial justice, but always pursuing them quietly, within the party structure—Diggs was fervently and openly committed to racial activism. His presence posed something of a dilemma. He came as a private citizen, but he was a duly elected congressman, the highest-ranking man in a racially segregated room. "Diggs sent in his card to Judge Swango," the Associated Press reported, "and the Judge arranged for the Congressman to sit at the Negro press table." Other reports said it was Sheriff Strider, maintaining his segregated courthouse, who insisted Diggs be sent to the back of the room. If there was any objection to this arrangement, no one recorded it.[20]

All of this took place in the midst of jury selection. Mississippi law required the defendants' presence during this process. The deputy sheriffs transported Milam and Bryant—each in a white shirt, khaki trousers, and no handcuffs—from the Charleston jail to Breland and Whitten's office, then the two walked with their lawyers across the street to the courthouse. The defendants took their seats facing the bench. Both appeared confident and in good spirits. To pick a jury, a special venire of 120 men had been called, most of them farmers, none too happy about being taken from their fields at the height of the harvest. The prosecution and the defense each had twelve preemptory challenges, allowing them to reject a potential juror without giving a reason, and all of the attorneys as well as Judge Swango could question the candidates and reject them for cause. "Because of wide publicity in this case," Gerald Chatham told the jury pool, "the prosecution will take special pains to see that fair and impartial men are selected to try the case on law and evidence and on nothing else."[21]

The process took longer than expected, all of Monday and part of Tuesday. Judge Swango pulled slips of paper from his own straw hat and handed them to Strider, who read each name aloud. Then the questioning began. Would you be prejudiced because of race, the prosecutors asked? Have any of Sumner's attorneys represented you in a lawsuit? The brothers' defense fund became an issue when a few of the prospective jurors admitted contributing to it or coming from families that had. Chatham asked one man if he would have contributed to the fund had he been asked. Breland objected, but Judge Swango allowed him to answer. When he said he was not sure, the judge dismissed him. Swango asked another prospective juror if he had any reservations about treating the race issue even-handedly. "I might not have," he replied. Stand aside, said the judge. For referring to the defendant familiarly as "J. W." another man was excused, and the judge dismissed yet another when he said he expected to be called as a defense witness.[22]

The state ended up using eleven of its twelve challenges. Chatham then presented the defense with twelve men the prosecution found acceptable. Breland asked each potential juror if he believed the state must prove beyond a reasonable doubt that the body in the river was Till's? Were they certain the crime took place in Tallahatchie County? And would the wide publicity the trial received influence their decision? The defense rejected two of the twelve based on their answers, so when Monday's proceedings were adjourned at 5:00 p.m., ten of the jurors had been chosen.[23]

Chatham purposely neglected to challenge potential jurymen on the death penalty. He had decided not to ask the court for this ultimate punishment but rather to let the jurors make the decision. As Clark Porteous wrote in his syndicated column in the *Memphis Press-Scimitar*, "Never in Mississippi history has a white man or woman been given death for killing a negro." If the jury wanted the death penalty, Chatham reasoned, they could order it, but he would not jeopardize his case over the matter. Still, Paul Holmes of the *Chicago Tribune* was impressed that Monday's jury selection "brought the racial issue frankly into the open," and he called the process "a soul-searching inquisition" into whether white jurors were capable of *fairly* judging the case. This was odd praise because Holmes also noted that no one mentioned the key fact of the case, "the Negro victim had insulted a white woman."[24]

Court resumed Tuesday morning. After just an hour, by 10:30 a.m., the final two jurors had been chosen, and Judge Swango empaneled his jury. The jurors had much in common in addition to being male and white: all but one was married with children; all but three were farmers (two were carpenters, one an insurance salesman); three-quarters of them were in their thirties or forties. Most lived up in the northeast corner of Tallahatchie County, the Hill Country, far from the scene of the kidnapping and murder, an area less dependent on cotton and with fewer black people than the Delta. Their names: Ed Devaney, L. L. Price, Howard Armstrong,

J. A. Shaw, Ray Tribble, Davis Newton, Bishop Matthews, James Toole, George Holland, Travis Thomas, Jim Pennington, and Gus Ramsey. The attorneys also agreed on an alternate juror, W. D. Havens, from Charleston. Some commentators later wondered whether the prosecution erred in avoiding jurors from the Delta, if poorer Hill Country folk would not be less likely to convict the brothers than more prosperous Delta planters.[25]

The trial was set to begin after a break for lunch when Chatham rose and surprised the court by announcing that new witnesses of "major importance" had been found. He requested a recess so that they could be subpoenaed and interviewed. Breland was on his feet before the prosecutor finished, objecting vigorously to any delay. Chatham retorted that the new witnesses were critical to the prosecution's case, that his staff needed time to question them and secure their testimony. Breland countered that the state had already subpoenaed thirteen witnesses as against the defense's nine. Over defense counsel's objections, Judge Swango granted a continuance until the following morning at 9:00 a.m. He ordered the bailiffs—four of them, double the usual number—to bring the jurors to their quarters in the Delta Inn, where they might watch television or listen to radio but not, Swango made clear, read newspapers or hear newscasts.[26]

Before adjourning, the judge noted that several photographers had violated his ban on taking pictures while court was in session, and he promised to punish additional infractions. Swango also mentioned the dangerous overcrowding: "This is your courtroom, it belongs to Tallahatchie County for the use of citizens, but we must keep these aisles clear; if a fire were to break out here it would be a great tragedy." Several times he asked the bailiffs to clear the aisles and doorways, and he promised he would not allow such hazardous and distracting conditions to continue. "After today," he said just before adjourning, "no one will be permitted to stand in the courtroom who has no official business here."[27]

CHAPTER TWELVE

MOSES WRIGHT

JUDGE SWANGO CALLED the court back to order on Wednesday morning, September 21, "wielding a heavy gavel that fairly rocked the building," as one observer noted. He sat raised above the proceedings, his back to the door leading to his chambers. He wore no robe. Once again, the sun hit the windows, its heat pouring in despite the drawn shades. The ceiling fans barely made a difference as the temperature outside soared into the nineties. "The trial progressed," one reporter wrote, "in an oven-hot, smoke-filled courtroom that was jammed to the walls with spectators," though now bailiffs kept the aisles more or less clear.[1]

Swango looked out on a room filled mostly with white men, some fanning themselves with their hats, a few women with handkerchiefs held to their faces. The judge conceded much to the heat: he dropped the formality of coats and ties, saw to it that pitchers of ice water kept circulating, and allowed smoking. But he also made his rules clear. Photographers and sketch artists, for example, had free rein—until the proceedings started. The judge "severely reprimanded" one NBC cameraman who tried to shoot some footage during the first day of testimony. "A fair and wise judge who makes you toe the line," one attorney said of Swango before the trial. Thinking back on him years later, Murray Kempton recalled, "Curtis Swango was the best judge I ever saw; before or after I never thought there was one better. He ran the trial with complete informality and at the same time gave it tremendous grace and gentility." Even the *Daily Worker* agreed that Judge Swango presided with "dignity and decorum."[2]

The courtroom had a classic feel. A railing separated participants from the crowd; the defendants and their wives sat with their backs to it. Between them and the judge were two large tables, one for the defense and one for the prosecution attorneys. To Swango's right was the jury, to his left, the witness stand. On the railing's other side sat rows of newsmen, photographers, and local citizens. All the way in back along the wall were a dozen or so African American spectators, and in the corner, at a table too far away at times to hear the witnesses, their view partially obstructed, sat the African American press corps. "Good Morning, Niggers," Sheriff Strider cheerfully greeted them each day, explaining that "the colored people will be in one section and the white in another.... We've kept the races separated for a long time and we don't intend to change now." With testimony beginning, bailiffs sequestered the day's witnesses in back rooms until they took the stand, so Mose Wright, Mamie Till Bradley, and the others were nowhere to be seen.[3]

Whether justice would be served depended on whom you asked. The *Greenwood Morning Star* argued that Milam and Bryant likely would never serve time but not because anything was amiss, quite the contrary, the prosecutors simply did not have a case. It further noted that the scene in Sumner was emblematic of southern good feelings across the racial divide. The writer contrasted this with the "many white people in the north who have bitterness in their hearts for negroes," and he quoted from the *South Deering Bulletin*, a newsletter from a racially troubled Chicago neighborhood, which said of Emmett Till, "Evidently he thought he was back in Chicago where it is the common and accepted thing for black bucks to toss rude, insulting and suggestive remarks to white women." The *Morning Star* noted the "mounting resentment by the people of the Delta toward the radicals who have invaded that peaceful community where the races have lived in comparative harmony for many years," and he singled out the "red-tinged newsmen" spreading propaganda about Mississippi. Still, he insisted, justice would prevail.[4]

Dr. T. R. M. Howard of Mound Bayou, on the other hand, had no doubt that justice was the farthest thing from the jury's mind: "This trial will demonstrate to the nation just what Mississippi justice means to the colored man." Howard told reporter James Hicks that the men sitting on the jury had the same mind-set as the murderers: "The punishment will be just about what it always has been for white people who kill colored people." Shooting a deer out of season brought longer prison terms than killing a black man in the Delta, and he added that as long as the federal government stood aside, "Mississippi will continue to kill colored people."[5]

The prosecution called its first witness, and the courtroom buzz gave way to silence.

Short and wiry, with the wrinkled skin of a man who had spent decades under the southern sun, Moses Wright came to court neatly dressed in dark slacks, white shirt, blue tie, and suspenders. He "pushed his way firmly through the crowded courtroom and sat down in the big witness chair," one journalist wrote. Wright's age and size notwithstanding, he proved a bold witness. One reporter wrote that the old preacher "answered questions without hesitation in a loud voice. Now and then he pounded his fist on the table before him." Another said that Wright testified with "a confident air," and yet another wrote that this slight man spoke "unflinchingly" while Bryant and Milam "listened intently to his testimony," the former showing little emotion, the latter sucking on a cigarette and shifting nervously in his seat.[6]

Wright's determination was especially striking because the month had taken its toll on him. Though blameless for what happened, his nephew had died in his care, and he would carry that weight for the rest of his life. Of course, physically resisting Milam and Bryant was not an option. Wright had perhaps been overconfident that he could always dodge trouble in Mississippi. Mose's wife, Elizabeth, had wanted to leave for years (she did just that after the kidnapping, swearing never to return). Mose loved the land, loved the life of a farmer, but now time had run out. His testimony to the grand jury helped secure the indictments against Milam and Bryant, and everyone knew he intended to bear witness against them at the murder trial, so he was not long for his home state.[7]

In the days before the trial, out-of-town reporters had dropped by Mose Wright's home, where he repeated his story for them—how Emmett almost missed his train south, how Milam and Bryant kidnapped him, how he identified the body three days later. Wright told the newsmen that he wasn't afraid, and that no one had bothered him, but he kept a loaded shotgun handy, and he expected to follow the rest of the family out of Mississippi after the harvest. He also told members of the African American press corps that in the days leading up to the trial, he and his boys never slept at home. Mamie Till Bradley wrote years later that after the trial ended, carloads of white men came looking for Wright in the night; they ransacked his house as he hid out in his car, parked by the Money Cemetery.[8]

Chatham signaled part of his strategy right from the beginning by addressing Wright as "Uncle Mose." Honorifics such as "Sir" and "Ma'am" were reserved for whites in the Jim Crow South; enough gray hairs might earn black people "Uncle" or "Auntie." The prosecutor knew that his job was to make himself and his case appear deeply southern, to seek justice within the white norms of Jim Crow, to avoid alienating the jury. This was no put-on. Chatham believed in segregation.

He began by taking "Uncle Mose" through a series of questions to win the jury's sympathy—how Wright lived for almost ten years on Mr. G. C. Frederick's plantation in Leflore County, how he was known as "Preacher" because of his ministry in the Church of God in Christ, how he raised twelve children and picked countless bales of cotton over the years. The message: Uncle Mose was a good old-time Negro.[9]

Now Chatham brought the witness back to the early hours of Sunday morning, August 28. Wright, along with his sons, grandsons and nephew, went into Greenwood on Saturday evening. By day, cotton obsessed Greenwood, as men brokered, processed, and shipped tons of the white filaments. But on Saturday nights, Greenwood was the place for socializing, for shopping, for meeting friends, chatting, gossiping, listening to music, dancing, going to movies, eating, and drinking. Wright and his boys returned home about 1:00 a.m. and went to bed.[10]

Chatham asked Mose Wright to describe what happened while everyone slept:

Chatham: What was the first thing that attracted your attention to the fact that there was someone about your premises?

Wright: Well, someone was at the front door, and he was saying, "Preacher—Preacher." And then I said, "Who is it?" And then he said, "This is Mr. Bryant. I want to talk to you and that boy."

Chatham: Do you know Mr. Bryant?

Wright: I just know him since he came up here. I couldn't see him that night so well, only with that flashlight there, and I could see that it was this other man, Mr. Milam. But I know Mr. Milam.

Chatham: You know Mr. Milam, do you?

Wright: I sure do.

Chatham: And then what did you do?

Wright: Well, I got up and opened the door.

Chatham: And what did you see when you opened the door?

Wright: Well, Mr. Milam was standing there at the door with a pistol in his right hand and he had a flashlight in his left hand.[11]

Now came the moment. Everything about the scene was intimidating—Milam and Bryant facing Wright, the skeptical looks of the all-white jury, the attorneys, the spectators, the very layout of the courtroom, embodying the state's power. But the defendants had invaded his home, terrorized his family, tortured and killed his nephew. Chatham asked Wright to rise, look around the courtroom, and say if he recognized the man with the gun. The courtroom fell dead silent. Wright did not hesitate, stood straight as an arrow and spoke in a loud, clear voice. Across the country, Americans read the AP lead: "Mose Wright pointed a knobby finger at J. W. Milam Wednesday and said, 'There he is'—identifying him as one of the men who abducted his nephew." Asked if he recognized the second kidnapper, Wright pointed right at Roy Bryant, "There he is."[12]

Journalists wrote that this was the first time a black man had testified against a white one in a Mississippi courtroom, and certainly the first time in a capital murder trial. Everyone knew Wright's moment on the stand was earthshaking, everyone knew the risks he was taking. Wright himself felt them acutely.[13]

Wright described how Milam took over, walking from room to room, bed to bed, gun and flashlight in hand. Milam asked Wright if he had two boys from Chicago in the house:

Chatham: And what did you say?
Wright: "Yes, Sir."
Chatham: And will you tell the jury who those boys were?
Wright: Wheeler Parker, my grandson, and Emmett Till.
Chatham: How long had they been visiting in your home with you?
Wright: They was there a week that same day.
Chatham: Now Uncle Mose, after you told Mr. Milam that you did have two boys there from Chicago, and that they were there in your house, what did he say and do then?
Wright: Then Mr. Milam said, "I want that boy that done the talking down at Money."[14]

Once Milam identified the boy he wanted—they had never seen each other before—the big man ordered him to get up and get dressed. While Till did so, Milam told Wright and his wife that if this was not the right boy, they would return and put him back to bed. But after this lame effort to assuage their fears, Milam asserted his power. He asked Wright how old he was, and said on hearing the answer, "Well, if you know any of us here tonight, then you will never live to get to be sixty-five." "No, Sir, I don't know you," Wright replied. The old man pleaded with Milam and Bryant to give his nephew a beating but not take him away. No answer. Elizabeth begged them to take money rather than Emmett. Milam replied, "You get back in that bed, and I mean, I want to hear the springs." Did Wright ask Milam and Bryant what they were going to do with Emmett? Attorney Chatham queried. "No, Sir, I sure didn't."[15]

The two men walked their captive out to a vehicle parked fifty feet from the house. It was pitch dark, and Wright testified that he could not see much, or tell what kind of car it was or what color. But standing at his screen door, Mose heard a voice. One of the two kidnappers asked someone unseen if this was the boy? "Yes," came the response. "Was that a man's voice or a lady's voice?" the prosecutor asked. "It seemed like it was a lighter voice than a man's," Wright replied. Then the kidnappers drove back in the darkness toward Money.[16]

Chatham asked Wright if Milam and Bryant ever brought his nephew back? "No, Sir, they haven't." And when was the next time you saw Emmett? "I saw him when he was taken out of the river."[17]

Chatham now turned to Wednesday, August 31, the day they found the body. Wright described being taken by a deputy sheriff to the Tallahatchie River, where several people, white and black, had gathered.

Chatham: When you got there, was the body of Emmett Till laying on the bank?
Wright: It was in a boat.
Chatham: I want you to tell the jury whether or not you could tell whose body it was?
Wright: Yes, Sir.
Chatham: And who was it?
Wright: Emmett Till.
Chatham: During the time you were there where you first saw the body, did you notice whether or not the undertaker or any Deputy Sheriff took a ring off of Emmett's finger?
Wright: Yes, Sir.
Chatham: And was that ring taken off his finger in your presence?
Wright: That's right.[18]

Wright explained that undertaker Chester Miller removed the ring as he prepared to transport the body back to the funeral home in Greenwood.

Chatham: And you stated you were present there when Miller took the ring off of Emmett's finger?
Wright: I was looking right at him, that's right.
Chatham: And what did Miller do with that ring?

Wright:	He put it on the seat there when he taken it off.
Chatham:	Do you mean the seat in the funeral coach?
Wright:	That's right.
Chatham:	Was the ring ever given to you?
Wright:	That's right. I asked for it.
Chatham:	When did you ask for it?
Wright:	Shortly after they got the body in the coach.
Chatham:	Now I hand you a ring, Uncle Mose, and I ask you to tell the Court and Jury if that is the ring that Chester Miller took off of Emmett's finger and gave to you that morning?
Wright:	Yes, Sir, it is.

Wright described how he gave the ring to Leflore County deputy John Ed Cothran when Cothran brought him home, and how that was the last time he had seen it until this moment.[19]

During Chatham's questioning, Breland repeatedly objected to points large and small: How could Wright possibly recognize Milam and Bryant in the dark? How could Wright know what happened to the body since he never saw it again once it was taken out of the river? How could he identify the deputies if he did not even know their names? Judge Swango mostly overruled the objections, but not before Chatham blurted out in exasperation, "The old man is endeavoring to tell the truth. Do you object to that?" Then just a few moments later, after yet another objection, Chatham declared, "Mr. Breland, we will conduct this examination, if you don't mind." Judge Swango admonished the attorneys to refrain from arguing with each other and to address all of their remarks to the bench.[20]

His questioning complete, Chatham said, "Take the witness," turning Wright over to Sidney Carlton, who conducted the cross-examination for the defense. Carlton's strategy was to challenge what Wright saw that dark night, and to test the reliability of his memory, to catch him in contradictions of fact in order to shake his credibility. First, there was a series of questions about Wright's home, and who was sleeping in which room and in which bed. Then questions about the lighting. Were the house lights ever switched on? Was there more than one flashlight? Did Milam or Bryant ever shine the light in their own faces? And when the kidnappers woke Emmett up and had him get dressed, what kind of clothes did he put on? Wright could not remember.[21]

In the midst of establishing who was sleeping in which room, Carlton asked casually, "Well, how did you know what boy they were looking for?" How did Wright know, in other words, whom Milam and Bryant had come for?

Wright:	I heard someone say that this boy had done something or had done some talking down at Money. I think that was on Thursday or maybe Friday.
Carlton:	You already knew about it, did you?
Wright:	That's right.
Carlton:	Had you talked to Emmett about it?
Wright:	I sure did.
Smith:	We object to that, if the court please.
The Court:	The objection is sustained.
Carlton:	Did you punish Emmett for that?
Smith:	We object, Your Honor.
The Court:	The objection is sustained.

But Carlton had gotten his point across. Emmett said or did something to anger the brothers, Mose Wright found out about it a day or two later, talked to Emmett, but apparently did nothing to punish him.[22]

Carlton returned to the problem of identity. Whoever first knocked on the cabin door referred to himself as "Mr. Bryant"? "Did you ever see this man that you pointed out as Mr. Bryant, did you ever see the light shining on his face that night?"

Wright:	I did not.
Carlton:	Had you ever seen him before that night?
Wright:	Not to know him.
Carlton:	Had you ever been in his store?
Wright:	I never have.
Carlton:	And the first time you ever saw him was in the courtroom this week, wasn't it?
Wright:	The first time I saw his face, that's right.

So if you'd never seen Mr. Bryant before, Carlton asked, how could you recognize him in a dark room? And the same for Mr. Milam, you never saw him before, you just knew he was big and bald. No, Mose Wright insisted, he saw Milam's face on the night of the kidnapping.

Carlton:	The first time you ever saw him was in this courtroom, isn't that right?
Wright:	No Sir. I knowed him that night.
Carlton:	And the reason you say you know him is because the man had a bald head, isn't that right?
Wright:	Well, I noticed his face and his stature. And I knowed his face just like I see him there now.

Round and round they went, Carlton suggesting it was too dark to see anything, Wright insisting that he knew Milam's face by the flashlight's glare. Chatham again grew frustrated: "If the court please, I would like to ask Mr. Carlton to please give the witness time to answer his questions." Swango again told the prosecutor to direct his remarks to the bench.[23]

Carlton switched gears again. Now he focused on giving the jury a mental picture of Emmett Till:

Carlton: How old is Emmett Till?

Wright: Fourteen.

Carlton: What grade was he in?

Wright: The ninth.

Carlton: And how did he walk? Did he walk natural?

Wright: He walked right.

Carlton: Did he walk good?

Wright: That's right.

Carlton: And how did he talk?

Wright: Well, he had a stammering speech. Sometimes he couldn't get a word out.

Carlton: Did you understand him all right?

Wright: Yes, when he got it out.

Carlton: And he could make you understand him, is that right?

Wright: That's right.

Carlton: And how tall was he?

Wright: Well, it looked like Emmett was about five feet and three or four inches.

Carlton: And how much did he weigh?

Wright: One hundred and fifty.

Carlton: Did he look like he was pretty well grown? Was he a pretty good-sized man?

Wright: He looked like a man.

There was a reason for this line of questioning. A black fourteen-year-old the size of Emmett Till was a man in the Mississippi Delta in 1955, in the sense that while he might attend the brief semesters of a segregated school, he was a worker now, old enough and big enough for full-time hard labor in the fields. In the North, where high school had become routine for teenagers, most people thought of a lad like Emmett as a boy. And of course, Carlton's unspoken point: An able-bodied man, five feet four inches tall and weighing a hundred and fifty pounds might easily overpower a small woman like Carolyn Bryant.[24]

Now came another turn in the questioning. Down at the river, as he walked from the deputy sheriff's car toward the body in the boat, at what point did Moses Wright recognize his nephew? Was he still several yards away? The implication, of course, was that Wright had no idea whose body it really was. No, Wright insisted, he recognized Emmett Till only when he stood right over the body. And the ring? When did you see your nephew wearing it?

Wright: Well, he didn't wear it all the time. He didn't wear it every day. I think they had to put some tape around it or something. It was too big.
Carlton: Do you mean to say that he was there in your home all week and you didn't see that ring?
Wright: I sure didn't.
Carlton: Then you had never seen that ring before?
Wright: No, Sir....
Carlton: And you don't know of your own knowledge that it was Emmett's ring, do you?
Wright: Yes, Sir, I do.
Carlton: Just how do you know that, Mose?
Wright: Simon [Simeon] and Robert [Wright's sons] told me.
Carlton: Somebody told you it was his ring, is that right?
Wright: Simon and Robert told me.

Carlton turned to the bench with an objection, and Breland followed; this was hearsay evidence, the court must instruct the jury to disregard it. Swango agreed.[25]

Carlton returned now to the issue of darkness; no electric lights, no auto headlamps, no moon illuminated the night. Could you be sure who you saw in darkened rooms on such a black night? A night so dark that when they drove away, you couldn't tell what make or model or color of vehicle they drove, couldn't even tell whether it was a car or a truck? Yet you claim that you recognized two men you had never seen before? Wright stuck to his story: the two men sitting in front of him here in court were the very ones who invaded his home three weeks ago.

Carlton: Was there anybody else there at the time?
Wright: There was one man who stood there at the screen door.
Carlton: How was he standing?
Wright: Well, he was standing kind of with his head down like this here [demonstrating] peering. He was trying to hide, it looked like.

Carlton: In other words, you think he was trying to hide to keep you from seeing him?

Wright: That's right.

Carlton: And I believe you told me before that you thought he was a colored man, isn't that right?

Wright: He acted like a colored man.[26]

Carlton kept hammering away at how dark it was, asking over and over if Mose Wright could tell if the car was a Ford or a Chevy, if he could even see a vehicle at all. Chatham finally had enough: "Your Honor, I think that is about the third time he has gone over that. We will be here all week if he keeps up that type of questioning." Judge Swango asked the defense attorneys to refrain from such repetitiveness; Carlton returned to the same line of questioning; Chatham objected once again. Judge Swango sustained the objection, and Carlton let the witness stand down.[27]

Throughout Wright's testimony, the twelve jurors remained still, save for a few who puffed away at cigarettes. The whole courtroom was quiet and attentive, perhaps mesmerized as much by the novelty of a black man incriminating whites as by Wright's words. Carlton's cross-examination ended with questions hanging in the air: Whose voice came from the unseen car, confirming that the boy was in fact "the one that did the talking down at Money"? Who was lurking on the porch, trying not to be seen or recognized? Did Mose Wright actually recognize the two brothers in the dark or just say he did? For that matter, did he really recognize the corpse by the river? Sowing such doubts was the defense attorneys' job. But it was Wright's courage—he sometimes even omitted the obligatory "Sir" while answering Carlton's questions—that staggered the *New York Post*'s Murray Kempton. Despite the attorney's badgering and J. W. Milam's cold stare, Moses Wright, unbowed, had endured "the hardest half hour in the hardest life possible for a human being in these United States."[28]

CHAPTER THIRTEEN

UNDERTAKER CHESTER MILLER

COURT ADJOURNED SHORTLY before 10:30 a.m. for a brief recess. Back in session a few minutes later, the judge and attorneys quickly worked out details for the newly subpoenaed witnesses, all African American, the same individuals for whom Chatham sought an early adjournment the day before. That settled, the prosecution resumed calling its witnesses.[1]

Chester A. Miller, an undertaker with sixteen years' experience, most recently as manager of the Century Funeral Home in Greenwood, was next on the stand. Whites and blacks had separate mortuaries, funeral homes, and cemeteries. White undertakers occasionally handled black bodies, but only by mistake would white people seek out a man like Chester Miller to care for one of their own. The very fact that the Leflore County Sheriff's office called on the services of a black funeral home indicates its belief that the corpse was African American.[2]

Assistant District Attorney Robert Smith questioned the witness for the prosecution. Miller told the court that he had received a call on the morning of Wednesday, August 31, from John Ed Cothran, the Leflore County deputy sheriff, asking him to drive thirty miles up from Greenwood to the Tallahatchie River, just past the town of Philipp. Miller and an assistant arrived around 10:00 a.m. They knew they had come to the right place when they found a gathering of people—Robert Hodges who first found the body floating on the river, Hodges's father, their landlord B. L. Mims, and Sheriff Strider and his deputy Garland Melton. Cothran and deputy Ed Weber stopped on their way to the river to pick up Moses Wright, whose day had begun hours before in the cotton fields. Miller testified that he found all of these people gathered around a boat pulled out of the water on the riverbank. Inside the boat lay a body, along with a muddy gin fan. The body was naked except for a silver ring on its finger and a strand of barbed wire around its neck.[3]

Prosecutor Smith asked Miller a series of detailed questions about his profession, about the body, and finally about the ring:

Smith: Would you recognize that ring if you saw it again?

Miller: Yes, Sir.

Smith: I hand you here a ring that has marked on it, engraved on the front of it, "May 25, 1943," and with the large initials "L.T." I will ask you if that is the ring you removed off the finger of that dead body?

Miller: Yes, Sir.

Smith: You can positively identify that as the same ring?

Miller: Yes, Sir.[4]

Miller described how his assistant removed the ring and handed it to him, and how he in turn placed it on the floorboard of his ambulance. They loaded the body, bloated with water and gas, into a wooden casket, put the casket in a metal shipping container, then loaded everything into the car. Smith kept questioning Miller, even as J. J. Breland objected repeatedly.

Smith: Did anyone present there at the scene identify the body as any particular person?

Miller: Yes, Sir.

Smith: And who did they identify it as being?

The Court: That is, if you know.

Breland: We object, Your Honor. That calls for a conclusion.

The Court: The objection is overruled.

Smith: Who did they identify that body as being, if you know?

Miller: The body of Emmett Till.

Breland: We object, Your Honor, because that was a statement made there.

The Court: The objection is overruled.

Breland here argued that Miller's answers went beyond mere assertions of fact to conjectures, opinions, or second-hand information. Judge Swango disagreed.

Smith:	Did you later find out who the person was who identified the body that you testified to?
Miller:	Yes, Sir.
Smith:	And who was that?
Miller:	Mose Wright.
Smith:	Have you seen Uncle Mose since then?
Miller:	Yes, Sir, I have seen him since then.
Smith:	And you know that was Mose Wright?
Miller:	Yes, Sir, I know him well.
Smith:	Now then, I will ask you, in your business as an undertaker for sixteen years, have you seen a number of dead bodies in that time?
Breland:	I object to that leading form of the question.
The Court:	Objection overruled.
Smith:	Have you or not seen lots of dead bodies during the time you have been in your profession?
Miller:	Yes, Sir.
Smith:	In your opinion, was the body that was there in the boat that you took out of the boat and put in your ambulance, was it possible for someone who had known the person well in their lifetime to have identified that body?
Miller:	Yes, Sir.
Breland:	I object to that, Your Honor. That definitely calls for a conclusion.
The Court:	The objection is sustained. And the jury will disregard the answer.[5]

This was a significant point. Although Swango clearly was losing patience with Breland's objections—at one point the judge uttered with ill-disguised exasperation, "Let's proceed,"—the identification of the corpse was critical. Chester Miller's testimony supported Mose Wright's assertion that the body in the boat was that of Emmett Till. The ring was proof, but Miller confirming Wright's visual identification was important too. The defense attorneys sought to cast doubt on the corpse's identity, and by disallowing Miller's conjecture that kin might recognize the body, Judge Swango let that doubt linger.[6]

Chester Miller stepped down and the prosecution called C. A. Strickland of Greenwood. Strickland worked for the Greenwood Police Department, documenting car wrecks, accidents, and crime scenes. In his few moments of testimony, he described how he photographed the body and the gin fan at the Century Funeral Home on the morning of August 31, shortly after Chester Miller brought them back from Tallahatchie County. The prosecution entered Strickland's photos in evidence and then dismissed him.[7]

Next, the prosecution called George Smith, the Leflore County sheriff. Smith was an important witness because he interviewed Roy Bryant just hours after the kidnapping. George Smith could place Bryant and Till together on the night of August 28, so defense attorneys strove to exclude his testimony. The defense's main line of attack is summed up in the phrase "corpus delicti," which in legal jargon does not mean corpse but "body of crime." For example, you cannot prove that a man robbed a bank without evidence that the bank had been robbed; no robbery, no robber, no loot, no crime. Similarly, you cannot prove someone committed homicide without demonstrating that a killing had been done; the corpus delicti, the "body of crime," includes the murder, the murderer, and the murdered. In the Till trial, the identity of the body found in the river and the likelihood of foul play were crucial to establishing the corpus delicti. While everyone from sheriffs to journalists to attorneys had all assumed that the body was Till's, the defense strategy was to make the prosecution prove it. Persuade the judge that the body might not be Till's and he could throw the case out; persuade the jury and they would acquit Milam and Bryant.[8]

Here is where Sheriff Smith's testimony was crucial. The prosecution intended to show the jury that Roy Bryant confessed that he had kidnapped Emmett Till. Defense council argued that any such confession was inadmissible until prosecutors demonstrated that a kidnapping had taken place. Without that, Breland argued, the corpus delicti had not been established. Moreover, how did anyone know that the body in the river was Emmett Till? Or how that person died? The prosecution must establish those facts. Judge Swango asked the jurors to leave the courtroom, then listened for a few minutes to Smith's testimony and to arguments as to why it should or should not be admitted at this juncture. The judge agreed that the prosecution had not yet established the corpus delicti. He dismissed Sheriff Smith from the witness stand and brought back the jury. In response to the judge's ruling, the prosecution recalled Chester Miller.[9]

Seeking to prove the identity of the corpse and the cause of death—the "body of crime"—Prosecutor Robert Smith probed for details:

Smith: Will you give the jury a description of that body as to size, age, weight and so forth?

Miller: Well, it looked to be about five foot four or five inches in height; weight between one hundred and fifty or sixty pounds. And it looked to be that of a colored person.

Smith: Could you tell whether or not it was the body of a young person, or middle age or an old person?

Miller: Yes, Sir. Well, the flesh in the palm of the hand, well, it looked like it was the body of a young person. And from certain parts of the body—well, in my experience in handling those kind of bodies, by certain parts of the body it looked like a youth more so than a grown person or an older person.[10]

Miller delicately referred here to the body's genitals and pubic hair (or lack thereof). The corpse he described clearly fit the description of Emmett Till. But was there evidence of murder? Attorney Smith asked about the condition of the body.

Miller: The crown of his head was just crushed out and in, you know, and a piece of his skull just fell out there in the boat, maybe three inches long or maybe two and a half inches wide, something like that.
Smith: Now don't tell what your conclusion is [Miller's earlier use of the words "bullet hole" brought vehement objections from Breland], but just state what the wound was there about the head....
Miller: I saw a hole in the skull.
Smith: And how big a hole was it?
Miller: Oh, about maybe half an inch square, something like that.
Smith: And where was that hole? Will you point on your head to where it was?
Miller: It was somewhere around there, above the ear [indicating with his hand].
Smith: And that is about three-quarters of an inch above your right ear, is that right?
Miller: Yes, Sir.
Smith: Was there any hole or similar thing on the other side of his head?
Miller: Well, it was crushed on the other side. You couldn't tell too much it was crushed so. And it was all cut up and gashed over the top there.

Now Attorney Smith ventured beyond the physical evidence of injuries to their possible effects:

Smith: Will you state whether or not the wounds which you have described here were sufficient to cause his death?
Breland: We object to that, Your Honor. He is no expert to that. And the jury knows as much as he does about that. I think that is within the province of the jury.
The Court: I am going to let the witness answer the question.

Smith: Will you state whether or not the wounds which you have
            described here were sufficient to cause his death?
Miller: Yes, Sir.[11]

Smith turned the witness over to the defense for cross-examination.
Breland was ready and quick. A hole through the victim's skull might
look like a bullet wound, but without an autopsy one couldn't conclude
that, could one? And the same was true for all of the bodily trauma; it was
impossible for a layman to say what exactly caused these injuries. Nor
could anyone but a medical examiner tell for sure *when* the wounds occurred; they could even have happened in the river, long after death,
wasn't that so? In fact, the body from the Tallahatchie had undergone no
forensic analysis. Rural sheriff's departments were poorly equipped,
African American deaths simply were not considered that important, and
besides, the body was shipped back to Chicago the day after it was found.
Breland asked Chester Miller just a few simple questions:

Breland: Now, what you saw about the condition of that man as to his head,
           you couldn't tell whether it was caused before or after his death,
           could you?
Miller: No, Sir.
Breland: And you couldn't tell whether it was caused in a car accident or
           otherwise, could you? You couldn't tell that to be truthful about it,
           could you? You couldn't tell, could you?
Miller: No, Sir.

The defense strategy was clear. The prosecution must prove Milam and
Bryant guilty beyond a reasonable doubt. Here was doubt: a murder conviction required a deliberately killed body, not an accident victim. Could
the prosecution bring forth witnesses or evidence that showed how the
person in the river died, or when? Could they prove without an autopsy,
to the judge's satisfaction, that the corpse belonged to Emmett Till? And if
they got past the judge, could they convince the jury?[12]

Miller repeated that he and his assistant finished up at the river, drove
the corpse back to Greenwood to prepare it for burial, then loaded it back
into the ambulance and drove it to Money, where a shallow grave awaited.
But Miller no sooner got there than the plan had changed. Miller was told
to bring the body back to Greenwood, where he received new instructions: Seal the remains for transfer to Tutwiler, forty miles north of
Greenwood. Emmett Till's uncle Crosby Smith was good as his word to his
kin; he personally retrieved his nephew's body in Greenwood and drove

it to Tutwiler, where it was quickly embalmed, then Smith accompanied Emmett on the train to Chicago.[13]

After Miller finished at 11:45 a.m., the court recessed for three hours, allowing defense attorneys to interview the new witnesses subpoenaed by the state. The long break gave everyone else time to eat lunch, to get out of the stifling courtroom, and to ponder the morning's dramatic testimony.

When they returned shortly before 3:00 p.m., the prosecution, still working to establish the corpus delicti, called Robert Hodges. "I seen two knees and feet," the young man testified of his gruesome discovery when he went down to the river to check his trotlines on the morning of August 31. Hodges told how the body was upside down in the river, its head and torso dragged under by the gin fan tied round its neck with barbed wire. He described how he and several others came back to pull the body out, how it was badly cut up on its back and hips, and how the head was smashed in several places. Then Hodge's landlord, Mr. Mims, took the stand, outlined the same grisly scene, and added, "we could tell by looking at it that it was a colored person."[14]

Taken together, the testimonies of Miller, Hodges, and Mim established the corpus delicti to Judge Swango's satisfaction; he allowed the prosecution to recall Sheriff George Smith, followed by Smith's deputy, John Ed Cothran.

CHAPTER FOURTEEN

SHERIFF GEORGE SMITH AND DEPUTY JOHN ED COTHRAN

GEORGE SMITH CAME forward once more. He had served as Leflore County sheriff for the past four years, and he recently ran unsuccessfully for a seat in the state legislature. Mose Wright's home was in Leflore County, so Sheriff Smith's office in Greenwood was the Wright family's first contact with legal authorities after the kidnapping. Sheriff Smith spearheaded the investigation himself between Sunday, when Wright first reported the kidnapping and Wednesday when the body in the river emerged—just over the line in Tallahatchie County, and out of Smith's jurisdiction.[1]

Gerald Chatham led Sheriff Smith through a series of questions before a hushed courtroom. Till was abducted about 2 a.m. on Sunday morning, and the authorities were informed not long after daylight. Early that afternoon, Smith drove over to the grocery store in Money and awakened Bryant; the two men spoke in the sheriff's car. Chatham asked Smith if he had threatened or intimidated Bryant in any way or had offered him any reward or immunity from prosecution. No, said Smith; Bryant made his statement freely and voluntarily.

Chatham: Mr. Smith, go ahead and tell about the statement that Mr. Bryant made to you that Sunday afternoon.
Smith: Well, I just asked him about it.

Chatham: What did you ask him?

Smith: I asked him about going down there and getting that little nigger.

Chatham: Will you please go over that again.

Smith: I asked him why did he go down there and get that little nigger boy, and he said that he went down and got him to let his wife see him to identify him, and then he said that she said it wasn't the right one, and then he said that he turned him loose.

Chatham: And where did he say that he turned him loose?

Smith: He said right in front of the store....

Chatham: Did he tell you where he went to get Emmett Till?

Smith: To Mose Wright's.[2]

Sheriff Smith noted that it was about three miles from the grocery store back to Wright's house, and he asked Bryant why they didn't bring young Till home. Bryant replied that the kid knew the way back. Then Attorney Chatham asked the sheriff about Roy Bryant himself on that Sunday:

Chatham: And when you drove up to Roy Bryant's store in Money that Sunday afternoon, was the store open?

Smith: No, Sir.

Chatham: Where was Mr. Bryant at that time?

Smith: He was asleep in the back of the store.

Chatham: And what time of day was that?

Smith: It was around two o'clock approximately.

Chatham: Did he offer any explanation to you at that time as to why he was asleep?

Breland: We object to that, Your Honor. That has nothing to do with the case at all.

The Court: The objection is sustained.

Chatham: Did he say where else he'd been the night before other than going down to Mose Wright's house?

Smith: He said he went to some of his people—I don't remember just who he said now—and he said he played cards there the rest of the night.

Sheriff Smith's testimony was brief, but it established that Bryant had admitted kidnapping Till from Mose Wright's home, established it not in the words of an old black sharecropper, but from Bryant's own mouth to the ear of a white officer of the law. The conversation in Sheriff Smith's car put the brothers in direct contact with the murder victim shortly before he was last seen alive.[3]

Now Breland began his cross examination, not to contradict anything Smith said, which would be pointless, but to imply that Bryant's confession, if that is the proper word for it, was not freely given. Breland asked Sheriff Smith if he and Roy Bryant were friends, if they trusted each other, if Bryant supported Smith in his bid for the legislature. Yes to all of these questions. Then Breland asked about the members of Bryant's family who began to gather at the grocery store just as Smith took Roy out to the car, and about Smith's own deputy, John Ed Cothran, who was also at the store, all of whom the sheriff failed to mention during the prosecution's examination. Breland's point was clear: Smith had broken trust, violated some unwritten rule of comity. The sheriff had manipulated Bryant, abused the confidentiality that his friend freely gave, extracted information without a warrant, never properly advised Bryant of his rights, even as he separated the man from his kinfolk.[4]

Breland: Now Mr. Smith, when you came up there to see Mr. Bryant, and he came out to your car and got in the car, and you got in the car with him there, you didn't tell him that you had come to arrest him, did you?

Smith: Not at that particular time.

Breland: I mean, until he made that statement to you, isn't that right?

Smith: Well, my general purpose was to go up there and arrest him.

Breland: But you didn't tell him that, did you?

Smith: Well...no, not right then.

Breland: And you didn't have a warrant for him, did you?

Smith: Not at that time.

Breland: Did you tell him that you were investigating the case for the sheriff's office?

Smith: Yes, Sir—well, he knew that.

Breland: I am asking you if you told him that?

Smith: I wouldn't say that I told him exactly that.

Breland: But you went up there that afternoon as far as appearances were concerned, and as far as a reasonable man would think, where he might have been concerned, you went up there just as a friend to talk privately with him, isn't that right?

Smith: Well, I got him in the car, yes, Sir.

Breland: Of course. And you didn't tell him that any statement that he might make to you anywise incriminating him might be used against him, did you?

Smith: There wasn't no statement hardly made, Mr. Breland.

Breland: But you didn't tell him that, did you?

Smith: No, Sir, I did not.

Breland: And did you later arrest him?

Smith: Yes, Sir....

Breland: And you took him right on to jail in Greenwood, did you?

Smith: A few minutes later, yes, Sir.

Breland: In other words, you waited for him so that he could dress and
           change clothes?

Smith: Well, he waited on some customers and so forth first.

Breland: And you didn't have him in handcuffs or anything like that?

Smith: No, Sir.

Breland: You just took him along with you to Greenwood and put him in
           jail, is that right?

Smith: Yes, Sir.[5]

The extra time and lack of handcuffs might be merely a gracious gesture, but Breland invited the jury to see it as a violation of trust among friends. Smith had gulled Bryant with fake courtesy. Worse, the sheriff had deprived the accused of his rights. Breland asked the Court once again to exclude Smith's testimony on grounds that Bryant's confession of abducting "that little nigger boy," was not free and voluntary, and more, that his client was not properly advised of his rights. Judge Swango refused, noting that Smith was simply investigating a crime, doing his job as sheriff, and Bryant must have known it. The defense had no further questions, so Sheriff Smith stood down.[6]

The prosecution now called its last witness of the day, John Ed Cothran. A peace officer for nearly a decade, Deputy Cothran arrested J. W. Milam at the Leflore County courthouse in Greenwood on Monday, August 29, the day after Sheriff Smith brought in Roy Bryant. Milam turned himself in on the kidnapping charge, it was later said, to keep his brother Roy from inadvertently making self-incriminating remarks. Cothran had a conversation with Milam inside the latter's jail cell. Just as Smith's testimony connected Till with Roy Bryant, Cothran's linked the youth's abduction to Milam. But Cothran's testimony before the court had hardly begun when defense counsel once again asked that the jurors be sent out of the room. When they were gone, attorney Sidney Carlton objected to them hearing Cothran's testimony because Milam's alleged confession of abducting Till from Mose Wright's home was "made under improper circumstances without the defendant being properly advised of his rights." Carlton also reprised the earlier defense objections that the corpus delicti still had not been properly established, that there was no good evidence that the body in the river was Till's, or that its death was caused by criminal agency.[7]

"The objections will be overruled," Judge Swango replied simply. "Let the jury come in." Carlton knew by now that Swango would rule against him, but the defense attorneys were establishing a record for an appeal in case the jury convicted Milam and Bryant.[8]

Under questioning by Chatham, Cothran described his brief conversation with Milam. Did you threaten the defendant in any way? No, Milam's statement was made of his own accord. Did you offer or promise him anything? No.

Chatham: Now will you tell the jury, Mr. Cothran—and speak out so the last
        man sitting over here on the back row can hear you, will you
        state what you had to say to "J. W." that day in the jail and what
        he had to say to you in regard to the murder of Emmett Till?
Cothran: I asked him if they went out there and got that little boy and if
        they had done something with him. And he said that they had
        brought him up there to that store and turned him loose, there at
        Roy Bryant's store.

Cothran was a man of few words—quiet words at that, since a juror at one point requested that he speak up—but Milam and Bryant's stories mostly matched: They picked up Till at Mose Wright's home a few hours before dawn on Sunday morning, they brought him to Bryant's store, talked to him, then let him go. Bryant specifically mentioned showing Till to his wife Carolyn, while Milam omitted that detail. Bryant said he then played cards with his family all night, while Milam claimed to have gone straight home to Glendora and to bed.[9]

Next, Chatham walked Cothran through the scene at the riverside on Wednesday morning. When he arrived, the deputy said, the gin fan was still in the boat and the barbed wire around the victim's neck. Cothran brought the gin fan, mud and all, down to the sheriff's office in Greenwood, and now identified it in the courtroom. Chatham asked if Cothran had seen many dead bodies in his years of service? Yes, Sir, I have. Had he seen ones that were maimed, beaten and shot? Yes, Sir. Could he describe the body in the boat?

Cothran: Well, his head was torn up pretty bad. And his left eye was
about out, it was all gouged out in there, you know. And right up in the
top of his head, well, there was a hole knocked in the front of it there....
And then right over his right ear...well, I wouldn't say it was a bullet
hole, but some of them said it was....

And what about the ring? Cothran described it as silver, possibly home-made, bearing the initials "L.T." and a date in May 1943, he couldn't recall it exactly. The ring was on the body when Cothran got to the river, then Chester Miller's assistant removed it and handed it to Mose Wright. But have you seen the ring since, Chatham asked? Yes, when they left the river, Cothran drove Mose Wright back home, where the old man showed the ring to his son, then gave it to the deputy, who had it in his possession ever since.[10]

"If the court please," Chatham announced, "we at this time will offer this ring in evidence as Exhibit 1 to the testimony of Mr. John Ed Cothran." Chatham also asked the deputy for a description of the gin fan, how much it weighed, how it was caked in mud, how it had been attached to the body with barbed wire. Finally, Chatham took Cothran through each wound and gash he could remember, having the deputy point out for the jury on his own head where the piece of skull came loose and where it appeared a bullet had entered above the right ear. That finished, Chatham turned to the defense table and said, "Take the witness."[11]

Defense counsel Carlton cross-examined Cothran much the same way Breland had questioned Sheriff Smith. Carlton established that Milam and Cothran were friends who trusted each other; indeed, Milam's whole family supported Cothran's unsuccessful bid to become sheriff. Carlton implied to the jury that the deputy manipulated that trust, exploited it. Was anyone else privy to your conversation with Milam in the Greenwood jail? Did you tell him that any statement he made could be used against him? Did you warn him before he spoke that he was being charged with a crime? Did you indicate that by answering your questions, Milam might incriminate himself? Cothran answered no to every question.[12]

Next Carlton asked about the gin fan. What did it weigh? About seventy pounds. But it came out of the river full of mud? Yes, it could have weighed double that with all the mud. How many blades on that fan? Carlton waited while Cothran counted out eighteen. Are they sharp? Yes. With a big heavy hub in the middle? Yes. And we can't tell if the wounds were made before the body went in the river or after, can we? No, not for sure.

Carlton: Those wounds on the left-hand side of his head were such that they could have been made by this fan dropping on the head, isn't that right?

Cothran: Yes, Sir. If it had hit him, it would have.

Carlton: And the depressed place in the forehead of that body, the gash there, that could have been made by the fan blades or by the hub, too, couldn't it?

Cothran: Yes, Sir.

Carlton: In your best judgment, was it possible for that place, the wound over his right ear, was it possible for that to have been made by a snag in the river?

Cothran: Yes, it could have been.

So a postmortem accident might explain the head wounds? Cothran agreed. What about other injuries?

Carlton: Now John Ed, I believe you testified on direct examination that there was no mutilation of this body except around the head?

Cothran: That's right. If there was, I didn't see any.

Carlton: Had the boy's privates been mutilated?

Cothran: No, Sir.

Carlton: Did his back show any signs of any bruises or any wounds at all on the back?

Cothran: Now you are asking me a pretty hard question there. That body was in pretty bad shape, and I couldn't hardly tell. And I wouldn't want to answer that "Yes" or "No." At least, you couldn't see any.[13]

Now Carlton returned to the identification of the corpse. He asked Cothran what Mose Wright said when he first saw the body at the river? Cothran replied that Mose's first words were, "I believe that's him," meaning his nephew, Emmett Till. Was Mose Wright close to the body? Roughly fifty feet away, with the corpse face down in the boat. What about the ring, what did Mose say about that?

Cothran: He said he didn't know about the ring, but that he would ask his son about it.

Carlton: And Mose said at that time that he didn't know anything about the ring?

Cothran: That's right....

Carlton: Now when Mose got up close to the boat and saw the body there, did he make any statement to you such as, "I could be mistaken that it might could not be him"?

Cothran: He did.

Carlton: At the time the ring was taken off his finger, did the skin come off with the ring?

Cothran: Yes, Sir. . . .

Carlton: What was the position of his tongue there at the scene?

Cothran: It was swelled out of his mouth.

Carlton: And what was the condition of the body all over as regards swelling?

Cothran: It was bad.[14]

And again, less delicately this time, Carlton asked about the body's genitals. His import was clear: Were these the private parts of a boy or of a man?

Carlton: And was he a well-developed body?

Cothran: Yes, Sir.

Carlton: And what was the condition of his private parts there when he was turned over?

Cothran: It was in bad shape.

Carlton: Were they swelled or stiff?

Cothran: Well, swelled or stiff.

Carlton: And were they well-developed privates?

Cothran: Yes, Sir.

Carlton: How old would you estimate this body to be?

Cothran: I wouldn't.[15]

With that, the defense dismissed the witness. Attorney Chatham asked to enter a photo of the gin fan into evidence, then the prosecution too rested. Judge Swango adjourned court until 10:00 a.m. the following morning.[16]

It had been a good day's work for the prosecutors. The judge permitted them to examine witnesses and enter evidence that clearly tied the defendants to the disappearance of Emmett Till and that also connected Till to the body in the river. Mose Wright made his dramatic identification of Milam and Bryant as the men who invaded his home; young Robert Hodges recounted his gruesome discovery of a corpse floating on the river; Chester Miller gave solid testimony about the horrible wounds on the body and the telltale ring on its finger; Sheriffs Smith and Cothran testified that the two brothers admitted kidnapping the kid from Chicago out of Mose Wright's home. And Judge Swango allowed the jury to hear it and allowed all of it to stand.

But the defense did well too. Milam and Bryant's attorneys undermined Wright's story about what he saw on that dark, dark night; they shook the jury's confidence that Smith and Cothran dealt fairly with the brothers; and they planted doubts about Chester Miller's veracity. Above all, defense council pushed a wedge of doubt between the missing boy and the body in the river. Cothran's testimony about the corpse's wretched condition, and about Wright's identification of his dead nephew foreshadowed the defense's most effective ploy: Was Emmett Till really dead?

CHAPTER FIFTEEN

MAMIE TILL BRADLEY

JUDGE SWANGO CALLED for order on Thursday morning and a long, steamy day of testimony began. The first witness was C. F. "Chick" Nelson, the mayor of Tutwiler, Mississippi, and also that town's funeral director. His brief time on the stand affirmed that a body, said to be that of Emmett Till, had been brought to his place of business, where "we prepared it the best we could and shipped it to Chicago."[1]

When Nelson stepped down, the prosecution called Mamie Till Bradley. "A way was opened down the center aisle," wrote reporter Clark Porteous, "as a hush fell over... the hot, humid little courtroom." Mrs. Bradley wore a conservative gray-and-white summer suit with a gray-and-black jacket. There were many reasons the prosecution brought her down to Mississippi—to make the tragedy more palpable; to show the jury the grieving mother; to let her pain humanize the case; most important, to have her confirm that the body in the river was Emmett's. After all, she had powerful reason to not recognize her son in that decomposed corpse, for then there would be hope that he was still alive.[2]

She knew the drill: the lawyers would call her "Mamie" and she would address them as "Sir" or "Mister." She had given some thought to how, as a black woman and a northerner, to deliver her testimony. She knew of course that the defense would analyze and pick apart her words, and she was determined to present herself as clear and certain of her opinions, but not angry or emotional. She would explain in detail how she knew that the body was Emmett's. Above all, she would keep her feelings in check to win over the jury.[3]

Robert Smith asked Mrs. Bradley a series of questions about Emmett's age, where they lived, who his father was, how Louis Till died. Then Smith got to the heart of the matter, the identification of the body. She explained that she first saw the corpse after its long train ride from Tutwiler to Chicago. She described examining her son's mortal remains:

Bradley: I positively identified the body in the casket and later on when it was on the slab as being that of my son, Emmett Louis Till.

Smith: Will you please tell the court and the jury how you looked at it and what you did in identifying it?

Bradley: I looked at the face very carefully. I looked at the ears, and the forehead, and the hairline, and also the hair, and I looked at the nose and the lips, and the chin. I just looked at it all over very thoroughly. And I was able to find out that it was my boy. And I knew definitely that it was my boy beyond a shadow of a doubt.

Bradley's eyes went to the jurors as she answered Smith's questions, trying to form a human connection with them. But she never looked at Milam and Bryant, recalling fifty years later, "If I had any chance at all to appeal to that jury, to reach out to them, then I could not let them see me challenge those two monsters. And that is how it would have been interpreted if I had been seen looking at them."[4]

Now Smith turned to Emmett's ring, formerly the ring of Private Louis Till, who died in the European theater during World War II.

Smith: I now hand you a ring, Mamie, that has engraved on it "May 25, 1943," with the large initials "L.T.," and I ask you if that was among the effects that were sent to you which were purported to be the effects of your dead husband?

Bradley: Yes, Sir.

Smith: What was your husband's name?

Bradley: Louis Till.

Smith: In other words, his initials were "L.T."?

Bradley: Yes Sir.

Smith: And after you got this ring along with his effects, what happened to it?

Bradley: I kept the ring in a jewelry box, but it was much too large for the boy to wear. But since his twelfth birthday, he has worn it occasionally with the aid of scotch tape or string. He had to have something else on with it to make it fit his hand tightly enough.

But usually though it was kept in his personal jewelry box, and
on the morning of...August 20 when he got ready to board the
train, he was looking in his jewelry box to get some cuff links,
I think it was, and when he looked in the box there, he saw this
ring, and he put it on his hand, or on his finger, and he shook his
hand, to make sure that it would stay on there and not fall off. And
I remember that I casually remarked to him I said, "Gee, you are
getting to be quite a grown man."

Smith: Did he then put the ring on his finger?
Bradley: Yes, Sir.
Smith: And he left Chicago with it, did he?
Bradley: Yes, Sir.
Smith: And you definitely say that was the ring that he left there with?
Bradley: Yes, Sir.
Smith: And that was the ring he had when he came down here to
             Mississippi?
Bradley: Yes, Sir.[5]

Now Smith asked Mrs. Bradley to look at a photograph of her son's mutilated body, a photo taken at the Century Funeral Home in Greenwood,
the same image placed in evidence the day before, a photo Mamie had
never seen until this moment. "Oh," she remembered decades later, "everything just washed over me again. The force of it rocked me in that old
cane chair, back and forth. I bowed my head. I had to do that to collect
myself. I mean, the tears were welling up and I wanted so much to hold
them back. I wanted to hide them. No one should see them. I had to be
strong up there. I couldn't be weak. I had to be strong for Emmett." Her
voice lost all emotion as she answered Smith's questions.

Smith: And I hand you that picture and ask you if that is a picture of your
             son, Emmett Till?
Bradley: Yes, Sir.
Smith: That is him, isn't it?
Bradley: Yes, Sir.

As Attorney Smith passed the photograph to the jury, Mrs. Bradley's composure cracked just for a moment. She shook her head from side to side,
sobbed once, then just as quickly removed her glasses and furtively wiped
her eyes. Smith turned the witness over to the defense.[6]
    J. J. Breland began with a series of questions about Mississippi and
Chicago. He remained in his seat and spoke quietly, almost casually. He

established that though she was born less than three miles from where the trial now took place, Mamie Till Bradley had no memory of this; her family left the town of Webb in Tallahatchie County when she was two years old and moved north for good. The prosecutors objected to Breland's line of questioning as irrelevant, but not before he established for the jury that here was a Mississippi family that turned its back on its home state. By simply raising the issue Breland began a new line of thought—that Mamie and her family were "Chicago Negroes," ungrateful for their former lives in the South.[7]

Next, Breland asked if she held any insurance policies on her son. The prosecutors objected but Judge Swango overruled them. Mamie revealed that she had two policies covering Emmett, that she had purchased them when he was a baby, ten cents weekly for one, fifteen cents for the other, one payable to herself, one to her mother, together worth about four hundred dollars. Policies like these were very common in northern black communities, hedges against the formidable cost of a proper burial, something terribly important to people of limited means and all-too-often foreshortened lives. The defense unwittingly did the prosecution a favor asking this set of questions, because rumors had been rife in the Delta that Emmett's mother held policies worth $10,000 or even $15,000 on her son. Mamie gave detailed answers and stood her ground.

Breland: And have you collected on those policies?
Bradley: No, Sir.
Breland: Have you tried to collect on them?
Smith: We object to that, Your Honor. That is highly irrelevant.
The Court: The objection is overruled.
Breland: Have you tried to collect on those policies?
Bradley: I have been waiting to receive a death certificate.
Breland: Have you contacted the insurance companies about the policies?
Bradley: Yes, Sir.
Breland: And you and your mother, both have done this?
Bradley: Yes, Sir.

Once again, Breland's strategy was to cast doubt, all of it implied, never explicitly stated: Mamie Till Bradley had a financial stake in identifying the body. Maybe she would lie for cash. And if the insurance company failed to pay off on the policies, perhaps they too suspected that Emmett Till was not really dead. It was all part of a larger battle between the attorneys to control the impressions received by the jury and the larger public, the prosecution portraying her as warm and caring, a respectable middle-class mother, filled with unspeakable grief, while defense council's questions implied she was cold and calculating, a woman who would monetize her dead son.[8]

Milam and Bryant's attorney kept hammering away. Black Chicago itself became his focus.

Breland: Now, Mamie, what newspapers do you subscribe to in Chicago?
Smith: We object to that, Your Honor.
The Court: The objection is sustained.
Breland: Do you read the *Chicago Defender*?
Smith: We object to that, Your Honor.
The Court: The objection is sustained.
Breland: Your Honor, I think this is important because I have some
            exhibits that I want the witness to identify.
Chatham: If the Court please, I think it is perfectly obvious what he is trying
            to get at. And I think counsel should be counseled not to ask any
            more questions like that.
The Court: The objection is sustained. Now, will you gentlemen of the jury
            step back in the jury room a moment, please?[9]

When they were gone, Judge Swango said he was willing to consider Breland's line of inquiry, but he insisted on previewing it in the jury's absence. The *Chicago Defender* was as close to a national newspaper as existed in black America, carried south by Pullman Porters, distributed surreptitiously. Its first crusading publisher, Robert Sengstacke Abbott, long championed the Great Migration, urging African Americans to leave the land of their oppression and come north, if not quite to the promised land, at least to a better life than they had known in the Jim Crow South. In 1940, his nephew John Sengstacke took over the newspaper and helped lead the equal rights cause. For African Americans, the *Defender* was a voice of hope and a lightning rod for organizing, while white Mississippians often considered it a pack of lies and propaganda, stirring discontent among otherwise happy people.[10]

Attorney Breland continued his questions with the jury absent.

Breland: Have you been reading the *Chicago Defender* since the trial of this
            cause?
Bradley: Yes, Sir.
Breland: And also since the incident happened that has been referred to
            here?
Bradley: Yes, Sir.

Breland: And you have been getting it, have you?
Bradley: Yes, Sir. I read it every week.

Breland produced photographs and asked Bradley about the one that appeared in the *Defender* along with the story about Emmett's funeral. She'd seen it, yes; it was of Emmett in his coffin. What about this one of him smiling, reprinted by the *Memphis Press-Scimitar*? Yes, that one and three others were taken just two days after Christmas, 1954, and given to the press after Emmett's murder.[11]

Breland played a subtle game here, asking that the photos be entered as exhibits for the jury's perusal. One would think these before-and-after photos would benefit the prosecution, making the horror of the murder visceral for the jury. Breland gambled that the images would have the opposite effect—How could that smiling happy lad be the mangled body pulled from the river? The corpse was too far gone, no reasonable man could infer that these were the same human being. Breland also wanted the jury to believe that Mamie Till Bradley had shamelessly publicized this whole event. She had given pictures to the *Chicago Defender*, that rabblerousing rag smuggled into the South to stir up unrest. Just as bad was the *Memphis Press-Scimitar*—from which Breland clipped the photos of a smiling young Emmett—perceived as a white renegade sheet. Clark Porteous, one of its reporters, had made a name for himself investigating lynchings. He had even befriended the former NAACP executive secretary Walter White. Porteous was in this very courtroom, covering the trial, turning his treacherous gaze on the Till murder.[12]

Judge Swango had had enough. He let Breland go on with the jury out of the courtroom, but then, according to Murray Kempton, with "a sudden sharpness in his habitual courtesy," Swango cut Breland off: "Every question you have asked will be excluded, and there'll be no reference to it." For the remainder of the trial, the judge ruled, attorneys would make no reference to what newspaper witnesses did or did not read. "Just this once in Mississippi," Kempton concluded, "they'd try a murder case and not Chicago, and, having made that guarantee, Curtis Swango told the bailiffs to bring the jury back into the courtroom."[13]

But not quite yet. Breland said he had one more line of questioning for the witness, and he suggested he pursue it while the jury was still out of the room, since there would be objections from the prosecutors. Swango told Breland to proceed. Breland asked Mamie Till Bradley about her warnings to Emmett before he left Chicago. Did she caution him about how to behave himself in Mississippi? Yes, she had. And was this press quotation accurate (Breland read aloud): "I told him several times before he left for Mississippi that he should kneel in the street and beg forgiveness if he ever insulted a white man or white woman"? She said that she was not sure about her exact words, but she repeated the gist of it for the court:

> *Bradley*: I told him when he was coming down here that he would have to adapt himself to a new way of life. And I told him to be very careful about how he spoke and to whom he spoke, and to always remember to say "Yes, Sir" and "No, Ma'am" at all times. And I told him that if ever an incident should arise where there would be any trouble of any kind with white people, then if it got to a point where he ever had to get down on his knees before them, well, I told him not to hesitate to do so. Like, if he bumped into somebody on the street, well, and then they might get belligerent or something, well, I told him to go ahead and humble himself so as not to get into any trouble of any kind.[14]

Had Emmett ever been in Mississippi before, Breland asked? Yes, when he was about fifteen months old, then around age four or five, and then when he was nine years old, always visiting his Uncle Mose.

> *Breland*: And did you specifically indicate to him and caution him not to do anything to any white man so as not to bring on any trouble?
> *Bradley*: Yes, Sir.
> *Breland*: And from the newspaper quotation, the newspaper report says that you did that several times, is that true?
> *Bradley*: I did. I impressed it on him very carefully as to how he should act while he was down here....
> *Breland*: And did you caution him in those conversations you had with him not to insult any white women?
> *Bradley*: I didn't specifically say white women. But I said about the white people. And I cautioned him not to get in a fight with any white boys. And I told him that, because, naturally living in Chicago, he wouldn't know just how to act maybe.[15]

And here was Breland's point: If Emmett Till had been to Mississippi before, why did he need so much counseling? It was a classic no-win inquiry. Bradley attempted to show she was a good mother and her son had been instructed properly. So why all of this coaching? Why did she think Mississippi was so touchy? More to the point, what kind of troublemaker was Emmett Till?

Breland: Prior to his coming down to Mississippi, and prior to his leaving
          Chicago, while he was living there in Chicago, had he been doing
          anything to cause you to give him that special instruction?
Bradley: No, Sir. Emmett has never been in any trouble at any time.
Breland: And he has never been in reform school?
Bradley: No, Sir.
Breland: And he never had any trouble in any way with any white people?
Bradley: No, Sir.

A glimmer of doubt: If Emmett was such a good lad, why so much prep-
ping for his trip? Was he an accident waiting to happen?[16]

Breland pursued one more line of questioning with the jury still out of
the room. "I believe you live on the South Side of Chicago, the black
belt," Breland asked. Merely invoking that place was a goad. On Chicago's
South Side, African Americans who had moved north from Mississippi
and neighboring states, lived free of Jim Crow laws. And the people on
the South Side, Breland went on, are they all colored people or white
people? Mamie Bradley replied that there were a few white people living
there. These were the final brush strokes in the defense's portrait of
Emmett Till and his family: The *Chicago Defender*, reform school, the "black
belt." Breland evoked a series of stereotyped racial fears, and left a question lingering in the air: Maybe Mamie Till Bradley schooled her son so
carefully on how to behave because she knew he was trouble, knew that
he would provoke white people. Maybe Emmett Till was yet another hotheaded Chicago Negro, shaped by the angry politics of that seething black
world.[17]

Judge Swango was having none of it. When told the defense was
finished, the judge made his ruling: "The objections to all that testimony
will be sustained, and there will be no questions along that line whatsoever.... And there will be no further reference to it, and there will be no
questions asked concerning that after the jury comes in."[18]

When the jurors came back to the courtroom, Breland returned to the
newspaper photographs from the funeral, entered them in evidence and
showed them to the jury, this time with their origins blotted out.
Mrs. Bradley had the last word. When Breland asked if the photo of her
son was what she saw in the Chicago funeral home, she replied in her
soft, matter-of-fact way, no, not exactly. This picture was taken, after the
body had been cleaned up.

Breland: And everything was the same except that clothes had been put on
          the body the second time you saw him, is that right? That is, it was

the same as it was when you saw him the first time when he had no clothes on, is that right?

Bradley: No, Sir. The first time I saw him, he had a hole in his head up here [indicating with her hand], and that was open. And he had another scar. I can't tell you exactly where it was. It was either over the right eye or the left eye. I can't remember just now.

And he had a gash in his jaw, and his mouth was open and the tongue was out. That is the first time when I saw him without his clothes on. But from this picture here, it seems like his mouth has been closed, and that gash was sewn up, and that piece of his forehead up there has been closed up. That is the way it looks to me.

The defense rested, and the prosecution had no further questions for Mamie Till Bradley.[19]

CHAPTER SIXTEEN

AN INTERRACIAL MANHUNT

THROUGHOUT THEIR STAY in Mississippi, the African American reporters sitting at the segregated table in the back of the courtroom had good reason to fear for their personal safety. Tallahatchie County deputies in the courthouse and thugs on the road did their best to intimidate them. The newsmen found evidence that their hotel phones had been tapped; a few reported strangers knocking on their doors in the middle of the night; they were followed on foot and by car. Some spoke only half-jokingly to one another about diving out one of the courtroom's second-story windows if necessary or grabbing a deputy's gun in the event that violence broke out.[1]

The danger only strengthened their resolve to do more than merely cover the story. The Till trial offered an example of the limits of "objective reporting." More precisely, good journalism was impossible if that meant simply taking things at face value. Getting the full story required unusual, even courageous, action that had an impact on the case itself. Writing about it a few months after the trial, Simeon Booker from *Jet* magazine described an "interracial manhunt," involving "Negro and white reporters, top Negro leaders, and Mississippi law enforcers working together in a hard-hitting team at a time most of the U.S. thought the Dixie state was doing nothing about gaining convictions in the case." Between the eve of the trial on Sunday, September 18, and Thursday morning, September 22, when Mamie Till Bradley testified, Booker's "hard-hitting team" took great personal risks to identify and bring to court several key witnesses.[2]

The veteran black journalist James L. Hicks learned that something was up before the trial even started, and he followed his reporters' instincts deep into the Delta. Recall that Hicks made it to Sumner in time for Kid Townsend's funeral service on Sunday, the day before jury selection began. Hicks described how, as he stood outside the church after Townsend's service, a man came up to him and asked if he was in town for the trial. Hicks replied he was, and the man pointed to a woman standing behind a parked car and suggested that the reporter go speak with her. She furtively told Hicks to go down to the tiny town of Glendora to a juke joint called Kings and ask about a man named "Too Tight." Don't talk to any white people, don't let anyone know what you're looking for, and be sure to get out of town before dark. She drifted away and the first man sidled back up to Hicks, just to let him know that Glendora, seven miles distant, the home of J. W. Milam, was "one of the roughest towns on colored people in the county."[3]

Later that afternoon, in a back alley crowded with black folks, Hicks found Kings, a club with music blaring, couples dancing, food and beer coming out of the kitchen. Hicks struck up a conversation with a man who appeared to be the owner of the place. After some idle chat, Hicks asked whatever happened to Too Tight. "The man stopped as if I had hit him in the face." Talk to that chick over there, King's owner said.[4]

Observing the scene, Hicks saw that the best approach was simply to ask the woman to dance, which she willingly did. Too Tight is in jail, she told him on the dance floor. For what? I don't know—they came and got him last Monday. How do you know this? Too Tight was living with me and my husband, who is in jail too. What did they get him for? She replied that she didn't know, but that both worked for one of those white men who kidnapped that boy from Chicago. Hicks asked what jail they were in, and she said she didn't know that either. She was afraid to talk to anyone about it; she wasn't even certain that they were in jail. Hicks also found out that Too Tight's real name was Leroy Collins, and that the woman's husband was Henry Lee Loggins. Hicks asked if they could go look for them tomorrow. "I'd like to do it," she said, "but I'd get a beating," and she explained that at harvest time, the white man she worked for "came around and whipped everyone who didn't go out into the cotton fields and pick his cotton." She added, "even if they are sick, he whips them."[5]

Hicks returned to his room in Mound Bayou before dark. The story might have ended there, but it turned out he was not the only one gathering information. On Tuesday morning, Hicks learned from T. R. M. Howard that more news had come to light. After midnight, a field hand named Frank Young slipped into Mound Bayou and told Dr. Howard that Milam and Bryant had been spotted just hours after Till's kidnapping near Drew, Mississippi, on the plantation supervised by J. W.'s brother, Leslie Milam. Young mentioned the names of Add Reed, his grandson Willie Reed, their neighbor Amandy Bradley, and one or two others. Willie Reed claimed he saw Emmett Till on the morning after the kidnapping in the back of a green and white pickup truck carrying several men, both black and white.[6]

Hicks wanted to break the story immediately, and Ruby Hurley, the NAACP director for the southeast region, agreed; the trial might end without new witnesses testifying if the journalists failed to get the word out. But there was a problem. Interfering with workers at the height of the harvest would not go down well, and a bunch of black reporters calling those folks out as witnesses would put them in danger. If Sheriff Strider was arresting field hands and doing God knows what else to them to keep them from talking, then anyone revealed as a witness might disappear, or worse. Loggins and Collins, after all, were still nowhere to be found. Publishing the story prematurely was simply too risky.[7]

The best solution was to quietly bring the witnesses to Mound Bayou—that rarest of Mississippi places, an African American sanctuary, a well-armed, well-organized, all-black town—to persuade frightened people to do something truly terrifying, give evidence against white men in a court of law. Exactly how Hicks, Howard, and the others found the witnesses and brought them in is not entirely clear. Apparently Ruby Hurley, Medgar Evers (Mississippi field secretary for the NAACP), and Moses Newsome (a reporter for the *Tri-State Defender*) dressed up as field hands, went out to the plantations, and mingled among local workers to encourage witnesses to gather that evening in Cleveland, Mississippi, a few miles south of Mound Bayou. The witnesses never showed up, but the word was out in the fields that their testimony mattered.[8]

Dr. Howard now reasoned that the only way to bring the witnesses in was with the help of local law enforcement officials, and more, that the best way to persuade them was through the intervention of some of the white newspaper reporters. Howard told a few newsmen about the witnesses, including the only one he fully trusted, Clark Porteous. The plan worked, and a handful of sheriffs and prosecutors from counties bordering Tallahatchie joined the search.[9]

On Tuesday afternoon, District Attorney T. J. Townsend and Prosecutor Stannie Sanders from Sunflower County, Sheriff Smith and Deputy

Cothran of Leflore County, and a special investigator named Gwin Cole, sent by the governor, drove out to the plantation near Drew, Mississippi, where Leslie Milam lived. They searched the shed on his property for signs of a beating or a murder, but they found no bloodstains or other evidence. They also spoke with local workers, who repeated stories about what went on there a month earlier. That night, the law officers met up with several journalists, black and white, including Porteous, Jimmy Hicks, and Simeon Booker.[10]

They made the decision to find the witnesses and convince them to come to Mound Bayou. Rumors had swept the plantations about the white men who came earlier, frightening local people. The white officers made it clear they could not force anyone to leave the cotton fields, but they agreed to drive the journalists and activists out to the plantations to persuade those with information to come forward. Simeon Booker, the *Jet* reporter, quoted Sheriff Smith as saying, "These witnesses have a story to tell. We've got to find them if it takes all night." With that, a few groups took off, sheriffs in their squad cars accompanied by reporters and local community leaders, other vehicles trailing behind, all on wild chases over dirt roads at seventy-five miles an hour in the hot Delta night.[11]

They found and persuaded Amandy Bradley, Add Reed, and most important, Willie Reed, to come to Mound Bayou. All were terrified and reluctant to testify. Dr. Howard promised them that he and other NAACP workers—Hurley, Evers, Amzie Moore, Aaron Henry—would make sure they got safely out of Sumner after the trial. Chatham and Smith were briefed by their Sunflower County counterparts. Finally, all the attorneys in Sumner interviewed the new witnesses and prepared the rest of their case.[12]

It was a victory but only a partial one. Frank Young, who tipped Dr. Howard about the new witnesses, never testified, and it is impossible to know what he might have said. Two others subpoenaed by the prosecution also failed to appear. More important, Too Tight Collins and Henry Lee Loggins were never located before the trial ended. Rumors persisted that Sheriff Strider had locked them away in the Charleston jail, though, according to Clark Porteous, Sheriff Smith looked long and hard for them with no luck. Loggins and Collins might or might not have been willing to testify, no one knew for sure if they were even involved in the Till case, but as Dr. Howard told reporters, there was plenty of reason to believe that those two were in a position to "split this thing wide open."[13]

Jimmy Hicks later regretted that he failed to publish a story about Collins and Loggins until after the trial ended. Mississippi had frightened him. He had been watched during his week in Sumner and felt that his life was in danger. He feared for Collins's and Loggins's safety if their whereabouts were publicized, but he feared for his own even more. Chatham told Hicks that a prosecutor could not produce witnesses if the sheriff failed to. Hicks asked what Chatham thought happened to Loggins and Collins? "I wouldn't like to say," the DA answered, underscoring Hicks's own fears.[14]

CHAPTER SEVENTEEN

WILLIE REED

WILLIE REED FOLLOWED Mamie Till Bradley to the witness stand. Reed was the most important of the surprise witnesses. Eighteen years old, tall, wiry, and dark, Reed lived with his grandfather, Add Reed, on Clint Shurden's plantation near Drew, Mississippi. J. W. Milam's brother, Leslie Milam, supervised the workers there. Shortly after dawn on Sunday morning, August 28—roughly four hours after Milam and Bryant kidnapped Emmett Till—Reed walked from his home to a nearby store, stopping along the way to fetch a bucket of water for his neighbor, Amandy Bradley. That walk took him right by Leslie Milam's place.[1]

The arc of the trial testimony so far went from Mose Wright's vivid account of the kidnapping, through Robert Hodge's and Chester Miller's descriptions of the scene by the river, to Sheriff Smith and Deputy Cothran's assertions that the brothers admitted kidnapping Emmett Till, then through Mamie Till Bradley's stark description of the body she buried in Chicago. Now Willy Reed put the jury literally within shouting distance of Emmett Till's torment.[2]

His testimony was almost painful. Reed had serious weaknesses as a witness, weaknesses exploited by Milam's and Bryant's lawyers. He had difficulty comprehending some questions and formulating answers. Clearly, he was terrified. An "uneasy witness," one reporter called him, "squirming uneasily in his chair." His normally soft voice grew all but inaudible, and Judge Swango urged him repeatedly to speak up. His testimony had a jerky quality to it, more like snapshots than a movie. As Robert Smith tried to elicit the young man's story, the defense attorneys interrupted repeatedly, vigorously objecting to his questions and to the witness's answers. Judge Swango sustained some particulars but overruled the major objections, permitting the larger picture Reed painted to emerge. The young man took the jury to the crime scene; his words allowed the court to visualize the penultimate moments of Emmett Till's life.[3]

Prosecutor Smith led Reed with a series of simple questions.

Smith: In going from your house to the store, what place do you have to pass by?
Reed: I pass by Mr. Milam's.
Smith: Then Mr. Milam lives out there, does he?
Reed: Yes, Sir.
Smith: That is Mr. Leslie Milam, is that right?
Reed: Yes, Sir.
Smith: And not Mr. J. W. Milam?
Reed: No, Sir.
Smith: Is there any shed, or barn or other building on the place there?
Reed: Yes, Sir.
Smith: What kind of building was that?
Reed: Green.
Smith: Well, what kind of a building was it? Will you tell the jury what kind of a building it was?
Reed: It was a barn.
Smith: A barn?
Reed: Yes, Sir.[4]

Before he got to Leslie Milam's home and barn, however, Willie Reed said a truck passed him, traveling in his direction. Reed's description was precise—1955 Chevrolet, green body, white top.

Smith: And who, if anyone, was in that truck that you saw?
Reed: Well, when the truck passed by me I seen four white mens in the cab and three colored mens in the back. And I seen somebody sitting down in the truck back there....
Smith: And you say there was somebody down in the back end of the truck?
Reed: Yes, Sir. I seen another colored boy.

So a truck carrying seven or eight people, it was a little unclear, passed Reed: four white men in front, three or four blacks in back, one of them, a boy, sitting on the floor bed, looking out of the back of the truck.

Smith: How close did you get to that truck?
Reed: I was about as far as from here to the door back there [pointing with his hand].
Smith: Well, how far would you say that was? Would that be fifty feet?
Reed: It may be. I don't know.[5]

Reed said he did not recognize any of the men in the truck—perhaps he was afraid to name them, more likely he had never seen most of them before—but he recognized the boy.

Smith: Now later on did you recognize a photograph or anything that indicated to you who the one sitting down in the back end of that truck was?
Reed: Well, when I looked at this [news]paper I was sure—well I seen it, and it seemed like I seen this boy someplace before. And I looked at it and tried to remember, and then it come back to my memory that this was the same one I seen in the paper.
Smith: And it was Emmett Till?
Reed: I don't know if that was him but the picture favored him.
Breland: We object to that, Your Honor.
The Court: The objection is sustained....
Smith: Willie, I have a picture here that has been offered as Exhibit 1 to the testimony of Mrs. Mamie Bradley for purposes of identification....
Breland: We object, Your Honor. That is not in evidence here.
The Court: It has been offered or introduced for purposes of identification, and it may be used as such.

Judge Swango had no problem with photographs already accepted by the court as evidence, but he would not let attorneys lead the witnesses— Willie Reed must connect the photo to the boy in the truck on his own.

Smith: Now I ask you to look at that picture, and I ask you whether or not does that or does that not resemble the person you saw sitting there in the back of that truck on that particular day?

Breland: We object, Your Honor.

The Court: The objection is sustained.

Smith: Is that the boy you saw in the back of that truck?

Breland: We object.

The Court: The objection is sustained. But you can ask him if he had ever seen that boy before.

Smith: Have you ever seen that boy before?

Reed: It is a picture of the boy I seen on the back of the truck.[6]

A few minutes after they passed him on the road, Reed walked by Leslie Milam's farm, and there he saw that same truck again, empty, parked in front of the barn.

Smith: Now, later on in the morning, did you see Mr. J. W. Milam out there?

Reed: Yes, Sir.

Smith: Where did you see him?

Reed: Well, when I passed by he came out by the barn to the well.

Smith: And was that Mr. J. W. Milam, the man who is sitting over there [pointing to the defendant, Mr. Milam]?

Reed: Yes, Sir.

Smith: Will you state whether he had anything unusual on about his person?

Reed: Yes, Sir.

Smith: What did he have?

Reed: He had on a gun.

Smith: Was it a pistol, a rifle, or a shotgun?

Reed: He had on a pistol. He had it on his belt.

Smith: And what did Mr. J. W. Milam do when you saw him?

Reed: He just came to the well and got a drink of water.

Smith: What did he do then?

Reed: Then he went back to the barn.[7]

Next came a series of objections that Judge Swango sustained, but Attorney Smith persisted, drawing Reed out with more precise questions, until the judge finally allowed the testimony to enter the record:

Smith: Did you see or hear anything as you passed the barn?

Reed: I heard somebody hollering, and I heard some licks like somebody was whipping somebody.

Smith: You heard some licks and you also heard somebody hollering, is that right?

Reed: Yes, Sir.

Smith: What was that person hollering?

Reed: He was just hollering, "Oh."

Smith: You heard someone hollering "Oh," is that right?

Reed: "Yes, Sir."

Smith: Did they holler once or was it more than once, or was it two or three times, or what?

Reed: They hollered more than once.

Smith: And what about the licks? Was it just one lick you heard, or was it two, or were there several licks?

Reed: There was a whole lot of them.

Smith: You heard a whole lot of licks?

Reed: Yes, Sir.

Smith: And was that a human being you heard or was it some kind of animal?

Reed: Well, it sounded like a human being.[8]

Reed described how he stopped at the next house down the road, Amandy Bradley's place. She was one of Leslie Milam's tenants, well along in years, and she asked Reed to fetch a bucket of water from the well for her. Not too much time would have passed—five minutes, ten?—but Reed testified that when he went back to the well, he heard more hollering coming from the barn. He brought Bradley her water and continued with his errands. He went to the grocery store, then passed the barn once again, and finally returned home to get ready for Sunday school. The prosecution concluded:

Smith: On the way back, did you hear or see anything, or hear or see anybody?

Reed: No, Sir, I didn't see anything. They were gone.

Smith: Was the truck gone?

Reed: Yes, Sir.[9]

When the prosecution rested, J. J. Breland immediately rose and moved to exclude Willie Reed's testimony on grounds that it was not sufficiently tied to the defendants, that his story had no connection to the body in the river, and that Reed never properly identified Emmett Till. Judge Swango overruled the motion without comment.[10]

Attorney Kellum cross-examined Reed. He asked a series of questions—had Reed ever seen the truck before (no), did he know both Milam brothers (yes), how many times had he seen J. W. Milam in the past (three or four times). But more important, Kellum hammered away at Reed's competence as a witness, his knowledge and intelligence. After establishing that Reed was eighteen years old and currently enrolled in school in the ninth grade, Kellum asked in what direction Reed was walking when the truck passed him. It became clear that Reed did not know east from west. Were you walking toward the truck or did it pass you going away? Reed answered both ways. How fast was the truck going? Kellum made Reed's nuanced answer—fast coming off the main road, slow as it turned uphill onto gravel—seem muddled. Most striking, Reed simply could not estimate distances.[11]

Kellum: Willie, how far do you live from this barn or shed that you mentioned?

Reed: I don't know, but I don't live too far down.

Kellum: Would you say you lived a quarter of a mile away or a half-mile away?

Reed: I just wouldn't know how far.

Kellum: When you passed by this shed or barn, how far were you from the barn?

Reed: Well, I wouldn't know, Sir, just how far I was from the barn. But I wasn't too far from it.

Kellum: Well, how many steps would it be from this spot where you passed by the barn over to the barn?

Reed: I wouldn't know, Sir.

Kellum: Well, would you say it was a hundred yards?

Reed: I just wouldn't know how far it was.

Kellum: You don't know how far it was?

Reed: No, Sir....

Kellum: This person that you testified to was Mr. Milam, he was how far from you when you first saw him?

Reed: I wouldn't say how far because I wouldn't know.

Kellum: Then you don't know whether you were one hundred yards away, or two hundred yards, or five hundred yards away from him?

Reed: No, Sir.

Kellum highlighted Reed's ignorance to undermine his credibility as a witness. How reliable was a young man who could not tell the difference between a few yards and a few hundred?[12]

But there was another point to this line of questioning. Interviewed by the defense attorneys on the day before he took the stand, Reed apparently told them that Milam was four hundred yards away when he saw him at the well, nearly a quarter mile. Perhaps Reed agreed to that figure to be polite, or maybe the five lawyers in that tiny office intimidated him. Either way, doubts remained: Had Reed lied to them in their office, or was he lying on the stand? Was he really close enough to see anything? If he was so sure he saw Milam at the well, why didn't he recognize anyone in the truck when it passed just a few yards away? More precisely, why didn't he recognize anyone except a boy he had never seen before, Emmett Till? And of course Reed never looked inside the barn itself, never *saw* anyone whipping anyone.[13]

Kellum raised serious questions about the young man's credibility and about the accuracy of his testimony, but in the end the attorney never entirely dispelled the terrifying picture Reed painted:

Kellum: But you didn't see anybody in the barn at all, did you?
Reed: No, Sir.
Kellum: And you don't know whether that was somebody hammering there, trying to fix a wagon or a car, or something like that, do you?
Reed: It was somebody whipping somebody.[14]

In his redirect examination, Smith undid a little of the damage. No, Reed could not estimate abstract measurements of feet or yards, but Smith got him to show how far he was from J. W. Milam that morning. From the witness stand Reed pointed to the scene just outside the window. Yes, Reed said, Milam was about that far away. About fifty, sixty, maybe seventy yards, Smith asked? I just really wouldn't know, Reed replied. But Smith had made his point; Reed was close enough to Milam to see him clearly that Sunday morning. And another authenticating detail: Did you see Milam come to the well before or after you first heard the hollering? After I heard it, Reed replied. Beating a boy was thirsty work.[15]

Willie Reed was excused from the witness stand, and Breland rose and asked for the jury to retire so he could make a new motion. When they were out of the room, he moved that the court dismiss Reed's testimony on grounds that the prosecution failed to prove its connection to Emmett Till or to the body in the river. Overruled. At the very least, he then argued, the jury must disregard Reed's testimony with respect to Roy Bryant, "because Roy Bryant has not been identified in any way or in any respect as being any person present on the occasion testified on by this witness." Smith countered that Milam and Bryant could have opted for separate trials any time before the jury was empaneled; they failed to do so, and testimony like Reed's, aimed at one defendant but also implicating the other, was admissible against them both. Judge Swango agreed with the prosecution and dismissed Breland's motion.[16]

Spoken through fear, Reed's timid and halting sentences were all the more powerful. John Herbers reported for the AP that when Reed identified Milam, "a murmur of excitement swept through the crowded second-story courtroom." Clark Porteous wrote, "Defense Counsel put Willie thru a stern cross-examination, but could not shake his testimony. The most they could do was mix him up on his estimate of distances." James Featherston of the *Jackson Daily News* concluded that Willie Reed, "electrified the court."[17]

Milam and Bryant barely reacted to Reed's testimony, but it must have given their lawyers pause, especially if it emboldened other new witnesses to come forward. The day after Willie Reed took the stand, the *New York Post* noted how frightened he appeared, almost whispering his answers. Yet, like Mose Wright, when the time came he "arose and pointed his finger at J. W. Milam." The defense proved that Willie Reed could barely count and that he did not know the difference between forty feet and four hundred yards, "but he clung to his story and he was as close to a solid witness as the state could get." Mississippi would likely fail to punish the brothers, the *Post* concluded, but not due to any lack of courage from Willie Reed.[18]

Judge Swango recessed his court for lunch at 11:45 a.m.

When everyone returned, the prosecution finished its case by calling two more witnesses. Add Reed, Willie's grandfather, testified that he saw Leslie Milam and a pickup truck near the shed as described by his grandson. However, he could give no further details. Then the Reeds' neighbor, Amandy Bradley, took the stand and confirmed in broad outline much of Willie Reed's story. When Reed told Bradley what he had seen, she looked out her window toward Leslie Milam's place where she saw four white men. She noted that one of them, tall and baldheaded, went to the well for a drink of water, but all of them were too far away to identify for sure. Mostly "they was just coming in and out from around the barn there, just going back and forth there in and out around the barn." Finally they backed a truck up to the barn, and a while later, drove away, four men in front, the back of the truck covered with a tarp.[19]

And with that, the prosecution rested. Once again, Breland rose and requested that the jury be sent away. This time, after they left the room, he asked that the court direct the jury to return a verdict of not guilty. In other words, he wanted a dismissal not just of particular testimony but of the whole case, because, he said, the evidence was totally insufficient for a conviction. One more time, Judge Swango denied the request, stating that the evidence produced by the state raised issues that the jury itself, not the bench, must decide.[20]

In fact, the evidence was strong but far from airtight. The jury saw Mose Wright point to the accused and declare that Roy Bryant and J. W. Milam came in the night and kidnapped his grandnephew, Emmett Till. On top of eyewitness testimony to kidnapping, the accused admitted the crime to Leflore County sheriffs. Yet another eyewitness swore that four hours later he saw J. W. Milam, a pistol at his belt, in the presence of Till, and that he heard the sounds of a beating coming from a barn where Milam and several others had taken Till. Three days after that, a naked body, to all appearances shot and badly beaten, floated up in the Tallahatchie River, a heavy gin fan tied with barbed wire around its neck. The corpse was first reported as black, it wore a ring belonging to Emmett Till, and Mose Wright identified it as his nephew. And Emmett Till's own mother affirmed on the witness stand that the body was her missing son, "beyond a shadow of a doubt." The case was heavily circumstantial, but juries convicted defendants in the past with far less evidence.

The court took a brief recess, and at 2:30 p.m., the defense attorneys began to call their witnesses.

CHAPTER EIGHTEEN

CAROLYN BRYANT

THE CASE PRESENTED by the defense was really quite streamlined, just four substantial witnesses examined for a total of two and a half hours on Thursday afternoon, then another hour on Friday morning for a few citizens to attest to Milam and Bryant's good reputations in their communities. But even before defense attorneys began calling witnesses, their two-pronged strategy was clear. First, convince the jury that the body in the river was not—or might not be—Emmett Till. There was no need for subtlety here, so the five defense lawyers pounded away at it.

The second strategy had to be handled more delicately, especially since the jury was not the only audience for the trial, and every word uttered in the Sumner courthouse might be reported nationally, even internationally. The key here was to undermine the state's emotional advantage: a dead child, a grieving mother, two heartless thugs, racial bullying. Prosecutors implicitly and explicitly argued that Emmett Till was an innocent, goofy kid who did not understand Mississippi's racial codes, and was tortured and murdered by a couple of unfeeling brutes.

The defense chose to depict just the opposite: Till was the living embodiment of the white South's worst fear—a big, out-of-control, sexually rapacious black buck, a product of Chicago's "black belt," where African American appetites went unchained. These two defense strategies were mutually contradictory: Emmett Till was not dead, but he had it coming anyway. No matter. The defense's case hinged not on its internal logic but on piquing racial fears already rubbed raw in the summer of 1955, then denying the presence of racism.

Breland, Whitten, and the others did not have to spell it out. The trial took place a little more than a year after *Brown v. Board of Education*. Then just months before Emmett Till traveled to Mississippi came *"Brown 2,"* the implementation plan. In fact, *Brown 2* was very vague as to how and when schools must integrate. "With all deliberate speed," the Supreme Court had said, which turned out to mean more deliberation than speed. But in the summer following *Brown 2*, much of the white South reacted as if a federal invasion were imminent. If nothing intervened, many white southerners feared, blacks like Till—teenaged, man-sized, filled with primal lust—would soon be going to school with their daughters.[1]

Few said that in so many words, but the defense attorneys designed their line of questioning to stoke such fears. They coaxed the jury to put Emmett Till in a familiar cultural category—the brutal black rapist. Yet Milam and Bryant's attorneys knew that not everyone who picked up a newspaper in New York or Omaha or even Greenwood believed such nonsense. And even confirmed bigots in Mississippi in 1955 knew that it was not always appropriate to flaunt one's racism. Defense counsel could only go so far painting Till as a black monster; some code words were necessary, even in the Mississippi Delta. Their best hope in pursuing this half of their strategy was Carolyn Bryant—that is, if the judge allowed the jurors to hear her testimony.[2]

Carolyn Bryant—Mrs. Roy Bryant, as she referred to herself when asked to state her name—was a magnet for newsmen's eyes: "A trim little brunette," one reporter wrote; "black-haired, brown-eyed, shapely and slender," said another; "she took the stand in midafternoon, look-ing lovely in a high-necked black dress topped by a white collar," de-clared a third. Sex was in the air. Yet in court, Mrs. Bryant's demeanor was anything but glamorous. "Prim and demure" was how one writer described her, "she averted her gaze to the floor with delicate hands clasped in her lap." Bryant spoke in a soft, reluctant voice. Her quiet words were her first in public since the episode began, and she had the whole courtroom's rapt attention. As one observer wrote, "Spectators shifted to the front of their chairs as she told her story," which all began when someone she'd never seen before came in to buy some bubble gum.[3]

Attorney Carlton opened by asking her about her stature—five feet, two inches tall, one hundred and three pounds. He asked about her chil-dren, their names and ages, Thomas and Roy Junior, two and three years old. She filled in how she and her husband were married in April 1951, when she was seventeen and Roy was twenty-one. He was in the army back then and served for three years, from June 1950 through June 1953. In little more than a dozen brief questions and answers, Carlton got his witness to sketch out the Bryant's wholesome family life: handsome couple, healthy children, patriotic service.[4]

"Now Mrs. Bryant," Carlton asked, "I direct your attention to Wednesday night, on the 24th day of August, on that evening, who was in the store with you?" Knowing this was coming, prosecutor Smith jumped to his feet and objected to the defense bringing up anything that happened so many days before Milam and Bryant kidnapped Emmett Till. Breland just as quickly shot back that the defense would show how the two events were connected. Before it went any further, Judge Swango asked the jurors to retire to the jury room.[5]

The lawyers argued it out for several minutes. The prosecution, Carlton insisted, first brought up the incident at Bryant's Grocery Store when their own witness, Mose Wright, quoted J. W. Milam's phrase, "the boy that did the talking down at Money." In so doing, the prosecution introduced the subject of Wednesday night's events and opened a door for the defense, or as Carlton put it:

> The State having introduced that testimony has raised inferences which the defendants believe they are entitled to explain and to show what happened.
>
> And the State having opened the inquiry as to the occurences on that occasion has given the defendants the right to explain those occurences.
>
> And further, the defendants believe that these occurences are part of what the state alleges is one entire transaction, the beginning and inception of the incident. And as such, the occurances[sic] there on that occasion are a part of the res gestae of the case. And as such the defendants should be permitted to offer testimony in that particular.

In other words, all of the events from Wednesday night at Bryant's store through the beginning of the next week when Bryant and Milam were arrested, were part of the full sequence of the case, the res gestae, the legal term for the whole of the alleged crime from beginning to end. The prosecution admitted as much when their own witness, Mose Wright, mentioned "the talking down at Money."[6]

Smith responded that the prosecution had confined itself entirely to events that transpired from Sunday morning at 2:00 a.m. forward, and that in no meaningful way had they invoked events at Bryant's Grocery

Store days earlier. Until now, Carolyn Bryant's name had not even come up in the trial. Smith went further: "The Supreme Court of Mississippi has many times held that former difficulties where not a part of the res gestae cannot be brought in as evidence." In other words, animosities between parties followed by violence were not to be considered in a court case. Smith added that even if the concept of res gestae might on occasion apply to events that took place days before a felony, this had no bearing on the Till case because nothing that happened in Money, Mississippi, on Wednesday night was a justification for murder. Those events, Smith concluded, were "wholly incompetent and irrelevant in this case."[7]

Breland disagreed with Smith's first point about Supreme Court rulings, arguing that incidents could be separated by days or even weeks, so long as they were connected. He declared that if an act or event, "forms a background for a later happening, then that can be considered as part of an entire transaction."[8]

Judge Swango was skeptical. Yes, the Mississippi Supreme Court allowed evidence to be introduced as part of the res gestae in cases where there had been an altercation or incident between parties when the deceased had been the aggressor. "Then such evidence would be admissible," he ruled, "but without such a showing, it would not be admissible." In other words, the defendants' attorneys were not suggesting that Till was a threat or that Milam and Bryant acted in self-defense.[9]

Or were they? Attorney John Whitten now rose to speak. He repeated his colleague Sidney Carlton's point that the state's own witness, Mose Wright, had raised the issue of the encounter in Bryant's store by quoting Milam's phrase about "the boy that did the talking down at Money." But more, far more, Whitten said, "the State, by its own witness, has raised in the minds of this jury some question as to whether what happened down there at the store in Money was just mere talk."[10]

A door had just swung open: Emmett Till, a black man, two inches taller and fifty pounds heavier than Carolyn Bryant, posed an imminent physical threat. It was the white male code of honor, men defending their homes and families. And more particularly in the context of Jim Crow Mississippi, white men defending their women against black men.

What happened Wednesday night must be admissible because the accused, in Whitten's words, "have the same right to protect their families as they do themselves." What Emmett Till said, did, and intended in Bryant's Grocery Store was more than rude or distasteful or insulting: it was a sexual assault. Bryant and Milam defended hearth and home. Their attorneys had suggested this line of defense to reporters a week before the trial, and they deployed it now in court.[11]

Judge Swango agreed that res gestae might encompass not just minutes or hours but days, and he also agreed that the concept could include situations where citizens came to their family's defense. And he agreed that, "any accused in any criminal case can bring out anything relating to a continuation of any part of an alleged crime." But he disagreed that the principle applied here. Till, when he was kidnapped in the early hours of Sunday morning, was no threat to Carolyn Bryant nor to her family; there was no credible evidence that he was an aggressor, that he committed some overt act against the defendants. Judge Swango therefore ruled that the jury would not be allowed to hear Carolyn Bryant's testimony.[12]

Breland asked that Mrs. Bryant be examined anyway, without the jury present. It was critical to create a record if the defense attorneys ended up appealing the case. Besides, though the jury would be sequestered after today's testimony ended, seasoned attorneys like Breland understood that news reports and rumors had a way of leaking past the bailiffs to the jurors. Swango then agreed to let Mrs. Bryant testify, and Sidney Carlton resumed his questions before an empty jury box. Once again everyone in the courtroom shifted to the fronts of their seats to better hear her quavering voice.[13]

Carlton asked Carolyn Bryant if she was alone in her store on Wednesday night? Yes, though her sister-in-law, Juanita Milam, along with her two children, were visiting in the living quarters behind the shop. Carlton asked Mrs. Bryant to describe what happened after dark, at about eight o'clock that night. "This nigger man came in the store and he stopped there at the candy case." She told how sweets were displayed along the sidewall and how she came out from behind the counter in back to wait on him.

Carlton: And what transpired at the candy counter?
Bryant: I asked him what he wanted.
Carlton: And did he tell you?
Bryant: Yes....
Carlton: And did you then get the merchandise for him?
Bryant: Yes. I got it and put it on top of the candy case.
Carlton: And what did you do then?
Bryant: I held out my hand for his money....
Carlton: And did he give you the money?
Bryant: No.
Carlton: What did he do?
Bryant: He caught my hand.
Carlton: Will you show the court just how he grasped your hand?

Bryant demonstrated, seizing one hand in the other.

Carlton: And was that a strong grip or a light grip that he had when he held your hand?
Bryant: A strong grip.
Carlton: And will you show the court what you did? How did you get loose?
Bryant: Well, I just jerked it loose, like this [demonstrating]....
Carlton: And just what did he say when he grabbed your hand?
Bryant: He said, "How about a date, baby?"

Horrified, Bryant raced toward the back counter of the store, but the assailant caught her at the cash register.

Carlton: You say he caught you?
Bryant: Yes.
Carlton: How did he catch you?
Bryant: Well, he put his left hand on my waist, and he put his other hand over the other side...
Carlton: Now Mrs. Bryant, will you stand up and put my hands just where he grasped you? Will you show the court and jury?
Bryant: It was like this [demonstrating by putting Mr. Carlton's hands on her body].
Carlton: He grabbed you like that, did he?
Bryant: Yes.
Carlton: In other words, with his left arm around your back?
Bryant: Yes.
Carlton: And his left hand on your left hip.
Bryant: Yes.
Carlton: And he had his right hand on your right hip?
Bryant: Yes.
Carlton: Did he say anything to you then at the time he grabbed you there by the cash register?
Bryant: Yes.
Carlton: What did he say?
Bryant: He said "What's the matter, baby? Can't you take it?"
Carlton: He said, "What's the matter, baby? Can't you take it?"
Bryant: Yes.
Carlton: Did you then try to free yourself?
Bryant: Yes.
Carlton: Was it difficult? Did you succeed in freeing yourself?
Bryant: Yes.

Carlton: Did he say anything further to you at that time?
Bryant: Yes.
Carlton: What did he say?
Bryant: He said, "You needn't be afraid of me."

Carlton then asked his witness if the man who made this assault said anything else, uttered any words, made any suggestions? Yes, he uttered a word that Carolyn Bryant would never use.

Carlton: Can you tell the Court just what that word begins with, what letter it begins with?
Bryant: [The witness did not answer verbally but shook her head negatively.]
Carlton: In other words, it was an unprintable word?
Bryant: Yes.

The *New Orleans Times-Picayune* reported the sentence and the unprintable word as, "'I've [...] white women before.'"[14]

So in just a few moments of testimony, Carolyn Bryant described how her unnamed assailant with a "Northern brogue"—a "nigger man" whom she'd never seen before—propositioned her, grabbed her, pursued her, taunted her, grabbed her again, told her not to be afraid, and said he'd had white women before. How did she ever escape? "This other nigger came in the store and got him by the arm," she told the court.

Carlton: And what happened then?
Bryant: And then he told him to come on and let's go.
Carlton: Did he leave the store willingly or unwillingly?
Bryant: Unwillingly.
Carlton: How did the other negro get out of the store then? How did they leave?
Bryant: He had him by the arm and led him out.
Carlton: Were there any white men in the store at the time this occurred?
Bryant: No.
Carlton: Were there any other negro men in the store at the time?
Bryant: No.
Carlton: Were there any other persons outside the store?
Bryant: Yes.
Carlton: Were they white men or colored men?
Bryant: Colored.

Carlton: Were there a number of them out there? How many of them were out there?

Bryant: Oh, about eight or nine.[15]

Surrounded by black men, the only thing that saved Carolyn Bryant was someone dragging her assailant away. (She failed to mention that her rescuer was Simeon Wright, Emmett's smaller, twelve-year-old cousin.) After they left the store, Bryant called to her sister-in-law, Juanita Milam, to come watch her. With that, she ran out the door to Mrs. Milam's car to fetch a pistol from under the driver's seat. As she did so, she saw the person who had grabbed her standing by one of the pillars on the front porch.

Carlton: Did he say or do anything at that time?

Bryant: He whistled and then came out in the road.

Carlton: Can you give a sound something like the whistle that he made there? Was it something like this? [Mr. Carlton demonstrated by giving two low whistles.]

Bryant: Yes.

Carlton: When you got your pistol, Mrs. Bryant, where was this boy then? Or should I say where was this man?

Bryant: When I turned around, he was getting in a car down the road.

Carlton: Have you ever seen that man before?

Bryant: No.

Carlton: Have you ever seen him since?

Bryant: No.[16]

Carlton's final questions highlighted how terrifying the situation was for Carolyn Bryant, how her assailant was so much taller, heavier, a black stranger. It was difficult enough running a small general store with a mostly black clientele and her husband away at the Gulf Coast hauling shrimp, the time and date of his return uncertain. "Did you have any white men anywhere around to protect you," Carlton asked? No, she answered, just her sister-in-law and her little nephews, "so that I wouldn't be alone." Asked her overall feelings about that night, Carolyn Bryant replied, "I was just scared to death."[17]

It was powerful stuff, and Carlton asked Judge Swango once more to let Mrs. Bryant repeat it for the jury, since after all, it was the prosecution, not the defense, that first brought up what had happened in Money. Her testimony, Carlton said, was essential "to remove from the minds of the jury the impression that nothing but talk had occurred there."[18]

Judge Swango answered quietly that the court had already ruled, and that Carolyn Bryant's testimony was not admissible.[19]

"We have no further questions, Your Honor," Carlton said when the jury returned to the courtroom. "No questions," Gerald Chatham responded. Carolyn Bryant stepped down from the witness stand. It was a miraculous act, this transformation of a fourteen-year-old boy who walked into Bryant's Grocery Store looking for bubble gum, into the black predator of fevered Mississippi imagination.[20]

CHAPTER NINETEEN

SHERIFF CLARENCE STRIDER

EVEN THOUGH THE JURY never actually heard Carolyn Bryant, her mere presence in the courtroom was a reminder of what was at stake. For one week in September 1955, Sumner, Mississippi, was ground zero in the violent fusion of race and sex.

After Bryant finished, the defense called her sister-in-law, Juanita Milam. Mrs. Milam's testimony was a brief confirmation of her husband's good character, how he and she had been married for six years, how they now raised two young sons, how he served his country honorably in World War II. Juanita's few minutes on the stand indicated that defense counsel had no intention of letting J. W. or Roy testify; there was nothing to be gained.[1]

Next, the defense called Clarence Strider, the Tallahatchie County Sheriff. The day after the body rose on the river, on September 1, Strider signed a death certificate for Emmett Till, describing him as a fourteen-year-old Negro male from Chicago. It labeled Till's death a homicide and attributed his injuries to "Gun Shot or Ax."[2]

But a few days later, Strider no longer was sure about any of this. By September 6, as Till's family buried their child and the grand jury indicted Milam and Bryant, the sheriff told reporters that the body was too decomposed to be identified, and certainly too far gone to have been in the water for only three days. More, Strider said he could not tell if the corpse was black or white. Tallahatchie County's chief law enforcement officer, the man charged with bringing criminals to justice, gave no assistance to the prosecution. Quite the contrary, in his brief testimony, he became the defendants' most important witness.[3]

Defense Attorney Whitten examined Sheriff Strider:

Whitten: Now tell the jury about the appearance and condition of that body as you saw it that morning.

Strider: Well, it was in mighty bad shape.

Chatham: We object to that, Your Honor.

Swango: Just state the physical facts, not your own conclusions.

Strider: Well, the skin had slipped.... I would say it had slipped on the entire body. The fingernails were gone from the left hand. A ring on the right hand was holding the skin that held the fingernails on that hand. And the entire body, the skin was slipping or it had completely gone off it.

Whitten: What was the condition of the head? What did you observe there?

Strider: There was a small hole about one inch above the right ear. There was two...well, maybe two or three gashes on the head...

Whitten: This hole you speak of that was over the right ear, did you determine whether it penetrated the skull?

Strider: I cut a stick about the size of a pencil and tried to find if it penetrated through the skull or not, and I was unable to find if it penetrated through the skull....

Whitten: Did you observe the tongue?

Strider: The tongue was extending, I would say, about two and a half or three inches. And the left eyeball was almost out, enough to almost fall out. And the right one was out, I would say, about three quarters of an inch.

Whitten: Was there any odor about the body that indicated it was decomposed or that decomposition had set in?

Strider: It was so bad that we couldn't examine the body until the undertaker got there, and then he opened a deodorant bomb. And even then we couldn't get too close, and he had to use a quart of some kind of liquid. I didn't ask him just what it was.[4]

With the water surface temperature around seventy degrees, and much colder at depths of twenty or thirty feet, Strider estimated that whoever's corpse they found must have been in the Tallahatchie River much longer than three days. How long? Whitten asked.

Strider: I would say at least ten days.

Whitten: Referring back to the condition of that particular body there, could you tell whether it was a white person or a colored person?

Strider: The only way you could tell it was a colored person—and I wouldn't swear to it then—was just his hair. And I have seen white people that have kinky hair. And the hair had slipped in some places on the head there, but some of it was there, and what I saw, it showed it to be sort of kinky, or that of a negro.

Whitten: Was that body recognizable to be that of any particular person?

Strider: Well, if one of my own boys had been missing, I couldn't really say if it was my own son or not, or anybody else's I couldn't tell that. All I could tell, it was a human being.

Whitten: Your witness.[5]

The prosecution had a formidable task in shaking the jury's faith in the sheriff. He was an imposing figure in Tallahatchie County, a man of wealth and political power. His word about the body in the river certainly had more credibility than a black undertaker, or an old sharecropper, or a grieving black mother from Chicago. Prosecutor Smith went to work, beginning with the police photograph of Till's body taken a few hours after it was pulled from the river. Strider agreed it was the very corpse he saw on Wednesday morning, August 31.

Smith: I will ask you if that photograph shows that the skin or flesh is sluffed [*sic*] off at any place?

Strider: Well, you can't tell in several places. You see, the darkness of this picture shows that the entire skin on the body had slipped. This was made hours later, and it had begun to turn dark. . . . At the time it was brought out of the water, he was just as white as I am except for a few places around that was just a little darker than other places. And except for that, he was just as white as I am.

So the skin only turned dark because it had dried out in the hours after it was taken from the river? Smith refused to accept this notion, and he pounded away until Strider grudgingly acknowledged that the photo indeed represented what everyone saw on the riverbank, a dark-skinned corpse.[6]

Next, Smith asked if the sheriff signed a death certificate for Emmett Till? Yes, Sir, Strider replied, I signed it. But then Strider denied ever intending to certify that the body taken from the river was that of the missing boy. "I said it was a dead body. I had never seen Emmett Till before, and I couldn't swear it was Emmett Till because I didn't know Emmett Till or what he looked like."[7]

Uncomfortable, Strider began to ad lib. He denied that Mose Wright definitively identified Till by the riverside. Asked if the body in the boat was Wright's nephew, the sheriff quoted Mose as saying, "I believe it is, but I couldn't say it is for sure." Strider said he then asked the old man if he recognized the ring on Till's finger, and Wright replied he didn't know, he'd have to check with his sons. The sheriff elaborated:

> And then I said to him, "Do you mean to tell me, Mose, that he has been staying there at your home for a week with this ring on his finger, and eating there at the same table with you, and you don't even know this ring, or that you didn't notice he had a ring on his finger?" And then he said, "No, Sir. I did not know about that ring. But my boys would know whether he was wearing that ring or not." That is what he said to me.

Attorney Smith was having none of it. He asked Strider point-blank, "[D]o you know whether that death certificate had the name of Emmett Till on it or not?" "No, I don't," the sheriff lied.[8]

What about injuries to the body? Strider testified that he saw no wounds except those to the head. The back had a reddish cast, but he could not tell if it was bruised, and he added, "there wasn't no broken places in the skin or anything like that... and his body wasn't bursted anywhere other than about his head." Then Strider repeated his doubts about the wound above the right ear being a bullet hole. Finally, Smith asked a question Strider anticipated, about a well-known principle of forensic science.

Smith: Mr. Strider, from your qualified experience in handling dead bodies brought out of the river, you know as a matter of fact, do you not, that a body that is wounded and beaten up and injured will decompose much quicker than a body that has not been. Isn't that true?

Strider: I would think so, yes, Sir.

Smith: And you also know that conditions will vary in different bodies which will cause one body to decompose much quicker than another?

Strider: Well, I wouldn't say too much about that. But I have taken bodies out of the river that were in there much longer than this.

Smith: But circumstances can make a difference, and circumstances can vary as far as a body is concerned, which might cause a body to decompose quicker or faster than another body?

Strider: Well, I thought it depended on temperature.[9]

This was the sheriff's mode: concede a bit, deny a lot, and above all muddy the waters. Smith's cross-examination made Strider appear more than a little bumbling, but actually he carried the day. From his position of authority, he legitimated skepticism. Strider's testimony enabled anyone so disposed to believe there was uncertainty about whose body bobbed up in the river with a necklace of barbed wire and a gin fan pendant.[10]

Smith made one more try to crack Strider's story. If the body in the river was not Emmett Till, Smith asked, then who was it? Someone died violently and ended up in the Tallahatchie River. Was it not the sheriff's job to solve such crimes?

Smith: Sheriff, have you made any investigation to find out who that body was? Who that person was?

Strider: Yes, Sir, I sure have.

Smith: And are you continuing your investigation?

Strider: Yes, Sir....

Smith: What efforts have you been making to find out whose body that was?

Strider: Well, I have had several reports about a negro who disappeared over there at Lambert. And I went out there and investigated that and one man would tell you that he saw him, or that he said somebody told him they saw him, and then someone else would tell me that someone else had told them something about it. And it would just carry you right around to where you started from.

It was a classic southern story, handed down by both blacks and whites since slavery times, and all the more believable because of its venerability. For whites, African Americans were chronically evasive and unreliable, especially when questioned by the authorities. For blacks, officers of the law were not to be trusted, so they gave them the runaround. Everyone knew the drill, especially Sheriff Strider:

Smith: But you got no information whatsoever to indicate whose body that was? You have not gotten any information about that as yet?

Strider: No, I have not.

Smith: That is all.[11]

CHAPTER TWENTY

DOCTOR L. B. OTKEN AND UNDERTAKER H. D. MALONE

THE DEFENSE ATTORNEYS HAD chipped away at the prosecution's case—darkness in Mose Wright's home making positive identification of Milam and Bryant dubious, underhanded practices by Sheriffs Smith and Cothran to extract kidnapping confessions, ulterior motives of Mamie Till Bradley, Willie Reed's ignorance, the assault of the "nigger man" against Carolyn Bryant. Those moments highlighted key emotional undercurrents in the case: the audacity of African Americans testifying against whites, the hubris of northerners—especially black ones—telling southerners how to run their affairs, the growing danger to The Southern Way of Life, the fear of federal power crushing "states' rights."

Such emotional issues influenced what jurors might decide, and it was Clarence Strider who offered them the excuse, the rationale, the indispensable fig leaf to cover their prejudices. The defense team's strongest legal move was convincing the jury that the body in the river might—*might*— not be Emmett Till's. It helped if the jurors believed that Mose Wright saw what he wanted to see, that Mamie Till Bradley was an opportunist, that Willie Reed was not too bright, that Carolyn Bryant looked scared to death. But the strongest legal defense was engendering doubt that the Tallahatchie corpse was Till's. So now the defense attorneys called to the witness stand a medical doctor, followed by the embalmer in Tutwiler who handled the body. Their job was simple; reinforce Sheriff Strider's story.

Back on Wednesday, August 31, after the undertaker Chester Miller packed up the corpse from the Tallahatchie River and hauled it back to the Century Funeral Home in Greenwood, the Leflore County Sheriff's office contacted Dr. L. B. Otken and asked him to examine it. Otken, a graduate of the University of Texas, was not a medical examiner or coroner. He had practiced general medicine in Greenwood, Mississippi, for almost forty years, and in that time he had seen hundreds of dead bodies.[1]

Otken told the court that he did not write a pathologist's report or handle the body in any way; he simply viewed it. Breland asked the doctor to describe it for the jury.

Otken: This body was badly swollen, badly bloated. . . . I would estimate that this body would have weighed two hundred and seventy-five pounds. It was that badly bloated. . . . The skin and the flesh was beginning to slip on it. The head was badly mutilated. The right eye was protruding. And the tongue was protruding from the mouth.

Breland: And what about the odor of the body.

Otken: Terrific.

Breland: What was the state of putrefaction of that body at that time?

Otken: Well, I would say it was in an advanced state of decomposition—or putrefaction if you wish to call it that.

Breland: Doctor, I want to ask this question, from the condition that you saw that body in, in your opinion, could anybody have identified any particular person as being that body . . . ?

Otken: I don't think you could. I don't think you could have identified that body.

Breland: Now suppose if the man had been another person's brother, could he have identified it, in your opinion?

Otken: I doubt it.

Breland: Or if it had been a person's son, could a mother have identified that body, in your opinion?

Otken: I doubt it.

Breland: Doctor, from your experience and study and your familiarity with the medical authorities, what, in your opinion, had been the length of time that the body had been dead . . . ?

Otken: I would say eight to ten days. . . .

Breland: Is that the minimum or the maximum?

Otken: That would have been a minimum.

Breland: And what would have been the probable maximum number of days?

Otken: Say two weeks.
Breland: Take the witness.[2]

On cross-examination, Robert Smith asked if Otken could tell if the body was black or white? Otken would not say for sure. Smith asked for details about wounds. Otken repeated that he merely viewed the body, never laid a hand on it, but that he observed a hole above the right ear and a triangular shaped gash on the forehead with some of the bone gone and the flap of skin pulled upward. On the left side behind the ear the head was "badly crushed in as if by some blunt object." There was also a mark that went entirely around the neck. Smith asked if the head wounds might have caused this person's death? "I would say so," Otken replied.[3]

To counter that last point about head wounds, Breland asked on redirect if Otken could tell whether those injuries were made before or after the victim died? "I couldn't," Otken replied. Breland had no further questions, but Smith did.

Smith: Doctor, is it true or not that a person who is fat and heavy and has a good deal of weight, fat weight, is it true that such a body will decompose faster than a body that is more slender and muscular?
Otken: That's right.
Smith: And that would affect the rate of decomposition?
Otken: That is right....
Smith: And doctor, is it not also true that a body that has been badly beaten or injured will decompose faster than one that has not been?
Otken: That is right.
Smith: That is all.

To which the defense countered:

Breland: Doctor, observing that body as you saw it, and with the wounds you saw on it, would that change your opinion as to the length of time that the body had been dead, as you saw it?
Otken: No.[4]

It was late afternoon and the court had gone without a break through the defense case. Except for testimony as to the good character of the defendants, Breland and his team were down to their last substantial witness, so Judge Swango let the proceedings continue. To strengthen the case that the corpse in the river was not Emmett Till, the defense called H. D. Malone, the man who had embalmed the body in Tutwiler before sending it on to Chicago. Breland established Malone's bona fides for the jury—licensed in Mississippi and Tennessee, a 1952 graduate of a respected mortuary school, experience handling hundreds of bodies. The attorney asked if Mr. Malone embalmed the body brought from the Miller Funeral Home in Greenwood to the Nelson Funeral Home, the Negro mortuary in Tutwiler, on August 31. "Yes, sir."[5]

Breland: State to the court and to the jury what the condition of that body was. Just give its general description, and then if there is any scientific or medical description, will you please explain such terms to the jury in layman's language.

Malone: The body was bloated and swollen so bad it was beyond any possible recognition, I think.... It was so bloated that the features were not recognizable. There was a prevalent skin slip all over the body.

Breland: Will you explain that to the jury?

Malone: Well, anywhere you touched it, the skin rolled up and slipped off. It just turned loose.

Breland: Go ahead.

Malone: And the entire skin on his left hand was off.... And the hair came out easy. There were multiple lacerations about the head. The left eye was hanging from its socket. And the entire body was a bluish-green discoloration.

Breland: And what did that indicate to you?

Malone: That indicated to me that the body had been dead possibly ten days or longer.

Breland: Do you mean possibly? Is that what you mean, possibly?

Malone: Possibly; very likely that it had. It is very possible it had.

Breland: And that means that the probability that it had, is that right?

Malone: Yes, Sir.

Breland: And the greatest probability that it had?

Malone: Yes, Sir.

Smith: Your Honor, we object to counsel putting words in the witness's mouth.

The Court: The objection will be sustained. Counsel will please refrain from testifying.[6]

Breland and Malone now took the jury on a journey through the science behind rigor mortis, the color of dead bodies, the initial delay of decomposition caused by lactic acid, the rapid onset of decay as a corpse's chemistry shifted from acidic to alkaline, and finally the buildup of tissue gas as it decomposed. Malone observed that a body in water— say, twenty-five or thirty feet deep, as Breland suggested, weighted down with a gin fan into the cooler depths—broke down more slowly.[7]

Taking account of all this, Breland asked Malone for the shortest length of time he thought the body plucked from the Tallahatchie River had been dead? About ten days. And the longest? Maybe twenty or twenty-five. Breland asked about the casket the body came in, how long was it? Six feet, three inches long.

Breland: How did that body fit in that casket? How completely did it fill the casket end to end?
Malone: It filled it very near full.
Breland: Do you mean from end to end?
Malone: Yes.
Breland: Did you measure the length of the body?
Malone: No, I did not.
Breland: What would be your estimate of the length of that body?
Malone: I would say the body was five feet, ten.
Breland: Five feet, ten inches?
Malone: Yes.[8]

So by Malone's estimate, the corpse was half a foot longer than Emmett Till. And one last thing: Is it possible, Breland asked, for a mortician or plastic surgeon to repair a body in such bad shape, to make it look "more like it's natural self." Yes. And would this be done, Breland continued, more in the cities or the country? Well, Malone acknowledged, more in the cities. Once again, Breland had planted a seed: a skilled mortician, in a big city like Chicago, could make one body look like another. The identity of the corpse in the river grew just a bit more uncertain.[9]

On cross-examination, Smith repeated his questions about fat bodies and abused bodies breaking down more quickly.

Smith: And isn't it also true that a body that is wounded and beaten and so forth, that such a body will decompose faster than one that is not?
Malone: Under normal conditions, yes sir.
Smith: But of course, you have no knowledge of the conditions where this body had been, do you?
Malone: No, Sir.
Smith: And what you are testifying to is what would happen under normal conditions, is it not?

Malone: That's right.

Smith: And isn't it true that if a person is fat, or heavy, and has more fatty tissue than the average person that such a body will decompose at a greater rate than one that is not so fat?

Malone: Yes, sir....

Smith: I think that is all.[10]

At just past five o'clock, Judge Swango recessed the court until Friday morning. Day two had been exhausting, but all that remained now was for the defense to present character witnesses, for the attorneys to make their closing arguments, then for the jury to decide.[11]

CHAPTER TWENTY-ONE

YOUR FOREFATHERS WILL TURN OVER IN THEIR GRAVES

AFTER A WEEK of temperatures well into the nineties, the last day of the trial—the first day of autumn—began with thunderstorms and a heavy downpour at dawn. The rain brought no relief inside the court-room, leaving it just as hot and more humid than ever. The meteorological fireworks outside tapered off just in time for Judge Swango to gavel his court to order at 9:30 a.m.[1]

The defense took an hour to present seven character witnesses for Roy Bryant and J. W. Milam—local farmers, merchants, and tradesmen from around Glendora and Money, all white men, mostly middle-aged. Attorney Kellum questioned them, asking each how long he had known the defendants and if they had good reputations for peace and order in their communities, to which each witness answered yes. The first character witness, Tallahatchie County Supervisor Lee Russell Allison, swore to Milam's solid standing. But under cross-examination, Gerald Chatham asked if Milam supported Allison's most recent bid for reelection?

Allison: I believe he did. Most of them did.

Chatham: And any way that you could repay that favor, you would be glad to do it, and that is what you are doing now, is that right?

Allison: I don't know about repaying any favor.

Chatham: But that would be the natural thing to do, isn't that right?

Allison: Well, if I could return a favor, I would.

Then Chatham challenged Milam's reputation for peace and order, asking Allison, "I want you to tell the jury if it is not an actual fact that he was convicted...or he was arrested and pleaded guilty to a charge..."; Breland cut in, "We object to that, Your Honor." Judge Swango sustained the objection.[2]

On it went, witnesses affirming that Milam and Bryant were good men, Chatham asking hard questions. He had the following exchange with Harold Terry, a farmer who knew Roy Bryant for the two years while the latter lived in Money:

Chatham: Do you do business with Mr. Bryant?

Terry: No, Sir, I do not.

Chatham: Do you know what his general reputation was for peace or
          violence before he came to Money?

Terry: I didn't know him before he came to Money....

Chatham: Now you stated that his general reputation in the community for
          peace and violence was good. I want to ask you how many people
          you heard discuss Mr. Bryant's reputation during the past two
          years?

Terry: I haven't heard Mr. Bryant discussed.

Chatham: Then you haven't heard his reputation discussed?

Terry: No, Sir.

Chatham: Well, then, how do you know what his general reputation is?

Breland objected, adding, "that is the best reputation a man can have, when nobody says nothing about him." Judge Swango said, "overruled." The district attorney continued:

Chatham: Who asked you to come here to testify today?

Terry: I volunteered to come up here.

Chatham: And you are in sympathy with Mr. Bryant, is that right, or is that
          wrong?

Terry: [The witness did not answer the question.]

Chatham: Why do you hesitate to answer, Mr. Terry?

Terry: [The witness did not answer the question.]

Chatham: You can stand aside.

After an hour of this, both prosecution and defense rested.[3]

Neither side had called the accused to testify, each fearing that there would be much more to lose than gain. Now Breland rose to request again that the court exclude all the evidence presented on behalf of the state and direct the jury to return a verdict of not guilty. One final time, Judge Swango said no.[4]

After a brief recess came the summing up.

Each side was allotted an hour and ten minutes. Both took their full time, with a break for lunch. No transcript survives, so the attorneys' arguments can be reconstructed only from newspaper accounts. The prosecution began, then it was the defense attorneys' turn, and after lunch each side gave their final words.[5]

Gerald Chatham spoke for almost fifty minutes. The trial had taken its toll, and he looked like a man who needed to step down from his job, which he would do in a few months. He died before a year had passed. But when Chatham rose on this late morning in Sumner, Mississippi, he was on fire. His style was dramatic, his voice deep and booming, audible outside on the courthouse square. Sweating freely though he'd shed his coat, he pounded the table, pointed at the defendants, and waved his arms. Journalists expressed admiration for the enthusiasm of his oratory and the quality of his arguments.[6]

At times, he spoke in the style of a Baptist preacher, giving a churchly feeling to the courtroom. The jurors listened with rapt attention, "unblinking attention," one newsman called it. Chatham brought tears to spectators' eyes, black and white, another wrote. One juror let the cigar in his mouth go dead, another stopped puffing and put away his pipe. Roy Bryant listened, his arm lightly around Carolyn's shoulder; J. W. Milam focused on the newspaper in his lap.

This was not just a random murder, Chatham began. The killing was planned from the start: "The first words that entered this case were literally dripping with the blood of Emmett Till." Those words were J. W. Milam's after he and Roy Bryant forced their way into Mose Wright's home: "I want the boy from Chicago who did the talking at Money." The brothers' intent was there all along, Chatham argued, and that is what made the killing not just cowardly and cold-blooded but premeditated murder in the eyes of the law.

The district attorney called the abduction at gunpoint "a command of summary court-martial with the death penalty," and Till had done nothing to deserve it. This was an important point. The testimony of Smith and Cothran established beyond a doubt that Milam and Bryant abducted Till. The brothers admitted it. Right there, Chatham argued, they assumed culpability in the eyes of the law: "When these two defendants took Emmett Till from the home of Uncle Mose Wright, they were absolutely morally and legally responsible for his protection." They kidnapped him, he turned up dead, the law calls that murder, no further evidence needed.

Chatham tiptoed around Carolyn Bryant's testimony. The story she told was the missing motive for murder, but of course no Mississippi jury would convict two white men under those circumstances. There was no advantage to bringing up Till's alleged violation of the region's sexual code, so the prosecutor merely hinted at it, but all the while taking his stand as a loyal southerner:

> I was born and bred in the South. I'll live and die in the South. The very worst punishment that could have occurred or should have occurred, if they had any idea in their minds this boy did anything, would have been to take a razor strop, turn him over a barrel and give him a little beating.

Yes, Chatham told the jury, I'm a southerner too, I understand the codes, but what Milan and Bryant did was way out of proportion. "I've whipped my boy. You've whipped yours. A man deals with a child accordingly as a child, not as a man to man."

The DA hammered at the facts as presented over the previous two days: Milam and Bryant kidnapped Emmett Till; they admitted it to the county sheriffs; an eyewitness saw Milam with Till hours after he claimed to have released the boy; Till's body was positively identified by his mother and by his uncle; the ring found on the corpse confirmed his identity. The defense says the body was too badly decomposed to be Till's, too badly decomposed to tell if it was black or white. Then why, Chatham asked, did officials without hesitation call a Negro funeral home to come pick it up?

The prosecutor drove his point home: "Everyone who has testified here has stated that this was the body of a colored boy. When the sheriff was first told of the body, his informer said, 'There is a little nigger boy in the river.' Everybody who saw the body said 'a nigger boy is in the river.'" But now Dr. Otken comes and says he could not determine if the corpse was black or white. "I tell you," the prosecutor thundered, "the people of this state are wasting their money sending a man to school and educating him to be a doctor when he is not able to tell a white man from a Negro," and Chatham added, "if he can't tell black from white, I don't want him writing any prescription for me."

Then the district attorney told a story about his son's dog, Shep. The dog had been missing for days when Gerald Chatham Jr. announced that he'd found his pet, took his father by the hand, led him to the ravine behind their barn and pointed to the badly decomposed body of a dog. "That dog's body was rotting and the meat was falling off its bones," Chatham told the jurors, "but my little boy pointed to it and said, 'That's old Shep, Pa. That's old Shep.'"

"My boy didn't need no undertaker or a sheriff to identify his dog," Chatham told the jurors. "And we don't need them here to identify Emmett Till. All we need is someone who loved him and cared for him." Mamie Till Bradley was "God's given witness to identify him."[7]

Chatham ended his closing statement by confronting the issue of southern identity head on. Outsiders were invading the region and trying to dictate how Mississippi ran its affairs, some newspapers claimed; we must acquit Milam and Bryant, this argument went, because the trouble-makers wanted them found guilty.

No, no, no, the prosecutor thundered, this was the road to perdition. Outsiders will only succeed if we betray what we believe in. "I am concerned with what is morally right or wrong," and right and wrong in this case means bringing the murderers to justice, regardless of external pressures. "If your verdict is influenced by anything except the evidence," Chatham told the jurors, "you will endanger every custom and tradition we hold dear." To be true to the South was to do justice, and doing justice meant a guilty verdict for Milam and Bryant. And with that, Gerald Chatham sat down.

Sidney Carlton led off the summation for the defense. Wearing a dark suit despite the heat, Carlton's style was less theatrical than Chatham's, less dramatic. But he addressed the prosecutor directly, turned to Chatham and said, "He's talked generalities because the facts just don't bear out the guilt of these defendants. Where's the motive? Where's the motive?"

Indeed. After weeks of newspaper coverage and rumors, everyone knew about this notorious "wolf whistle" case. Exactly what Emmett Till said or did might be in dispute, but clearly the trial centered on the blood-libel of black male predation against pure white womanhood. Long before Judge Swango empaneled the jury, editors stuffed Mississippi newspapers with stories about the black boy who "talked ugly" to "pretty and petite" Carolyn Bryant. Ubiquitous, too, in the papers was the charge by defense council that Till "assaulted" her.

But when Judge Swango rightly blocked the jury from hearing Carolyn Bryant's testimony, the question "where's the motive?" followed logically. Remove overt discussions of race and sex from the case, and the defendants' motive disappeared. Everyone knew what sent Milam and Bryant out into the night a month earlier without anyone saying a word. Now the defense made Carolyn Bryant's absence before the jury work for them.

"The state," Carlton declared, "did not link up the dead boy with the defendants," and if you believed that Milam and Bryant let Emmett Till go, and disbelieved that Willie Reed saw Till in Milam's truck hours later, and ignored whatever you heard about the events down in Money, and thought maybe the body in the river was a plant by the NAACP, then Carlton's assertion rang true. "Where's the motive?" If anyone bothered to notice, Carolyn Bryant never mentioned Emmett Till by name, calling him simply "this nigger man." And the jury never heard her anyway.

The defense could have it both ways. Till whistled at Carolyn Bryant, spoke terrible things to her, laid hands on her—he was a would-be rapist. But with Carolyn Bryant's testimony kept from the jury, where indeed was Milam and Bryant's motive? Carlton could honestly say to the jury that the only testimony connecting Till to the defendants *before* they allegedly kidnapped him was a vague remark about "the talk down at Money."

The old canard—white male honor avenging interracial sex—disappeared from the courtroom, or more precisely, it was hidden in plain sight, a sleight-of-hand trick, but it worked. The prosecution had every reason not to bring up such a volatile issue, not to remind the jury of Till's alleged transgressions, but the defense turned the absence of a motive against the state. And that absence offered twelve-white-men-and-true another fig leaf.

What about Mose Wright's testimony that Milam and Bryant abducted the boy, Carlton asked? How could Till's uncle tell who the kidnappers were in pitch blackness? How could he be sure one of them carried a pistol? Mose could not even make out what kind of vehicle they were driving. One man was big and bald, Mose said, the other called himself Mr. Bryant. Lots of men were big and bald, and "how many Mr. Bryants are there in the state of Mississippi?"

Besides it made no sense that kidnappers would reveal their real identities: "If any of you had gone to Mose Wright's house with evil intent," Carlton asked the jury, "would you have given your name? No one is that stupid; there's nothing reasonable about the state's theory." And he added, raising his voice, "If that's identification, if that places these men at that scene, then none of us are safe." Nor was it reasonable, as the state contended, that Milam and Bryant abducted Till in Leflore County, carried him west to Sunflower County, then doubled back to dump his body in Tallahatchie County.

But the prosecution argument finally turned on identification of the body. Several witnesses testified that the corpse was too far gone for anyone to identify it, and now J. W. Kellum took his turn to speak, faced the jury and hammered the point home that doubt mandated an acquittal:

"We don't have to prove to you that it was not Till's body," the defense attorney declared; "we only have to raise a reasonable doubt."

Kellum cited the testimony of Dr. Otken, who said that the remains he examined must have been in the water at least eight to ten days, whereas only three days had passed between Till's disappearance and the discovery of the corpse. To ignore that fact and convict the defendants, Kellum said, would mean that "freedom was lost forever." This was no mere murder trial. Liberty itself was at stake, and more, loyalty to southern honor. If you fail to acquit Milam and Bryant, Kellum concluded, "your forefathers will turn over in their graves."

The court then took a lunch break and resumed a little before two o'clock. John C. Whitten finished for the defense. The issue of race had been handled gently all morning, but Whitten concluded with a few carefully chosen words: "There are people in the United States who want to destroy the custom and way of life of southern white people and southern black people." There are people, he continued, "out to put us at odds who are willing to go as far as possible, to commit any crime to widen the gap between us." Whitten never uttered the letters NAACP; there was no need. "If these people had the opportunity to create a commotion, to stir up a trial such as this and focus national attention on Mississippi and focus national attention on the strained relations here, they would do it." Such people were capable of anything. They might even "go so far as to put a stinking body in the Tallahatchie River with the hope that it could be identified as Emmett Till."

Reasonable doubt once again, the trump card. I don't *know*, Whitten told the jurors, that these nefarious organizations came down here, planted a dead body in the river and claimed it was Emmett Till, but "I do know it is well within the realm of possibility." These "rabble rousers" inflicted terrible shame on Sumner, besmirched the tiny Delta town, dragged it into the national press to amplify the message, just as many citizens feared before the trial even started. To redeem the honor of Sumner, Tallahatchie County, the Delta, and the South, Whitten challenged the jurymen to prove, "that every last Anglo-Saxon one of you has the courage to free these men in the face of that pressure."

Attorney Smith now rose to conclude the prosecutions' case, and he aimed his words directly at Whitten. For two days, the lawyers largely avoided speaking openly about race, segregation, and white supremacy. Race was ever in the courtroom, of course—witness a black US congressman given a back seat at a card table, questions about who read the *Chicago Defender*, stirring stories about white folks rescuing black children—but during the trial race was mostly spoken of in code. Like

Whitten, Smith now brought race closer to the center but again with guarded words.

Yes, Smith agreed, "there is no doubt that outside influences are trying to destroy our way of life." But exonerating murderers to defend southern customs, southern honor, was the surest way to destroy them. "Once we take the life, liberty or pursuit of happiness from anyone we will be put on the defensive and become vulnerable in trying to justify our stand."

Smith continued, "If J. W. Milam and Roy Bryant are turned loose it will serve the purpose of the very organizations that have come down here to stir up trouble. If you convict them no one can use this to raise funds to fight us in our defense of southern traditions." Indeed, convict Milam and Bryant, Smith said, and you silence the agitators, because no one will believe that "the state of Mississippi didn't do its duty." The South, Smith declared, could survive only by defending the constitutional rights of every citizen, black and white, and that meant punishing those who deprived Emmett Till of his life.

Make no mistake, he concluded, it was Emmett Till whose body was pulled from the Tallahatchie River. How else explain the ring on his finger? How else explain that "good old country Negro" Mose Wright's clear identification of his nephew's body? How else explain Mamie Till Bradley's sad testimony, "because the last thing in God's creation a mother wants is to believe that her son is dead"? In the end, Smith called the defense's claim that, to divide blacks and whites, outsiders put a corpse with Till's ring on it in the river, "the most far-fetched argument I've ever heard in a courtroom." And with that, the closing arguments ended.

Writing for a syndicate of black newspapers, James Hicks called the prosecutors' summation the dramatic highlight of a drama-filled trial, and he singled out Chatham's performance as "one of the most passionate pleas ever made by a white man in the South on behalf of a Negro." Southern-born Chatham rose to an enormous challenge, Hicks asserted, asking an all-white jury to do something unprecedented: convict two of their peers for murder. Mamie Till Bradley sat next to Hicks during the closing remarks, and she turned to the reporter after Chatham finished and said, "He couldn't have done any better."[8]

She was right, but maybe in a way she did not mean. In the straitjacket of Mississippi, there were certain things one dared not question. Everyone—everyone—knew that this trial was about a deeply southern concept of racial honor, an old drama staged decade after decade with new costumes, props, and actors, yet the same basic plot. White men must protect the purity of white women from bestial black men. Any intimation of desire between them besmirched family honor. Lynch mobs might be out of fashion now, but for centuries white men beat, tortured, and killed black men for alleged violations of this extralegal code. It was central to the very definitions of white manhood and white womanhood, a cornerstone of The Southern Way of Life, of Jim Crow segregation. The defense took their stand on it, the prosecution had neither reason nor desire to openly challenge it, but the jurors, indeed the entire region, understood exactly what was at stake.[9]

VERDICTS

CHAPTER TWENTY-TWO

I'M REAL HAPPY AT THE RESULT

JUDGE SWANGO APPOINTED J. A. Shaw Jr. as foreman, discharged the extra juror from further duty, read aloud his instructions, and, at 2:34 p.m. on Friday, September 23, directed his bailiffs to lead the jury to their room to decide the fate of Milam and Bryant. Spectators and officers of the court milled around, waiting. Friends and family offered assurances to the defendants, who remained in their seats, next to their wives.[1]

Thirty minutes after the jurors left, a knock came from behind their door, and the courtroom went silent. But the jurors only asked for soft drinks, which Sheriff Strider brought them. Half an hour later came more knocking, and Judge Swango called his courtroom back to order. The jurors filed in at 3:42 p.m. They stood at their seats.

The Court: Have you gentlemen reached a verdict?
Mr. Shaw: Yes, Sir, we have.

Shaw handed a piece of paper to Charlie Cox, the clerk of the court.

The Court: Mr. Clerk, will you read the verdict?
Mr. Cox, the Clerk: "Not guilty."[2]

Reporters began their dash to the phones, but Judge Swango banged his gavel for order. He was not pleased that the jury had failed to use the proper language. He asked the jurors to return to the jury room and come back with "a correct verdict," using the form supplied to them. "During the delay," wrote one observer, "Milam sat smoking a cigar....He didn't bat an eye, didn't change his expression when the 'not guilty' was said or during the wait. Neither did Bryant, who sat holding his wife's hand." Finally, the jury returned to the courtroom.

The Court:	Have you gentlemen reached a complete verdict now? Has your verdict been made in accordance with the form that was given you?
Mr. Shaw:	Yes, Sir.
The Court:	Will you give the verdict to the clerk, please, Mr. Shaw. [A paper was handed to the clerk.] Will you now read the verdict, Mr. Clerk?
Mr. Cox [reading]:	"We, the jury, find the defendants: not guilty."

Judge Swango thanked the jurors, instructed them to go downstairs, and collect their pay warrants.[3]

"A gasp of released tension broke courtroom silence at the acquittal verdict," Edward Everett wrote for the AP, "then a wave of excited exclamation drove through the more than 300 persons in the room." In Everett's judgment the verdict would reverberate from "northern Negro centers down into the heart of the Deep South." Now, he concluded, "extreme racial antagonisms" would boil into the national consciousness.[4]

After Judge Swango thanked the jury, defense counsel moved to dismiss the kidnapping charges on grounds that jurisdiction rightly belonged to Leflore County. Prosecutors and the judge agreed, and Milam and Bryant were bound over to Sheriff Smith. Acquitted of murder charges in Tallahatchie County, the grand jury sitting in Greenwood would decide whether to indict Milam and Bryant for kidnapping.[5]

But first Sheriff Smith allowed the brothers a few moments of celebration. Cameramen and reporters closed in on the defendants. Friends and family widened the circle, reached in to shake hands, slap the two men on the back. Milam and Bryant's mother told reporters she didn't think the prosecution presented any real evidence; their sister remained in her chair, sobbing quietly. Back in the southeast corner of the room, a dozen black reporters stood and stared blankly. "Flashbulbs were popping all over the place," Clark Porteous wrote. "Each of the two couples was kissing, long and hard. Later they did it again for the photographers, but those first ones were for each other." Photographers climbed over tables and chairs to get good angles. Milam made a crack about buying a wig, there had been so much talk about a tall man with a bald head. Both defendants lit up fresh cigars. "I'm glad to get loose," said Roy Bryant; "I'm real happy at the result," Carolyn added. J. W. also expressed his pleasure, and Juanita, at his side, declared, "I was scared, but sure of the verdict."[6]

She was right to be confident of the outcome. Shaw, the jury foreman, a farmer from Webb, Mississippi, told reporters that the jurors voted three times. First, they polled nine for acquittal with three uncertain; then ten not-guilty votes with two still on the fence; and finally, a unanimous decision to free the brothers. In three ballots, not a single juror voted for a conviction. What convinced them all? "There was a reasonable doubt," Shaw said, and the key was "their belief that there had been no identification of the dead body as that of Emmett Till." Not only did the prosecution fail to prove to the jury's satisfaction that the corpse in the river was really Till, but when the jurors studied the police photo, they agreed that the body was too badly decomposed for anyone to identify it. And what did the jury think of Mamie Till Bradley's testimony that the body was indeed her son, that the ring on its finger was Emmett's? "If she had tried a little harder," Foreman Shaw answered, referring to the moment when she looked for the first time at that same police photo and fought to control her emotions, "she might have got out a tear." He added that Willie Reed's testimony also failed to impress them.[7]

Courthouse reporters never got the chance to ask Mrs. Bradley about the verdict. She, her father, Rayfield Mooty, and T. R. M. Howard left for Mound Bayou before the decision even came in. She recalled years later that it wasn't the look in the jurors' eyes as they retired to their deliberations that told her it was time to go, but rather the African American spectators along the back wall who quietly exited the courtroom, knowing when it was best to get out of harm's way.[8]

Mrs. Bradley and the others were not quite back in Mound Bayou when news of the verdict came over the car radio, celebratory sounds, like New Year's Eve, she recalled. "I wasn't surprised at all," she later told reporters; "I had already considered the possibility of acquittal, but it still struck me a little forcibly after the summation of the case by the state...." Congressman Diggs agreed: "I think the judge was fair, I think the prosecution of the case was impressive, but apparently the deep-rooted prejudices of the jurors would not permit any kind of objective consideration of the case." Diggs added, "Our first line of defense against this kind of injustice is thru the ballot box."[9]

After they packed their bags, Dr. Howard got everyone into cars headed to Memphis. A very friendly and talkative driver took Mamie and her father to the airport. Their conversation ended when the driver learned who they were. Terrified, he turned off his headlights, drove north through twilight over back roads, and almost neglected to collect his fare, so eager was he to get away from them.[10]

Asked what he thought of the jurors' verdict, Gerald Chatham, who looked even more weary and ill after court adjourned, said only that he accepted their decision since trial by jury was "one of the sacred guarantees of our federal constitution." Sheriff Strider assured the press that he would continue his investigation into the real identity of the Tallahatchie corpse and the whereabouts of Emmett Till. Sumner quickly returned to normal. Saturday morning shoppers from nearby farms strolled the streets. "Negroes and whites," Popham wrote in the *New York Times*, "formed their customary separate groupings on the Court House Square under the shady oak trees hard by the Confederate monument."[11]

A few years after the verdict, a young political scientist, Hugh Stephen Whitaker, returned to his home in Tallahatchie County. He studied the Till case and interviewed many of the participants for his 1963 master's thesis at Florida State University. Whitaker was told that members of local Citizens' Councils managed to contact all the jurors, even though they had been sequestered throughout the trial. No threats were made, but the goal was to make sure that they voted "the right way." It probably did not matter. Whitaker concluded the jurors believed that Milam and Bryant killed Emmett Till, and only one of them really thought the body in the river might not be Till's. The jurors told Whitaker that the northern press castigating the South had no impact on their votes. The simple truth, Whitaker concluded, was that a black male had insulted a white woman, and her husband would not be prosecuted for killing him.[12]

The legal battle now shifted to Leflore County. Sheriff Smith cut Milam and Bryant's celebration short, drove them back to Greenwood, and had them arraigned on kidnapping charges. Their lawyers were eager to free them on bail immediately, but the brothers ended up staying put for a week, waiting for the Tallahatchie court to deliver a full trial transcript and other documents. Only then could Judge Charles Pollard, sitting in Greenwood, set bail.[13]

Finally, Friday morning, September 30, at 10:00 a.m., the judge, Milam, Bryant, their lawyers—J. W. Kellum and Sidney Carlton—as well as the district attorney, Stanny Sanders, met in Pollard's tiny office for a hearing that lasted three minutes. Witnesses reported that Milam and Bryant appeared stiff and uncomfortable, standing against the wall. The judge set bail at $10,000 each, which was posted immediately by two Leflore County plantation owners, D. C. Walker and F. B. Steinback. Deputy Sheriff Ernest Stowers told reporters, "Why, they could have gotten up to a million dollars in bond if they needed it," because wealthy planters would "go the limit" to free them.[14]

Once again the brothers paused for pictures. Milam said he would go home to Glendora and start harvesting cotton; Bryant hoped to rest up a little then reopen the store in Money. Then their other brother Ed Milam drove up and sped them away. They were free for the first time in a month but would be back in Greenwood in five weeks. Two Mississippi laws covered kidnapping, one carried the death penalty, the other up to ten years in prison, so for a second time, a grand jury might put the brothers' lives in jeopardy or free them altogether.[15]

During the week that Milam and Bryant sat in their cells in Greenwood, a rumor flew around the Delta: Emmett Till was alive; he'd been spotted in Chicago, New York, Detroit, at Parchman Prison, at the movies. Deputy John Ed Cothran received a "siege of telephone calls." He added, "You couldn't investigate a cow killing without somebody telling you a rumor they'd heard." One caller even wanted to know "if Sheriff Smith had gone to Chicago to pick up the boy." Once again, Clarence Strider was instrumental in keeping the rumors alive. Several days after the trial ended, Strider said to reporters, "I definitely believe he's somewhere, but I don't know where." Strider admitted that no new facts supported his opinion, but in the Till case, facts were often irrelevant. From Chicago, Mamie Till Bradley called the rumors a "cruel hoax." She added, "If he were alive, I would know," and she offered to have Emmett's body exhumed if that would quell the rumors. No one took her up on it. Hearsay was nothing new in the Till case. Even before the trial began, there had been rumors, amplified by Sheriff Strider, of carloads of Chicago blacks coming down to the Delta to make trouble. After the acquittal, Sheriff Smith declared that "Negroes have begun a campaign of throwing rocks at whites." State highway patrolmen investigated but found nothing.[16]

Real enough, however, was the wave of fear that the Sumner verdict unleashed on Delta African Americans. One response, quiet and tentative, was a deepened commitment to self-defense, even fighting back. Ruby Hurley, the secretary of the Southeast Regional NAACP believed that African Americans were not looking for trouble, but the Till trial "convinced most Mississippi colored persons that if the law won't protect them, it is up to them to protect themselves." One local businessman told her, "I don't intend to sit quietly by and let anyone kill me for nothing," adding that he kept weapons at hand in every room of his home and office.[17]

But another response was that it was time to leave the Delta, leave Mississippi, leave the South. Those who had stood up boldly in court against Milam and Bryant began their inexorable trek away from their home state. On the night he abducted Emmett Till, J. W. Milam told sixty-four-year-old Mose Wright that he'd never reach sixty-five if he identified the kidnappers. Willie Reed saw six or seven men on the truck carrying Emmett to his torture and death, so there were at least that many people, maybe more, liable under the law for kidnapping, homicide, or accessory to murder. The last thing they needed was witnesses who might testify against them.

Wright, Willie Reed, and Amandy Bradley had broken the unwritten law of segregation: they spoke as equals in a court of law and singled out white men. At the very least the Citizens' Councils would make their lives miserable, and if past was prologue, a beating or worse, much worse, loomed in their future. The black press highlighted such fears. The *Houston Informer* was typical, describing "terror-stricken Negro witnesses" fleeing Mississippi, and others in the community fearing reprisals and talking about leaving. Milam and Bryant's acquittal, the *Informer* feared, "gives the go-ahead signal to lynchers all over the south."[18]

On the Friday that the verdict came down in Sumner, someone warned Mose Wright of trouble. He had been sleeping with guns by his pillow, but that was no longer good enough. "I put my three sons in the car and we hid out in the brushes near the cemetery," he recalled. Wright's neighbors reported that a few carloads of men came in the night, that they called out Mose's name, shone lights on his home, then went in and ransacked the place. Saturday, Wright packed up what he could and sold the rest, furniture and livestock, noting, "I had to take what I could get because everybody knew I had to flee." Worse, Wright said, "I had to leave about 16 bales of my best cotton in the fields." Saturday night, he and his sons again slept by the cemetery in their old Ford. The next day they drove to Winona to catch the Illinois Central to Chicago, where Mose's wife Elizabeth waited for them. Wright asked Crosby Smith to come pick up his old car and get what he could for it.[19]

Willie Reed made it to Mound Bayou, then to Chicago; he never even got the chance to say goodbye to his girlfriend. "We felt Reed would be safer in Chicago," Congressman Diggs told reporters; "He will go to school and get a job there." Reed moved into his mother's small apartment, but within a few days came a flood of threatening letters, so the Chicago police dispatched two plainclothes officers to stand guard outside. Shortly thereafter, Reed had a nervous breakdown, and his mother checked him into Michael Reese Hospital. Amandy Bradley also made a hurried escape on a Chicago-bound train, just ahead of thugs who came looking for her. They beat her husband, and then Leslie Milam kicked him off the plantation.[20]

As these stories circulated in the press, the *Jackson Daily News* began a campaign to discredit the refugees and defend Mississippi's honor. After all, a jury had found Milam and Bryant innocent, and the jurors questioned whether a murder had taken place at all. A series with banner headlines, splashed across the front page, told how the *Daily News* writer Bill Spell went to Chicago to obtain the truth. Spell led off with an incendiary charge—that Wright, Reed, and Bradley were "now being held 'captive' in the deepest part of Chicago's South-Side Negro Section by the National Association for the Advancement of Colored People." Spell found Willie Reed and asked him if anyone had threatened him? No, only that Milam and Bryant "looked hard" at him during the trial. It was the same with Amandy Bradley. "I left because I was scared," she told Spell, but she acknowledged that no one hurt her. In the middle of their conversation, a "middle-man" told her not to answer questions without a representative of the NAACP in the room, revealing that "Bradley is under the complete domination" of that organization."[21]

In his last article, Spell charged that the NAACP blocked him from interviewing Mose Wright, and he concluded that Wright's story about hiding in the cemetery while his home came under attack was just part of the "wave of propaganda spread against Mississippi out of Chicago." Besides, Spell asked, why did Willie Reed need police protection if Chicago was so much safer than Mississippi? And what did the NAACP do with all that money it raised off the Till story? Spell concluded that Reed, Wright, and Bradley were unwitting stooges for the NAACP, which used them to "spread world-wide hate against the State of Mississippi."[22]

More than exposing a few exaggerated stories, Spell claimed he had gone underground into the darkest recesses of the ghetto to uncover the NAACP propaganda machine. "What are the people of Chicago afraid of?" he asked; "What is the grim political power held by a single organization?" Spell spent little more than twenty-four hours in Chicago, but already he was being followed, he wrote, revealing the NAACP's insidious power, the thick webs of corruption in which it entrapped the city's highest officials. He contrasted his harassment—he offered no details—with the cordial welcome the press had received in Sumner.[23]

Spell's allegations got national traction when the Associated Press reprinted his reports. "That's the most fantastic story I've heard yet," said Amandy Bradley. "Nobody is keeping me here. I wanted to come, and I did, paying my own expenses. I haven't been threatened, but I don't want to return to Mississippi." Moses Wright also said that he came of his own free will, that he paid his family's way to Chicago, that he was afraid to live in Mississippi. But for those inclined to believe him, especially in

Mississippi, Spell's words did their work, transforming a story that evoked terrified slaves freeing their captivity on the underground railroad and Great Migration refugees finding shelter in the North into an exposé of "darkest Chicago."[24]

Soon an even more bizarre story broke. Before the Sumner trial began, the newsman James Hicks reported on the two African American men who allegedly abetted Till's abduction and murder. Although Willie Reed never mentioned them by name, it was assumed that Henry Lee Loggins and Levy "Too Tight" Collins were with Emmett Till in the back of the pickup truck as it approached Leslie Milam's property. During the trial, prosecutors tried without success to find them. Now with the Leflore grand jury meeting in a month, their testimony could be explosive, maybe enough to put Milam and Bryant away and even indict others. Hicks was certain that before the murder trial, Sheriff Strider locked them up in the Charleston jail, but Sheriff Smith as well as Robert Smith, the prosecutor, and several others investigated and found no trace of them.

A week after the Sumner trial ended, the *New York Post* reported widespread rumors in the Delta that the two men were missing and probably dead. Sheriff Smith dismissed the report, speculating that they were just lying low. Ruby Hurley quoted him as saying, "They'll show up. Nothing has happened to them. Both of them are devoted to Milam and will do anything he told them. They are his personal boys; they'd die for him if necessary." Hurley added she was sure that Collins and Loggins knew exactly who the other white men were on the truck with J. W. and Roy Bryant, but that they would never tell. J. W. ran illegal bootlegging and gambling out of his store in Glendora, Hurley said, with Loggins and Collins as his go-betweens to black customers.[25]

Sheriff Smith and Ruby Hurley were right; Loggins and Collins were indeed alive. The former turned up in St. Louis and the latter in Chicago. According to the AP, the *Chicago Defender* smuggled them out of Mississippi for their own safety—and to get their story—but the two refused to name names. Loggins simply clammed up; Collins, on the other hand, talked and talked. The editor of the *Tri-State Defender* (a Memphis affiliate of the *Chicago Defender*) L. Alex Wilson and legal counsel Euclid L. Taylor of the *Chicago Defender* spent hours interviewing Collins. He denied any involvement in Till's murder, denied that he'd been locked up in Charleston, denied reports that he was seen Sunday morning washing blood out of J. W.'s truck. Every question elicited evasion. According to Collins, both he and Loggins worked for J. W. driving cotton-picking machines until Saturday evening, August 27, then left Glendora for Greenwood, where they visited some girls. In other words, they were not even in Money or

Glendora during the kidnapping. Asked if on the following Tuesday he and Loggins discussed Milam's arrest, Too Tight said no. Did he even know about the arrest? No. Yes. Then, "when white people get to talking about something, I don't stay to see what they are talking about. I get out." Told that a friend quoted him as saying he knew more about the Till case than he let on, Collins replied, "I don't know anything about it."[26]

Even while insisting that he had nothing to do with Emmett Till, Too Tight Collins changed his story about where he was during the murder and trial. After Till disappeared but before his body emerged, Collins claimed that J. W. drove him and Loggins to Minter City, where they worked for Milam's brother-in-law, Melvin Campbell, hauling gravel. Or were they hauling gravel during the trial? Or were they working for Campbell for that whole month, from just after the killing through the "not guilty" verdict? All of the above. Collins disappeared again in early October, only to resurface in mid-November, *after* the Greenwood grand jury met. Toward the end of the year, he was seen working at a sawmill in a little town near Greenwood. Then he disappeared again.[27]

Months after Sumner, Henry Lee Loggins turned up again. According to T. R. M. Howard, Loggins was in jail. J. W. Milam had accused Loggins of stealing scrap iron from his yard and had him arrested, the real purpose being to keep him quiet. Once again, Howard hoped to coax a witness out of Mississippi, bring him to Chicago, and let him reveal what really happened. Howard said that Loggins's own father confirmed that Milam forced Henry Lee and another field hand to hold Till down in the back of the truck, and later, to wire a weight around the dead boy's neck and throw him in the river. Now Henry Lee Loggins promised to come north and tell the truth. According to one reporter, however, "after bail had been supplied, the alleged killers of Till appeared on the scene and Loggins refused to leave jail." A man who many believed might blow the case wide open was intimidated into silence.[28]

Two years later, Adam Clayton Powell, the New York City congressman, asked the FBI to investigate charges that Loggins and Collins had been lynched. Their families suspected their deaths and added that they, too, had been warned to stop talking about Emmett Till. The Justice Department replied to Powell that there was no basis for federal intervention.[29]

With that, the trail leading to Loggins and Collins grew cold and stayed that way until the FBI picked it up again—fifty years after Emmett Till's murder.

CHAPTER TWENTY-THREE

THE SOUL OF AMERICA

SOON AFTER the trial ended on September 23, the Oklahoma City *Black Dispatch* declared that "the conscience and virtue of a people" are revealed on editorial pages of local newspapers. Search those pages, the editor urged, for they "daily shape the conduct of the masses." He added that the very "soul of America" could be found on the opinion pages. If so, it was a pretty divided soul.[1]

Most southern editors cheered the jury's decision in the days following the verdict. The *Kingsport (TN) Times-News* epitomized the most common response: "Justice has been done in Sumner, Miss." The trial was fair, and the prosecution's case weak; "latter-day abolitionists" and "radical elements" notwithstanding, truth carried the day. The *Greenwood Commonwealth* accused "alien elements" of hurling unfounded accusations against Mississippi and its people, but the Sumner trial proved once again that the state could "handle its affairs without any outside meddling." The *Greenwood Morning Star* —which sometimes referred to the trial as "the Till Rape Attempt Case,"—declared that top newsmen like James Kilgallen, "were unanimous in their opinions that the trial was fair and impartial." Mississippi "proved to the world that this is a place where justice in the courts is given to all races, religions and classes." Two weeks later, the *Morning Star* was still railing against, "the rabble rousing, pink tinted press of the north, and the lousy sensation seeking magazines" for their biased coverage.[2]

There were, of course, dissident editorial voices in the southern press. The *Atlanta Constitution* called Till's murder a racial killing whose burden rested with Mississippi; the *Raleigh News and Observer* argued that the verdict offended the region's sense of justice, and that most southerners favored segregation but hated violence; Hodding Carter's *Delta Democrat-Times* editorialized that Sheriff Strider's duplicity misled the jurors: "The very man who was designated to lead an investigation into an obvious case of brutal murder was busy most of the time inventing diverting fantasies as to how the whole thing could have been arranged by someone else." But criticisms like these were rare on southern editorial pages, and Carter argued that if anything, the verdict pushed out moderation.[3]

The African American papers, of course, were scathing. "Every aspect of the trial was edged by flagrant racism," concluded the *Chicago Defender*. There is nothing new in the Mississippi trial, the *Baltimore Afro-American* added: "victim kidnapped and lynched; woman concocts story of sex attack, mob members arrested, tried and freed." The *Kansas City Call* headlined its editorial, "White Supremacy Wins Again." The Oklahoma City *Black Dispatch* accused the South of "hiding behind white women's skirts while the real purpose is to terrorize and intimidate Negroes in the exercise of their constitutional rights."[4]

Most of the northern press mercilessly castigated the jury, Mississippi, and the South. The *Chicago Sun-Times* described the defense attorneys' raw appeal to the jury's prejudice as "nothing less than a lynching." The *Detroit Free Press* editors were "disgusted" by John Whitten calling the jurors Anglo-Saxons whose forefathers expected an acquittal: "This was a vicious, bigoted slur on every American." The *New York Post* argued that mob rule had replaced justice in Mississippi. The Racine, Wisconsin, *Journal Times* said that the verdict put ready-made propaganda into the hands of America's enemies, that Sumner's principles were no better than those of the Communists. The *Christian Century*, a Chicago-based mouthpiece of mainline Protestantism, concluded that, "Justice died with all its formalities in perfect order."[5]

The veteran African American columnist Roi Ottley took away something more positive. Hearing an articulate black congressman and watching highly professional black journalists must have unsettled whites in Tallahatchie County, he argued, and amazed them too. The *New York Post's* Murray Kempton also detected glimmers of hope: "Curtis Swango and Mamie Bradley are the future. . . . Just the sound of their voices, speaking with dignity and without fear, is a death verdict for the beast that sits and swaggers all around them."[6]

The iconoclastic journalist I. F. Stone took a much darker view (though he sent a personal note to Kempton praising his coverage of the trial).

"There is a sickness in the South," Stone wrote; "Unless cured, there may some day spring from it crimes as evil and immense as the crematoria of Hitlerism." Stone went a level deeper, castigating the press and the public, cowed and complaisant: "To the outside world it must look as if the conscience of white America has been silenced." Stone indicted the whole nation, North and South, for acquiescing in white supremacy. Only a Gandhi, he concluded, might lead black America—and then black America might lead white America—against this "psychopathic racist brutality."[7]

Opinion-page letters-to-the-editor certainly lent credence to Stone's pessimism. The *Memphis Clarion-Ledger*, for example, kept printing them for weeks. "Many advocates of integration remind us of the Negro's pride," one man wrote. "What about the pride of the white man? Does he want his ancestry to become a mixed, mongrel race of cross-breeds? Where is the white father who favors his daughters to become brides of the colored man?" Another writer argued that in the past lynching kept predatory black men in check, but now they felt free to rape and murder. Milam and Bryant killing Till was a "spontaneous combustion generated by such criminal attacks upon a long-suffering people, and the Negroes have no one but themselves to blame for what happened." Yet another letter-writer declared that a Communist Party operative groomed Till then sent him south, and the feeble-minded kid acted precisely as his "mentor" knew he would. Thus, a new martyr was born, money flowed into Communist coffers, and Mamie Till Bradley became a "gold-plated" exhibit for the NAACP.[8]

Yet all of the editorials, opinion columns, and letters-to-the-editor were mild compared to many of the private missives people wrote about the Till affair. Neither self-censorship nor editors' blue pencils restrained these communiqués. Not many survive, but those that do give us a window onto unvarnished racism, sectional hatreds, and class tensions.

Defense attorneys Breland and John Whitten saved a handful of letters. One from Littleton, New Hampshire, for example, told Whitten that God would hold him responsible for Sumner, that had the writer been a black Mississippian, she would raise a mob and kill Milam and Bryant's children to end the chain of hate passed from fathers to sons. On the other hand, an attorney from Athens, Alabama, called Milam and Bryant "fine young men," but of Emmett Till he declared, "I suppose this young savage from the African jungles of Chicago felt like he could do as he pleased in Mississippi and that the NAACP and other South haters would come to his rescue." The journalist Westbrook Pegler agreed, writing from Rome, Italy, of "many horrible criminal assaults by negro beasts on white women in New York and Chicago."[9]

The best surviving source of letters, however, is the collection of more than 250 sent to and saved by Gerald Chatham, the district attorney. While certainly not a representative sample of how Americans reacted to the case, the collection contains a wide and uncensored range of opinion. Chatham had been a public servant his whole adult life, working not only as a prosecuting attorney but also as a representative in the state legislature, as county superintendent of education, and as chairman of his local school board. He took his charge seriously—to secure an indictment of Emmett Till's killers and prosecute them to the full extent of the law. Sick, depressed, and exhausted when the trial ended, he lived only another year, dying at age fifty. His family believed that he, too, was a victim of Till's murder, that the trial and its angry aftermath shortened his life.[10]

Once the case was over, Chatham had time to sit in the study of his farmhouse near Hernando, Mississippi, and read the mail that had accumulated for several weeks. It must have been a depressing slog. Of course, those who write to public officials are people with strong opinions. We cannot know if he replied to anyone, or why his family held on to the cache of letters over the years. Probably they sensed the trial's historic significance, that the correspondence captured the passions of the moment, ugly as they often were.[11]

Not all the letters made for grim reading; some thanked the prosecutor for his courage and eloquence. One man wrote at the beginning of the trial that the nation would "applaud your sincere and able efforts in seeing that justice be done and deserved punishment meted out to the two merciless killers of that poor innocent boy." A Mississippi writer praised the prosecutor's "courage and conviction," and one from Alabama wrote that Judge Swango and Attorney Chatham had turned the trial "into an historical event."[12]

But most of the letters were not so positive. Some writers, perhaps, did not understand that Chatham's goal was to put Milam and Bryant behind bars. Others thought he did a poor job, or even deliberately sabotaged the prosecution. Still others saw him as a cog in a system that denied justice to African Americans regardless of what role he played in the courtroom. Even as Chatham sincerely strove to secure the convictions of Milam and Bryant, his patronizing language toward blacks in the courtroom, as reported by the newspapers, made it clear that he fully accepted key assumptions of white supremacy.

Still, what must have been surprising to a man who valued his reputation for fairness, good will, and justice was the anger in letters written by African Americans. One Chicago woman noted that three-quarters of the world's people were dark-skinned, a fact recognized by Russia but apparently not by white America, and, she added, "As long as you continue to lynch Negroes you might as well burn up all the law books and stop telling…foreign countries all these lies that all men are created equal." She concluded, "The only way you white people got anywhere was by cheating, fighting, and stealing. You even stole this country from the Indians."[13]

Another unsigned letter from Chicago referred to Mississippi as, "that hell hole," the "least civilized" state in America. The writer called Mississippians dogs, skunks, and crackers. He accused them of cowardice, sneaking around at night, killing children one by one. He predicted that blacks would one day force Mississippi whites to fight in the open. Even more militantly, an unsigned note from Cleveland, Ohio, declared of Milam and Bryant, "KILL THEM RATS OR DIE YOURSELVES." Kill them, the writer added, or we'll blow up Sumner.[14]

Sheriff Strider made it seem as if only letters like these poured into his office. Chatham didn't get many of them, but there were a few. One man claimed to speak for four thousand like-minded veterans—African Americans, Puerto Ricans, and West Indians—all of them fed up with southern atrocities. We have spies, guns and cars, he wrote, and if the courts won't punish Milam and Bryant, we will. The South, he declared, is as repressive as Russia, and the first atomic bombs should have been dropped somewhere between Virginia and Florida. We will stop terrorism like Emmett Till's lynching, he signed off, "even if we have to start a revolution down south." Another former GI swore, "Those who died for a free America have not died in vain." Blacks shed too much blood in two world wars to countenance Till's murder, and the writer promised that he and other GI's would come south to extirpate American Nazis like Milam and Bryant.[15]

Such letters must have been terribly upsetting to a man who saw himself steering a moderate course, seeking justice not only for Till and his family but also a restoration of racial harmony. Liberal notions of progress and good feeling between the races took savage epistolary blows here, but far more came from racist whites—many of them northerners—than from militant blacks. "The little nigger asked for it and got precisely what was coming to him," a man from Morehouse, Missouri, wrote. A writer from Philadelphia, Mississippi, blamed the Supreme Court: "This gang of political shysters, in their desire to humiliate the South, encouraged Emmett Till to insult a white woman."[16]

"It did my heart good," wrote a woman from Chicago below a finely engraved letterhead of two lovebirds, "to read of men like Milam and Bryant, who do something about dirty rotten niggers that insult white women." Up north, she said, blacks daily raped, robbed, and killed adults and children with no consequences. As for Till, "this big gorilla type kid just forgot he wasn't in Chicago." Another citizen from the Windy City bemoaned the thousands of southern blacks pouring into her town, called them thugs and pigs, and concluded they all belonged back in Africa. Yet one more Chicagoan put it simply: "That dirty nigger...probably got what he had coming."[17]

The most vicious letters zeroed in on sex between black men and white women. One New Yorker complained about living in a city of "nigger lovers and mulattoes"; about "niggers" and "white trash" strolling arm-in-arm; about interracial classrooms, intermarriage, and the result of it all, mixed-race children. Convict Milam and Bryant, he warned, and it is "open season on white women...because if that nigger got away with it, word would spread around fast and there would be no stopping the niggers." Another New Yorker made explicit the ties between sex, Emmett Till, and the *Brown* decision, which "deliberately opened an attack upon our daughters in the schools..., opened the bedrooms of all the White Women." And again, a "200% American Mother," descended from "a venerable and patriotic American family," feared that black rapists stalked her "lovely white daughter." "God put them in Africa," she concluded; "if he wanted to mix the races, he would have done so in the beginning."[18]

Many of the letters were less concerned with black crime than refighting the Civil War. Inevitably, some questioned Chatham's loyalty to the South. One in particular no doubt stung him deeply: "Most Southern people, I mean real Southern people, think you are acting like a skunk in the stand you are taking regarding this matter." The writer argued that the NAACP tricked "good negroes" into hating white people. All true southerners knew this, but then again, you, Chatham, "may be a damn yankee...and think the nigger is as good as you are." There was no dearth of arrogance from white northerners either. The tone of most of these letters was deeply antagonistic toward the South, toward southern justice, and toward Chatham himself. One, for example, called the court system that Chatham labored in his entire adult life "a disgrace" and "a farce." Even the few notes that praised his efforts did so only to denigrate Mississippi.[19]

The depth of anti-southern feeling is striking. From Manhattan, Kansas, came an unsigned letter that referred to the jury and all of the attorneys as "Slimy southerners in their ignorant sadism." A man from Ysleta, Texas, wrote that he always had been proud of his region, yet both the murder and acquittal were disgraceful examples of "Down South Justice," and he hated everyone involved with them. A Tacoma, Washington, man agreed and wrote that the Sumner verdict made him ashamed to admit his southern roots. He marveled that poor whites so willingly did the bidding of the rich, then suggested what united them: "The southern gentry as well as the crackers...raped ten thousand negro women for every white woman ever raped by a negro."[20]

Others remarked that the United States was morphing into its totalitarian enemies. "If America tolerates such a gross miscarriage of justice," wrote a woman from Fort Worth, "then we can indeed be likened to the Gestapo of Hitler and the dreaded secret police of the Soviets," who, like Till's kidnappers, dragged citizens from their homes in the dead of night. What is the point, a mother wrote from Jamaica, New York, of sending men like her husband overseas to fight for democracy only to have it crushed here at home? One woman compared Mississippians to Hitler's blond-haired, blue-eyed Nazis, another admonished them to avoid the fate of the German "Master Race," and yet another lectured Chatham, "How the communists must gloat over such treatment of a minority group.... I presume every newspaper in Russia will carry headlines about it."[21]

Some writers emphasized how the Till verdict desecrated the Christian faith. A letter from San Jose, California, chastised Chatham, "You seem to forget that the colored people are God's children the same as you are." Others warned him of God's reckoning, told him he was "spiritually on trial." On hearing the verdict over the radio, Mrs. Mable Green in Hutchinson, Kansas, questioned whether the jurors really were Christians because their decision denied that Emmett, too, was created in God's image. She imagined the killers in an integrated heaven, with St. Peter enjoying their discomfiture. Others took up this theme, that justice denied on earth would be found in the afterlife: "I earnestly pray that the men who committed the crime, those who aided, those [who] gave testimony to prevent justice, will hear the screams of that boy until their day of judgment."[22]

Over and over again the writers expressed a powerful sense of shame, shame in whiteness, shame in the criminal justice system, shame in America. Mrs. Martin Gordon from Los Angeles wrote that for the first time in her life, "I'm ashamed of being white and I'm ashamed of being an American.... It was my race and my countrymen who committed the terrible crime and acquitted Milam and Bryant." Another man described feeling "cheap and sick inside" since skin color was all that mattered to the jury.[23]

Writers piled up their invective against Chatham and his state. "You must be proud of your juries," one woman wrote, and she asked if Chatham wanted Mississippi to offer bounties for dead Negroes? Another, after wishing leprosy on everyone involved with freeing Milam and Bryant, added that he could not bring himself to sign off with the word "respectfully."

"Feel proud," an anonymous writer said, "real proud of the sin you have committed—a sin the millions of other citizens of the United States will try to live down and explain to the World. He closed, "With deep shame that I am considered fellow Countryman to you and your kind."[24]

So Chatham's critics castigated him for betraying the white South and for doing its bidding, for selling out African Americans and for pandering to them, for undermining civil liberties, for destroying The Southern Way of Life, and finally for losing the trial. The prosecutor's belief in the importance of the Till case kept him on the job even while those closest to him knew that he should have stepped down. They paid for his sense of duty with phone calls in the middle of the night, unwanted attention from reporters and television crews for weeks after the verdict came down, allegations about his loyalty to his region, and charges that he betrayed judicial ethics. We will never know if the criticism made Gerald Chatham question his sense of duty as a Christian, a southerner, and an American. But he must have wondered, reading through his correspondence during his last days, if doing the right thing wasn't a fool's errand.[25]

CHAPTER TWENTY-FOUR

EACH OF YOU OWN A LITTLE BIT OF EMMETT

ON SUNDAY AFTERNOON, two days after the verdict, ten thousand people gathered at a Harlem church for a protest meeting, a third of them jammed inside, the rest listening to loudspeakers on the sidewalk. The crowd was so dense that New York City policemen closed Seventh Avenue between 130th and 133rd Streets. Anticipating the Sumner trial's outcome, A. Philip Randolph—a civil rights stalwart since World War I and president and founder of America's largest African American union, the Sleeping Car Porters—organized the meeting. Featured speakers included Randolph, Mamie Till Bradley, and Roy Wilkins.[1]

The crowd shouted its approval when Randolph called the Sumner trial "a national disgrace" and offered a resolution demanding a special session of Congress to pass an anti-lynching law. "If the United States can send its forces six thousand miles across the sea to Korea," Randolph said to loud, sustained applause, then "in the interest of world democracy it would appear that the federal government should use its vast powers to stop the lynching of Negro citizens by Mississippi racists."[2]

Next, Earl Brown, a New York City councilman, called for a Mississippi Refugee Committee to assist African Americans leaving the state, and he echoed Randolph's demand that the federal government do as much to liberate its own citizens in the South as those victims of Communist dictatorships in Europe. Following Randolph and Brown, the Reverend

David Licorish, associate pastor of the Abyssinian Baptist Church, suggested a march on Dixie, and then Roy Wilkins called for the Democratic Party to repudiate racist southern politicians and pass new civil rights legislation.[3]

But the star of the show was Mamie Till Bradley. As she started to speak, the thousands in the street surged forward, breaking police lines trying to get a glimpse of her. The *New York Post* described the crowd as "whipped into anger and bitterness by her soft-spoken, dispassionate words at the most emotion-packed rally since the Scottsboro upheaval in 1931."[4]

That same Sunday, handbills distributed by the Detroit branch of the NAACP invited citizens to a mass meeting at that city's Bethel AME Church. Six thousand people came to hear about the fight for justice in the Emmett Till case. Representative Charles Diggs attacked the "sheer perjury and fantastic twisting of facts" that he had witnessed in Sumner, while the NAACP's field secretary in Mississippi, Medgar Evers, reported on the campaign against segregation. The meeting raised $14,000, according to the press. Another two thousand people showed up for a rally at the Metropolitan Community Church in Chicago where they heard speakers call for White House intervention to stop "the wave of terror against Negro citizens of Mississippi." Meanwhile, CIO Packinghouse Workers and NAACP members picketed a Chicago meeting of James Eastland's Senate Internal Security Committee with signs reading, "Witch Hunts in Chicago Won't Stop Child-Lynching in Mississippi," and "Senator Eastland—Who Killed Emmett Till?" and "Mississippi Is the Real Threat to Internal Security."[5]

Many southerners accused the NAACP of cynically manipulating the Till case for their own purposes, sensationalizing the story with such phrases as "reign of terror" to raise money and attack the South. In a narrow sense they were right. The events in Money and Sumner were far from everyday occurrences. But the story of Emmett Till was a perfect organizing tool because it captured the brutal reality lurking just beneath the cordial facade of southern segregation, all of the editors' and politicians' protestations of harmony between the races notwithstanding. Emmett Till's murder made the system's violence and injustice palpable. Like lynching itself, this was daily life in extremis, the logical outcome of the gross imbalance of power, status, and wealth between white and black. The charge that the NAACP had some sort of hidden agenda beyond finding out who killed Emmett Till and bringing them to justice was, of course, correct, except that there was nothing hidden about it. It was there in plain sight: civil liberties for African Americans and the destruction of segregation.[6]

This was neither cynical nor disingenuous. After decades of organizing and protest, NAACP leaders knew an effective story when they saw one. Less than six months after taking over the reins of the organization, Roy Wilkins was handed a powerful narrative that exposed Jim Crow exploitation. If the slaughter of a million people is a statistic but the death of one a tragedy, then the Till story offered a bold dramatization of southern horrors. The torture and murder of a boy by grown men because he crossed some absurd racial line gave the lie to all the pious cant about good feelings between the races. The unwillingness of the killers' neighbors to bring them to justice struck increasing numbers of Americans as morally hideous.[7]

And so the rallies began, unprecedented in their size, frequency, and ubiquity. The same day as the meetings in New York, Detroit, and Chicago, the NAACP took out a seven-column ad in the *New York Times*, asking for contributions to "help end racial tyranny in Mississippi." The following day, Ruby Hurley sent out an appeal to all NAACP branch officers, with the opening sentence, "The story of Emmett Till, a 14-year old polio victim, and the victim of Mississippi 'justice' is now well known to you." Hurley asked these local leaders to take up collections in every church within their district, and she called on "each minister to make a strong appeal for these necessary funds." Meanwhile, an NAACP board member, Alfred Baker Lewis, suggested to Roy Wilkins that the organization "use the feeling engendered by the Till case" to elicit contributions from major union leaders like Walter Reuther, David Dubinsky, and George Meany. And even as these organizing efforts geared up, local NAACP youth councils initiated their own activities, beginning in Chicago with a memorial service for Emmett Till just a week after the jury finished its work in Sumner.[8]

Before September ended, rallies were planned from Atlanta to San Francisco, from Mobile Bay to Boston. Meetings took place not just in the great cities but in towns like San Antonio, Bridgeport, Dothan, Youngstown, and Little Rock. The spread of these events across time and space was something new in civil rights organizing. Tens of thousands of people were exposed to a range of ideas: Charles Diggs suggested that after the next election, Mississippi's congressional delegation not be seated on grounds that the state failed to secure all of its citizens the right to vote; Congressman Adam Clayton Powell called for a boycott of goods made in Mississippi; others wanted to raise funds for a mass migration out of the South, still others suggested prosecuting the Citizens' Councils as inimical to American security under the Smith Act. Emmett Till's death was the touchstone of mass organizing for the remainder of 1955 until the

Montgomery Bus Boycott (Dec. 1955–Dec. 1956) and Autherine Lucy's attempt (1956) to integrate the University of Alabama took over the headlines. For several months, the Till story turbocharged the civil rights struggle, as calls and letters and money continued to pour into NAACP headquarters in Manhattan.[9]

A powerful institutional network of churches, unions, civic, and civil rights organizations facilitated Till rallies and speeches. Houses of worship in black neighborhoods were the most important venues, eliciting donations, offering administrative support, and opening their doors for meetings. Local organizations engaged in a range of activities, as when the inter-denominational Council of Churches in Madison, Wisconsin, pressed Mississippi's governor, Hugh White, for action, and when Chicago ministers led a busload of congregants to picket the White House and demand justice from the federal government. America's leading spokesman for liberal Christianity, Dr. Harry Emerson Fosdick, organized a luncheon for 250 prominent citizens—Edward Bernays, Cleveland Amory, and the Reverend James A. Pike were on the guest list—at New York's Roosevelt Hotel, while the B'nai B'rith chapter in Massapequa, out on Long Island, sponsored a meeting under the banner, "Who Murdered Emmett Till?" to discuss the growth of anti-Negro and anti-Semitic organizations in the South.[10]

When the Reverend Adam Clayton Powell addressed upwards of twenty-thousand people in New York City on October 10, urging not only a boycott of Mississippi goods but also a special session of Congress to unseat Mississippi representatives, he shared the podium with clergymen white and black, Catholic, Jewish, and Protestant. "Rabble Rouser Urges Mississippi Boycott," declared the following day's headline in the *Hattiesburg American*.[11]

Then came a monster rally on October 11 in Manhattan's garment center, cosponsored by the NAACP and District 65 Retail, Wholesale, and Department Store Union-CIO. Unlike most of the mass rallies, this one did not take place in a black neighborhood, and the November issue of the NAACP's monthly magazine, *Crisis*, took note and called for more such integrated events. Labor's relationship to race historically had been troubled; many union locals, both North and South, were rigidly segregated, and racial issues were an ongoing struggle in the movement. But not all unions drew the color line, and a powerful strain of interracial organizing had grown up, especially in well-integrated industrial unions like the Packinghouse Workers, so a strong segment of labor got behind and helped organize the Till rallies. Indeed, from the week Emmett's body was discovered, petitions, resolutions, and letters of protest flowed from union locals to the government, and offers of aid poured into the NAACP.

Walter Reuther, president of one of America's most powerful industrial unions, the United Auto Workers, took the lead in condemning Mississippi for its handling of the Till case, saw to it that his locals contributed to the NAACP's "Fight for Freedom Fund," and organized a union-wide letter writing campaign to Congress to support federal civil rights legislation. Nonetheless, the Till rallies remained mostly African American affairs held in black neighborhoods. Interracial harmony was at times in short supply at these events, and one NAACP branch officer worried openly that the Till meetings might stir racial antagonisms. Referring to an early November event in Los Angeles, he told his staff, "had a white man bumped into a Negro on the street outside a race riot would have occurred."[12]

Such occasional troubles notwithstanding, the star of the Emmett Till rallies, measured by crowd size and newspaper attention, was Mamie Till Bradley. Her October schedule included visits to thirty-three cities in nineteen states. After the Harlem rally two days after the trial verdict, she appeared in Detroit at a twenty-four-hour-long meeting, during which twelve clergymen and local officials also spoke. She told the crowd that she was over her sorrow, that "now I'm angry—just plain angry." She spoke to four gatherings over two days in early October in the St. Louis area. At the largest venue, more than three thousand people in Masonic Hall listened with rapt attention, many with tears in their eyes, as she described her feelings when she saw Emmett's body: "Something happened to me—it was as if two bolts of electricity met in my body." Bradley told the crowd how she knew that she must tell her story: "I asked God what I should do. He said to me: 'If you go, I will go with you.' That is why I am here." She added that she did not hate Emmett's killers. Rather, his lynching must become a rallying cry for equality. "I'm not bitter," she said; "I'm rather proud to be the mother of the boy who died to free our bodies.... Each of you own a little bit of Emmett."[13]

Less than a week later, she was in Washington, DC, where people began showing up at noon for a 4:00 p.m. rally. Six thousand of them made their way into Uline Arena, and a second special meeting was scheduled for 8:00 p.m. for the thousands who failed to get seats earlier. The following week, the NAACP sponsored three big events, with Congressman Diggs in Mobile, Dr. T. R. M. Howard in Pittsburgh, and Mrs. Bradley in Des Moines. She told the gathering why she refused to respect Mississippi's wish that Emmett's casket stay closed. "It just looked as though all the hatred and all the scorn ever had for a Negro was taken out on that boy," she said of the moment she first laid eyes on her dead son. That was when she understood she must not be silent. "I gained interest in everybody's child under the sun....Then I knew it could happen to any boy as long as it happened to one. No one is safe."[14]

It was her mission now to tell people to organize, vote, pressure the politicians. Referring as much to herself as to her listeners, she said, "It is time for us to wake up. We have been asleep for a long time. We have been waiting for somebody to come and hand us something—and that is not the way it is going to be." She thanked the crowd for their prayers, letters, and support. "I lost Emmett," she reiterated, but, "I have millions of children to live for now." Spreading the word got her through her sorrow, for, "the more I talk the lighter my burden feels." Bradley ended, "With God helping me and you behind me, I don't think the devil stands a chance." A day later, in Omaha, she suggested that maybe Emmett's death would be the turning point for race relations in America, because now it was clear what everyone was up against. Now the real work could begin: "Don't feel sorry for my boy or me....He has done his job and mine has just begun."[15]

Mamie Till Bradley's rallies were Christian crusades, bearing witness to the horrors of racism. The suffering of her child and her own bereavement were sources of moral authority and strength. And while she certainly did not have to take on the crusader's burden, she never shied away from it, not for the rest of her life. Most important, she explicitly took it on as a woman and a mother. Her terrible loss became the source of her moral authority, of her wisdom, and of her right to speak out.[16]

CHAPTER TWENTY-FIVE

A PROPAGANDA VICTORY FOR INTERNATIONAL COMMUNISM

FORMER First Lady Eleanor Roosevelt wrote in her syndicated column that people around the world awaited Milam and Bryant's kidnapping trial in Greenwood, wondering whether "justice in the United States is only for the white man and not for the colored." Should Mississippi courts fail once more, then "we will have again played into the hands of the Communists and strengthened their propaganda in Africa and Asia." She was right. The Till case was not merely an American story. The murder, trial, and aftermath kept it boiling in the press for months, beyond the Delta, beyond Chicago, even beyond America's borders.[1]

Civil rights struggles were long connected to American foreign relations, and US officials were particularly sensitive to the country's image abroad. During both World War I and World War II, the black press and the NAACP argued that African Americans who served overseas made a down payment in blood on equality. Slowly the federal government responded. More precisely, Democrats recognized an opportunity to garner northern black votes. In 1941, under pressure from A. Philip Randolph and others, Franklin Roosevelt issued Executive Order 8802, banning discrimination in defense industries. At the end of the decade President Harry Truman desegregated the armed forces, also by executive order.[2]

Meanwhile, American civil rights leaders like W. E. B. Dubois and Paul Robeson joined the international movement to liberate Asian and African nations from European colonial rule. Decolonization overseas was part of a larger struggle of colored peoples for autonomy and equality. Before *Brown v. Board of Education,* American radicals—black and white, socialists, Communists, unionists, anticolonialists—were prominent in "the long Civil Rights Movement." Leftist attorneys represented African Americans unjustly accused of crimes, famously so in the rape trials of Alabama's Scottsboro boys. Left wing sports writers even championed baseball's integration long before Jackie Robinson broke in with the Brooklyn Dodgers in 1947.[3]

By the late 1940s, the Cold War had become a civil rights battleground. Simultaneously, as the United States and the Soviet Union confronted each other in an ideological struggle for allies, issues of racism and segregation grew ever more prominent at home. With the old colonial empires breaking apart, East and West vied for the loyalty of new nations. But how could countries in Africa, Asia, or the Middle East put much faith in American-style capitalist democracy when it was clear that our racial minorities were oppressed, denied basic freedoms, even killed when they got out of line? In radio broadcasts to the "Third World," the Soviet Bloc countries constantly raised the issue of American racial hypocrisy. The United States countered with stories of American freedom and black progress. By the time of Emmett Till's murder, the propaganda wars had been going on for years, so it is no surprise that the specter of "Communist subversion" had threaded its way through the Till case.[4]

Founded in 1953, the United States Information Agency was the State Department's news bureau, its clearinghouse for overseas reporting, and more accurately, its propaganda wing. The Cold War necessitated putting a good face on America, so the agency issued a steady stream of favorable news while attempting to counter negative stories. Even as Milam and Bryant awaited their Sumner murder trial, the USIA prepared an "Infoguide" about the Till case for friendly foreign reporters. Mostly a factual outline of events—wolf-whistle, kidnap, murder, funeral, indictment—the two-page document nonetheless advised how to spin the story. It suggested that overseas news agencies of America's allies emphasize three points in their treatment: (1) give the story "minimum reporting," (2) point out that it was a revenge killing, not a lynching, and (3) emphasize the fact that "the majority of Americans condemn and deplore such actions of violence and lawlessness."[5]

Efforts like these were not terribly successful. Foreign coverage of the Till case was both extensive and negative. For instance, days after the murder, Moscow Radio's English language service included in its report Bishop Lewis Ford's remark at Till's funeral: "until the Negroes attain full freedom in America, the US does not lead the rest of the world." A week later, another Moscow broadcast noted that the murder was not an isolated case, that "'racial atrocities' now beset the United States," including cross-burnings, lynchings, and black disenfranchisement. Rumanian announcers pointed out that in several American states, whites refused to abide by the Supreme Court's *Brown* decision, while the "judicial farce" of the Till trial "roused the indignation and protests of millions of people." From Prague came a broadcast beamed to Latin America arguing that the Till case was "proof of the many ways that the reactionary circles in the US violate all democratic rights of the people."[6]

American allies and nonaligned countries were equally critical: the *London News Chronicle*, for example, led with "Third Negro Lynching in Four Months"; Till made headlines in all the Australian papers, none of them good; Mexico's *Ultimas Noticias* called the murder "a crime left over from slavery"; the American embassy in Norway reported that angry press reaction in Oslo had damaged American prestige; in Leopoldville, Congo, came "severe anti-US publicity"; in Paris, newspapers reported that the American singer Josephine Baker co-chaired a meeting of the "International League Against Racism," where a thousand Parisians petitioned the American ambassador, stating that the Sumner verdict, "'consecrates the legality of lynching in the United States and insults the conscience of the civilized world.'"[7]

Americans at first knew little of international interest in the case. With the exception of the African American press, there was scant coverage of the global uproar. The *Memphis Commercial Appeal* was one of the few newspapers to mention that European dailies gave the story prime space throughout the trial. In France, *Le Figaro*, generally friendly to the United States, featured the jury's decision on the front page. So did the *L'Aurore*, which reported the verdict as purely racial in nature, and added sarcastically of Milam and Bryant, "Perhaps even tomorrow these two honest citizens of free America will go back to their usual occupations greeted, respected and the objects of ovations, as though nothing had happened."[8]

The Till story's foreign impact began to register more forcefully two weeks after the acquittal when Congressman Adam Clayton Powell returned from abroad and began making widely reported speeches. Powell's district included Harlem, and he had a clergyman's flare for the dramatic. He told a union-sponsored rally in New York City that no single incident caused as much damage to American prestige abroad as the Till case. In Africa and Europe, from which he had just returned, the Till trial was seen as a "lynching of the Statue of Liberty" and a propaganda victory for international communism. To counter such negative publicity and rehabilitate

America's image abroad, Powell proposed a new underground railroad, designed to bring victims out of the South; he pushed for a boycott of goods made in Mississippi; he insisted that the federal government intervene in the Till case. For months, Powell hammered home the importance of remedial steps to undo the overseas repercussions of Emmett Till's lynching.[9]

But it was the American Jewish Committee's report, "European Reaction to Emmett Till Case in Sumner, Mississippi" that forced many Americans to take note of Till's international impact. The AJC was founded in 1906 in an era of intense anti-Semitism in Eastern Europe. The organization took as its mission the protection of American Jews, many of whom had only recently fled pogroms. For decades the AJC promoted the ideals of equality, tolerance, religious freedom, and social justice for all peoples throughout the world. The committee often made common cause with other American ethnic groups against discrimination, filing a friend-of-the-court brief in *Brown v. Board of Education*, based on the agency's research on prejudice.[10]

In a well-orchestrated presentation complete with a news release, a press conference, and endorsements by such figures as Senator Paul Douglass of Illinois and New York Congressman Emanuel Celler, the AJC published its report on the Till case a month after the Sumner trial ended. The American wire services picked up the story immediately, and news outlets gave it prominent and extensive coverage.[11]

The report consisted mainly of long passages from European newspapers, framed by AJC commentary. The AJC took pains to note that these were all mainstream news sources and, if anything, the liberal and conservative papers were angrier at the verdict than Communist outlets. The AJC's opening sentence was widely quoted: "Europe's reaction to the trial and verdict in Sumner, Miss., was swift, violent and universal." Hundreds of newspapers from every country and political persuasion reported the Till story as it unfolded, often accompanied by editorial condemnations that the AJC described as "unanimous, total and unqualified." Some reports held Mississippi or the South itself accountable, but others "raised sharp doubts about the sincerity of the United States in proclaiming itself as a defender of human rights and oppressed people throughout the world."[12]

The AJC highlighted stories from half-a-dozen foreign newspapers. Words like "scandalous," "monstrous," and "abominable" dominated their headlines. *La Nation Belge* in Brussels declared itself "astonished" that such an incident could take place a hundred years after *Uncle Tom's Cabin*. Rome's *La Giustizia* stated that "the ignoble scar of racism, still so alive in the U.S." undermined American culture. The Communist newsletter *Das Freies Volk*, in Düsseldorf, claimed that "the life of a Negro in Mississippi is not worth a whistle.... Every hysterical woman can send a Negro to the electric chair by claiming that she was insulted," and the editors singled out Secretary of State John Foster Dulles and "other roving preachers of American democracy and freedom who babble about the 'American way of life.'" The anti-Communist Parisian daily, *Franc-Tireur*, said, "It is disquieting to see that in spite of the American laws condemning anti-Negro racism, the vilest passions can triumph unpunished.... Racism like Hitlerism is still spreading its poison over the world." Another Parisian daily, *Radar*, was simply incredulous: "A young Negro, Emmett Till, 14 years old, whistled in admiration at the young white woman, Mrs. Bryant. In Europe, this is a homage which provokes a smile. Here it was the equivalent of a death sentence." And *L'Action* in Tunisia concluded that before pointing to the sins of others, the US must put its own house in order.[13]

Such comments, the AJC argued, revealed that the Till case badly damaged American prestige abroad, overshadowing the universally praised *Brown* decision and necessitating federal action. The AJC made three recommendations to the US Congress: (1) pass new laws to make racial or religious attacks on individuals a violation of their civil liberties, (2) reorganize the Department of Justice to create a civil rights division with its own Assistant Attorney General, and (3) increase FBI personnel to better investigate civil rights violations. Above all, the AJC called on the federal government to guarantee black voting rights and end the Citizens' Councils' assault on civil liberties.[14]

A month after the acquittal in Sumner, the AJC report once again put the Till story in the headlines. The USIA did its best to weather the storm. One public information officer, Francis Hammond, made some suggestions. He wrote to the USIA chief Theodore Streibert just days after the AJC report appeared, arguing that the best way to deal with the Till story would be a steady stream of accurate reporting, which meant sending out news items "depicting the positive side of interracial progress in the U.S.A." An African American and a former professor of Philosophy at Seton Hall University, Hammond specialized in minority affairs. What would really help, he argued, would be a speech or a written statement from President Eisenhower, or even Vice President Richard Nixon, expressing sympathy for Till's family. "It would take some of the sting out of the communist barbs and other criticism of the fact that the government has not spoken out against this crime," Hammond reasoned. The Till murder, he argued, had "neutralized the gains we were making propaganda-wise" since the *Brown* decision; a strong statement against bigotry by the highest American leaders could turn the tide again.[15]

No such statement was forthcoming.

CHAPTER TWENTY-SIX

LOUIS TILL

TWO WEEKS AFTER the Sumner verdict, as Mamie Till Bradley spoke to thousands of people across America, *Life* magazine eulogized her son: "Sleep well, Emmett Till; you will be avenged. You will also be remembered, as long as men have tongues to cry against evil." *Life* draped the murdered lad in robes of Christian martyrdom. Emmett's soul was fashioned by God and given his seal: "This is my son, akin to all others, but unlike any one of them. Like each of my children he is unique, irreplaceable, immortal. I hereby send him among other men, who are his brothers." The child-killers and their abettors sacrificed their own immortal souls, while Emmett lost only his life, just like his soldier-father, "who was killed in France fighting for the American proposition that all men are equal."[1]

The pseudo-religious tone rankled many people, but their revenge came five days later, on October 15, when the staunchly segregationist *Jackson Daily News*, published the following:

> Shocking new information gathered by the *Jackson Daily News* Saturday further debunked some of the "hate Mississippi" propaganda used by the nation's press following the Till Trial at Sumner....It was learned today that Emmett Till's father had raped two Italian women and murdered a third while serving with the United States Army during World War II.

The report added details about Private Till's alleged crimes, including the fact that the army hanged him in Italy on July 2, 1945.[2]

The next day, the *Daily News* published an editorial, "About Till's Father," castigating the northern media for its coverage of father and son: "One after another national publication called the killing a 'lynching' and many so-called great magazines represented Till's rapist-murderer father to be a fallen war hero." The *Daily News* charged that Mamie Till Bradley made the same inference—that her husband gave his life for his country—in her national speaking campaign. Deploying such "rank Negro propaganda" to slander Mississippi, the NAACP raised "fabulous sums of money," by depicting the state as a battleground between the races.[3]

The *Daily News* exaggerated how much Louis Till's name had been invoked during the trial and its aftermath. His service during the war was mentioned, but it was a distinctly minor theme. Mamie Till Bradley mostly avoided discussing her former husband. Still, Louis Till had shadowed his son from the beginning—by his violence against Mamie, by their estrangement, by his absence from his child's life, and finally by his ring on Emmett's finger. Returned to Mamie by the army after the war, the ring became Emmett's, a measure of his maturity, a clue about the man he never knew, a personal emblem with its arcane markings: "L.T., May 25, 1943." The ring proved a sort of talisman; it could not protect Emmett, just as his father never protected him, but it guaranteed that no one could efface the boy's identity. It named him when they pulled his body from the river, rebuked those who lied about the murder.[4]

The army inducted Louis Till on July 9, 1942, listing him as twenty years old, raised in New Madrid, Missouri, five feet ten and 178 pounds. No parents were listed as next of kin, only his uncle, Lee Green, of Argo. Army records also show that although Till was separated from his wife, he had filed paperwork so that she received a dependents' allotment of $22 per month throughout his military service. Six months after his induction, Private Till shipped out to the Mediterranean Theater of Operations, where he served as a stevedore at the port of Civitavecchia, fifty miles north of Rome. In the months before his court-martial, he had been in trouble twice with the army, small infractions, once for being absent without leave (not the same AWOL charge as when he was visiting Mamie in Argo back before he went overseas) and once for leaving an assigned post without a pass.[5]

The *Jackson Daily News* did not mention that Till stood trial for rape and murder with an accomplice, another African American, Private Fred A. McMurray. The allegations against both men were identical, brought under the Ninety-second Article of War. On June 27, 1944, each, with malice aforethought, did "willfully, deliberately, feloniously, unlawfully and with premeditation kill one Anna Zanchi" and each man did "forcibly and feloniously, against her will, have carnal knowledge" of both Benni Lucretzia and Frieda Mari, who were Italian nationals, both pregnant. The defendants pleaded not guilty but were convicted by the military court, and a board of review upheld the convictions. Till and McMurray were hanged in Leghorn, Italy, two months after the war in Europe ended.[6]

Looked at closely, the story told in the court-martial proceedings seems less clear. Four men, including Till, McMurray, Private James Thomas, and an unnamed English soldier had been drinking at their base, around 10:00 p.m. on June 27, 1944. They consumed several bottles of wine, wanted more, and decided to go on a "raid" at a nearby "shack." They knew that a few women lived there. They wore masks and carried guns. Air-raid sirens, searchlights, and a long barrage of antiaircraft fire began just as they barged into the house, the noise and confusion providing them cover. Italian witnesses gave testimony that three "colored men" pushed their way in, pistol-whipped Ernesto Mari, and serially raped his daughter Frieda and her friend Benni. Both women testified that they resisted, that their assailants held them down, beat them, tore their clothes, spread their legs, entered them and ejaculated, saying as they did, "'You lavorare, lavorare!'" (work, work). One of the men, probably Till, threatened to kill them if they talked. He also sought to disguise their identity: "'No neri, bianchi! Tedeschi! Tedeschi!'" roughly, we're white, not black. German! German![7]

Ernesto, Frieda, and Benni all testified that despite the masks, they could see their assailants' hands by the antiaircraft flashes, and that they were black men. However, they could not identify their assailants. After roughly half an hour, the attackers left and split into two groups. About fifteen minutes later, Till and McMurray knocked on another door. "Un poco di vino, per favor," they requested. Told there was no wine, they demanded to come in and check. Trying to protect her son, daughter, and future son-in-law, Anna Zanchi, refused to cooperate, threatened to go to the authorities, yelled at Till and McMurray through the closed door. They shot at the door, a bullet hit Zanchi in the stomach, and she died within hours. Till and McMurray fled, but that same night, while investigating the incident, American military police found a soiled airmail envelope a few feet from Zanchi's house, addressed to Private Fred McMurray.[8]

They picked up McMurray and questioned him for several hours. Confronted with the envelope that placed him at the murder scene, McMurray gave a very detailed oral statement that was transcribed, signed, and entered into evidence. He described a lot of scrounging for wine, sharing of bottles, and brandishing of guns just before the raids.

McMurray told his inquisitors that when the antiaircraft attack began, Till said, "Everybody follow me: If anybody turns back I'll blast him." Till told McMurray that they were going to a house he knew where there were some women; he hoped the air raid might frighten them into sex. "By this time," McMurray told his inquisitors, "all of us were drunk."[9]

According to McMurray, Till went in first—the door was ajar—and used his .45 automatic to beat the old man blocking their way. Then Till and the English soldier said to the two women inside "Fiky-Fiky" and they replied "si," and "vieni qua," come here. Each took one of the soldiers by the hand and led him to a back room. There they found another woman in bed; "Thomas asked this woman to 'fiky-fiky' and she said 'si,'" so the two of them found a room. McMurray described how he now got into one of the beds, when, "Till came up to me with his cock in one hand and the .45 automatic in the other." They argued, but McMurray backed away, "because I was afraid of him." McMurray claimed he was the only one who did not have sex. They all left several minutes later. As they headed back to camp, Till persuaded McMurray to raid another house, this time for more wine. Told there was no vino, Till became abusive. A fight ensued, Till began firing, McMurray ran back toward camp, and moments later, he saw Till running up behind him. They returned to their bunks and went to sleep.[10]

In his confession, McMurray gave up his alleged accomplices, Thomas and Till. Till refused to talk during the whole proceeding, but Thomas confessed to being at the scene and testified at the court-martial. Presumably his cooperation and the fact that he was not present at the murder kept the noose from his neck. Thomas claimed that his only role during the first raid was lighting matches so the others might see what they were doing. His testimony initially downplayed the violence—he said that he saw no blows struck, that Till forcibly pushed one of the women on to the bed, that she did not struggle after that but rather, uttered the words, "Buone cose," good thing. The unidentified English soldier, he added, had sex with both women, and Thomas also described one of the women taking his own hand and asking if he would be back tomorrow. Thomas initially painted the whole liaison as more consensual than forced, but by the end of his testimony, he acknowledged that the women resisted Till and McMurray and that both men flashed their guns during the raid.[11]

Thomas and McMurray each did his best to deflect culpability. McMurray depicted himself as an unwilling accomplice, while Thomas's self-portrayal was as a guy who just showed up to light some matches. Both said that the sex they witnessed was consensual, but then described acts of force and violence. McMurray stated clearly that Louis Till instigated both raids, and repeatedly threatened the other soldiers with his weapon. McMurray and Thomas each claimed that the other had "carnal knowledge" of Frieda and Benni, though the women themselves described what can only be called a gang rape to the court, not consensual sex.

To muddle things even more, one witness to the murder, John Masi, said in his pretrial testimony that one of the assailants was black, one white. Then, a few months later, during the court-martial itself, he testified they were both African American, that he had spent twelve years in America and that he recognized their dialects as black English. While McMurray claimed he tried to stop the murder of Anna Zanchi, the military police found shell casings and bullet holes from both .45 and .32 caliber weapons in the dead woman's home; Till carried a .45, McMurray a .32. The US Army was not interested in the English soldier; he remained unnamed throughout the proceedings, and mostly invisible. One thing that comes through clearly is that everyone agreed that the largest of the assailants, the most aggressive and violent, the ringleader who carried a .45 caliber army pistol was Louis Till.[12]

During World War II, hundreds of cases like this ended up in military courts. As the fighting devastated much of Europe, women in the war zones sometimes resorted to prostitution to survive. Occasionally, in their towns and villages, it was safer to make false accusations of sexual assault rather than be exposed as promiscuous and so dishonored. Such cases are complicated, hard to read, and we certainly do not know enough about this particular one to determine exactly what happened. Maybe Thomas and McMurray were telling the truth, that Benni and Frieda did not resist the G.I.'s sexual advances; maybe their "shack" was more brothel than home. Unlikely, but possible.[13]

It is difficult to take seriously the claim that what happened in Civitavecchia was not rape. Men going to brothels do not usually wear masks or brandish guns. They do not plan "raids" where they force their way in and beat whoever gets in their way. Benni Lucretzia was sufficiently traumatized that she miscarried the next day; Frieda Mari was far along in her pregnancy and ended up giving birth prematurely. The same with the second raid; needless to say, unwillingness to share wine with strangers is not a legitimate reason to shoot people. Perhaps viewed through several bottles, the events seemed to the perpetrators like recreational sex for consenting adults, but the evidence makes the court-martial verdict reasonable.[14]

Unsurprisingly, the *Jackson Daily News'* rape-and-murder report received broad national coverage. But the whole Till story had become so fraught that even this fact, the extent of the coverage, was in dispute. The Citizens'

Councils issued a press release saying that not a single northern news outlet carried the *Daily News* story. The San Francisco–based newsletter, *Right*, castigated the "red and liberal press" for its "orgiastic shrieks of denunciation and hatred against the people of the South over their handling of the Till case," while the fact that "Till Sr. was hanged as a savage murderer and rapist seems to be overlooked by the lords of the press." Six months later, an article by William Bradford Huie in *Confidential* magazine repeated the erroneous charge that the national press "ducked the truth." The claim was patently false—the story was picked up by the Associated Press and the International News Service, and widely reprinted by northern and southern papers alike, and also by African American ones.[15]

But how did the *Jackson Daily News* obtain the story? More precisely, how did they get such detailed information, including the names of the victims, the charges, the place and date of the proceedings? The army withholds such sensitive information; military records like Till's are protected sources, not readily available to the press. The answer is that Mississippi's two senators, James Eastland and John Stennis, used their offices to obtain the documents from the army, then they passed them on to the *Daily News*. Although evasive when newsmen questioned him about his role in releasing the Till documents, Eastland wrote to one Fred L. Boon, chairman of a conservative political organization based in Los Angeles, "I cooperated with the *Jackson Daily News* in running down an anonymous tip which they received." Eastland told Boon that his goal was to discredit the NAACP, Mamie Till Bradley, liberal northerners, and all who sought to undermine segregation and the South. "It is a tragedy that our State is being subjected at present to so much vilification and calumny. We are going to fight back with every legal means at our disposal." And some illegal ones too.[16]

There was more at stake than simply Mississippi's reputation. William Henry Huff, the NAACP attorney who represented Mamie Till Bradley, suggested that the timing of the disclosure was meant to influence the grand jury sitting in Greenwood. Within just three weeks, they would evaluate the kidnapping charges against Milam and Bryant and decide whether to indict them. Huff told reporters, "Article III, Section 3 of the U.S. Constitution sets out that there shall be no corruption of blood. Whatever the lad's father did does not inure to the lad. This argument about the father coming from high sources is an attempt to condone the lynching of this child." Huff suggested that if Mississippi officials were so worried about the state's good name, they should stop filibustering against anti-lynching legislation.[17]

While Huff maintained that the *Daily News* story discredited neither Louis Till's child nor his former wife, that was precisely what the disclosure was meant to do. "Like father, like son," or, "the apple doesn't fall too far from the tree," or, "birds of a feather usually fly together," or "the sins of the fathers are visited on the sons," were the sorts of associations that Louis Till's story evoked. The "biology is destiny" assumptions about race that Judge Brady and his ilk espoused and that washed anew over the South after the *Brown* decision led directly to that conclusion. The image of Emmett Till as a sexual assailant seemed much more plausible if Louis Till was a "savage murderer and rapist." No one had to speak any of this; such ideas were just below the surface, deeply held, easily stirred.[18]

Before and after the trial in Sumner, Mamie Till Bradley never said much about Louis, beyond that he died in Europe during the war. She insisted she did not know about his crimes or his execution, only that the army sent her a telegram stating that Louis was dead, then a letter with the phrase "willful misconduct," followed by his personal effects, but no further clarification despite her requests.[19]

That is not quite the whole story. Back in 1948, Bradley's attorney, Joseph Tobias, had written on her behalf to the army. Tobias requested an "opportunity to examine all processes in this matter as the wife and child are in straitened circumstances." In other words, at issue was whether they were eligible for veterans' benefits. The army considered such requests private, and usually the family of a court-martialed soldier was not eligible. According to the *Memphis Commercial Appeal*, the army sent Tobias a copy of the court-martial report, a fact confirmed years later by the army. We will never know for sure whether Tobias shared the documents with his client, but suggestions that Bradley was less than truthful about Louis Till's death mattered now. Besides, as a public relations matter, the very fact that she married someone like him called her judgment into question, regardless of whether she knew how he died.[20]

As with every other part of the story, editorial pages went at it. The *Danville Virginia Bee*, for example, reminded readers that Emmett Till's Chicago funeral was "an anti-South orgie [*sic*]" and argued that Louis Till's crimes should put an end to the NAACP's "eulogies and oratorical flights of fancy." Silence was golden: "The whole nation would benefit and interracial relations would improve if the Emmett Till case, like the body of the slain youth, is permitted to rest in peace." The *Montgomery Advertiser* drew an analogy—Mamie and Emmett were no more responsible for the murder and rapes in Italy than the South was for Emmett Till's death.[21]

Northern newspapers mostly carried the court-martial story without comment, but the black press fired back. The *Baltimore Afro-American* accused the *Jackson Daily News* of suggesting that Louis Till's crime, "somehow explains, justifies, and absolves Mississippi for the foul manner with which it dealt with his son.... The inference is as dastardly as the deed." The *Chicago Defender* put the issue in a wider context, calling the Louis Till story a "smear campaign." The *Defender* added that the elder Till "was court-martialed and hanged under a Jim-Crow Army" and that often "battlefield courts-martial were... improperly prepared" and based on "flimsy evidence."[22]

The *Defender* had a point. During World War II black newspapers crusaded against the segregated military, singling out racial discrimination in courts-martial. Certainly, the Louis Till trial was no paragon of good judicial form. The evidence placing him at the rape and murder scenes came mainly from his accomplices, Privates McMurray and Thomas. They had good reason to deflect culpability from themselves and onto someone else. The army was wary of such evidence, a point made by the Review Board that examined the transcript and confirmed the verdict. During the trial, Till's and McMurray's council objected that, "except for the uncorroborated testimony of an accomplice (Thomas), no competent evidence was presented identifying the accused as the perpetrators of crimes alleged." The Italian witnesses failed to identify anyone, forensic evidence was weak. Defense council moved to dismiss the charges, but the court overruled the motion. Three months later, the trial's Review Board, citing the *Manual for Courts-Martial*, declared, "A conviction may be based on the uncorroborated testimony of an accomplice, but such testimony is of doubtful integrity and is to be considered with great caution." So noted, then ignored. The Review Board upheld the conviction.[23]

Even if we assume that Thomas and McMurray told the truth, that Louis Till, a man with a violent and abusive past, indeed committed rape and murder in Italy, there is still more to the story, and while the *Defender's* point about the Jim Crow Army does not exonerate him, it helps explain what happened in Civitavecchia. In fact, the role of race during the war was more complex and formative than even the *Defender* said.[24]

Recent historical studies make it clear that while America waged "the Good War" in Europe against the Nazis and while most G.I.s fought honorably, soldier misconduct was not uncommon. On the one hand, the US Army had a very strict policy against rape long before it became a war crime under international law. Where other countries sometimes encouraged rape as a means of terror or a right of conquest, the US military assumed that good relations with civilian populations in occupied territories was essential. But policy and implementation are two different things. Under the best of circumstances, rape is an underreported crime. In war zones in the 1940s, there is every reason to believe that only a tiny fraction of rapes committed by soldiers made it to the courts-martial. Just over nine hundred American cases were tried in Europe throughout the war. Using a rough criminologists' rule-of-thumb, the sociologist J. Robert Lilly calculates that only about 5 percent of actual rapes came to trial, meaning that the number of rapes committed by G.I.s was probably closer to eighteen thousand.[25]

This of course is only the roughest estimate, but here is the point: In the entire European theater of war, approximately 9.5 percent of servicemen were African American. The army executed seventy men for rape and/or murder. Fifty-five, 80 percent, were black. In France alone, 180 total cases of rape were brought in military courts, and 130 of the defendants were African American, nearly 75 percent. In the Mediterranean and North African Theaters of Operations, where again fewer than 10 percent of our troops were black, out of twenty-seven executions, fourteen were African American, more than half. Scholars further report that the tendency to disproportionately arrest and convict African Americans for all Military Code violations was especially skewed for sex crimes.[26]

There is not much research on Italy, where Till and McMurray met their ends, but work done on France, Germany, and England suggests some reasons for the disproportionate numbers. First, because southerners were thought to have the most experience with blacks, to "understand" them best, whites from below the Mason-Dixon Line were deliberately made commanding officers over African American companies, first in training camp, then in the war zones. This meant, of course, that many stereotypes about black men—their proneness to violence and their taste for white women, especially when under the influence of alcohol—became part of everyday army lore. Commanding officers were the very ones most likely to bring charges against troops. These same commanders often acted as defense counsel in courts-martial. Those who have studied the subject argue that most of the accused had very poor representation at their trials.[27]

Equally important, the segregated army usually kept black troops from the front. Most of them, like Louis Till, worked in support capacities. Till was in the transportation corps and listed as a stevedore, a dockworker, loading and unloading ships. Such assignments were the norm for African Americans. They worked as laborers in rigidly segregated units, and rarely were promoted above the rank of private. This meant that black soldiers spent more time in contact with local civilian populations, with more opportunity for casual mingling, including sexual liaisons. The American military outlawed any kind of "legitimate" sexual trade during the war, such as legalized brothels, so when young men looked around for sexual outlets, confusion reigned. The sex trade was underground, war's deprivations turned some women to prostitution to survive, language barriers made it hard to know what was being offered or refused, Americans were armed, women were needy.[28]

And something else: black soldiers often believed that Europe was a less racist place than the American South, that white women were more open to sex with them. This last point was doubly ironic, since there was plenty of racism to go around. Countries like France and Italy—imperialist nations with African colonies—had their own traditions of viewing black people as savage, hypersexual, and inferior, and it is clear from courts-martial records that prejudice sometimes nudged European women to accuse black men of crimes. This dovetailed with one final point: the historian Mary Louise Roberts suggests that the American command was determined to maintain the image of their soldiers as manly, clean, fighters for freedom. This was easier to do if crime came to be seen as a problem created mostly by black troops. Simply put, the bar was far lower for successfully prosecuting African American men for many crimes—especially rape—than white ones, because black men were expendable.[29]

Was Louis Till guilty of rape and murder? We will never know for sure. There was good evidence against him, though less convincing than the evidence against his son's killers. It is easy to imagine how defense attorneys in a civilian criminal court would cast doubt on the prosecution case against Louis Till. The main evidence against him was two eyewitnesses trying to save their own skins. The defense might have gotten an acquittal, assuming notions of race and sex and state loyalty and fears of outside agitators failed to poison the jurors' minds.[30]

But guilty or not, the story of Louis Till's court-martial and execution mattered profoundly. For those who wanted to believe Emmett Till himself was a would-be rapist who got what he deserved, here indeed was the missing link back to savagery. In the world of Judge Brady and the Citizens' Councils, the lesson could not be clearer. Even for many of those who saw Emmett Till's story as emblematic of the horrors of racism, his father's end gave them pause. Purely in the realm of optics, it was harder to think of the son as a martyr, much less a Christlike figure, when the newspapers blared out that his father was no freedom fighter but a moral monster. Senators Eastland and Stennis knew exactly what they were doing when they resurrected Louis Till's ghost.

CHAPTER TWENTY-SEVEN

EVILS SUCH AS THE TILL CASE ARE THE RESULT OF A SYSTEM

DESPITE THE REVELATIONS about her ex-husband, Mamie Till Bradley continued her tour through October 1955, visiting Grand Rapids, Des Moines, Omaha, Baltimore, and Indianapolis, drawing enormous crowds and raising money. She was hospitalized in early November for what the Associated Press described as "nervous strain." Just as she recovered and was ready to begin a two-week swing through the West Coast, the NAACP cancelled all her appearances. Money was the issue, according to Roy Wilkins's office. The original agreement called for the NAACP branch office in each town to pay her expenses and include an honorarium of at least $100, usually $150. In mid-October, Bradley asked that her father be allowed to accompany her. She wanted him with her for companionship, security, and to manage details. She also asked that he be paid, all of which the NAACP agreed to. Then, two days before the start of her trip, acting through an agent, Bradley asked for $5,000 for the western tour.[1]

Roy Wilkins immediately cancelled her engagements—a dozen West Coast speeches, including one at the sixteen-thousand-seat San Francisco Cow Palace—and refused to authorize future appearances. He explained in a letter to Milwaukee's branch president Dale Phillips, "The NAACP could not submit to what was virtually an extortion demand, made at the last minute in the belief that since our plans had been made we would have to accede to her demands."[2]

Mrs. Bradley, of course saw it differently. Having left her job, she had no income, and her debts were mounting. It must have pained her to make so little from the exhausting travel while newspapers said that her speeches raised tens of thousands of dollars. It did not help Roy Wilkins's mood when she told the press that she received living expenses only from the NAACP, conveniently forgetting the honoraria. Wilkins persuaded Mose Wright to pick up the western tour. Wright spoke to a large and enthusiastic crowd in Seattle on November 9. "He is not only the central hero of the trial," Wilkins wrote to promote Wright, "but is a country preacher who is articulate, is a colorful character, and tells a story that registers well with audiences."[3]

Wilkins was pleased to be rid of Mamie Till Bradley. Although the press carried stories about fabulous donations to the "Fight for Freedom Fund," the NAACP records revealed more modest amounts, often under a thousand dollars per rally. The figures are rough and incomplete, but from early October through early November, they show Bradley raising $12,400—far from the $100,000 the newspapers said she had raised—while her honoraria and expenses consumed about $4,500. Moreover, at the ten or so meetings where Congressman Diggs, Mose Wright, or Ruby Hurley appeared without Bradley, donations did not appear to suffer much. In other words, in financial terms alone, it was unclear that she was worth the extra money her agent asked for.[4]

But there is more to this story. Immediately after the trial in Sumner ended, a few ad hoc Till rallies came together before the NAACP took the matter in hand. Bradley spoke at these early rallies, which were cosponsored by radical organizations. "The left wing is already on the Till Case 'bandwagon,'" Roy Wilkins wrote to his branch officers. "This is further reason for keeping our lines straight and maintaining constant supervision and control over our several mass rallies."[5]

Going back to the late 1940s and through the red-baiting McCarthy era of the '50s, civil rights organizations and unions were terrified of being tarred with the Communist brush. Under laws like the 1940 Smith Act and the 1950 McCarran Act, the federal government had the legal power to destroy those institutions. The radicals who helped build progressive organizations now found themselves purged from them, and Wilkins had no intention of letting leftists back in. He hastily arranged a meeting in New York with Bradley on October 8 to explain the need to steer clear of the radicals. In St. Louis the next day, she declared that though she was willing to go wherever people would listen, she did not want to "wind up in a hot bed of Communists," and so the NAACP's national office would vet all of her future speaking engagements. The issue attracted scattered newspaper coverage: "Those who were fighting for justice in the Emmett Till case were reminded to be careful that their cause was not perverted by Red 'crusaders,'" warned one columnist about Communists and their dupes.[6]

After this shaky start came the news of Louis Till. When the story broke, Wilkins was relieved that he personally had never fallen into the trap of calling Emmett's father a war hero. But why had Mamie Till Bradley not warned others, said something about her ex-husband? And if she really did not know about his rape-and-murder court-martial, how could she be so ignorant? Certainly, marrying such a man and bearing his child complicated her story, made her appear naïve and foolish, Wilkins believed. And even if the charges against Louis Till were false, his story had a life of its own now. He was a public-relations nightmare, the very embodiment of the stereotyped black predator.[7]

Beyond the problems with money, Communists, and Louis Till, Mamie Till Bradley and her speeches fit uneasily with the NAACP's style and mission. Wilkins discussed some of this in private correspondence. The organization's biggest fight was against Jim Crow segregation, disenfranchisement, and the violence that enforced white supremacy. Congress and the courts were the main battleground. "This is a long struggle and may not appeal to those who are angry over [the] Till murder," Wilkins wrote to Junius C. Austin, one of Chicago's most prominent ministers. Wilkins carefully distinguished between atrocities like Emmett Till's murder and the larger context that enabled them. He was willing to use the Till story in the battle for civil rights, but he cautioned others about dwelling on the emotions of the moment at the expense of pushing for legal change, for desegregation, and for voting rights.[8]

Wilkins was most explicit in a long letter to the Reverend J. Raymond Henderson of Los Angeles's Second Baptist Church. Henderson was an NAACP stalwart, and his church sponsored an enormous Till rally headlined by Dr. T. R. M. Howard in mid-October. Henderson found it frustrating to work with the NAACP's national office. He asked what the NAACP was doing about the Till case since the killers had gone free, and, more pointedly, he wrote, "How shall we answer critics who say, 'the Assoc. is doing nothing—but using the case to raise money.'" Wilkins barely contained his anger. "Perhaps the great outrage and intense emotions involved in the Till case have prevented our people from seeing things clearly."[9]

For five more pages, Wilkins lectured Henderson. Emmett Till was dead. No rally could bring him back. Crimes like murder and kidnapping were matters for state courts. Not only was there nothing the NAACP could do about these things, but the very appearance of interfering in local affairs was a major tactical mistake. Although there was much talk of a civil suit—Mamie Till Bradley's attorney, William Henry Huff, spoke of suing Milam and Bryant for $100,000, even a million dollars, and later the Illinois chapter of the ACLU considered its own litigation—careful study indicated there was no chance of succeeding in Mississippi courts. The NAACP, Wilkins wrote, was not passively standing aside; there was simply nothing to be done.[10]

If any good came out of the Till tragedy, Wilkins wrote Henderson, it would be at the federal level. The key was for Congress to pass new laws. Legal change was the NAACP's main long-term strategy through court cases brought by their Legal Defense Fund headed by Thurgood Marshall and through lobbying for new legislation. Wilkins himself pounded away at these larger themes when he spoke at Till rallies, where he quickly moved from the acquittal in Sumner to black disenfranchisement, which made that "not guilty" verdict inevitable because it stacked the jury with white men. Wilkins told Henderson, "We do claim, and we insist, that evils such as the Till case are the result of a system in Mississippi and elsewhere in the South and that the only guarantee against more Till cases is the smashing of the system."[11]

The system was labor exploitation and Jim Crow segregation, abrogation of civil rights and, economic coercion, all of it enforced by corrupt laws, police, courts, and prisons. The solution was federal intervention through a powerful new civil rights division in the Justice Department, backed by anti-lynching, antidiscrimination, and voting rights bills. The latter especially would open up the court system, make politicians responsible to their whole constituencies, and blunt the power of the Citizens' Councils. Legal change was the real goal, Wilkins insisted. It took money, lots of it, to research issues, bring law suits, lobby Congress, and educate the public. That was where the Till case came in, Wilkins believed, but that was all: "An emotional outburst, no matter how great, is good only as ammunition to attack the basic evils.... We can't save the Till boy and we can't execute Milam and Bryant. We can work toward the day when we will not be confronted again with such a frustrating experience."[12]

Wilkins was willing to harness the power of the Till story to mobilize people, but deep outpourings of feelings made him uneasy. He was at pains to make sure that everyone understood that the goal of the rallies was not to raise money for the widow, or to pursue legal action against the killers. The NAACP was in it for the long haul, law and policy were its tools, the courts and federal agencies its venues. The agony of a martyred son and the heartbreak of a grieving mother exemplified the evils they fought, but, finally, people like Emmett and Mamie Till were small players in a large game. The phrasing Wilkins used publicly and repeatedly to explain why he would never consent to pay $5,000 to Mrs. Bradley—"The NAACP does not handle such matters on a commercial basis,"—is telling. He feared appearing to exploit raw emotions and cheapen the tragedy. Certainly, he wondered at Mrs. Bradley's need for an agent, and her vulnerability to those whose motives were far from pure. "Mamie's Circus," some southerners called the rallies, and Wilkins worried that there was an element of truth there.[13]

Mamie Till Bradley wrote to him on November 9, the day she was supposed to appear in San Francisco: "I feel very bad that the opportunity to talk for the Association would be taken from me," and she offered to restore the original cost-of-living-plus-honorarium arrangement. She described her motives with jolting words, "I set out to trade the blood of my child for the betterment of my race," and she had no desire to deviate from that course. "Please let me go forward for NAACP," she concluded, calling it her duty, and adding, "I would not want it said I did anything to shirk it."[14]

Wilkins wrote a long chilly response, detailing his understanding of their original arrangement, why he said "no" to paying the $5,000, and rejecting her offer to come back to work for his organization. Wilkins objected to her language—that the opportunity to be a speaker had been "taken" from her—and to her unwillingness to address the reasons for their falling out. He said she was paid over $2,000 plus expenses for her month of lecturing in October, a generous amount. And he signed off rather archly, saying that the NAACP was always available should she need consultation or advice.[15]

The split was a painful one and covered extensively by the African American press. The *Defender* described the rumors in the black community spreading against Bradley—that she capitalized on her son's slaying, became an arrogant celebrity, was filled with self-importance. But the newspaper argued that "faulty communications" caused her break with the NAACP, that greedy handlers took advantage of her, that she was ill-prepared for all that hit her beginning last summer. A *St. Louis Argus* editorial was sure that the two sides—Mrs. Bradley with her dignity and courage, the NAACP with its deeply held principles of justice—would settle their differences quickly.[16]

They never did. By December, The *Pittsburgh Courier* characterized her as at once "bitter" yet still hopeful of reconciliation. She was on her way to speaking engagements in Brooklyn, New Haven, and Jersey City, back on the road, on her own tour now, with day-to-day affairs managed by her father, who expressed his own anger at the NAACP for exploiting Emmett Till and Mamie: "It seems to me that as long as my daughter can be useful to them, everything's all right, but the minute she asks for something, it's a different matter."[17]

Wilkins had become the executive director of the NAACP just six months before the Till murder, and he would prove very hierarchical in his leadership style. He often grew dismissive of those he disagreed with, especially women. Wilkins and his organization were at home in the male world of Washington, of Congress, of courts and federal agencies, of insiders, experts and professionals. Temperament and policy merged here, for Wilkins was a little wary of grassroots organizers, fearful of more militant and radical elements in the movement, most comfortable with top-down reforms that came from leaders in business and government.[18]

Wilkins's emphasis on law and policy sometimes seemed a little cold and his approach to change one-dimensional. Going back to its founding in 1909, including its splendid magazine *Crisis*, the NAACP always emphasized civil rights as an enlightenment project, thoughtful, logical, rational. But as a mass movement, the freedom struggle increasingly needed strong elements of faith and emotion, anger and love. It needed not just position papers on legislation and court decisions but also visceral stories like Emmett Till's flesh-and-blood lynching. It needed great legal minds like Thurgood Marshall, but also people like Mamie Till Bradley, a loving, respectable, responsible mother who could bear witness to the sorrows inflicted by racism.[19]

The Emmett Till rallies continued on two tracks into 1956—those sponsored by the NAACP and Mamie Till Bradley's separate tour. They all drew large crowds, mostly in African American communities, and they helped bring people and cash into the struggle. Nonetheless, the rift between Roy Wilkins and Mamie Till Bradley exemplified a fissure in the movement. Mrs. Bradley embodied the aggrieved mother; she staked her claim to the nation's sympathy on it. Her anguish at her son's martyrdom gave her a voice, a woman's voice, to speak out about the oppression of her people. Her's was a moral stance, resonating with Christian imagery: Christ's agony and Mary's suffering, the betrayal of innocence and the spilling of guiltless blood. Turning pain into testimony, Mamie Till Bradley raised a prophetic cry against racism and brutality, and she spoke as the guardian of all children. She articulated a distinctly female perspective on the movement, one focused on families, a churchly maternalist vision. Above all, she was a witness against evil who compelled others not to look away: "Let the people see what they did to my boy."[20]

The NAACP could seem a little bloodless and technical, with its emphasis on law and policy, its role in brokering deals with powerful insiders. Its leaders tended to be middle class, and certainly Wilkins was not completely

comfortable with the deep emotions stirred by the Till rallies. He feare
that self-righteousness would become an end in itself, that it too easily
sated people before the real struggle even began. Policy changes—voting
rights, anti-lynching laws, Constitutional protections, a Justice Department
Civil Rights Bureau—mattered most to him.

These two ways of thinking about the growing freedom struggle—on
the one hand, a moral drama, redolent of faith and family, played out in
the streets, and on the other hand, a political, judicial and legislative
process—were neither contradictory nor mutually exclusive. Usually
they reinforced each other, moral imperatives powering instrumental
goals, the masses pushing the lawmakers. But in early November 1955,
Mamie Till Bradley's request for more money and Roy Wilkins's response
exposed deeper conflicts between them and hidden fissures in their
movement.[21]

CHAPTER TWENTY-EIGHT

AS FAR AS I KNOW, THE CASE IS CLOSED

MOSES WRIGHT PROMISED Sheriff George Smith that he would be back in Greenwood on November 7 when the Leflore County grand jury took up kidnapping charges against Milam and Bryant. "You won't even have to issue a subpoena for me," Wright told Smith.[1]

A week before the grand jury met, the *New York Times'* John Popham returned to Mississippi and wrote a column about what lay ahead. He reminded his readers that Mississippians initially reacted to the murder with horror, but then, "the touchy race relations phase...overshadowed all other considerations." Popham repeated the dominant line of the southern press: "Outside organizations" like the NAACP started throwing around the word "lynching"; obscene letters swearing revenge poured in; public opinion turned, and the acquittal surprised no one.[2]

Racial feelings once again threatened to defeat justice. A month previous, Popham argued that a kidnapping indictment would have been easy to obtain. Now, however, citizens' desire to see justice done was displaced by outrage over *Life* magazine's eulogy for Emmett Till, by the massive and emotional Till rallies in the North, and by the revelation of Louis Till's crimes. Especially the latter, Popham wrote, "has had powerful impact on broad community opinion in this area and is perhaps the most discussed item of the case at this time." Mississippians had dug in their heels: "Particular debates over NAACP, segregated schools, Negro voting, Citizens' Council activities and 'outside criticism' have become envisioned here as part of a great 'propaganda campaign' against Mississippi."[3]

Popham accepted too readily the notion that Mississippians merely responded to outside criticisms. Northerners, Communists, the NAACP, and the federal government muddied Mississippi waters, but not so much as Mississippians themselves when they decided that The Southern Way of Life meant segregation, and that segregation must be defended at all costs. The Till case never was a simple murder unencumbered by racism. On the contrary, it was a racial honor killing, a concept with a long, bloody history forged across decades. To keep insisting that all would have been well if not for outside interference was an old and willful lie, and to believe that lie took a powerful act of culturally-induced ignorance.[4]

Out on bail, J. W. Milam went back to Glendora to run harvesting machines and manage black laborers. Roy Bryant reopened the grocery store in Money, though at the end of October, having been abandoned by his black clientele, he advertised it for sale in the *Greenwood Morning Star*. Meanwhile, two attorneys prepared to present the kidnapping case to the Leflore County grand jury, Stanny Sanders from Indianola, thirty-six years old, the prosecutor for Mississippi's fourth judicial district, and, assisting him, John J. Frasier Jr., a thirty-year-old attorney for the county. There was no need to prove the identity of the body since there was no murder charge. The jurors' only question was whether Emmett Till had been kidnapped and by whom. If they chose to indict the brothers, they also must decide which kidnapping statute applied: the one carrying the death penalty, the other a maximum ten-year sentence. Four witnesses were expected to appear, Sheriff George Smith and Deputy John Ed Cothran, Mose Wright, and Willie Reed.[5]

The grand jury, twenty citizens strong, reviewed several cases between Monday, November 7, and Wednesday, November 9. Wright and Reed came back to Greenwood on Sunday night and stayed with friends. Prosecutor Sanders mentioned to the press the possibility that black citizens might serve on the jury, but when the court narrowed the venire of sixty-four men down to twenty, no African Americans remained, so once again the jury consisted entirely of white males. The courtroom scene was nothing like Sumner. The Greenwood courthouse was much larger and could have better accommodated a show like the one that took place in September. But grand juries met in private, and those who participated were asked to say nothing to anyone about their deliberations. A handful of newsmen came to Greenwood, including representatives from the major wire services, but compared to the murder trial six weeks earlier, coverage was quite limited.[6]

The newsmen played a waiting game. The grand jury revealed their decisions only at the end of the session, so there was little to report. Daily coverage mostly reprised the scene six weeks earlier in Tallahatchie County. News stories repeated Congressman Diggs's description of the Sumner trial as "sheer perjury and fantastic twisting of the facts," and the Citizens' Councils charge that the NAACP was a Communist organization. The *Chicago Defender* concluded, "The world waits for the verdict from Greenwood as millions ask: Did Emmett Till die in vain?"[7]

The jurors took up the Till case on Tuesday afternoon, November 8. Mose Wright and Willie Reed sat outside the jury room, chatting, dozing, waiting. "The two negroes said they had no fear of being harmed in Greenwood, but seemed nervous and anxious to return to Chicago," one observer wrote. Attorney Frasier called Wright at 2:21 p.m.; he was with the jurors for twenty-four minutes. Then at 3:15 p.m. came Willie Reed's turn, and he spent twenty minutes inside. Then the jurors recalled Mose Wright for a brief time. Finally came Deputy Sheriff Cothran, then Sheriff Smith, each spending just moments in the jury room. All told, hearing testimony and deliberating, the jurors spent about three hours on the case. We do not know what questions they asked the witnesses or what they said to each other. They had a copy of the trial transcript from Sumner but had no time to study it. They adjourned Tuesday afternoon.[8]

The grand jurors heard other cases into Wednesday, then late that day the circuit judge Arthur Jordan addressed the few reporters and photographers in his courtroom. "Gentlemen, in the case you are interested, there was a no bill returned." No true bill meant the jurors chose not to charge Milam and Bryant. Their docket had included thirty-four cases, and they handed down twenty-seven true bills. An indictment required a dozen votes out of twenty. "That's the end of the case as far as this county is concerned," Prosecutor Stanny Sanders told the newsmen. Asked if the Leflore grand jury could decide otherwise in the future, Sanders said simply, "As far as I know, the case is closed," and he added "beyond that I can make no statement." The grand jury foreman June Broadway told reporters that he would like to comment but was sworn to secrecy. And that was that.[9]

Opinions about the decision ran in familiar channels. The *Greenwood Morning Star* argued that Emmett Till molested Carolyn Bryant, grabbed her, made indecent proposals. Any husband would protect his wife under those circumstances. If Roy Bryant had been present during their encounter in his store, he would have shot Till dead on the spot, and no southern jury and few northern ones for that matter would indict him for it. The *Jackson Daily News* blamed the usual suspects—the NAACP, the Supreme Court, the northern press—for turning the rest of America against the South. Mississippi reacted with defiance, "and the sooner the people of the North recognize this fact, the sooner we in Mississippi will overcome our antagonism and revive our former friendly attitude toward the Negro people."[10]

But much of the southern press was not so sure this time. Far more than in Sumner, the Greenwood decision gave editors pause. They agreed that outsiders had provoked the region, and they certainly remained opposed to desegregation, but they feared Mississippi looked foolish to the rest of America. The *Memphis Commercial Appeal* argued that if men broke into private residences and took people away with impunity, "it could mean that no home is safe from invasion, no person safe from violence at the hands of others." The *Florence (SC) Morning News* said the decision gave the South the worst black eye since the lynching era, and it noted that the Greenwood jurors slunk away from the courtroom, as if to acknowledge that blacks could not get justice. The northern press and the African American newspapers agreed, summed up by a *Milwaukee Journal* editorial that called the grand jury's decision, "sheer viciousness and consummate bigotry."[11]

Local officials deflected criticism by blaming the witnesses. "I've been in this business for 22 years and I know what you can get and what you can't get," Sheriff Smith told reporters. Negroes, "have their rights just like anyone else and if they won't talk I can't make them." Stanny Sanders added that he received "no cooperation" from these witnesses. Such claims at best were disingenuous. Wright and Reed feared for their lives, yet they came back to Mississippi and gave eyewitness testimony placing the accused with the victim. Smith and Sanders also complained that Mamie Till Bradley refused to come down, and that she dissuaded Emmett's cousins—Simeon Wright and Wheeler Parker, both of whom witnessed the abduction—from going. Again, this was nonsense. After Sumner, why would Bradley expect a different result in Greenwood? And why would she and her family put those young boys back in harm's way? Besides, none of their testimony was essential. Milam and Bryant had confessed to Sheriff Smith and Deputy Cothran, more than enough evidence for a trial. Yet Sheriff Smith told reporters, "I don't think . . . the Negroes wanted an indictment. They want something to hold up as an example of injustice to keep attacking us on." The charge was false and absurd. This hardly seemed the same man who acquitted himself very professionally throughout the initial investigation and murder trial—that is, in a county not his own, where he need not worry about voters and reelections.[12]

So why, with confessions and eyewitness testimony, did the grand jury decide not to issue a true bill? Perhaps, eyeing Sumner, the jurors decided that there was no point to it, since a criminal court would probably free Milam and Bryant anyway. Maybe it was just like the *Jackson Daily News* suggested, that the grand jurors decided that their state was not going to be pressured by outsiders. Or it could be that the jury felt the case already had been adjudicated sufficiently in Sumner, that there was no reason to reopen the wound. Or perhaps, as John Popham hinted, the story of Louis Till, the war hero-turned-rapist, pushed them over the edge. Maybe it was as simple as this: anything that struck a blow for black political, economic, legal, or social equality was unacceptable. Still, even with the questions raised in Sumner about Milam and Bryant's confessions, about Willie Reed's reliability, and Mose Wright's night vision, the evidence for a mere indictment on kidnapping charges was quite strong, just not strong enough in Greenwood, Mississippi, in the fall of 1955 before a jury of white men.[13]

Shut out from the NAACP rallies, Mamie Till Bradley bore one more burden: "Just about everything has run out on me now," she told reporters when asked about the grand jury decision. How, she asked, could they fail to indict? She considered filing a civil suit against Mississippi and against Milam and Bryant, but the NAACP's William Henry Huff no longer represented her, and she could not afford her own lawyer. What rankled most of all, Mrs. Bradley said, was the charge, repeated like a mantra in the Delta, that justice failed because of outside agitators, northerners, uppity blacks, and radicals. If only we'd kept our mouths shut and not been so demanding, then the good white people of Mississippi would have done the right thing. That, on top of everything else, was too insulting to bear.[14]

However, Mamie Till Bradley was wrong, not everything had run out on her. Later in the week after the Leflore grand jury's decision, she was out speaking on her own tour. In Flint, Michigan, she stood before five thousand people at a rally called by Buick Local 599 of the United Auto Workers. She was back on the road. And she would not stop speaking out about her son's death until the day she died.[15]

CHAPTER TWENTY-NINE

WE CALL UPON THE PRESIDENT OF THE UNITED STATES

FROM THE BEGINNING, the Eisenhower administration preferred to keep its hands off the Till case. The African American press, the NAACP, the unions, and many private citizens pushed for federal action, and at times it seemed that Washington might intervene. Although much of the northern black electorate was still up for grabs between Republicans and Democrats, the Eisenhower administration remained inactive and mostly silent. The White House ignored the telegram that Mamie Till Bradley sent hours after her son's disappearance, and it did its best to dodge the Till case ever after.[1]

One important exception to the administration's inertia was the FBI, at least in terms of observing the situation in Chicago and in the Delta. Memos began flying within the agency less than twenty-four hours after Till disappeared, and J. Edgar Hoover's men monitored the case for the next several months, but not for the purpose of bringing the guilty to justice. Instead, Hoover continued to act on his long-standing obsession with Communists, indeed, with anyone critical of America, the Justice Department, or his agency.[2]

He was half-right. The Communist Party USA quickly recognized that the Till case united many civil rights, labor, and anticolonial activists. A week after the Sumner jury acquitted Milam and Bryant, the Party's National Administrative Committee issued a long memo to all members, noting the mobilization already taking place in American cities. A great struggle loomed on the horizon; the Emmett Till story revealed the depth of southern intransigence. Now, as emotions ran high, it was time to articulate a true leftist agenda, and to press the administration to back new civil rights, voting, and anti-lynching legislation.[3]

Near the end of the year, a thoughtful Marxist analysis appeared in *Political Affairs*, arguing that the Till case had aroused workers, sharecroppers, and the black bourgeoisie more than any event in recent years, and it called for left-wing leadership on a range of federal initiatives. Hoover feared precisely this sort of activism, not only because the Communists stood to make converts but because their protests and demonstrations made federal agencies look bad. He sent out a stream of memos warning department heads of coming agitation.[4]

Yet the Communists were always marginal to the Emmett Till story. Unlike the trials of the Scottsboro Boys back in the early 1930s, when the Communist Party played a lead role in defending nine young African Americans accused of rape, civil rights organizers kept them at arm's length in the Till case. More important, by 1955, the Communist Party was deeply weakened, with far smaller numbers and fewer resources than in its heyday during the Great Depression. Red-baiting from the Right, congressional hearings led by the House Committee on Un-American Activities and by Joseph McCarthy in the Senate, prosecutions under tough new laws, purgings of radicals from labor unions and progressive organizations, the ongoing revelations of Soviet barbarities—all took their toll.[5]

The Communist Party USA's national committee issued a strong statement at the end of September calling for a range of actions in response to Sumner, including impeaching Senator Eastland, refusing to seat Mississippi's congressmen until blacks could vote, as well as civil rights and anti-lynching legislation. Yet the CP USA did not have much clout. In a country of nearly one hundred seventy million people, the FBI estimated the party's total membership at twenty thousand, fewer than fifteen hundred of them African American, both figures showing a small fraction of their totals less than two decades earlier.[6]

So it is particularly striking that Hoover could not resist focusing on the party. Even as he noted their declining strength and acknowledged the rise of non-Marxist civil rights activism—black and white, North and South, most of it completely independent of the Communists—he continued to search for Reds in the growing uprising against southern segregation. Week after week, the FBI's confidential "Current Intelligence Summary," highlighted Communist involvement with civil rights rallies, slight as it was.[7]

Fully six months after Till's murder, Hoover still viewed the case through a red lens. He told Eisenhower's cabinet that while the Citizens' Councils were of concern, they were nonviolent, and he worried more about Communist infiltration of the NAACP, even though that organization had purged its membership and disavowed the CP USA. Communists, Hoover said, "used the Negro" to mobilize politically, pit class against class, and weaken the United States. The Communists, "claim that the unfortunate and brutal killing of 14-year-old Emmett Till is the finest thing that has happened from their standpoint. For public consumption they claim that the Till case is an historic event and the turning point in the Negro struggle for liberation." As evidence, Hoover cited party efforts to support the *Brown* decision, to lobby Congress for civil rights legislation, to persuade Mayor Richard Daley to write to the White House on behalf of Mamie Till Bradley (Hoover hastened to add, "Mayor Daley is not a Communist").[8]

In the shadow of the Till murder, as the great mass movement for civil rights gathered steam, and as the forces of reaction organized in both the North and the South, Hoover still battled the Reds. He told Eisenhower's cabinet he had "reliable information" from the Communist Party's "highest levels" that a Negro Communist leader, "has had a secret conference with NAACP leaders in New York on a campaign on the Till case." Then he reassured the cabinet that the FBI continued to monitor black organizations that might have ties to the Communists—the "Afro-American Congress of Christian Organizations," the remnants of Marcus Garvey's Back to Africa Movement, and the "Muslim Cult of Islam," with its thousand members.[9]

Digging up or even inventing evidence of Communist subversion was an effective political tool; Red-baiting discredited enemies. But Hoover was neither totally cynical nor delusional. One party member who followed the Till case closely was Pettis Perry. He read about it while serving a three-year term in federal prison for violating the Smith Act by advocating the overthrow of the US government. Perry was born to a sharecropper family in 1897 in Marion, Alabama. By age ten, he was working in the cotton fields, three years later in a cottonseed mill, then for the next fifteen years he traveled across the country as a mill hand, railroad worker, and iron molder. Aroused by the trumped-up rape charges against Alabama's Scottsboro Boys in 1931, and learning of the International Labor Defense's spirited work on their behalf, Perry joined the Communist Party and rose through its ranks to leadership positions. The federal government prosecuted him and several other officials in the mid-1950s.[10]

Perry followed the Till case by reading newspapers in the prison library, and he included his thoughts about it in letters he wrote home to his wife, Rose. Though convinced the Till trial was a farce, Perry saw in it a great opportunity, because suddenly the eyes of the world were on Mississippi. In his faith that a fresh start awaited America, Perry told Rose that he hoped activists would keep the Till case alive, for here was an instance where African Americans and white workers could make common cause. Mose Wright, T. R. M. Howard, and especially Mamie Till Bradley were grassroots leaders whose courage was a beacon for others. The NAACP, Perry wrote, should "start calling upon the white masses of the South to get into this struggle," and black organizations especially must reach out to white church leaders. Then, with a fully interracial movement, the real voice of America would be heard behind the iron curtain of Georgia, South Carolina, and Mississippi. Yes, the fight was against segregation and the plantation system, but more broadly it was a battle for all poor and working people.[11]

Delighted that the Till case was still in the news months after the trial ended, Perry believed it might yet rally millions of trade unionists, teachers, and church leaders across racial lines in a fight for freedom. He romanticized the situation from his prison cell, but dreams of solidarity like his still gave nightmares to others, J. Edgar Hoover prime among them.[12]

Aside from the FBI looking for Communists, the Eisenhower administration failed to move. More precisely, the White House and the Justice Department acted at home just like the United States Information Agency did overseas, spinning the story, managing it, keeping it under control. A week after the "not guilty" verdict in Sumner, W. Beverly Carter, publisher of the African American *Pittsburgh Courier*, wrote to E. Frederick Morrow, the Administrative Officer for Special Projects, and the first black man to hold an executive position in the White House. Morrow was the Eisenhower administration's Negro, the man whose impossible job it was to explain black America to the White House and vice versa. In his letter, Carter urged that someone high up in the administration—Attorney General Brownell, chief of staff and former governor Sherman Adams, even Vice President Richard Nixon—make a public statement that "the Federal Government looked with dismay" on the Till incident. Carter told his friend that even without federal action, a simple condemnation of the murder and acquittal by a high official would go a long way toward mollifying world opinion and signaling to African Americans that Washington was paying attention. It might even secure new black votes for the Republicans in 1956.[13]

Morrow took his friend's suggestion seriously, quietly pushed for such a public statement in October and November, but nothing ever came from the administration, and Morrow felt increasingly isolated. With an office in the White House, he was literally closer to the president than any African American official before him, yet he lacked power or influence. An attorney with experience in journalism, business, and government, a former field secretary for the NAACP, Morrow sought to help the administration work through the explosive civil rights issues of the mid-1950s. But no one seemed interested in the advisor's advice.[14]

His frustration mounting by late November after Leflore County refused to indict Milam and Bryant on kidnapping charges, Morrow wrote a "Memorandum for the Record," and a week later sent it to the secretary of the cabinet Max Rabb, the administration's point man on civil rights, immigration, and ethnic affairs. Continuing to ignore the Till case, Morrow wrote, would lead to embarrassment or worse for the administration. "There are visible indications that we are on the verge of a dangerous racial conflagration in the southern section of the country....The one theme on the lips and in the minds of all Negroes is the injustice of the Till matter, and the fact that nothing can be done to effect justice in this case." Murrow warned Rabb that the situation—the mass meetings, the unceasing publicity, the sermons from pulpits across America, the White Citizens' Councils with their "economic terrorism," the rumors of a militant Negro underground in the South—threatened to spiral out of control.[15]

Morrow noted that his own mail had been heavy and angry on the Till issue. He accepted the Justice Department's position that it was not a federal case. But people needed a signal that the administration cared. He proposed that a high official, perhaps the vice president, invite a dozen prominent Negro leaders to Washington to exchange views. "It will be a demonstration to the whole country that the responsible leaders, white and Negro, have a deep concern about this situation." He emphasized that "meetings of this kind always have a steadying effect upon responsible Negro leaders for they are able to go through the country and assure Negro citizens that the head of the nation is concerned about their welfare....By the same token it notifies any racist element that the administration frowns upon their un-American tactics." Given how volatile Morrow considered the situation, this was awfully tepid advice, and the suggestion that a few words from the White House would mollify "responsible negro leaders" was patronizing at best.[16]

Yet even this was too strong for the Eisenhower administration. No such meeting took place. Morrow—perhaps at Rabb's urging, the record is not clear—sent a new version of his memo to Sherman Adams two weeks later in which he expunged any reference to the Till murder, praised the administration for its fine efforts in civil rights, mildly chastised blacks for not appreciating all that had been done for them, said that his goal was to secure black votes for the Republican Party, omitted any mention that his proposed Washington conference might feature a high-ranking official, and suggested that only black ministers be invited to avoid heated confrontations.[17]

Morrow's experiences were the norm. The administration met the pressure for federal intervention with vague responses—thank you for your message, the president is aware of the situation, federal jurisdiction is limited, "states' rights" makes this a very touchy subject, we're doing all we can to the full extent of the law, and so forth. The drumbeat for federal action only grew louder with time. Back on September 7, just after Emmett Till's funeral, Roy Wilkins, Thurgood Marshall, Clarence Mitchell, Ruby Hurley, and Medgar Evers met with Assistant Attorney General Warren Olney in Washington to press for action on Mississippi's "Reign of Terror." Days later, Wilkins wrote a follow-up letter to President Eisenhower: "We believe the government of the United States which has protested brutality and violence throughout the world should not stand mute and inactive when brutality and violence are used against United States Citizens.... We call upon the President of the United States to use the immense powers of his great office, including that of public denunciation, to put a halt to the shameful intimidation and killing of citizens whose only 'crime' is their attempt to live as Americans." He received no reply.[18]

The evasions lasted for months, well into 1956. Civil rights organizations and the black press pushed for action, and the administration gave vague and conflicting answers. Fifty Chicago demonstrators arrived in Washington in late October arguing for prosecution of Till's abductors under federal kidnapping statutes; Arthur Caldwell, the Justice Department attorney, told the group that no federal laws had been violated. Days later, responding to an inquiry into the Till case by a New Jersey congressman, Warren Olney wrote, "The department is presently conducting extensive investigations concerning alleged deprivation of the civil rights of Mississippi Negro Citizens." By the end of October, the Attorney General himself pledged that the Justice Department would "give immediate and continuing attention to the entire civil rights field." But Brownell's office responded to the dozens of congressmen and senators who wrote at the behest of their constituents to urge action with the same answer: the Till case involved no violation of federal law so there would be no federal intervention.[19]

Everyone knew their part by the time the Leflore County grand jury declined to indict Milam and Bryant on November 9: The governor of Illinois renewed his call for an investigation; the governor of Mississippi told the press that he "feared federal action against us"; Brownell once again said he would look into it; another assistant attorney general declared the Justice Department had no jurisdiction, to which the NAACP asked why then was the FBI involved in a purely intrastate New York kidnapping trial. Brownell himself then confirmed again that there would be no federal action on the Till case; another deputy attorney general bemoaned the lack of justice for Till's family; the Attorney General's office repeated it had no basis to intervene. When Congressman Harrison Williams of New Jersey asked why the Justice Department had failed to enforce the Fifteenth Amendment in Mississippi, he received no reply.[20]

With the New Year came a nasty flare-up between Dr. T. R. M. Howard and J. Edgar Hoover. Back in September, two days after the Sumner trial ended, Howard gave a speech suggesting that the government investigate white southerners working as FBI agents. "It is a strange thing," he told over two thousand NAACP members in Baltimore's Sharpe Street Methodist Church, "that the FBI can never seem to work out who is responsible for killing Negroes in the South." He called upon black leaders, the attorney general, and the president to discuss why the FBI was unable to solve southern crimes, more particularly the murders of George Lee, Lemar Smith, and Emmett Till. Howard added that he himself was a marked man, that he always had bodyguards at his side.[21]

Howard kept banging away at this theme in speeches and writings, until J. Edgar Hoover finally responded with an open letter that he sent to several newspapers. Hoover accused Howard of "a complete disregard of the facts." He explained that his bureau acted at the behest of the Department of Justice: "The FBI is not a policy-making organization and we merely conduct fair and impartial investigations and submit the results of such investigations to the Department of Justice," which then decides which cases to pursue. Hoover also accused Howard of conveniently forgetting that the FBI "was largely responsible for the virtual elimination of lynchings in the South and . . . for the breaking up of the K.K.K. in the Carolinas and Georgia." Dr. Howard, Hoover charged, made "irresponsible and false charges," and was not at all interested in the truth.[22]

It was vintage Hoover—deflecting criticism, attacking enemies, protecting his agency, and all of it disingenuous. The bureau and its director had wide latitude in selecting which cases to pursue and how. Moreover, it was absurd to claim that the FBI was responsible for the decline of the

KKK and of lynching. For years the Feds did their best to stay out of such matters. Dr. Howard's response did more than simply point out such inaccuracies. Hoover had unwittingly set a trap for himself, and Howard sprung it:

> I do not understand how the FBI was able to take effective action to 'virtually eliminate' lynching in light of your statement that the Department of Justice can act only when Federal statutes have been violated. If the Federal Government was able to act in this area of lynching, in the absence of a federal anti-lynching statute, is it possible to undertake similar action in...the George Lee, Lamar Smith and Emmett Till cases in light of a similar claimed lack of applicable Federal Statutes?

Howard characterized himself as a concerned American citizen, exercising his right to criticize the government. The real issue, he wrote, was that Negroes were being murdered and the killers were going unpunished. Howard added that condemnation of such crimes from respected men like the Director might help stop them in the future.[23]

The dustup between Hoover and Howard got a lot of attention in the press, both white and black. *The Los Angeles Tribune* accused Hoover of squelching public debate; the *Kansas City Call* asked why it took Hoover so many months to explain to an eager public his agency's inertia on the Mississippi murders; the *Philadelphia Tribune* wondered how it was that the Feds captured John Dillinger and solved Brinks Armored Car robberies yet were powerless when black citizens were murdered for registering to vote? The *California Eagle* pointed to the larger issue: "There is a rising tide of criticism at federal inaction in the face of wholesale denial of civil rights buttressed by the murder of those who cry out against those denials."[24]

Here was the heart of the matter. Racist violence was one thing, but the key question was how to deal with local institutions that enabled it. Only federal laws, agencies, policies, and court decisions might overrule the intransigence of state and local governments. The issue arose again and again as the long freedom struggle unfolded, but never more clearly than in the case of Emmett Till. What was to be done if a mere boy, a child, could be murdered with impunity for some breach of racial etiquette? Who but the federal government could stop the abuse of constitutionally guaranteed rights?

Federal civil rights legislation—anti-lynching, desegregation, voting rights, a strong Federal Employment Practices Commission—was not in the cards, not in the mid-1950s. The Eisenhower administration backed some tepid reforms, and the president spoke vaguely in his 1956 State of the Union message about judging each citizen "by what he is rather than his color, race or religion." When Democrats made big gains in the Congress in 1956, Attorney General Brownell finally backed new legislation to establish a civil rights division within the Justice Department and extend federal jurisdiction over voting rights. A tepid bill moved through Congress in 1957, further weakened when Senator James Eastland of Mississippi, head of the Judiciary Committee, crippled its enforcement powers.[25]

Frederic Morrow wrote his memo to Max Rabb advocating a summit of black leaders and White House officials in November 1955. A year and a half later, as the anemic civil rights bill slowly made its way to the president's desk, Murrow and Rabb were still talking about it—how many leaders would be too many, would it look like the White House was pressuring southern congressmen, what about other ethnic groups that might demand the administration's attention? In August 1957, Eisenhower's already flaccid support for the bill weakened further. Morrow dreaded going to his own office each day, where letters and phone calls from irate black citizens piled up. They were, he wrote in his diary, "fed up with the President's moderate stand on civil rights.... They accuse him of refusing to assume the moral leadership of the country at this time." Morrow added, "I feel ridiculous standing on platforms all over the country, trying to defend the administration's record on Civil Rights."[26]

Yet with high-minded resolve, Morrow wrote in his diary just a few days later, "I could never be disloyal to Dwight Eisenhower. I realize that he is straining every nerve to serve, to the best of his ability, the interest and welfare of all the people of the United States." Morrow stayed through the administration's end in 1961, and his diary is a call-and-response of slights to black people, followed by rationalizations for presidential inaction.[27]

Chief Justice Earl Warren was less forgiving. After retiring from the bench in 1969, he criticized Eisenhower for never speaking out forcefully in support of black rights, a missed opportunity given the president's popularity. Warren told a story in his memoirs about the early days of the administration, before the *Brown* decision. Just as the case came under submission to the Supreme Court, Eisenhower invited the chief justice to the White House. Taking Warren aside after dinner and speaking about the South and southerners, the president told him, "These are not bad people. All they are concerned about is to see that their sweet little girls are not required to sit alongside some big overgrown Negroes."[28]

The waning days of 1955 gave little reason to think that the Emmett Till story would have lasting impact. The rallies at which Mamie Till Bradley and others spoke were a revelation, with tens of thousands of people turning out. Yet despite support from unions and religious organizations, most of those in the crowds were African American, angry, inspired, energized—and without much access to the levers of power. Meanwhile, Milam and Bryant were free, no one pursued their accomplices, and the Sumner and Greenwood travesties exemplified the ongoing imperviousness of the criminal justice system. People of good will were horrified by Emmett Till's murder and the freeing of his killers. That, however, did not bring change, not yet, and certainly not from the federal government. The language of racism and white supremacy, whether raw or refined, remained louder and more pervasive than calls for freedom, rights, and equality.[29]

After one more big burst at the beginning of 1956, Emmett Till's story threatened to pass into oblivion.

MEMORY

CHAPTER THIRTY

THIS IS A WAR IN MISSISSIPPI

THE TILL STORY'S biggest aftershock came four months after Sumner. William Bradford Huie had made a name for himself as a crusading reporter. A native of Alabama, he started writing for the Birmingham newspapers as a young man, then gradually worked his way up to the editorship of H. L. Mencken's old journal, *American Mercury*. He also co-hosted *Chronoscope*, one of the earliest television news and commentary programs.[1]

Huie had enormous drive and ambition as well as a real talent for sniffing out marketable stories. By the early 1950s, he had moved back to his native state and become a freelance writer. He wrote articles, novels, éxposes, screenplays; more precisely, he uncovered sensational tales, then turned them into best-selling paperbacks and movies. For three decades, he wrote about military scandals, covered courtroom dramas, and worked the "race beat," in such books as *The Execution of Private Slovik, The Americanization of Emily, The Revolt of Mamie Stover, The Hero of Iwo Jima*, and *Three Lives for Mississippi*. At the end of his long career, he claimed that he had sold forty million books, though none of them were still in print when he died in 1986. His one goal—the guiding principle that he never tired of repeating—was uncovering the truth.[2]

Two weeks after Milam and Bryant kissed their wives and smiled for the cameras in Sumner, Huie wrote a letter to Roy Wilkins proposing that the NAACP bankroll a book on the Till murder. Huie told Wilkins that he had already set it up with the brothers' attorneys, Breland and Whitten, and he noted that their firm was the most prominent in Tallahatchie County, that they represented the big planters and farm equipment companies, all of whom stood behind Milam and Bryant. The attorneys could bring their clients to the table and help obtain their confessions.[3]

As an eighth-generation southerner, Huie told Wilkins that he and the lawyers spoke one another's language. To show how close he had gotten to them, Huie quoted Breland at length, revealing where the real power lay in Tallahatchie County:

> Bryant and Milam? Sure, they're rednecks—peckerwoods. We've sued Milam a couple of times: he's bootlegged all his life. He comes from a big, mean, overbearing family. He's got a chip on his shoulder. That's how he got that battlefield promotion in Europe: he likes to kill folks. But hell, we've got to have our Milams to fight our wars and keep the niggahs in line.[4]

The attorneys claimed they never asked if their clients were guilty, but Breland assumed that they were: "They shouldn't killed that nigger. They should'a just given him Thirty-Nine [lashes] and turned him loose. But you know how these things go. They're likkered up. They start off whippin' him and he sasses one of 'em, and maybe they hit him with the axe, and then they got to finish the job." Then Breland—unreconstructed, a leader of the local Citizens' Council, certain that the *Brown* decision could be resisted and black activism stopped—took his stand:

> The whites own all the property in Tallahatchie County. We don't need the niggers no more. There ain't gonna be no integration. There ain't gonna be no nigger votin'. And the sooner everybody in this country realizes it the better. If any more pressure is put on us, the Tallahatchie River won't hold all the niggers that'll be thrown into it.[5]

The journalist burnished his credentials with Wilkins by giving an insider's view of how local elites like Breland thought. The Delta no longer needed so many laborers now that machines harvested much of the cotton. Huie explained that the recent "wave of terror" was about keeping remaining blacks in line, but its other purpose was to drive thousands more away at the behest of "the Powers in Mississippi." Milam working black crews with cotton-picking machines and African Americans fleeing the Delta in response to horrors like Emmett Till's lynching were all part of deep social and economic changes.[6]

Huie assured Wilkins that he could write a book about the slaying better than anyone else in America, because "I have the hardest-hitting style in the business." More, "using nothing but facts, I can dramatize the abduction, torture, and murder of that boy in a way that will be more explosive than *Uncle Tom's Cabin*—and a lot more honest."[7]

So why did Huie write to Roy Wilkins? He needed money to pay off the brothers, Carolyn Bryant, two unnamed members of the "torture-and-murder-party" as well as Breland and Whitten. Huie would interview the killers, buy their story, and pay them to sign releases: legally binding documents giving the author the right to portray them however he chose, in print or on the screen. These releases were to reassure skittish publishers and movie producers that they need not fear a lawsuit. Huie planned to write his book without actually saying that the murderers confessed; "I would write the facts of the crime without ever stating that either of the defendants 'told' me anything." Milam and Bryant could deny they ever confessed to anyone, satisfying their attorneys and giving them plausible deniability with their families and friends. Huie asked Wilkens for three thousand dollars in payoff money to buy everyone's cooperation.[8]

No record survives of Wilkins's response. Given his desire to keep his organization above reproach, he probably dismissed Huie as a crank and simply ignored the letter. The last thing the NAACP needed was a scandal, and in most people's eyes, paying murderers to tell their stories— "checkbook journalism," some called it, or in Huie's words, a "secret deal," a "pay-off" —was unethical. Still, the killers' confession, or at least a good facsimile of one, must have tempted the head of the NAACP.[9]

After a week of silence from Wilkins, Huie sent a similar letter to editors at *Look* magazine and to the Knight newspaper group. Details changed, but the basic idea remained. Huie expanded on the white power structure in the Delta:

> This is a war in Mississippi. These men are playing for keeps. Far from "giving an inch" in the racial struggle, the [Citizens'] Councils are organized for an offensive against the Negroes. A man like Breland honestly believes that they can force the Supreme Court to reverse itself—"just like Prohibition." And while he "don't approve of murder," he is quite willing to "turn the rednecks against the niggers and let the chips fall...."

Channeling Breland, Huie offered a clear vision of the social forces roiling the South to those whose money he needed: noblesse oblige was easy before the activists and the Supreme Court hammered away at Jim Crow, before the heady egalitarian rhetoric of World War II and the anticolonialist impulse in its wake challenged white supremacy. But by the mid-1950s, segregation was embattled, and men like Breland intended to fight for The Southern Way of Life with everything they had.[10]

Ever the chameleon, Huie backed off his social justice rhetoric when the target of his letter became white magazine publishers, not the head of the NAACP. Now he was the objective reporter, neither a liberal nor a crusader, quite the contrary: "I only write about the human race, I don't try to reform it." His work commanded an enormous readership, Huie said, because he never took sides, merely told the truth. And he got along just fine with men like the Milam and Bryant and their attorneys, all of them "members of the lodge," southern white boys.[11]

Despite his loud allegiance to veracity, Huie was devoted even more to his career. His personal correspondence was filled with schemes—hiding his earnings or fudging tax deductions, acquiring syndication rights, threatening and avoiding law suits, parlaying articles into books and books into movies. But more than scheming, he was duplicitous. Huie told the editors at *Look* and at Knight that his conversations with Milam and Bryant revealed that four men tortured and killed Till. When two of them, fearing arrest, refused to cooperate, Huie had no problem writing his article as if they did not exist, as if Milam and Bryant acted alone. Or again, Huie wrote Roy Wilkins, "I have a clear understanding of the worldwide revolt of colored men against white domination," implying that he and Wilkins shared an anticolonialist political outlook. But later, Huie wrote to the attorney John Whitten that his Till book, "will be a bitter dose for the NAACP and the 'liberals'...particularly for the chapter on the late Pvt. Louis Till." Huie even offered to send Whitten some of the court-martial documents to be "read aloud at all meetings of the Citizens' Councils."[12]

Huie paid Breland and Whitten for access to their clients, and he promised everyone that the money would keep rolling in as he found new ways to sell his version of the Till story. A year after his first article about the murder appeared, Huie wrote to Whitten that he was hopeful they would soon hit the jackpot with a fat Hollywood contract. At the very least there would be one more big article and a book.[13]

Look closed the deal with Huie. He spent several hours late in October interviewing Milam and Bryant, parking his car just outside Sumner and walking in to Breland and Whitten's office under cover of darkness. Whitten even sent Huie some of the firm's stationary so that their correspondence would not carry a suspicious out-of-town return address. Huie took down Milam's and Bryant's words and worked up his notes.

He also spoke at length with Breland and Whitten, especially the latter, getting their perspective and gaining entrée to the world of Tallahatchie County. Huie assured his publishers at *Look* that he spent days in Sumner and in Chicago, interviewing people, checking details, and taking photographs.[14]

Breland and Whitten drew up the releases granting Huie the right to portray Milam and the Bryants any way he saw fit, to "report any and all of the details" of their lives especially regarding their relationship to Emmett Till. But then the kicker: "The forgoing consent is in no way to be regarded or considered as an admission by me, express or implied, that I am a killer or possessed of any other reprehensible characteristics, criminal or otherwise, which Mr. Huie may, in the work, attribute to me." The clause allowed the two attorneys to keep their clients safe from further prosecution.[15]

But publishers at *Look* were not yet satisfied. They wanted their own lawyer to oversee the wording and execution of the contracts. Huie gave very specific instructions about the sort of man they should send from New York, an "Anglo" (someone without a foreign sounding last name, and certainly not a Jew), preferably not a "liberal," someone not afraid of the South or of rough customers like Milam and Bryant, a man accustomed to tough talk and strong whiskey. As Huie put it, "Let's don't send a preacher to the whorehouse." All of the attorneys approved the arrangements, everyone signed releases, and Huie pledged never to testify against the brothers or show the signed agreements to anyone except New York publishers and Hollywood producers as needed. Then he wrote his article.[16]

Huie's work on the Till murder was not, as some have called it, America's first experience with checkbook journalism, but it certainly was a striking example of the practice. The attorney that *Look* sent from New York, Frank Dean, acted as bagman, carrying a satchel with thousands of dollars in cash to Mississippi. Exactly how much Huie earned and paid out over the next few years is unclear. He offered his first Till article to Knight newspapers for $5,000, plus half of all syndication fees, but he ended up publishing it in *Look* for $7,500, and later the article was abridged in *Reader's Digest*, with a circulation, Huie estimated, of ten million copies. A second article appeared in *Look* a year later for $5,000. Huie turned his initial articles into a paperback book published by Signet; he also signed a $25,000 contract with United Artists for a Hollywood screenplay, which he delivered in 1960. *Look*'s initial payments to Milam and the Bryants totaled a little over $3,000, not a small amount in 1955 dollars (Mamie

Till Bradley, for example, earned about $3,600 working for the federal government in 1954), while Breland and Whitten split $1,260. Future earnings were divided at 20 percent for Milam and Bryant, 10 percent for their attorneys, 10 percent for Huie's agent, and 60 percent for Huie.[17]

"The Shocking Story of Approved Killing in Mississippi" appeared in the January 24, 1956, issue of Look, but it actually hit the newsstands two weeks earlier, on January 10. Look's editors included a solemn preamble, declaring that Emmett Till's murder revealed "man's inhumanity to man," and the brutality of racial conflict. Here for the first time, they said, was the true story, "the story no jury heard and no newspaper reader saw." Huie echoed the editors in his very first line: "Disclosed here is the true account of the slaying in Mississippi...." There actually was not that much new in the article for those who followed the case as it unfolded. Even the jurors never said the brothers were innocent, just that the prosecutors failed to prove their guilt.[18]

Moreover, in his effort to present "the facts," Huie elides a lot of what is most interesting. He never parses conflicting evidence—for example, Willie Reed saw four white men in a truck while Huie mentions only two—in order to assert a simple narrative line. To this day the Till story is filled with factual uncertainties: How many killers, did Emmett's friends egg him on, exactly what did Till say to Carolyn Bryant? None of this was clear, but writing in a declarative style—telling a "shattering" story—left no room for ambiguity.[19]

One thing, however, was both new and important, and it was the basis of Huie's claim to authenticity: for the first time in the Till saga, readers heard the killers' voices. More precisely, J. W. Milam said what was on his mind during the night of the murder, what he did and why, and his justification for killing Emmett Till. Or so it seems. "Approved Killing" is "the truth," if truth is defined as taking an informant at his word and letting him speak without probing beneath the surface. Assuming, of course, that Milam really spoke the words attributed to him. Huie never writes "Milam said," or "Milam told me." Quotation marks appear around words and the reader is led to infer that they issued from Milam's mouth. Roy Bryant apparently had nothing to say; at least we never hear his voice.[20]

Huie sets the scene by sketching the brothers' extended Delta family: "This is a lusty and devoted clan. They work, fight, vote and play as a family." The Bryants ran a grocery store that served a clientele of black field hands, usually on credit. Roy and Carolyn were poor, owned neither car nor television. Roy was away on Wednesday, August 24, trucking shrimp from the Gulf Coast while Carolyn waited on customers in their dusty crossroads shop. According to Huie, Carolyn never stayed overnight in the living quarters in back of the store whenever Roy was away. A relative always came to get her and the kids, and, foreshadowing the danger to come, Huie notes that white women in the Delta refused to travel without a man after dark.[21]

"Approved Killing" describes how Emmett Till and seven friends arrived by car just as it was getting dark. A dozen other black youths were already outside, playing checkers on the porch. Till started bragging about dating white girls, showed a picture of one that he carried in his wallet. Bo's companions goaded him to go in the store and ask for a date with the "pretty little white woman."[22]

Huie's description of the encounter in the grocery store closely follows Carolyn Bryant's trial testimony—Till grabs her hand, asks for a date, puts his hands on her waist, says I've been with white women before, wolf whistles; Carolyn goes for her gun as Till and his friends make their getaway. Carolyn tells her sister-in-law Juanita Milam what happened and both agree not to tell their husbands. By the time Roy Bryant gets back home on Friday, the story has spread, and a black customer reports to him about the Chicago boy staying at Preacher Wright's place. Roy confronts Carolyn and she confirms the story. "Once Roy Bryant knew," Huie writes, "in the opinion of most white people around him, for him to have done nothing would have marked him as a coward and a fool."[23]

Roy tells J. W., who whips into action, and after midnight on Saturday the brothers drive out to Mose Wright's place. Now Huie writes with much more authenticating detail, giving the reader the sense of being there, no doubt because from here on he tells the story from his informants' perspective: "There was no moon as they drove to Preacher's House: 2.8 miles east of Money.... Big Milam drove the pickup in under the trees. He was bareheaded, carrying a five-cell flashlight in his left hand, the .45 in his right." Huie added hints of "Negro dialect" in describing the confrontation: Mose "sho' had" talked to the boy about his behavior in Money; Emmett wanted to go home, but Elizabeth Wright urged him to "finish yo' visit."[24]

Years later, Simeon Wright, who was at Bryant's Grocery Store and in the cabin when Milam and Bryant kidnapped Emmett, wrote in his memoir that despite Huie's claim that he came up to Chicago to learn more about the Till family, no one recalled meeting him, and he got countless details wrong—Bryant's store was cash only; Emmett arrived with five friends, not seven; he had no picture of a white girl in his wallet; he never bragged about dating white girls from school (McCosh School in Chicago was all black anyway); and begged *not* to be sent home after the incident. Huie was a master of verisimilitude. The trouble was he made much of it up, accepted what he was told uncritically, or bent the details to make his story more dramatic.[25]

The first half of "Approved Killing in Mississippi" could have been written from newspaper accounts of the trial. Little was new. The article becomes interesting only in the second half, when Huie switches to a first-person account based on his interviews. Milam knew a place along the river—the Mississippi River, not the Tallahatchie—with hundred-foot bluffs and deep waters below. He described his plan to take Till up there, pistol-whip him, make him think they intended to throw him in the river. "Brother, if that won't scare the Chicago -------, hell won't." But after driving more than an hour to get there, Milam and Bryant could not find that spot on the river in the dark, so they drove all the way back to Milam's house in Glendora, arrived at 5:00 a.m., three hours after leaving Money, all of it with Till in the back of the pickup truck.[26]

Milam told Huie that they never tied Till up. So why didn't he jump out and run? This, Huie wrote, was the most remarkable part of the story: "Bobo wasn't afraid of them! He was tough as they were. He didn't think they had the guts to kill him." And here Huie quotes Milam: "We never were able to scare him. They had just filled him so full of that poison he was hopeless." The brothers brought him to a tool shed on Milam's property and took turns pistol-whipping him. Emmett never hollered, but told them what he thought of them: "You bastards, I'm not afraid of you. I'm as good as you are. I've 'had' white women. My grandmother was a white woman."[27]

They beat Till until he wore them out. "Well, what else could we do," Milam asked? "He was hopeless."

I'm no bully; I never hurt a nigger in my life. I like niggers—in their place—I know how to work 'em. But I just decided it was time a few people got put on notice. As long as I live and can do anything about it, niggers are gonna stay in their place. Niggers ain't gonna vote where I live. If they did, they'd control the government. They ain't gonna go to school with my kids. And when a nigger even gets close to mentioning sex with a white woman, he's tired o' livin'. I'm likely to kill him. Me and my folks fought for this country, and we've got some rights. I stood there in that shed and listened to that nigger throw that poison at me, and I just made up my mind. "Chicago boy," I said, "I'm tired of 'em sending your kind down here to stir up trouble. God-damn you, I'm going to make an example of you—just so everybody can know how me and my folks stand."

The brothers ordered Till back in the pickup and drove to the town of Boyle, where they had noticed an old discarded gin fan. They forced Till to load it in the truck. It was daylight now, and Milam and Bryant grew worried about being seen.[28]

They drove east and then north, to the Tallahatchie River, to a secluded spot that Milam knew. In Huie's words:

> Big Milam ordered Bobo to pick up the fan.
> He staggered under its weight, . . . carried it to the river bank. They stood silently . . . just hating one another.
> *Milam*: "Take off your clothes."
> Slowly, Bobo sat down, pulled off his shoes, his socks. He stood up, unbuttoned his shirt, dropped his pants, his shorts.
> He stood there naked.
> It was Sunday morning, a little before 7.
> *Milam*: "You still as good as I am?"
> *Bobo*: "Yeah."
> *Milam*: "You've still 'had' white women?"
> *Bobo*: "Yeah."
> That big .45 jumped in Big Milam's hand. The youth turned to catch that big, expanding bullet at his right ear. He dropped.

Milam and Bryant tied the gin fan around Till's neck with barbed wire and dumped him in twenty feet of water. They brought his clothes back to Glendora and set them on fire; his thick crepe-soled shoes took three hours to burn. Huie's last brief paragraph concludes with the observation that the majority of white Mississippians approved of this murder, or at the very least they did not disapprove of it enough "to risk giving their 'enemies' the satisfaction of a conviction."[29]

Once again, Emmett Till was in the headlines. *Look* took out advertisements in newspapers across the country, a photo of him in the corner and block letters at the top, "For the first time . . . THE TRUTH about the Emmett Till killing!" The NAACP, the black press, and liberal organizations immediately seized on Milam's and Bryant's confessions, pushed again for a federal antilynching law, voting rights legislation, and a new civil rights division of the Justice Department. Congressman Charles Diggs had a copy of "Approved Killing" read into the *Congressional Record*, pointing out that the killers' confession ought to revive the kidnapping charges and silence those who said justice had been done in Sumner. In response, Congressman Mendel Rivers of South Carolina charged that *Look* had slandered Mississippi "with unmitigated vituperation," and other southern congressmen and senators made clear they would block any new expansion of federal powers.[30]

"Approved Killing" gave with one hand and took back with the other: Emmett Till was the defiant black man southerners feared, but Milam and Bryant confessed that they killed him, sold out their defenders for cash. The *Jackson State Times* was whipsawed in its reaction. On January 9, the paper's headline said approvingly, "*Look* Says Till's Boastful Defiance Spelled His Death." Two days later, the headline read, "Baseless Reporting: *Look* Sinks to New Depths in Till Case." Huie's blanket condemnation of Mississippi—the "approved" killing promised in the title—was reduced to a throwaway line at the very end, but it rankled most. How dare a respected national publication condemn the whole state when it was clear that most citizens deplored Till's murder and wanted to see justice done?[31]

Mississippi's governor-elect J. P. Coleman thrashed around the story like he'd been thrown into quicksand. *Look* reprinted a tape-recorded interview he gave in Texas saying that Milam and Bryant "should have been convicted and electrocuted." Coleman denied he had ever said such a thing, noting that "Mississippi no longer electrocutes; we use the gas chamber." Roy Wilkins called Coleman on it, wrote an open letter asking him to convene a new grand jury: "The whole nation is horrified and stands humiliated in the eyes of the civilized world that these vicious men should walk free and unashamed while boasting of their depravity." Coleman replied that only a circuit judge, not a governor, could convene a grand jury. (In Leflore County, Judge Arthur Jordan agreed but conveniently declared himself too busy to seek a new kidnapping indictment.)[32]

Governor-elect Coleman was not done commenting on the confessions. He told the United Press that the state of Mississippi "did everything in the world we could to bring these two men to justice" He argued that the NAACP wanted the Sumner acquittal for propaganda purposes, "and unfortunately the jury, being stirred up as they were, proceeded to give them that propaganda." Had northern blacks left well enough alone, Mississippians would have "darn near taken those fellows and strung 'em up." Then Coleman denied that he had ever blamed the NAACP for the acquittals and also affirmed that the people of Mississippi did not condone killing young boys.[33]

"Approved Killing" complicated the murderers' lives too. J. W. Milam initially denied speaking to Huie, denied he had been paid for his confession, and asked John Whitten to sue *Look*. Milam knew that his lawyer had collaborated with Huie all along, but the public remained ignorant of that fact. Of course, he had no intention of suing. Like Whitten, he stood to profit from Huie's future work on the Till case, including the *Reader's Digest* condensed version of "Approved Killing," coming out in April.[34]

A few days after his initial talk about suing, Milam opened up to reporter Jay Milner. He was no longer too disturbed by the article, he said, and in fact was pleased with all the publicity. Milam mentioned that he received offers for books, movies, even television shows. "I'll say one thing for the article. It was written from a Mississippi viewpoint. I've gotten a lot of letters from people complimenting me for what *Look* said I did." Milam pulled fourteen letters from his pocket, "today's batch," and quoted a man from California who wrote that the *Look* story, "gave me a big thrill."[35]

Initially, however, most readers of "Approved Killing" were so shocked by the confession that it took them a while to absorb the part about Emmett Till as a defiant black man. Mamie Till Bradley's remarks to the African American press a few weeks after the article first hit the newsstands expressed the deepest outrage. She declared Huie's description of her son's final hours to be filled with lies. Milam and Bryant were indeed murderers, she told reporters, but Emmett was not at all like the boy depicted in "Approved Killing." They were "just trying to justify why they did it" in order to live with themselves and their community. "They lied about my child," she said flatly. "'Bo' would never brag about women he had. How could he? He was only 14. He didn't know enough about that kind of thing to be bragging about the relationship."[36]

Emmett was so innocent, Mrs. Bradley said, that just a few weeks before he was murdered, she had given him five dollars for a "date"—his first—with a local girl. Emmett paid for the bus ride to the movie and the popcorn. Moreover, the description of Emmett as unafraid and defiant simply did not match his personality: "Emmett was no superman and saying that he took all that beating without begging for mercy or that he kept talking back to them to the very end just isn't true." That a black boy plucked from bed at gunpoint by big angry white men reacted with defiance defies both what we know about Emmett Till and common sense.[37]

Why was Huie so uncritical? Why did he take Milam's word at face value? Because the myth of the sexually rapacious black man was self-evident to him and also to much of his audience. Certainly the "revelation" about Till's defiance made the story more dramatic. It was easy, too, since Huie simply followed the path cut by Breland and Whitten in their defense of the murderers. Huie tipped his hand in his description of Emmett Till in "Approved Killing," calling him five feet five, 160 pounds, and muscular. Actually, he was a little shorter, a little lighter, and everyone who knew him described him as "roly-poly." Indeed, when Huie finally delivered a screenplay to United Artists a few years later, he made his fictionalized "Bobo Wilson" seventeen years old and a lot bigger than Emmett Till.[38]

Like Mamie Till Bradley, the veteran black journalist Roi Ottley was skeptical of the story. He called "Approved Killing" slick, because it cut the case down the middle and refused to take a moral stand—yes, the brothers killed Till, but he goaded them into it, half-deserved it. Writing as if there were two sides to the story, Huie reinforced white supremacy. By repeating Carolyn Bryant's claim that Till had grabbed her (it defied reason, Ottley wrote, that any black male would violate this taboo, the consequences being so well-known and dire) Huie had given white men all they needed to justify the killing. But Huie went even farther, depicting Till bragging about the women he'd "had." The self-styled truth-teller Huie had relied on that tired old lie, that all black men in their hearts were rapists of white women. Huie, Ottley charged, had written an article about child murder without a trace of indignation, enabling people to read about it and "nod their heads with approval."[39]

Long after it appeared, "Approved Killing" colored the way Americans— white Americans—thought about the Till case. Yet the article is filled with half-truths and make-believe. For example, when he described the scene in the grocery store, Huie wrote that Till jumped in front of Carolyn Bryant and grabbed her with both hands—exactly as she had testified in court. However, the first time Carolyn Bryant told her story, less than three weeks before the trial, she said nothing about Till clasping her waist, nothing about him boasting of his girlfriends, nothing about his having white women. We know this because her attorneys took notes as she spoke. They gave the notes to William Bradford Huie. In other words, Bryant embellished her story, added details that were not originally there. The testimony she gave in court elevated a childish prank into an assault, and *that* was the version Huie chose to write for *Look*. Telling the story that way projected the specter of Emmett Till that Breland and Whitten raised in court. Huie transformed a pudgy fourteen-year-old kid into a sullen, hotheaded black man, the white South's worst nightmare—Louis Till's son.[40]

"I told the truth," Huie said, and no doubt he believed that, even though the truth meant accepting uncritically the most extreme version of the accusations against Emmett Till. It also meant paying the murderers for their story, men who had plenty of reason to lie. The Emmett Till described in "Approved Killing" was not a person but a waking nightmare, a militant Chicago black man filled with toxic ideas about his rights: "I'm not afraid of you, I'm just as good as you are." A fourteen-year-old beaten so hard that his eye popped out of its socket and his skull cracked could not have said those words. But a phantom could. Huie did not make it all up on his own. Newspaper editorials, Citizens' Council propaganda, barbershop gossip had inflamed white fears for months, ever since the *Brown* decision. The words Huie put in Emmett Till's mouth were echoes of Sumner, now legitimated by a respected organ of American journalism.[41]

Emmett Till may have been just a boy visiting family, but he represented something larger and more threatening. Northern whites were starting to express their displeasure with Jim Crow segregation—their own cities' ugly segregation and racist violence notwithstanding. White southerners might try and reaffirm their faith in the old myth of "happy Negroes" and improving race relations, but evidence to the contrary abounded. The very day that "Approved Killing" went on sale, the Interstate Commerce Commission ordered the integration of railroad and bus waiting rooms for routes crossing state lines, an order that the Mississippi legislature answered with a barrage of defiant new bills reinforcing segregation with steep fines.[42]

"'Chicago boy,' I said, 'I'm tired of 'em sending your kind down here to stir up trouble." African Americans were now organizing as never before to fight American apartheid. In not too many years, months really, black southerners, many of them just a little older than Emmett Till, would launch a children's crusade against Jim Crow. And they would win. "I stood there in that shed and listened to that nigger throw that poison at me..." Over and over southerners repeated the myth of their own innocence, of how outsiders reviled and victimized their region. "I just decided it was time a few people got put on notice.... Me and my folks fought for this country, and we've got some rights." So William Bradford Huie had indeed captured a truth, one encrusted in lies, when he gave voice to Emmett Till's murderers and their fears of the end of white supremacy.[43]

For the next three decades, "Approved Killing," helped shape the way white Americans thought about the Till murder. That is, if they thought about it at all, because now dropping the subject got a lot easier. If those who trumpeted Mississippi justice were shamed by the confessions, then at least Till's alleged defiance, his insistence that he had been with white girls and was as good as his abductors, made murder understandable, even justifiable in their eyes. If "Approved Killing" bolstered segregation's foes with Milam and Bryant's admission that they indeed killed Emmett Till, Huie balanced the books by depicting their victim as a black menace. When you boiled it down, "Approved Killing" was a confession in which no one really confessed, a series of allegations about Emmett Till's behavior that made no sense, a channeling of J. W. Milam's voice that more accurately might have been ascribed to Breland or Whitten or Huie himself. Just as Roi Ottley wrote in the *New York Amsterdam News*, the article was a moral muddle.[44]

After its moment in the sun, "The Shocking Story of Approved Killing in Mississippi" helped push the Till story off the front pages. The passage of time would have done that anyway, time and new stories. Just a month before "Approved Killing" appeared, the Montgomery Bus Boycott began, and that story kept growing for a year until the Supreme Court ruled there would be no more racial segregation on public conveyances. Then in September 1957, President Eisenhower called out federal troops to maintain order and integrate Central High School in Little Rock, Arkansas. As new terrors and triumphs of the freedom struggle filled the headlines and nightly television news in the late 1950s and early 1960s, Emmett Till's story was set aside and mostly forgotten.

Mostly.

CHAPTER THIRTY-ONE

FEW TALK ABOUT THE TILL CASE

WE THINK of memory as beginning in clarity then fading with time, but it is rarely so simple. Terrifying events get repressed while things that at first seemed fleeting or ephemeral grow in importance as the years pass. Conversations that felt inconsequential come flooding back, filled with new meaning. Remembrance of things past suddenly brings whole epochs into sharp focus. We reconstruct memories belatedly, imperfectly often through the needs of the present.[1]

What is true for individuals is also true for whole cultures. Emmett Till's name mostly vanished from print a few months after Huie's article appeared. One major newspaper database, for example, lists more than three thousand articles about him during 1955 and 1956, the vast majority published in the six months following his murder. The whole of the 1960s brought only three hundred articles. In the 1970s, fewer than fifty stories appeared. From there the numbers picked up slowly, almost150 articles in the '80s, nearly 250 in the '90s. Then suddenly two thousand in the first decade of the twenty-first century. Books take much longer to write and publish than newspapers, but something similar happened: a handful of books about Till in the 1960s and '70s, then a rising tide from about the mid-1980s all the way into the new century.[2]

That the number of stories about Till declined sharply with time is no surprise. But given how big the story had been, it seems odd that there were so few remembrances of him on the tenth and twenty-fifth anniversaries of his death. It was as if those who wanted to put the story to rest after Sumner finally got their way—a willful erasure for some, an embarrassed silence for others. But not everyone forgot. Some remembered Emmett Till as the decades passed, a few fiercely so. Most unexpected was the awakening that came at the end of the twentieth century and into the twenty-first.

The Emmett Till story stayed alive in the headlines through 1955, sometimes in unexpected ways. For example, turmoil engulfed the Chicago community of South Deering during the early 1950s, usually involving black families seeking to move into this white working-class neighborhood. South Side towns experienced riots, bombings, and assaults, and not just in Chicago, for such vigilante action bedeviled many segregated northern cities. Ten days after Till's body rose, renewed tensions provoked an editorial in the *Newsletter of the South Deering Improvement Association*, an organization dedicated to keeping the town white. The editor praised Mississippi for controlling its black population and condemned as "brazen hypocrites" those upset by Till's killing. In our "mongrelized city" the editor wrote, "thousands of White women, girls and even small children are raped and/or murdered by negroes each year."[3]

Behind the editorial was a long history of de facto segregation in Chicago, first on the South Side, then in a new West Side ghetto, all of it enforced at midcentury by federal housing laws, local ordinances, red-lining, restrictive covenants, "block busting" by corrupt real estate brokers, and banks refusing to loan to African American customers. Violent assaults against black families seeking to move into white neighborhoods were merely the end-game of institutional racism. South Deering offered a little reminder, should anyone need it, that all of the high-horse condemnations of the South masked the urban North's own brand of segregation.[4]

On the other hand, the *Westport (CT) Town-Crier* condemned the Sumner verdict but refused to turn criticism of the South into a praise song for the North. The *Town-Crier* editor declared that a small lynching occurred every time restrictive covenants kept black families out of neighborhoods, every time African Americans were denied educational or employment opportunities, every time whites stereotyped blacks. It was as if the *Town-Crier* was taking direct aim at places like South Deering. Of course, Westport was a wealthy and distant suburb of New York City; the issue of African American families moving in was more abstract than in South Deering.[5]

Throughout 1955, Emmett Till's name evoked a range of responses from whites, North and South, all of them coming to grips with a world destabilized by mass African American migration, the budding freedom struggle, and changing ideas about equality. His story provided a way to think about these issues. But even before William Bradford Huie published his article in *Look*, Till's name had begun to fade.

In late November, a friend of J. W. Milam named Elmer Kimbell murdered a black man in cold blood. Clinton Melton, father of four, had pumped gas and fixed cars at Lee McGarrh's service station for ten years. Melton was highly respected. The Glendora Lions Club called his murder an outrage. A peace officer picked up Kimbell at J. W. Milam's house. Kimbell showed a superficial wound and claimed Melton shot him first, overcharged him for gas, and then spoke abusively to him. McGarrh, a respected white business owner, witnessed the whole event, and swore in court there had been no improper language from his black employee, that Kimbell drove up drunk in Milam's car (the two had gone hunting that day), and that the only gunfire came from Kimbell's shotgun. The grand jury charged Kimbell with murder, and the judge (Curtis Swango, it turned out) denied his request for bond. Three months after the killing—two months after J. W.'s confession of the Till murder in *Look*—Kimbell was tried in the Sumner courthouse. Sheriff Strider leaned in for the defense and Attorney J. W. Kellum represented Kimbell. An all-white jury acquitted him after deliberating for four hours.[6]

Coverage of the trial, what there was of it, referred back to Emmett Till. The *Delta Democrat-Times* pointed out that this time the victim was not some Chicago "smart alec" but a highly respected local black man, that there was no issue of white southern womanhood involved, that the NAACP stayed away—"No flashbulbs popping, no television cameras, no reporters from all over the world milling around"—no one could say that Mississippi was backed into a corner, there was nothing to be defensive about. Still, the *Democrat-Times* noted, "no matter how strong the evidence nor how flagrant is the apparent crime, a white man can not be convicted in Mississippi for killing a Negro."[7]

David Halberstam agreed. The young reporter returned to the Delta and wrote "Tallahatchie County Acquits a Peckerwood." Mississippi, he noted, was divided into "the good people" like the jurors, and the peckerwoods like Kimbell, troublemakers prone to violence and intent on "keeping the niggers in their place." The good people saw themselves as above the peckerwoods, above murder and mayhem. But they were every bit as invested in protecting their white supremacist birthright. "I suspect," Halberstam wrote, "that the jurors who may have had misgivings were thinking that they had to go on living in the county, and how could they explain any other verdict to the neighbors...." The logic of white supremacy meant that even against their better judgment, the good people must close ranks with the peckerwoods. As Halberstam also pointed out, the Melton story barely got reported.[8]

Before Emmett Till's story faded further from view, the South's most famous writer, William Faulkner, weighed in. He had written a widely reprinted open letter from Rome two weeks after they found the body. Faulkner asked if the white race, a mere quarter of humanity, could continue to commit crimes against colored people and survive? Perhaps the Till case might "prove to us whether or not we deserve to survive." Emmett Till's murder, Faulkner argued, gave the lie to America's Cold War talk of freedom and justice: "If we as Americans have reached that point in our desperate culture when we must murder children, no matter for what reason or what color, we don't deserve to survive, and probably won't." Having raised this disturbing point, Faulkner pulled back, urging African Americans to go slow, to be patient, to not push white southerners too hard. Black and white shared a culture, so together, gradually, they might eradicate the absurdity of racism.[9]

Faulkner returned to the Till case nine months later in the June 1956 issue of *Harper's Magazine*. He marveled at the progress African Americans had made in the course of three centuries—from savages eating rotten elephant meat in African jungles to George Washington Carver and Booker T. Washington (!). Commenting on William Bradford Huie's article, Faulkner asked what were whites so afraid of:

> If the facts as stated in the *Look* magazine account of the Till affair are correct, this is what ineradicably remains: two adults, armed, in the dark, kidnap a fourteen-year-old boy and take him away to frighten him. Instead of which, the fourteen-year-old boy not only refuses to be frightened, but, unarmed, alone, in the dark, so frightens the two armed adults that they must destroy him.

Faulkner simply accepted Huie's take on the Till story, especially the absurd notion that a fourteen-year-old boy frightened two big armed men. What, he asked, had caused southerners to fall so far from the valor of their ancestors, what now made them so fearful as to believe that, "as soon as the Negro enters our house by the front door, he will propose marriage to our daughter and she will immediately accept him?"[10]

For all of his hedging and misplaced faith in moderation, Faulkner was on to something. If Emmett Till did not scare Milam and Bryant, the *idea* of assertive black men certainly frightened the white South. It went deeper than the old sexual fears of black men, Faulkner argued, to include the idea of blacks seeking justice and competing successfully in all areas of society against whites. "Fear, not hatred, is what I've experienced from Southern people," Faulkner told a radio interviewer. He was right, fear was as much a part of white supremacy as hatred. Racism merged them, entwined them in bad faith, because fear rationalized hatred. Hatred could not justify child murder, but fear could.[11]

Equally as powerful as hatred and fear was forgetting, even denial, as a young screenwriter named Rod Serling learned. Twice he attempted to bring the Emmett Till story to television. A few months after Sumner, he wrote a screenplay called "Noon on Doomsday" for ABC's *United States Steel Hour*. Sponsors refused to approve a drama focused on Till and the South. They believed that anything overtly about race risked alienating a large portion of their audience. Serling tinkered with his original concept, set his drama in New England, made the victim Jewish, and emphasized the broad themes of scapegoating and tribalism. ABC thought it still evoked Till too strongly. Then word got out, the Citizens' Councils mobilized a letter-writing campaign, and network executives asked the young playwright for more changes.[12]

"Noon on Doomsday" finally aired on April 25, 1956, and the *New York Times* critic Jack Gould, who had praised Serling's earlier writing, said this play strained credulity about narrow-mindedness in a small town, adding, "His work seemed artificially supercharged instead of genuinely powerful . . . and his characters emerged more as stereotypes in a superfluity of plot than as people of persuasive dimension." Precisely such fuzziness, of course, made sponsors and the network more comfortable.[13]

Serling returned to the Till story a couple of years later. He outlined a script for CBS's *Playhouse 90*, this time with an African American subject. Five out of six sponsors said no, for fear of offending white southern audiences. *Playhouse 90* finally produced "A Town Has Turned to Dust" in June 1958, but not before turning the story into a Western. Serling agreed to set the action in the Southwest of the 1890s and to make his victim a nineteen-year-old Mexican named Pancho Rivera. The *Times*'s Jack Gould liked this one, calling it, "a raw, tough, and at the same time deeply moving outcry against prejudice." Ironically, Gould also praised Serling and *Playhouse 90* for fighting executive interference with the story. But Serling was not happy: "By the time 'A Town Has Turned to Dust' went before the cameras, my script had turned to dust. . . . They chopped it up like a room full of butchers at work on a steer." Serling died in 1975, but in 2008, students at Ithaca College, where he had taught off and on for years, staged a reading of his original play about Emmett Till, set in the South with black and white characters.[14]

Even without the censorship of corporate sponsors and television executives, interest in the Till story drained away quickly. As we have seen, Huie hoped to parlay his *Look* article into something much bigger. He wrote to John Whitten of his plans to do another essay for *Look*, merge it with the first article, expand them into a book, and then score some real money with a blockbuster movie. If all went well, Huie told Whitten, he soon would be sending more checks to Sumner.[15]

Huie did the work as promised, but the big payoff never came. His new article, "What's Happened to the Emmett Till Killers?" appeared in *Look* in January 1957, exactly a year after "Approved Killing," and it detailed the fate of Milam and Bryant since their acquittal. Huie reviewed the "facts" of the case—how Till bragged to his Mississippi pals about his white girl-friends back in Chicago, his encounter with Carolyn Bryant, how he told Milam and Bryant, he was as good as they were. The brothers believed that the "not guilty" verdict signaled their neighbors' approval of the murder. Any "red-blooded, Anglo-Saxon, southern white man" would do what we did, Milam told Huie. As it turned out, white Mississippians did not want the blood-soaked confession rubbed in their faces. Sexual mingling between the races remained anathema, violence might be justified, but bragging about it for pay embarrassed them.[16]

Huie wrote that disillusionment and misfortune dogged the brothers now, that their neighbors made them pariahs in their own land. Milam had no regrets about killing Emmett Till, but he resented the hardships that followed. African Americans refused to trade with the family, so the stores in Money, Glendora, and Sharkey all closed; black workers stopped picking cotton and running farm equipment for them. Milam was forced to go back to farming, but no one in Tallahatchie County would rent to him, least of all the big men who had helped pay his lawyers. He finally found a place in neighboring Sunflower County, after Whitten intervened to secure a bank loan for him. Meanwhile, Roy Bryant struggled to find a job after losing his store. His family moved to Indianola, where he attended welding school under the GI Bill. J. W. worried that this would go hard on his brother, since welding often ruined a man's eyesight, and in fact, Bryant eventually went blind.[17]

Milam clearly expected sympathy, and Huie wrote in a manner to bend the readers' emotions that way, to castigate the hypocrisy of Delta elites. "I had a lot of friends a year ago," but now those friends were "making excuses," Milam lamented. "I got letters from all over the country congratulating me on my 'fine Americanism' . . . but I don't get that kind of letters any more." Now he was back to sharecropping, living in a cabin in Sunflower County with no running water. "My wife and kids are having it hard," he told Huie; "I don't know nobody and nobody knows me." On top of all that, the sheriff ordered Milam to stop carrying his gun, despite the fact that death threats were the one type of letter that never stopped coming.[18]

A Tallahatchie citizen explained the situation to Huie: "We figured we might as well be rid of them. They're a tough bunch. And you know there's just one thing wrong with encouraging one o' these peckerwoods to kill a nigger. He don't know when to stop—and the rascal may wind up killing you." Huie concluded, "As landless white men in the Mississippi Delta, and bearing the mark of Cain, they will come to regard the dark morning of August 28, 1955, as the most unfortunate of their lives."[19]

Huie hoped for a big splash with his article, but compared to "Approved Killing," he got little attention. Once again, *Look* took out newspaper ads: "EMMETT TILL KILLERS PUNISHED," the headline read, and the copy added that "the awakening conscience of the South" was giving Till's murderers "the punishment they deserve." The African American press reported on the *Look* article, leading with the death threats against the brothers and re-counting, indeed reveling, in their hardship. But the mainstream media failed to give the story much play; readers had lost interest in Emmett Till. Huie finally published *Wolf Whistle and Other Stories* in 1959 as an expanded version of the two *Look* articles. He filled it out with more tales of his own courageous truth-telling, and with new and even more dubious "facts"— now, when Preacher Wright rose in court he described Milam and Bryant as the men, "who come in de night and got de boy"; now, there were twenty teenagers in front of Bryant's store; now, Emmett's friends in Chicago attested to his sexual precocity; now, Mamie raked-off five thousand dollars and acquired a new wardrobe from donations at Emmett's funeral; now, Till was an even bigger sexual aggressor, boasting to Milam about what "he did to a white girl in Chicago." Signet paperbacks published *Wolf Whistle*, but it was not a big seller. The following year, Huie submitted his screenplay to United Artists. The film was never made.[20]

"After Two Years, Few Talk about Till Case," headlined a United Press story on the murder's second anniversary. As one Tallahatchie County citizen put it, "the Emmett Till case isn't mentioned around here any-more." Nor was there much notice a year later when Mamie Till Bradley filed suit against *Look* for a million dollars. Her attorney alleged that the depictions of herself and her son held them both up to ridicule, injured their reputations, and violated Illinois libel laws. The case was thrown out. For whites, at least, the story had all but disappeared.[21]

For the next thirty years, only stray references to Emmett Till made their way into mainstream American culture. The trial scene in Harper Lee's 1960 novel *To Kill a Mockingbird* evoked Sumner, but Lee did not explicitly make that connection. The following year, Jay Milner, who had written about the Till case for the *Delta Democrat-Times*, published a novel, *Incident at Ashton*, in which a newsman covers a similar story only to face violence, desertion by his friends, and anger from his readers. Milner's book failed to sell out its first printing. In 1962 Bob Dylan, an obscure but promising young folksinger, wrote "The Death of Emmett Till": "For the jury found them innocent and the brothers they went free / While Emmett's body floats the foam of a Jim Crow southern sea...." Dylan renounced the song two years later, calling his motives "phony," meaning that he had written a protest song but knew little about the subject.[22]

Emmett Till had faded quickly from white American popular memory. Except for this coda:

In 1975, Susan Brownmiller published her best-selling book, *Against Our Will: Men, Women and Rape*. It was a landmark work for the feminist movement, which had revived in the 1960s, part of a larger social awakening that included civil rights and protest against the Vietnam War. To understand rape, Brownmiller argued, was to understand the power that men wielded over women in daily life. *Against Our Will* was a historical study, piling example on example of rape as the most extreme form of gendered domination and inequality. Brownmiller argued that the crime was not an outlier, not merely a personal offense or an aberration in human conduct. Rape was a social act, an atrocity, the clearest example of women's subordination to men. Rape was the most extreme act along a continuum of slights, intimidations, abuses, and violence.[23]

Brownmiller included a chapter on race, with discussions of black subjection to white, including the rape of slave women by their masters. As she moved into the modern era, she noted a handful of radical black men, leaders of anticolonial and civil rights struggles who suggested that in some cases, rape was a weapon of liberation. Brownmiller exploded. Rape was violence against women, pure and simple, designed to keep them in their place: "Rape is to women as lynching was to blacks . . ., the ultimate physical threat by which all men keep women in a state of psychological intimidation." Rape was men controlling women.[24]

And then *Against Our Will* took an odd turn. By 1975, the mainstream media rarely mentioned Emmett Till anymore, but citing William Bradford Huie as her authority, Brownmiller argued that "the Chicago braggart" had provoked his tormentors. She described the murder as, "a case of white male retaliation for black male transgression." Till displayed his white girlfriend's photo, asked Carolyn Bryant for a date, whistled at her. He was not just some kid who failed to understand the codes of the South.

In fact, he understood all-too-well male privilege over women, something he shared with his killers. Emmett Till did not deserve to die, but he was no innocent victim:

> Rarely has one single case exposed so clearly as Till's the underlying group-male antagonisms over access to women, for what began in Bryant's store should not be misconstrued as an innocent flirtation. Till's action was more than a kid's brash prank and his murder was more than a husband's revenge.... Till was going to show his black buddies that he, and by inference they, could get a white woman and Carolyn Bryant was the nearest convenient object. In concrete terms, the accessibility of all white women was on review.... [25]

Brownmiller argued that Till and Milam both understood that the wolf whistle was no mere compliment to a pretty woman but "a deliberate insult just short of physical assault, a last reminder to Carolyn Bryant that this black boy, Till, had in mind to possess her." And here Brownmiller turned history into memoir, because Emmett Till—Huie's Emmett Till—had taught her a personal lesson that began in 1955: "At age twenty and for a period of fifteen years after the murder of Emmett Till whenever a black teen-ager whistled at me on a New York City street or uttered in passing one of several variations on an invitation to congress, I smiled my nicest smile of comradely equality—no supersensitive flower of white womanhood, I." But finally, Brownmiller wrote, she came to "understand the insult implicit in Emmett Till's whistle, the depersonalized challenge of 'I can have you' with or without the racial aspect. Today a sexual remark on the street causes within me a fleeting but murderous rage."[26]

It was not lost on Brownmiller's critics that her indictment of Emmett Till smacked of scapegoating, just as rape victims were often blamed for the crime that befell them. The social activist and scholar Angela Davis argued that *Against Our Will* made Emmett Till nearly as guilty as his murderers, and she attributed this to Brownmiller's racist assumptions about black men as would-be rapists. Davis accused Brownmiller of dwelling on a handful of black liberationists' most "absurd and purposely sensational words" as if they represented the thoughts of all African American men. Davis went on to take other '70s feminists to task for accepting the old stereotypes of black males so readily. In a word, Brownmiller's laser focus on gender threatened to occlude her view of racial oppression.[27]

The politics of race and gender aside, it is striking how "The Shocking Story of Approved Killing in Mississippi" so easily dominated Brownmiller's thinking. She had lived through the Till murder, but all of the twists and turns of the case, its multiple racial valances, disappeared before her eyes, save for Huie's stereotype of the sexually rapacious black Chicagoan. For most Americans—white Americans—the Emmett Till story long since had been put aside. When Susan Brownmiller took it down off the shelf twenty years later, it was the *Look* magazine version she reached for. William Bradford Huie's "Approved Killing" had done its work.

CHAPTER THIRTY-TWO

THE TIME HAD COME. I COULD FEEL IT. I COULD SEE IT.

THE TILL RALLIES that began two days after the Sumner verdict revealed how black activists instantly recognized the importance of the story. So did African American artists and intellectuals. Late in 1955, Louis Burnham, editor of the monthly journal *Freedom*, penned an incisive social analysis, showing how Till's case was part of a much larger system of labor exploitation in the South. Also late in the year, Ernest Withers, a Memphis photographer who had covered the story in Mississippi and Chicago, published a small book of images, for sale through the black press. And James Hicks continued to write new and expanded essays, adding texture and detail. Poems also began to appear, some in black newspapers, some in leftist publications, including one by Langston Hughes.[1]

African Americans never swallowed Huie's account of the Till murder, and certainly black writers refused to give him the last word, refused to cede history's final image of Emmett Till to *Look*. In early 1956, the Los Angeles–based *California Eagle* published a five-part reprise of the Till saga, probably ghost-written by Dr. T. R. M. Howard, arguing that Huie covered up a conspiracy that went far beyond Milam and Bryant. Olive Arnold Adams agreed, and her brief book *Time Bomb* called Huie's work "vicious propaganda" that demeaned Emmett Till by damning him with the old stereotype of the black rapist.[2]

Then in the spring of 1956 came a series of long interviews with Mamie Till Bradley by the *Chicago Defender* reporter Ethel Payne. One of Bradley's reasons for opening up was to counter "that terrible article in *Look* magazine, full of Milam and Bryant's lies." She gave intimate details about the three agonizing days awaiting word of Emmett's fate, and she reasoned persuasively that at least half a dozen men—four white, two black—murdered her son. She also described how a "presence," a "voice" visited her in the night and told her that Emmett's death was ordained from the beginning of time, that he "died blameless like Christ," that spreading the word made her an instrument of her peoples' redemption. As if to underscore her point, the *Baltimore Afro-American* ran an article on the first anniversary of her son's death titled, "A Little Child Shall Lead Them."[3]

It is too simple to say, as some have, that the Civil Rights Movement began with Emmett Till, that once people saw the funeral photos the scales fell from their eyes, or that activism began when Milam and Bryant walked free. Lobbying, rallying, organizing, petitioning for a whole range of changes, including voter registration, antilynching laws, desegregating the armed forces, equal employment opportunities, ending housing discrimination—all started decades before 1955. Equally important, so did the intellectual crusade against racism by social scientists, journalists, and activists in both scholarly and popular journals. Till's murder was taken up as a civil rights cause because a thick web of black rights groups, labor unions, churches, and liberal organizations was already in place. The "Long Civil Rights Movement" began decades before Emmett Till boarded that Illinois Central train and would have continued had he never gone to Mississippi.[4]

Still, the phrase "The Emmett Till Generation," perfectly describes the group of young black activists born mostly in the 1930s and 1940s who went on to create the greatest mass movement in twentieth-century America. Till's story embodied the evils of segregation, racism, and a warped justice system. Even as his killers struck fear in peoples' hearts, they also unwittingly engendered courage. The activist Joyce Ladner is credited with coining the phrase, "Emmett Till Generation" to describe Mississippians like herself. "I can name you ten SNCC workers who saw that picture...in *Jet* magazine who remember it as the key thing about their youth that was emblazoned in their minds." That photo "galvanized a generation," she said; "that was our symbol."[5]

In 1966, the Harris-Newsweek Poll interviewed more than one thousand African American adults about their memories of key events in the

Civil Rights Movement, from the Scottsboro Boys trials in the 1930s to the assassination attempt on James Meredith in 1966. Harris also asked them about their political engagement—had they worked in voter registration, marched in demonstrations, joined a sit-in, or picketed a store? The political scientist Fredrick Harris reaggregated all of this data and found a clear correlation between activism and remembrance. Those with the deepest historical memories were also the most politically engaged, and the correlation was strongest for *Brown*, Montgomery, and Emmett Till's lynching. *Brown* and Montgomery should not surprise us; they were major victories in the Civil Rights Movement. But the Till murder was an act of terrorism designed to engender fear, to keep people in their place. That stomach-turning photograph seared the story into black peoples' memories, and the killers going free doubled the effect. Nevertheless, Harris's study shows that for many African Americans coming of age in the 1950s and '60s, Emmett Till's murder was a call to arms.[6]

Memoirs confirm the data. "I was shaken to the core by the killing of Emmett Till," the civil rights leader and future congressman John Lewis wrote in his autobiography, *Walking with the Wind*. "I was fifteen, black, at the edge of my own manhood, just like him. He could have been me. *That could have been me*, beaten, tortured, dead at the bottom of a river."[7]

John Lewis grew up in Troy, Alabama. He was in the thick of it all during the '60s: beaten during the Freedom Rides, arrested dozens of times, an organizer of the March on Washington, head of the Student Nonviolent Coordinating Committee with its Mississippi Freedom Summer, gassed and bludgeoned by police in the march from Selma to Montgomery. Lewis recalled how the hope engendered by *Brown* was answered by the horror of the Till murder—the brutality of the killers, the callousness of the Citizens' Councils, the cowardice of the Sumner jury. The Till story pushed him hard down the road to justice. "By the end of that year, I was chewing myself up with questions and frustration and, yes, anger—anger...at the system that encouraged and allowed this kind of hatred and inhumanity to exist." But out of the Till murder and its aftermath, Lewis wrote in his memoir, came a new feeling, not just outrage but determination: "The time had come. I could feel it. I could see it."[8]

The agony and turmoil and courage that went into the freedom struggle is nowhere better described than in Anne Moody's *Coming of Age in Mississippi*. Her opening words, "I'm still haunted by dreams of the time we lived on Mr. Carter's plantation," were an evocation of slavery in a mid-twentieth-century memoir, for the word "plantation," with all of its resonances, was still current a hundred years after emancipation. An exceptional child, a straight-A student but with a rebellious streak, Moody's adolescence and her racial coming-of-age came in the mid-1950s as the war over segregation boiled into public life.[9]

Emmett Till's murder was the moment of her awakening, and it coincided with her working as a part-time housekeeper for Mrs. Burke, a local organizer for the Citizens' Council—here called "the Guild"—who was determined to break Anne's spirit. Mrs. Burke told Moody that Till "got out of his place" with a white woman and "stirred up a lot of trouble." Burke added, "it's a shame he had to die so soon," noting that Anne and Emmett were the same age. The story had the desired effect: "For the first time out of all her trying, Mrs. Burke had made me feel like rotten garbage. Many times she had tried to instill fear within me and subdue me and had given up. But when she talked about Emmett Till there was something in her voice that sent chills and fear all over me."[10]

Fear, yes, but also the seed of racial awareness. The Till story terrified Moody's mother, who told her daughter never to talk about it. But one of Moody's teachers quietly explained what had happened to Emmett Till, and she told Anne how the NAACP worked for basic rights for African Americans. In the coming months, the local Citizens' Council put Moody's town, Centreville, through a witch hunt. White men who crossed the sex/race barrier were publicly exposed, black men who did the same were beaten and worse, and entire families were burned out of their homes. By the end of the 1956 school year, Moody said, she hated white people for the murders and beatings, and hated black people too, especially black men for doing nothing about it, "smiling in a white man's face, addressing him as Mr. So-and-So, saying yessuh and nossuh..." Like John Lewis, it would be a few years before Anne Moody hitched her fate to the burgeoning Civil Rights Movement, but it was the Till murder that first opened her eyes to the racist brutality that warped Mississippi life.[11]

Over and over again, Emmett Till's story moved men and women, some of them unlikely gladiators for equality. In his memoir, *The Greatest*, Muhammad Ali (born Cassius Clay) described driving through his hometown of Louisville, Kentucky, with his mother, in the early 1970s. She remarked on how rigidly segregated Louisville had been just a few years earlier, and how sensitive he was as a child to stories of injustice. "Then your father'd come home, dramatize what happened, make it worse. Like the thing about Emmett Till. You remember when they lynched Emmett Till in Mississippi, how upset you were?" Switching from his mother's voice to his own, Ali compared himself to Emmett Till, claimed that he and Emmett were born on the very same day (in fact, Ali was six months younger), said he felt "a deep kinship" to the Chicago boy. "A week after he was murdered," Ali recalled, "I stood on the corner with a gang of boys, looking at pictures of him in the black newspapers and magazines. In one, he was laughing and happy. In the other, his head was swollen and bashed in." In retaliation, Ali wrote, he and his friends threw some switches and derailed an incoming locomotive in a deserted train yard.[12]

Years later, the Till story kept gnawing at Ali, and it merged slowly with his dawning racial consciousness. He told an interviewer that he thought a lot about Emmett Till's killers going free, how often that sort of thing happened, and in the next sentence he said, "In my own life, there were places I couldn't go, places I couldn't eat. I won a gold medal representing the United States at the Olympic games, and when I came home to Louisville, I still got treated like a nigger. There were restaurants I couldn't get served in. Some people kept calling me boy...." When the US Army drafted Ali in 1967 during the height of the Vietnam War, he refused induction, and for the next several years, stripped of his championship, he spoke out against the war, always emphasizing that racism was the font of his unwillingness to serve: "The real enemy of my people is here." Muhammad Ali belonged to the Emmett Till generation.[13]

So did Cleveland Sellers, a key leader of the Student Nonviolent Coordinating Committee in the 1960s, who recalled how the "cold-blooded callousness" of the Till lynching touched everyone in his hometown, Denmark, South Carolina. For weeks, in barbershops and grocery stores, Till was the only subject on peoples' lips. Myrlie Evers-Williams, the widow of Medgar Evers and an activist in her own right, wrote that the key to understanding the Emmett Till case was its typicality—a black male lynched and no one punished for it—followed by the atypical, explosive reaction. Till's story became "a rallying cry and a cause...that ignited protests around the world... ." As an eight-year-old in New York City, the basketball star Lew Alcindor, who later changed his name to Kareem Abdul-Jabbar, remembered seeing Emmett Till's death photo in *Jet* magazine and hearing his parents talking about it. Then as a young adult in 1969 he read Anne Moody's book and the story came flooding back: "The murder shocked me; I began thinking of myself as a black person for the first time, not just a person. And I grew more distrustful and wary. I remember thinking: *They killed him because of his color.* In a way, I lost my childish innocence."[14]

Remembering Emmett Till sharpened black identity, prodded commitment, and motivated action. The metaphor underlying all of this was the death of innocence, but innocence was complicated. Some tellings of the story emphasized that Emmett was innocent as children are innocent, without knowledge of the adult world of sex and its taboos. Others stressed innocence as the undeserved suffering of a high-spirited kid who did nothing to deserve death. Innocence in other accounts meant that Till was not guilty of illegal or inappropriate acts—never wolf-whistled at Carolyn Bryant, never touched her, never carried a photo of a white girlfriend. Till's innocence was multivalent: innocent like an outsider, innocent like a child, innocent like someone unjustly accused, innocent like a holy naïf, innocent like Jesus— the *Sacrificial Lamb of the Civil Rights Movement*, as one writer called him.[15]

The companion to innocence is martyrdom. Emmett Till was a victim of white supremacy, a martyr to racism. So long as nonviolence dominated the Civil Rights Movement, stories of unrequited suffering remained powerful. In Christian mythology, suffering affirmed righteousness, and out of empathy with suffering came moral commitment. This worked in reverse too. Years after he graduated, the self-described conservative Shelby Steele decried the unearned victimhood that he and his fellow college students claimed. "The single story that sat atop the pinnacle of racial victimization for us was that of Emmett Till," Steele recalled. "By telling his story and others like it, we came to feel the immutability of our victimization, its utter indigenousness, as a thing on this earth like dirt or sand or water."[16]

Vicarious martyrdom gave Steele and his friends a sense of racial solidarity, helped them endure their vulnerability on a white college campus. But in retrospect, Steele argued, these feelings were inauthentic. He and his friends were privileged; their personal stories were nothing like Emmett Till's. Meanwhile, at the other end of the political spectrum, many militant activists also grew dubious about Christlike innocence and suffering but for very different reasons. Groups like the Nation of Islam and the Black Panthers rejected nonviolence in favor of active, even armed resistance. If someone lays a hand on you, send him to the cemetery, Malcolm X famously said. Recruiting converts on the streets, the Nation of Islam invoked Emmett Till's name as a prime example of the viciousness of the white man, the emptiness of his justice, the futility of seeking his help. Ticking off a litany of dead martyrs, including Emmett Till, Malcolm X concluded it was time that white people started dying. Innocent suffering was no virtue, and martyrs were to be avenged, not merely wept over.[17]

A few African American writers embraced William Bradford Huie's depiction of a defiant Emmett Till. James Baldwin wrote in the preface to his 1964 play, *Blues for Mr. Charlie*, "I do not know why the case pressed on my mind so hard—but it would not let me go." Baldwin based his play loosely on the Till story. A black man is accused of an indiscretion toward a white woman at a crossroads grocery store, and her husband kills him. However, Baldwin's main character, Richard Henry, is not young and innocent but full-grown, politically aware, defiant, armed. For Baldwin, desire across the racial divide is palpable, explicit for blacks and whites. Richard is an urban hipster who declares at one point, "I've got a whole gang of white chicks in New York. Man, you ought to watch a white woman when she wants you to give her a little bit. They will do anything, baby, *anything*." Baldwin channeled Huie's Till into a story of black defiance and desire. Freedom meant not just voting and citizenship, but love and sex. Till's story for Baldwin moved beyond innocence and martyrdom to personal liberation.[18]

All of this took a particularly dark turn with Eldridge Cleaver. Raised in Los Angeles and twenty years old in 1955, he wrote that Emmett Till's murder and his killers' acquittal, "turned me inside out." Cleaver was then serving time in Soledad Prison on a drug charge. Soon he joined the Nation of Islam and eventually became a founder and leader of the radical Black Panther Party. But back in 1955, he dwelled on a photograph of Carolyn Bryant, felt "tensions of lust and desire" when he looked at her picture, wondered if Emmett Till had felt the same about the woman responsible for his death.[19]

Cleaver wrote that he hated Bryant yet wanted her, and so "flew into a rage at myself, at America, at white women." He had a nervous breakdown, and when he recovered, began studying radical critiques of American society and capitalism. He came to think of himself as an outlaw, and, as a matter of principle, cultivated "an antagonistic, ruthless attitude toward white women." All of this merged into one thought: "Rape was an insurrectionary act," Cleaver wrote in his memoir, *Soul on Ice*. "It delighted me that I was defying and trampling upon the white man's law, upon his system of values, and that I was defiling his women—and this point, I believe, was the most satisfying to me because I was very resentful over the historical fact of how the white man has used the black woman. I felt I was getting revenge." He literally became white supremacists' worst nightmare made flesh, proudly claiming to enact the deepest fears of men like Milam and Bryant. For Cleaver, the Till story was not about innocence but revenge, "bloody, hateful, bitter and malignant." He served time for rape in Folsom Prison.[20]

Cleaver illustrates how the Till case was never just about race. Sex—more precisely, the relationship between black men and white women—propelled the story. No one understood this better than the Pulitzer Prize–winning poet Gwendolyn Brooks. Her brilliant 1960 poem "A Bronzeville Mother Loiters in Mississippi, Meanwhile, a Mississippi Mother Burns Bacon" reenvisions the Till story by telling it through Carolyn Bryant's eyes. Beginning with the South's long-standing fascination with Sir Walter

Scott, Brooks opens her poem with Bryant imagining the events of 1955 as a tale of chivalric valor. Carolyn pictures herself as the "maid mild" of the old English legends and ballads that she learned in school. Two manly knights had saved her from "the Dark Villain." But something was wrong. The Dark Villain was more like a child than an ogre chewing his enemies' bones. From what, exactly, had she been saved?[21]

Abruptly, Brooks shifts her poem away from Carolyn daydreaming medieval idylls to the Bryant's kitchen in Money, Mississippi, just days after the acquittal. Carolyn cooks for the family. She throws away the bacon she's burned and begins to fry a new batch. She steals a moment to pretty herself in the mirror before Roy comes down to breakfast. The reality of the Till murder crashes in on her:

> Had she been worth the blood, the cramped cries, the little stuttering
>   bravado,
> The gradual dulling of those Negro eyes,
> The sudden, overwhelming little-boyness in that barn?

Roy must never think she was not worth it; she would be a good wife.[22]

But at the breakfast table he rambles on about showing up Mamie Till Bradley and those northern intruders at the trial. The children start fighting, and Roy leans forward to slap one of them. Both begin to howl, and something snaps inside Carolyn Bryant. She leaves the table as the children scream. "She could think only of blood," and now she is filled with fear "tying her as with iron." Carolyn stares out the window, worried about her whimpering children and how she cannot protect them. Roy comes up behind her, consoling, but

> Still gripped in the claim of his hands.
> She tried, but could not resist the idea
> That a red ooze was seeping, spreading darkly, thickly, slowly,
> Over her white shoulders, her own shoulders,
> And over all of Earth and Mars.

Roy turns Carolyn around to face him and kisses her mouth:

> Then a sickness heaved within her. The courtroom Coca-Cola,
> The courtroom beer and hate and sweat and drone,
> Pushed like a wall against her. She wanted to bear it.
> But his mouth would not go away and neither would the
> Decapitated exclamation points in that Other Woman's eyes.[23]

Not heroic rescue as in the old legends here, but revulsion at "the claim of his hands," at Sumner, at her husband's kiss, at his violence, at her own dependence, at the phantom blood on her white shoulders, at the incriminating gaze of "that other woman," that Bronzeville mother. Old English ballads often ended with a rose and a briar entwining out of the graves of estranged lovers. Brooks added her own variation, a blossoming in Mississippi out of the corpse of Carolyn's love:

> ...A hatred for him burst into glorious flower,
> And its perfume enclasped them—big,
> Bigger than all magnolias.[24]

In the end, the romance turned to blood and loathing. The South's own version of chivalry—of white men "defending" their women against black depredations—was a trap, a steel cage of fear and violence. On the eve of the women's movement, Brooks suggested that to be protected was to be controlled. A well-ordered white society and a well-ordered white family were part of the same oppression, violence and power masquerading as love. Carolyn Bryant probably never harbored such thoughts but Gwendolyn Brooks, in her poetic imagination, revealed the intertwining of white supremacy and patriarchy.[25]

So in an era of tremendous intellectual and social ferment—of sit-ins, marches, and boycotts, of Freedom Rides, Freedom Summer, and the Freedom Democratic Party, of the NAACP, SCLC, and SNCC, of Watts, Harlem, and Detroit, of Black Muslims, Black Power, and Black Panthers—African American activists and intellectuals kept Emmett Till's memory alive. Perhaps the most important testament to the power of the Till story came just months after his murder. On December 1, 1955, Rosa Parks refused to give up her seat and move to the back of a Montgomery, Alabama, bus. Just a few nights earlier, she had attended a lecture by Dr. T. R. M. Howard. He spoke about organizing activities in the state, castigated the FBI for its inertia, and gave a vivid description of the Till case. Parks said later that Emmett Till was on her mind when the police hauled her off the bus and into jail: "I thought about Emmett Till and I could not go back."[26]

It was a matter of justice: "People always say that I didn't give up my seat because I was tired, but that isn't true. I was not tired physically, or no more tired than I usually was at the end of a working day....No, the only tired I was, was tired of giving in." Parks was no political innocent; she was the secretary of her local NAACP chapter and active in the Montgomery Improvement Association that organized the famous boycott of the city's buses. The young minister who gave the benediction at Dr. Howard's talk the night Parks was in the audience, and who also helped lead the boycott, was the twenty-six-year-old Dr. Martin Luther King Jr. He referred often in his speeches to "the crying voice of little Emmett Till."[27]

For years, decades, Emmett Till's memory was segregated, whites mostly forgetting, many blacks remembering and turning it into a weapon of liberation. If Till's murder was not the beginning of the Civil Rights Movement, his story made black oppression real, palpable, and thereby helped open new visions of freedom, visions that grew clearer with every march, every demonstration, every organizing drive.

CHAPTER THIRTY-THREE

WE'VE KNOWN HIS STORY FOREVER

THE EMMETT TILL GENERATION CARRIED his memory into Montgomery, Little Rock, Greensboro, Birmingham, Selma, and countless other places where they marched and demonstrated. At first their victories were local: a transportation system integrated, an all-white school enrolling black kids, new voters on election day. And then, through their efforts came colossal federal laws—the Civil Rights Act of 1964 and the Voting Rights Act of 1965, which swept aside southern segregation laws. Along with voting rights came black power in politics and in the criminal justice system.[1]

But the activism of the Emmett Till generation was not typical. Most African Americans' memories of him were as much personal and cultural as political. Emmett's was an intimate tale, told at kitchen tables, passed from one generation to the next about the treachery of the white world. "I was told that story the way you warn a child about traffic lights, seatbelts, and talking to strangers," recalled the writer Wesley Morris; "Till's age ensured that you never missed the point: He was 14."[2]

The historian Jonathan Holloway refers to stories like these as "Jim Crow Wisdom." Holloway recalled an Easter dinner party shortly after the twenty-first century began where he met an older African American gentleman, "stately and debonair" a "self-made success" who rose from rural Louisiana to Palos Verdes Estates in Los Angeles. Holloway was born after Emmett's murder, but he knew that his parent's generation braided the Till story into their own struggles with racial shame and humiliation. Holloway's dinner companion explained how he resolved to leave the South almost fifty years earlier because of the Till murder. "His voice wasn't quavering when he told us this story; too much time had passed for that. It was plain to see, however, that after so many years the bitterness was still present. The memories of lost time, broken families, and humiliations that ran the spectrum from racial epithets to lynching were as alive as the day of their first discovery."[3]

For most African Americans, Emmett Till's story did not become iconic immediately; it took years before his name became part of their saga as a people, their mythos. Memories of brutality and humiliation were not easy to embrace or talk about, especially in an age that promised brighter things. In the first few decades after the murder, Emmett's story was folk memory for most black Americans, recalled quietly, person-to-person, sometimes with anger, sometimes with sadness. Meanwhile, most whites were content to forget troubled times, or even to assume that America's racial turmoil had been addressed and solved. Ten years after the Till case dominated the headlines, his name threatened to disappear completely from mainstream culture. Newspapers, magazines, television, and even the African American press, including the *Chicago Defender*, mostly failed to note the tenth anniversary of his passing in 1965. The same was true in 1980 on the twenty-fifth anniversary, as America embarked on the Age of Ronald Reagan and decisively turned away from the social activism of the previous generation.[4]

Clenora Hudson-Weems recalled how she was traumatized as a ten-year-old by the photos of Emmett Till in *Jet* magazine and how the adults around her vowed "No more!" But casting about for a research topic in graduate school thirty years later, she reviewed works of academic and popular history and found only a sentence here and there about him. The story was still too painful—too raw, too brutal, too sexually charged—with no big victory at the end, no laws changed or facilities integrated, only the humiliations of Sumner, Louis Till, and William Bradford Huie. It was easier for civil rights leaders, the black bourgeoisie, white liberals, and historians to, in Weems's words, shovel earth over Emmett Till and focus on people like Rosa Parks. Emmett's cousin Wheeler Parker witnessed something similar. During the mid-1980s, Chicago teachers asked him to come and speak to their classes. Parker found that the students knew little of Emmett Till, the story made them uncomfortable, they had to be coaxed into listening. "For thirty years," Parker recalled of his family, "nobody interviewed us about it, and we were almost shamed to talk about it."[5]

This was about to change. Just when Hudson-Weems noted Emmett Till's absence from the pantheon of heroes, African American studies was enjoying a resurgence. Academic departments added courses and programs, and new scholarly books proliferated about slavery, reconstruction, Jim Crow, and the freedom struggle. Equally important, black history developed cache in American popular culture. The biggest initial push came from a powerful mix of fact and fiction, a dramatic family saga across generations from Africa to the slave South. In 1977, the television serial *Roots*, based on the eponymous novel by Alex Haley, riveted American families, black and white, to their screens. *Roots* proved that there was a market for African American history.[6]

Television, more than any other medium, also brought Emmett Till back into mainstream American culture. In the 1950s the networks broadcast fifteen minutes of national news each weeknight. Glimpses from Sumner came into American homes, allowing citizens North and South to hear a few words from Mose Wright, Mamie Till Bradley, and others. By the early 1960s, television revealed the sheer brutality of southern resistance to demands for civil rights: Attack dogs and water cannons in Birmingham, mounted police beating trapped protesters with truncheons in Selma. To many Americans, the freedom struggle protesters seemed like models of courage, self-restraint, and dignity.[7]

Television also created a civil rights archive for future generations. After a thirty-year hiatus, the Till story returned to broadcast news, first in Chicago in May 1985, when reporter Rich Samuels produced a segment for WMAQ's nightly report. Samuels opened by asking African Americans on the streets if the name Emmett Till meant anything to them? After a few "no's," Samuels used old video footage to reprise the story. Two months later, Samuels expanded it into a half-hour documentary, *The Murder and the Movement*. He included file footage, photographs, and interviews with Mamie Till Bradley, Wheeler Parker, Simeon Wright, even John Whitten. Most important, Samuels showed the picture of Emmett Till in his coffin. As it flashed on the screen, the writer James Baldwin, clearly shaken by his memories, says, "It was myself in that coffin, it was my brothers in that coffin. . . . I can't describe it so precisely, because it had been so mutilated, it had been so violated. It was him but it was all of us."[8]

For the first time in the mainstream media, whites saw the photograph, saw what the killers had done to Mamie's son, what tens of thousands of African Americans witnessed at Emmett's funeral back in 1955, what hundreds of thousands more stared at in *Jet,* the *Defender,* and other black publications. Samuels managed to end his program on an upbeat note. As its title implied, *The Murder and the Movement* linked Till's death to the freedom struggle, and the final minutes featured footage of Greenwood's now racially-mixed city council, of Mississippi blacks soliciting white votes and assuming positions of power. Out of suffering, the viewer might reasonably conclude, came progress. NBC's *Today Show,* America's longest-running morning news program, ran part of *The Murder and the Movement* in July 1986, bringing the Till story back to a national audience.[9]

The key breakthrough, however, came at the beginning of 1987. An independent African American film company called Blackside released a six-hour documentary, aired as part of Public Television's *American Experience* series. *Eyes on the Prize: America's Civil Rights Movement* covered the decade between *Brown* and the Voting Rights Act, and the opening episode, "Awakenings" made Emmett Till its first big story. Much of the footage was familiar to anyone who had seen *The Murder and the Movement.* There were some dubious details—Emmett carrying a white girl's photo, Huie on camera calling Emmett "belligerent," the assumption that there were only two killers, putting the words, "Thar he" in Mose Wright's mouth.[10]

Far more important, *Eyes on the Prize* made Emmett Till part of the freedom struggle's origin story for a national audience, placed his name squarely in its pantheon of heroes, moved him from private remembrance back into the public realm. The images from Money, Chicago, and Sumner, the interviews with participants, made it all come alive. At the center was the funeral, with gospel music over file footage, and embedded in the middle of it all, the two photos: Emmett smiling on Christmas Day 1954, the same picture Mamie pinned to his satin coffin-lid; and the ruin of Emmett's face after they dragged his body from the Tallahatchie River. *Eyes on the Prize* won several Emmy Awards for documentary filmmaking and became a staple in American classrooms for the next several years.[11]

Eyes on the Prize was part of a much larger rethinking of the Civil Rights Movement and the ferment of the 1960s. It is no coincidence that the documentary appeared just a year after the first observance of Martin Luther King Day. By the 1980s, few Americans would disagree publicly that southern segregation was wrong and that ending it had been a just cause. Embracing the accomplishments of the Civil Rights Movement as part of American history opened the possibility of acknowledging the savage past that had made it necessary. Emmett Till's lynching and the freeing of his killers were egregious acts; once the Civil Rights Movement grew less controversial, as overt racism got pushed into darker corners of American culture, it became harder to ignore such barbarities. *Eyes on the*

Prize helped make the freedom struggle central to the story of American progress, and the Till story was central to *Eyes on the Prize*.[12]

Like television, print journalism began to revisit it all in the 1980s. Simeon Booker covered the Sumner trial for *Jet* back in 1955, and he wrote a retrospective for his old magazine, that now venerable staple of the black middle class. Booker's title captured it all: "How Emmett Till's Lynching Launched the Civil Rights Drive." Booker reminded readers that Emmett Till's name had been all but forgotten for decades, but thirty years ago his story prodded masses of African Americans to march and contribute money and agitate for civil rights. He recalled how Mamie Till Bradley's pledge that her son had not died in vain "became a battle cry for a new corps of politicians, news people, civil rights leaders, and thousands of 'little' people who were sick and tired of being 'beaten down' and denied their rights." Mrs. Bradley, Booker wrote, fought the good fight, dedicated the rest of her life to educating Chicago's children, teaching them about tolerance. She embodied the spirit of change inspired by her son's death.[13]

Booker made explicit what *Eyes on the Prize* implied, that the Civil Rights Movement began with Emmett Till. Another Sumner veteran, Clotye Murdock, revisited Mississippi for *Ebony* magazine. The Till case, she wrote, was the most unforgettable story she had ever covered. Having lived abroad in subsequent decades, she wondered whether her friends now painted too rosy a picture of contemporary life in the Magnolia State, or, as she put it, "could democracy truly have come to the black man's mental Auschwitz?" Truckloads of men with rifles slowly driving by Mose Wright's home, Sheriff Strider's daily "Mawnin', niggers," the vendors in the courthouse who curtly refused to sell drinks to blacks, the "open, raw, vulgar menacing hate"—had it just disappeared? Yes, Murdock concluded, it had, not all of it but enough so that she felt comfortable as a black visitor. People were polite, shops integrated, African Americans occupied positions of power. Whites seemed relieved that "the day has finally come when they need no longer assert their Whiteness *all* the time." Above all, hope replaced pessimism, and no one could have predicted that thirty years ago. If Mississippi could be turned into a promised land, Murdock concluded, there was hope for America. And it all began with Emmett Till.[14]

Murdock failed to mention one of the most impressive changes of all, the Mississippi press, more precisely the *Jackson Clarion-Ledger*, which had recently merged with the old *Daily News* to become by far the state's largest newspaper. On the thirtieth anniversary of the verdict in Sumner, the *Clarion-Ledger* devoted a whole section of the Sunday paper to the Emmett

Till story, including comments by the old journalists who covered the trial. William Minor said that after Till, "you couldn't have a quiet little lynching" in Mississippi anymore; John Popham suggested that the case "was the first step of the changes that eventually came to the whole South"; Murray Kempton was still struck by the grace and gentility of Judge Swango; John Herbers remembered Mose Wright, "that slight man in his white shirt and suspenders rising from the witness stand and pointing his gnarled finger at Milam and Bryant as they sat stone-faced." The new *Clarion-Ledger* even acknowledged how much the old one had fostered a "stifling climate of opinion" back in 1955. It was all a little starry-eyed, even smug, but while racism and poverty endured, Mississippi *had* changed a lot.[15]

As the end of the twentieth century approached, works about Emmett Till grew not only more frequent but more substantial. In 1988 the historian Stephen J. Whitfield published the first book-length academic study of the case, *A Death in the Delta*. Several scholarly articles followed, most notably Ruth Feldstein's "I Wanted the Whole World to See: Race, Gender and Constructions of Motherhood in the Death of Emmett Till." The murder's fortieth anniversary in 1995 saw a new round of media attention and, more than ever, Mamie Till Bradley became memory's voice, giving countless interviews and speeches.[16]

The Till story also made its way into literature. Louis Nordan grew up in the Delta in the 1950s, and he placed Till at the center of his novel *Wolf Whistle* because, Nordan said, the story was, "a buried chunk of my self's permanent foundation, the granite cornerstone of something formative and durable and true." Another fictional rendering, Bebe Moore Campbell's *Your Blues Ain't Like Mine* was published in 1992, recounting the murder of fifteen-year-old Armstrong Todd, who spoke French to a white woman in a small Delta town, for which he was beaten and shot by her husband and his brother. The novelist Elizabeth Spencer never wrote about Till in fiction, but her 1998 memoir described how a family argument about his murder sent her permanently into exile from her native Mississippi with the words *"you don't belong down here anymore"* ringing in her ears. The poet Anthony Walton returned to the land of his parents long after they had fled Mississippi, where he wrote "The Lovesong of Emmett Till," which reimagined Till as a romantic adolescent, filled not with lust but with youthful infatuation for the Chicago schoolgirl—maybe Irish or Italian—whose photo he carried in his wallet. "He died," Walton's poem ends, "refusing to take back her name, his right to claim he loved her."[17]

The historic significance of the Till story kept growing with time. The veteran journalist William Minor wrote in 1994, "Those of us who covered the trial of Milam and Bryant in the cramped, steamy courtroom... had really no notion at the time of what the historic impact of the event would be." As the fiftieth anniversary approached in 2005, a flood of stories appeared in the media. Most of them summarized the murder and trial, sketched the lives of Emmett and Mamie Till, and marveled at how distant the Jim Crow South now seemed. They were more than a little self-congratulatory. Mid-twentieth-century America was long gone, they seemed to say; we can all breathe a sigh of relief that the nation has transcended its blatant old racism. The Till story had become part of a larger liberal narrative, proof of America's moral advancement, no longer a best-forgotten chapter of a benighted past, but the beginning of national enlightenment, a tale about the transformation of moral depravity into human progress.[18]

A few articles sounded a darker, less triumphal note. Paul Hendrickson wrote a long piece in the *Washington Post:* "Nearly every Mississippi story sooner or later touches this one," the tale of the callow, roly-poly kid from Chicago who, "didn't understand, not nearly enough, about the pridefulness and bigotries and paranoias and taboos and potentially lethal rages of the Jim Crow South." The Till story, Hendrickson wrote, was a key to unlock the enigma of race. Yet driving through Tallahatchie and Leflore Counties, talking to locals fifty years after Emmett's death, Hendrickson felt not the glories of racial progress but the tragic southern past as Faulkner had understood it, always dragging us back to its old darkness.[19]

Richard Rubin in the *New York Times* echoed this theme of ancient and indelible tragedy. Like Hendrickson, Rubin went to Mississippi, interviewed two elderly men—a juror and an attorney who participated in the Sumner trial—and came away wondering if anything fundamental had changed in fifty years. "We've known his story forever," Rubin wrote of Emmett Till. "Maybe that's because it's a tale so stark and powerful that it has assumed an air of timelessness, something almost mythical."[20]

But of course we had not known his story forever. What changed, articles like Hendrickson's and Rubin's signaled, was remembrance itself. Not only was the Till story reintroduced in American culture late in the twentieth century, it was told in the larger frame of the Civil Rights Movement, which exploded into popular memory in these years. In the South, local libraries and historical societies had remained mostly silent about the African American past into the 1970s—slavery, Jim Crow, lynching, and the rest received little attention. But as blacks acquired political power in the 1980s, the old institutions charged with keeping historical memory began to change. By the 1990s, black history moved toward the center of popular remembrance as new civil rights museums opened in Memphis,

Birmingham, and Savannah, with many more to follow. The freedom struggle itself became a key story in telling southern history, although too often as a triumph of American democracy and enlightened thinking rather than the product of mass organizing and political struggle against brutal resistance.[21]

Not just in the South but throughout the United States, African American history and the Civil Rights Movement expanded into popular memory through museum exhibits, high school and college classes, and even best-selling books. The growing attention to the accomplishments of the movement was a welcome antidote to silence, but much popular history was not terribly sophisticated. Almost fifty movies and television programs dramatized the Civil Rights Movement in the last decades of the twentieth century, the majority of them released in the 1990s. Most emphasized the victories of the sixties as a triumph of reconciliation and tolerance, as the expansion of compassion and understanding by individual whites. In reality, far more important were angry emotions, boycotts, law-breaking, violence, and finally victories through mass mobilizing. Long-suffering leaders like Martin Luther King and Rosa Parks were crucial to the movement's success, but they would have been the first to say that what really mattered were the thousands in the streets, risking their necks. And they would have cautioned against the smug assumption that the battle against racism and exploitation had been won.[22]

Rediscovering the Emmett Till story was part of this larger revival of civil rights memory. One simple measure of his newfound popularity was the proliferation of road signs marking the stations of his martyrdom. In 1955, Leon Despres, a Chicago alderman and a white liberal from the heavily black Fifth Ward, presented a resolution to the city council for naming a park after Till. The council referred Despres's resolution to the Forestry and Parks committee, where it died. But forty years later, in 1998 the city renamed a stretch of Seventy-first Street on the South Side "Emmett Till Road." Speeches and prayers commemorated the event, and in attendance were Mamie Till Bradley, Rosa Parks, and Mayor Richard M. Daley, son of Richard J. Daley, who had asked for federal intervention in the Till case back in 1955. Argo also renamed a street in honor of its native son, and Chicago's McCosh School, where he last took classes, was rechristened Emmett Till Math and Science Academy.[23]

By the early twenty-first century, historical markers bearing Emmett Till's name were everywhere. In the Delta, part of U.S. 49 East running through Leflore and Tallahatchie counties was rechristened the Emmett Till Highway. Plaques went up in front of the ruins of Bryant's Grocery

Store in Money, at the entrance to the courthouse in Sumner, and at the Roberts Temple of the Church of God in Christ in Chicago, each describing the building's place in history. The state of Mississippi added several other signs, including one marking the spot where Emmett's body was found in the Tallahatchie River (photos of this sign riddled with bullet holes became an Internet meme in 2016). Delta State University in Cleveland, Mississippi, created an Emmett Till archive and mounted an exhibit, sponsored in part by the National Endowment for the Humanities and the Mississippi Humanities Council. In tiny Glendora, Mayor Johnny Thomas oversaw the conversion of an old cotton gin into an Emmett Till museum, along with a twenty-acre park and nature trail. Mayor Thomas was the son of Henry Lee Loggins, one of the black men who allegedly took part in Emmett's abduction and death. The mayor told reporters that the new Glendora facilities were part of "a healing process."[24]

But television remained the single most powerful driver of the revival; film transformed Emmett Till into an icon. Evening news programs featured new Till stories, especially when current events like Mamie Till Bradley's death in January 2003 made it newsworthy once again. Most of these reports, like the ten-minute segment on CBS's popular show, *60 Minutes*, gave the truncated version of the story, much like *The Murder and the Movement*, and *Eyes on the Prize*.[25]

Then came two full-length Emmett Till documentaries, both created by black filmmakers intent on passing the torch of remembrance forward. Stanley Nelson produced and directed *The Murder of Emmett Till*, which, like *Eyes on the Prize*, received wide distribution as part of the *American Experience* series on public broadcast television. The film traced the story chronologically—Till's trip South, the incident at Bryant's Grocery Store, the kidnapping, murder, discovery of the body, funeral, trial, and acquittal. Along the way, the voice of actor Andre Braugher described lynching's reign of terror, the *Brown* decision, and the Citizens' Councils, but mostly the film stuck very close to Money, Chicago, and Sumner, emphasizing the viciousness of the crime, the innocence of the victim, and Mississippi's staunch defense of the murderers.[26]

Keith Beauchamp's 2005 documentary, *The Untold Story of Emmett Louis Till*, also highlighted the hellishness of the Jim Crow South, but it was a bit more ambitious. On the one hand, it followed the same well-worn conventions—blues for Delta scenes, gospel for the funeral, a melodramatic delineation of villains and victims; there was little room for ambiguity in the story. But Beauchamp had uncovered new photographs and video footage of the funeral and trial, and he eschewed an omniscient narrator for a series of on-camera witnesses—Emmett's cousins, his friends, his mother.[27]

Most striking was Beauchamp's suggestion at the end of the film that this was no closed case, that here on the fiftieth anniversary of Emmett Till's lynching, witnesses and perpetrators were still out there, waiting to be questioned, maybe brought to trial. Beauchamp combined filmmaking with advocacy. Not only was the past not dead but justice demanded keeping it alive, so even as he publicized his film, he crusaded for reopening the case. Praising the filmmaker and the film, a *New York Times* editorial declared, "Backed by Emmett's relatives, Mr. Beauchamp now asserts that there were actually 10 people—several of them still alive—present at the murder.... Family members and members of Congress are urging the federal government to investigate this case."[28]

Beauchamp's claims came in a context of ongoing federal investigations into other old civil rights crimes. Recent success in prosecuting Bryan De La Beckwith, who assassinated Medgar Evers in 1963, and in convicting two Klansmen whose bomb killed four little girls in Birmingham's Sixteenth Street Baptist Church strengthened federal resolve to reopen more cases. The passage of civil rights legislation and the creation of the Civil Rights Division in the Justice Department made this all possible. Beauchamp recruited a few congressmen to the cause, and the new district attorney for Leflore and Sunflower counties, an African American woman named Joyce Chiles, agreed that the guilty might yet be prosecuted. The young filmmaker's crusade paid off: the Justice Department opened a new Emmett Till investigation on May 10, 2004.[29]

CHAPTER THIRTY-FOUR

A WHISTLE OR A WINK

FBI AGENTS spent nearly two years on the case. They gathered old documents and interviewed everyone they could find. They were diligent this time, and their investigation offered important new insights. Their findings take us closer than ever before to the literal truth of what happened back in the summer of 1955, and closer also to some metaphorical ones. As it turns out, Willie Reed, the eighteen-year-old whose trembling testimony the Sumner jury ignored, got a lot of details right. Four white men in the cab of J. W.'s truck, two or three black men in the bed, along with Emmett Till—that's what Reed reported he saw early Sunday morning, August 28, on the Shurden plantation managed by Leslie Milam. Next, he heard the screams of someone being beaten in a barn. He identified J. W. Milam, a pistol at his belt, emerging for a drink of water.[1]

The FBI's interviews confirmed most of Willie Reed's account. Equally important, the federal agents refuted key parts of William Bradford Huie's version of the murder—that it was all J. W. Milam and Roy Bryant's doing, that they drove to the Mississippi River and back, that they alone beat Emmett Till in a shed in Glendora. Rather than focus on just the two brothers, the FBI concentrated on their extended family and communities. The Milams and the Bryants lived driving distance from each other in Leflore, Sunflower, and Tallahatchie counties. They ran tiny retail grocery stores that catered mostly to sharecroppers in Money, Glendora, Swan

Lake, Minter City, Itta Bena, and Ruleville. J. W. owned the store in Glendora and was part owner of the one in Money. Roy made deliveries for him when he and Carolyn were not busy tending to customers.[2]

Being small business owners was respectable enough, but in Mississippi black people were supposed to serve whites, not the other way around. Mom-and-pop grocery stores were well off the high road to status, and the Milams and the Bryants were hardly esteemed in their communities. The FBI agents noted that many locals, both white and black, referred to the family as "white trash" and "peckerwoods." Their sideline business, bootlegging, didn't help. One former police officer remarked on the family's arrogance, and he told the Feds, "Anybody they could push over they would," especially when several of the brothers got together.[3]

One name that came up repeatedly in the investigation was Melvin Campbell, who married into the family and ran a store in Minter City with his wife. Campbell died in 1972 but not before confessing to an unnamed source that he was with Roy Bryant the night of the kidnapping. Another FBI informant quoted J. W. as saying that Campbell was there when they tortured Emmett Till. The Feds also heard from an anonymous witness that Milam's friend Hubert Clark was with the brothers on the night of Till's murder. Other testimony revealed that yet one more of Milam's friends, Elmer O. Kimbrell, was seen at Bryant's store with Roy and J.W. on the night of the kidnapping. Kimbrell was the man charged with murdering Clinton Melton in Glendora three months after the Till killing. All of these potential accomplices were long dead by the time the FBI came calling.[4]

And then there was Leslie Milam, who lived on the property where they beat Till. A local peace officer described him as, "cocky, kind of a bully." As he lay dying of cancer in 1974, Leslie Milam confessed his involvement in Till's murder, but he did not specify exactly what he did. Emmett Till's beating, if not the murder itself, took place in the barn on the Clint Shurden plantation; Leslie Milam ran the farm, and Add Reed, Willie Reed's grandfather, identified Milam as being among the white men going in and out of the barn. So it is clear that either J. W. Milam had lied to William Bradford Huie to protect his family and friends when he said that he and Roy alone beat Emmett in a shed in Glendora, or perhaps Huie himself lied in his article because he could not obtain contractual releases from the others.[5]

As to the black men Willie Reed saw in the back of J. W. Milam's pickup truck, the FBI could not identify them with certainty, but two names that the journalist James Hicks heard before the trial in Sumner even began— Levi "Too Tight" Collins and Henry Lee Loggins—came up again and again in the FBI interviews, along with one other, Otha "Oso" Johnson. All of them worked off and on for J. W. Milam in Glendora, were dependent on him for their meager and irregular livelihoods—driving tractors, making deliveries, running mechanical cotton pickers, and, some informants suggested, selling bootleg whiskey. No doubt, some combination of threats, need, and loyalty to J. W. accounted for their presence on the truck, and probably also for their silence.[6]

Loggins and Collins never admitted their involvement, although several witnesses fingered them, while Otha Johnson confessed to his son that he had accompanied Milam and Bryant on the night they murdered Emmett Till. The three were probably there to make sure the boy did not escape, and perhaps, as some sources alleged, they held him down and even helped beat him. They also cleaned up the barn after the beating and washed the blood out of Milam's truck. By the time the FBI reopened the case, only Loggins remained alive.[7]

Because the Sumner trial turned on the identification of Emmett Till, the state of Illinois at the behest of the FBI ordered the Cook County medical examiner to unearth the body buried in Burr Oak Cemetery and conduct an autopsy. On June 1, 2005, almost fifty years after Till took the Illinois Central south to Mississippi, the coroner exhumed the remains and transported them to the office of the chief medical examiner. In case there was any doubt, dental records, DNA evidence, and other tests confirmed that it was indeed Emmett Till whom they had buried in 1955. The medical examiner ruled the death a homicide by gunshot wound to the head.[8]

The beating Emmett took was even worse than seemed apparent in 1955. When they pulled him from the river, an eye was out of its socket, his tongue protruded from his mouth, and a piece of bone fell from his head. A CT scan revealed extensive fractures of Emmett's skull, a break in his left leg, and fractures of both wrists, perhaps from trying to protect himself while being pistol-whipped. The medical examiner also observed a "vertical symphyseal fracture of the thyroid cartilage," which is to say his Adam's apple had been crushed. Metal fragments were embedded not only outside his skull but also inside. J. W., who long boasted of his marksmanship, had executed Till with an army-issue Remington cartridge filled with lead pellets, making his pistol a mini-shotgun. No wonder Big Milam could shoot a bumblebee out of the air with his Colt .45, as his friends attested.[9]

While the autopsy revealed the horror of Emmett Till's last night on earth, it refuted some of the gruesome "facts" that had arisen over the years. Till's torturers did not knock his teeth out. They did not castrate him or cut his tongue out. One local story had a dozen people attending his beating and murder, watching from bleachers inside the barn, which in the past had doubled as a venue for cockfights. In this telling, Till's tormentors repeatedly punctured his body with an awl, and finally killed him by drilling a handheld brace bit into his head. The examination found no evidence that the killers assaulted him with such implements, and FBI agents were convinced that the barn was never used for cockfighting, or that it had ever held bleachers.[10]

Though apocryphal, such details were part of the story's larger horror, and fifty years after Emmett Till's lynching, local people in Leflore and Tallahatchie counties reported fresh terrors to the federal agents. Some of the scenes they described were implausible, contradicting the known facts of the case. But these were less like lies than nightmares, fearsome tales, possessed of their own logic, metaphors of dread frozen in time, horror stories of black life at midcentury in the Mississippi Delta. The FBI's job was to gather legal evidence, but much of what they collected was testimony from trauma survivors. One moment young people sat with Emmett driving into Money, or they played games with him in the evenings after the harvest, or they laughed as he imitated the era's great comedians. Days later, his body turned up in the river, mutilated, shot in the head. Mere facts failed to capture the chaos and horror of that experience. Emotional truth demanded more. The FBI informants, most of them elderly now, mixed their personal memories with rumors, newspaper reports, their own imaginations, and incorporated it all into narratives of their times. If their stories were not strictly accurate in every detail, they were true in the way that bearing witness in church is true.[11]

Above all, the stories channeled elemental fear. One man recalled that he sometimes bought candy at Bryant's store, never had any trouble there because "I knew how to act." But then he remembered seeing a pickup truck one day, Milam and Bryant driving in the cab, and he heard screaming coming from beneath a tarp covering the back. A woman who spent her youth in Money said she knew Bobo Till and the Wright family, and that she had witnessed the kidnapping itself, that two or three hundred cars came screaming down the Dark Fear Road toward Mose Wright's home, following a snitch's lead. She speculated that Emmett's offense was that he had put money directly in Carolyn Bryant's hand rather than on the counter as interracial custom dictated. Yet another FBI informant recalled seeing several individuals around the Tutwiler Funeral home late in August 1955, when the director, who was drunk, asked "You want to see a dead nigger?" The informant was then shown the body of Emmett Till, and was told that citizens in town were organizing to free Milam and Bryant in case a jury convicted them.[12]

Such stories were filled with inaccuracies, improbabilities, inconsistencies. That is beside the point. They bespoke a world of terror in the Delta. Stay away from J. W.'s store, one boy from Glendora recalled his parents telling him, or risk getting cussed out or beaten up. Then he remembered standing outside the store one morning with friends, watching Too Tight Collins cleaning out J. W.'s truck. Too Tight offered them thirty-five cents each to help finish the job, washing out lumps of blood, "thick like jelly." Later he heard it was Too Tight who held Emmett down while Milam and Bryant cut out his tongue then cut off his genitals and stuffed them in his mouth.[13]

Another woman from Glendora described how for a lifetime she suppressed savage memories from her youth, things her parents hushed up, but now in old age they came flooding back, overwhelming her. She recalled men burning clothes in a barrel at night, Emmett's clothes, and one mental image in particular haunted her: a partly burned shoe, Emmett's shoe. "I remember them saying they found this man in the river," she told the FBI agents; "A lotta times really, they were finding people in the river." Whole families fled Mississippi for their lives after the trial, the agents were told.[14]

One witness, his fear still fresh after fifty years, recalled walking by the gas pumps in front of Milam's store in Glendora and seeing two black men standing in the bed of a pickup truck, blood running out the back, J. W. standing to the side. "This is what happens to smart niggers," Milam said. The man who told this story reported that he buried this memory for years, but later recalled his father dragging him through hedges away from the bloody truck, the branches cutting up his arms and legs. When they got out of earshot, his father told him never to speak of this incident or men would come to kill him and throw him in the river.[15]

The man who told this story was Johnny Thomas, son of Henry Lee Loggins. Thomas became mayor of Glendora decades after the murder. Out of guilt over his father's role in the crime, he said, he established the town's museum in an abandoned cotton mill, devoted to Emmett Till's memory. Even fifty years after the murder, his father was still afraid to admit he had been involved. Told by FBI agents that an informant accused him of being Milam's accomplice, Loggins burst out, "no that's a lie, that's a lie, that's a lie. What he said done tell a lie." Told that witnesses saw him and another black man riding in J. W.'s truck on the day of the murder, Loggins said, "I don't know nothing about that. I didn't see nothing about that....I ain't saw shit." But then Loggins admitted that shortly after the murder, Milam had him arrested on a trumped-up charge, and when he got out of prison six months later, Loggins's family, fearful for his life, gave him money to get out of Mississippi.[16]

There was plenty of hate to go around in the Delta at midcentury, and more than enough in the Milam/Bryant clan to murder a black boy. But as William Faulkner pointed out, fear was at least as important as hate in the Till story. Fear was racism's white-hot core. The memories revealed to the FBI fifty years after Emmett's murder attest to how deep that fear ran.

Fear stalked whites as well as blacks, though not the same fear, not as deep, or as visceral. White southerners feared that blacks, radicals, the NAACP, Communists, and the federal government were intent on burying Jim Crow. Lurking behind fear of those who would destroy their Way of Life was fear of intimacy with blacks, fear of competition from them, fear of reprisals for the injuries done to them, fear of sharing power, maybe even fear of one's own hate-begotten guilt. Somewhere just on the other side of a fourteen-year-old boy buying bubble gum in a grocery store lay whites' old fear of black male lust and violence. White fear grew out of the very system of racial oppression they created and perpetuated, but it manifested itself differently for men and women.[17]

Fear tinged the FBI interviews with the wives of J. W. Milam and Roy Bryant. Elderly now, their husbands long dead, they were still haunted by the Till story. In 1955, the Leflore County sheriff George Smith had written out a warrant for Carolyn Bryant's arrest but never served it, probably because the main evidence against her was Mose Wright's recollection that he heard a "lighter voice" confirming Emmett's identity from the kidnap vehicle. Carolyn Bryant and Juanita Milam gave long interviews to the FBI, yet each repeated over and over that she could not remember much, that her family kept her in the dark, that she had nothing to do with the kidnapping or killing, that she just did not know what really happened back in 1955.[18]

Carolyn Bryant had long since divorced Roy, and he died in 1994. She remarried, moved to Brookhaven, Mississippi, divorced, married again, and moved to Greenville. Each time the Till story lurched back into public notice, reporters tracked her down, looking for comments, and hate mail flowed again to her home. She did her best to ignore it all. When the FBI caught up with her, she told them that she had just received a phone call telling her to rot in hell for what she did to that little boy. We know what you look like, the caller said, and the same thing that happened to Emmett Till could happen to you. The federal agents told her they would help local police track down harassing calls and letters. They also reassured her that her conversations with them were strictly confidential, that probably no one would be charged with crimes, that the FBI was just setting the record straight, giving people the opportunity to clear their consciences. "Well, I didn't have a conscience to clear," she responded.[19]

Bryant told the agents that she had not spoken to anyone about Emmett Till since 1955. She could not even remember who drove her away from the store after they arrested Roy. She volunteered that he was a good husband and father most of the time, that they were very poor when all the trouble happened, that they owned a television but neither a car or a telephone, so in order to make a little extra money, Roy worked delivery jobs for his brother. In fact, the evening Emmett Till came into her store, Carolyn Bryant now recalled, was the first time that her husband was away overnight. Memory is a funny thing, one of the FBI agents remarked. Yes, she replied, "when you're scared to death," almost the exact words she uttered at the conclusion of her testimony in 1955. Mostly Carolyn Bryant repeated her story from the Sumner trial.[20]

Juanita Milam was even more closemouthed—at first. She convinced herself, or at least tried to convince her FBI interlocutors, that she was not in the building when Emmett Till walked in but, rather, in Greenville visiting her parents. She offered a few platitudes: J. W., who died of cancer in 1981, was a good man, everyone in the community liked him, he didn't talk about things that might worry her, and so he never discussed Emmett Till. Then she stonewalled. No, she'd not read Huie's article in *Look*; no, J. W. was not the type to kill anyone but he might have covered for his brother; no, she had no idea what became of her husband's gun. Juanita Milam added a few grace notes: Not only did J. W. not hate Negroes, he was an honorary member of the NAACP; Roy Bryant, unlike her husband, could be a little hot tempered; after Carolyn Bryant divorced Roy, she remarried multiple times and she drank too much.[21]

The federal agents asked Mrs. Milam what she thought had happened to Emmett Till. I still don't know, she replied. But what do you *think* happened? She said that she didn't think about it. The Feds persisted, arguing that all the stories from Carolyn Bryant and other family members didn't add up.[22]

And suddenly Juanita Milam let her guard down. No, they didn't add up, she agreed; Carolyn getting so upset over a whistle or a wink, "that's the point that don't make sense to me." The Feds saw their opening: "[Carolyn Bryant] told us and apparently she said at the trial back then that he grabbed her. Grabbed her wrist and grabbed her waist and said that basically he wanted to have his way with her and that he would be back. That's what she told us a month ago. . . . What do you think happened? It was more than that, wadn't it?" Juanita Milam said something quite unexpected: "Uh, the only way I can figure it is that she did not want to take care of the store. She thought this wild story would make Roy take care of the store instead of leavin' her with the kids and the store. That is a female point of view."[23]

The agents were incredulous. They asked if she was saying the whole thing never happened, that Carolyn Bryant had simply made up the story of the assault to get out of working at the grocery store. Well, Juanita Milam replied, Till might have winked or whistled, his cousins even said that he whistled. And then, seemingly unrelated, she started talking about how she had been around black people all her life, how she had good black help, how she never expected them to bow down to her, how she was not afraid of black people. The implication was clear: Carolyn Bryant made up her story about Emmett Till, worked a whistle or a wink into an accusation of sexual assault, to a near-rape, because she was scared to death of being alone with black men. From the "female point of view," they terrified Carolyn Bryant, and only her husband could protect her, take her away from this lonely store, rife with what a young white Delta girl had been taught to fear more than anything.[24]

Juanita Milam was the only one who ever told the story this way. She was in a position to know—she had been there, in the store and in the family, and the two sisters-in-law were intimate, they talked about the incident shortly after it happened. Simeon Wright, who was also right there, always maintained that when he went into Bryant's Grocery Store to bring his cousin Emmett out, nothing was unusual, no one seemed upset. Simeon and Wheeler Parker both denied that anyone had egged Emmett on at Bryant's store, or that they witnessed any tension or heard any commotion. They recalled that after he exited, Emmett stood with them watching a checkers game on the porch for a few moments. Only after Carolyn Bryant came out of the store did Emmett whistle at her.[25]

Juanita Milam's story is as plausible as any other, maybe more so. That fourteen-year-old Emmett Till was a sexual predator defies everything those who knew him best said about him. And we know for certain that Carolyn Bryant changed her story, making it more lurid in the days between her first discussion with her attorneys and the trial itself. Though not terribly specific, in 2016 she finally admitted to the historian Timothy Tyson that she had embellished the truth, made things up. Her fear of "this nigger man"—maybe any black man, as Juanita Milam suggested— felt entirely real to her. "I was just scared to death."[26]

After Bryant's encounter with Emmett Till, the two women agreed to say nothing to their husbands for fear of how they might react. But word of the incident quickly spread around the community. Someone—a

"Judas Nigger," currying favor with the white man, T. R. M. Howard later wrote—mentioned it to Roy Bryant on Friday after he got back from the Gulf Coast, and he pried the details out of his wife.

Maybe when confronted by her husband, Carolyn magnified a "whistle or a wink" into something much uglier. Stories about the lust of black men and about white men protecting their women from such depredations were in the very air Mississippians breathed. Or maybe she worked the story up after the murder, either on her own or coached by others, knowing that a mere "whistle or a wink" would not be enough in court, perhaps, too, not enough to quiet her own conscience after what happened to Emmett Till. Either way, if Juanita Milam's version was true, then the murder resembled more than ever an old-style lynching, where a black man's fate turned on a white woman's false accusation, an accusation she made for her own reasons but within the logic of white sexual honor.[27]

Carolyn Bryant mentioned one last thing to the FBI. Agents asked her about a recent article in the *Delta Democrat-Times* claiming that Mamie Till Bradley, shortly before she died, expressed a desire to talk to Carolyn Bryant about that night so long ago. "I wished many a time that I could have too," Carolyn told them. "But nobody ever contacted me..., and I didn't contact her because I didn't figure she would...wanna talk to me." It was a wistful moment, a fleeting longing for reconciliation that was not to be. The two daughters of Mississippi, two mothers of sons, never met.[28]

Not everyone longed to be reconciled. Carolyn Bryant's nephew carried the old rage of his father. J. W.'s son told the agents who came knocking on his door that in 1955, Mamie Till Bradley sent Emmett Till to Mississippi because he had raped a girl in Detroit. He described the "bull shit" that Till had thrown in his aunt's face. Young Milam asked his Dad "what got the kid killed" back then? J. W. replied, "you don't walk into a white man's store and tell a man's wife that you ain't been fucked till I fucks you." So far as Carolyn Bryant's nephew was concerned, Emmett Till was guilty as hell, and he told the FBI agents that his father, a man who took shrapnel from a German tank during World War II, wept as he recounted how his world collapsed after Money and Sumner.[29]

Through all of the news stories and all of the testimony over the years, Roy Bryant was the silent one, whose voice was rarely heard, even though it was his wife who allegedly was assaulted. In a 1985 interview he denied knowing anything but said he might remember more "for a bunch of money." Bryant added, "if Emmett Till hadn't gotten out of line, it probably wouldn't have happened to him."[30]

Roy Bryant was long dead when the FBI reopened the case, but they managed to find a brief tape-recording of him made years earlier by an unnamed informant. Bryant's words probably take us as close as we will come to the mood, the utter callousness, of the night they butchered Emmett Till. Asked if everyone had been drinking, Bryant replied "Yeah, hell yeah we was drinkin'," though he insisted nobody was drunk. He said he did not personally kill Till, but his contempt rings clear: "Well, we done whopped the son of a bitch, and I backed out of killin' the mother-fucker.... And we gonna take him to the hospital. But we done whopped that son of a bitch. I mean it was the carryin' him to the hospital wouldn't have done him no good (laughs).... Put his ass in the Tallahatchie River."[31]

In the end, the Federal agents simply reported their findings and made no recommendations regarding prosecutions. District Attorney Joyce Chiles decided to bring one case to the Leflore County grand jury, against Carolyn Bryant as an accomplice to her husband and brother-in-law. The jurors refused to endorse a true bill, the evidence was just too thin. Too many people were dead, too many memories cloudy, too few witnesses willing to cooperate. None of the nineteen jurors—twelve women and seven men, divided about evenly along racial lines—voted to indict.[32]

Beyond the shabby circle of the Milam-Bryant clan and their friends, the FBI turned up no proof of a major conspiracy, no KKK, no big lynch party. But certainly the good folks in the Citizens' Councils had done their part, poisoning the well of public opinion without getting their hands dirty. The same was true of many members of the local legal establish-ment, and of Mississippi politicians and editors too: they shed no blood, but they made sure that those who did never paid for it. In the end, the torture and lynching of Emmett Till was just cruel, sordid, and petty, com-mitted by roughly half-a-dozen people, from a little-respected white family, joined by two or three black workers who were compelled to assist. The larger Emmett Till's legacy grows, the sorrier his killers and their abettors become.

EPILOGUE

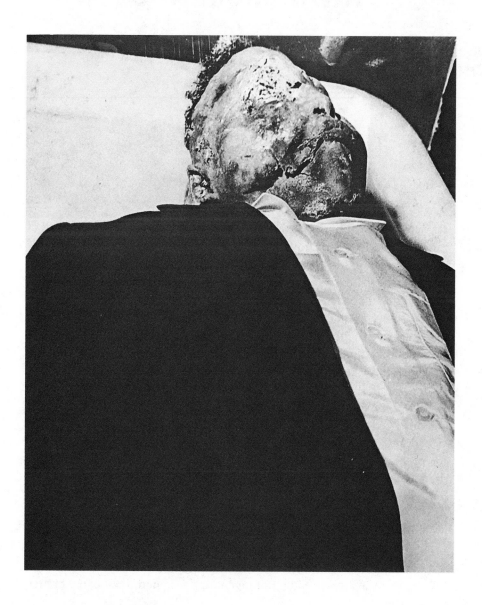

"YOU MUST NEVER LOOK
AWAY FROM THIS"

JUANITA MILAM'S REMARK that just "a whistle or a wink" started all of
the trouble reminds us how precarious the Emmett Till story was. As his
uncle Crosby Smith said, local officials hurriedly tried to spill the lad's
body into a shallow Mississippi grave; if they succeeded, we never would
have heard the name Emmett Till. Later, the civil rights leader Aaron
Henry observed that for decades the lynching of African American boys
had gone mostly unremarked by whites, but somehow the Chicago kid's
murder broke the silence.

The story of Emmett Till continues to grow and change. After the FBI
completed its investigation in 2007, a formal apology from Tallahatchie
County came to the Till Family. A year later, Congress passed the Emmett
Till Unsolved Civil Rights Crime Act—sponsored by Rep. John Lewis and
signed into law by President George W. Bush—which provided resources
for reopening cold cases. Since then, new Emmett Till documentaries,
dramas, websites, children's books, and museum displays have appeared,
and more are on the way.[1]

With heritage tourism seen as a path to community revival, plans
emerged to restore Bryant's Grocery Store in Money, and the courthouse
in Sumner. Chicago officially named the Roberts Temple a historic landmark in 2007, and local residents are seeking the same designation for the
Till home on the South Side. Heritage tourism sometimes creates strange

bedfellows—restored plantation mansions up the road from civil ri
memorials. Down in Tallahatchie County, the Emmett Till and Clar
Strider Memorial Highways intersect in the town of Webb, where Mamie
Till Bradley was born. And vandals have defaced, shot at, and erased
some of Emmett Till's historical markers in the Delta, including the one in
front of Bryant's Grocery Store.[2]

Three new Till books have come out in the last few years, all of them
widely and well-reviewed. Devery S. Anderson's *Emmett Till: The Murder
That Shocked the World and Propelled the Civil Rights Movement* (2015) is deeply
researched and tells the story in fine-grained detail, often through the
eyes of Mamie Till Bradley. The novelist and essayist John Edgar Wideman's
Writing to Save a Life (2016) focuses on Emmett Till's father, Louis, not so
much as straight history but as a meditation on the lives of black men.
Wideman uses documents, memoir, even bits of fiction to understand
the Tills, father and son. Timothy Tyson's *The Blood of Emmett Till* (2017)
focuses tightly on the South in those months when the story swept the
nation, and the book gives us Carolyn Bryant's confession that her sworn
testimony was not the full truth. New films are also appearing. A short
drama, *My Nephew Emmett*, tells the story through Mose Wright's eyes; it
was nominated for an Academy Award in 2018. And celebrities like
Whoopi Goldberg, Jay Z, and Will Smith have put their names and resources behind a forthcoming movie and a television miniseries.[3]

Perhaps the biggest Till event came in September 2016, when the mag-
nificent new National Museum of African American History and Culture
opened on the Mall in Washington, DC. On a floor devoted to the Jim
Crow era, in a room set apart, visitors arrive at the Emmett Till Memorial.
The exhibit has the feel of a chapel. Front and center rests the coffin in
which Emmett's body lay in Burr Oak Cemetery for fifty years before the
FBI exhumed it. Behind it, the entire wall is covered with a photo-mural
of the funeral service at the Roberts Temple. The effect is to transport
guests back in time to that traumatic moment, to State Street, Chicago,
1955. Visitors describe the Till Memorial as one of the most moving displays in the new museum. Oprah Winfrey called it "profound," and many
others summed up their experience as "sacred."[4]

Emmett Till's story has taken its place among the civil rights movement's holy of holies. In a stunning irony, by trying to silence "the boy
that did the talking down at Money," Milam, Bryant, and their accomplices gave Emmett Till a voice that has slowly grown louder with time.
But it was never a certainty that his story would become iconic. For thirty
years it had mostly disappeared from public discourse, his flame fed
mainly by those who put their lives on the line in the freedom struggle.

Today, activists in the Black Lives Matter movement know Emmett Till, keep his name alive by telling his story, the same way they keep alive Michael Brown, Eric Garner, Laquan McDonald, Philando Castile, Tamir Rice, and all the other African Americans, mostly men, whose names otherwise would sink into oblivion after the police took their lives. Once again, Oprah Winfrey struck the common chord: "When you look at the story of Emmett Till . . . and when you think about what's happening in our country today with black men unarmed being shot, it's like a new Emmett Till every week."[5]

When George Zimmerman shot seventeen-year-old Trayvon Martin to death in Sanford, Florida, in 2012—Martin was visiting family, but Zimmerman thought he looked "suspicious"—news stories routinely mentioned Till, and a photo-meme swept the Internet showing Trayvon and Emmett arm-in-arm. As the roll call of young African Americans killed by police came in over the next few years—in Ferguson, Missouri, on Staten Island, in Cleveland, Columbus, Chicago, Baltimore, Minneapolis, seemingly without end—newspapers and social media invoked Emmett Till's name again and again. The shootings were united by the assumption that young black men posed a threat, and by the fact that our criminal justice system exonerated the killers, not their victims.[6]

Of course, Emmett Till's murder was not precisely like these more recent deaths. The incidents in our own day are not honor killings or extralegal lynchings, not about interracial sex or regional antipathies. Our contemporary bloodletting takes place more often in the segregated North than in the South, and police, not civilians, are the killers. Urban racism and poverty form the backdrop, not Jim Crow sharecropping.[7]

Still, the comparisons to Emmett Till are appropriate. He was a young black man onto whom his killers projected their deepest racial hatreds and fears. He may not have been murdered by the police, but the criminal justice system failed him just the same, making a mockery of due process of law. Today's stories resonate with Emmett Till's lynching because they all still assume that young black men are dangerous, that they must be watched, that they can be killed with impunity. And just like decades ago in Sumner, families are denied justice.[8]

Emmett Till's story is invoked again and again today because it has become our foremost civil rights tale of innocence violated, of undeserved suffering and death. More, it is a horror story of institutional racism. No matter the fairness and good will of men like Judge Swango and Gerald Chatham, Mississippi's criminal justice system, law enforcement, politics, and social structure enabled Emmett Till's killers, protected them. Institutional racism is the beating heart of the Till story, far more than mere bigotry.[9]

The overaggressive policing that led to recent killings belies the notion that America ever became a "post-racial" society, a naïve presumption reinforced by the 2008 election of Barack Obama. The 2016 presidential election put an end to such wishful thinking, but several books had already demolished that myth. Michelle Alexander's *The New Jim Crow* (2010) focused on the carceral state, more particularly on the millions of African Americans in prison, on probation, or under the control of the law, way out of proportion to their numbers and often for slight causes. Alexander argues that the mechanisms of criminal justice have created a new racial caste system, not at all dependent on old-fashioned racism.[10]

Bryan Stevenson's *Just Mercy* (2014) took the story that Alexander constructed out of statistics and legal exegesis and personalized it, revealing in intimate detail how the legal system crushed real lives of real Americans. Ta-Nehisi Coates's *Between the World and Me* (2015), an open letter to his son, is more wide-ranging, less concerned with legal mechanisms—slavery, Jim Crow, the prison-industrial-complex—than with violence. His words cannot help but evoke memories of Emmett Till. Racism, Coates writes, "is a visceral experience," one that "dislodges brains, blocks airways, rips muscle, extracts organs, cracks bones, breaks teeth. You must never look away from this. You must always remember that the sociology, the history, the economics, the graphs, the charts, the regressions all land, with great violence, upon the body."[11]

There is a triumph of sorts in the fact that Emmett Till's story is better known now than at any time since his murder, that it is recognized as an American tragedy with deep historical roots, casting long shadows into our own day. We are closer than ever to fulfilling Mamie Till Bradley's wish that the world would know what they did to her child, acknowledging not only the barbarous violence of his killers but also the social and cultural evil out of which it arose.

Still, when Carolyn Bryant broke her decades-long silence and confessed that Emmett did not do the things she said he did back in 1955, some members of the Till family reacted with anger. The Internet was filled with headlines like, "Emmett Till's Family Calls for New Investigation," and "Emmett Till's Family Still Wants the Truth." Their need to know the full story and their desire for justice are understandable, righteous. They are owed more than a mere apology from Tallahatchie County and Mississippi for the loss of their child. But there can be no prosecutions of the dead, and the evidence only grows fainter with time. Remembrance—keeping Emmett Till's flame alive—is the main form of justice remaining.[12]

In spring 2017, someone painted a vile epithet on the wall outside the home of LeBron James, one of America's most celebrated sports stars. He lamented that even with his fame and success on the basketball court, he could not shield his children from gutter bigotry. But James also said that the first thing he thought of when he saw the word scrawled on the wall was Emmett Till's mother. He recalled the next day at a press conference how she refused to cover up racism and its terrible price. Like her, he must not remain silent. For LeBron James, Mamie Till Bradley was an icon of resistance, and a model for our own day; she and her son lived in his heart.[13]

A few months later, at the end of 2017, the comedian Dave Chappelle ended an hour-long television special with the Till story. He told a truncated version, with lots of errors and even a few comical flourishes. Chappelle acknowledged the courage of Carolyn Bryant for finally admitting her lie, and praised even more the bravery of Mamie Till Bradley for insisting that the world join her in bearing witness. Chappelle's version of the story was far too rosy, with Emmett's tragic death leading straight to enlightenment, to the Civil Rights Movement, to that very moment when an integrated audience listened to a successful black entertainer speak about Emmett Till. Chappelle marveled at the strange irony of it all, how Carolyn Bryant's lie resulted in a murder that "set in motion a sequence of events...that made this very night possible."[14]

That is too simple, of course, but Chappelle's words contain a great insight: that thoughtless remarks, surges of deep courage, senseless acts of cruelty, unexpected displays of integrity all mattered deeply. Sometimes small things take on enormous meaning, and Emmett Till's story was built up out of small things—a ring and a photograph, and little gestures like a whistle or a wink, and unknown places with names like Money and Argo, and innocuous phrases like, "there he is," and "let the people see...."

In profound social traumas and history-changing events, such small things suddenly can assume unexpected importance. In March 2017, a controversy erupted at the Whitney Biennial art exhibit in New York City, and for a week it filled social media and newspapers. A young white artist named Dana Schutz displayed her painting called *Open Casket*. It was instantly recognizable as an expressionist version of Emmett Till's death photograph, with a triangle of white shirt framed by a dark jacket on the right side of the canvas, and on the left, Emmett's face, a slashing abstraction of browns.

From the Biennial's first day, *Open Casket* elicited powerful critiques, especially from African American artists. Some compared it to old lynching photographs, death porn that invited whites casually to view violence against black people. Others argued that a white painter should not profit from black pain, especially pain inflicted by racist terror. A petition, signed by thirty artists, called for *Open Casket* to be taken down and destroyed, because the subject of the painting belonged to African Americans. One artist even stood in front of it to block others' view. He wore a shirt with the words "Black Death Spectacle" and advised visitors to look online for the original photograph in order to see the real agony of Emmett Till, not this distanced and abstracted version.[15]

Dana Schutz apologized for any offense she might have given, explained that she could not fully imagine Mamie or Emmett Till's pain, but that as a mother she felt empathy, and as a painter, she must express it. Other artists and curators weighed in, many of them angered by the idea of censorship, by the notion that art "belongs" to any particular group, and by the suggestion that creative works cannot transcend their makers' social background. A wide-ranging discussion commenced, spilling out of the art world and into the media. Who "owns" particular stories? Can we truly understand each other across chasms of race or other identities? By what right do the beneficiaries of privilege presume to depict the experiences of those less fortunate? Is there an obligation to identify and condemn oppression across barriers of wealth, race, gender, ethnicity, or other social categories that divide us? When does creative expression become exploitation? Is censorship ever appropriate, especially in our politically charged times?[16]

Lost in this discussion was the very object that sparked it. Whether we admire *Open Casket* or not, underlying the controversy were the deep emotions stirred by a photograph, the living record of every blow that cut Emmett Till's face and broke his skull and destroyed his innocent young body. Dana Schutz did not just paint a likeness of Emmett Till, she painted his photograph, *that* photograph, a sacred object, now more than ever the palpable image of suffering, the record on one child's face of centuries of brutality and exploitation, the record too of African Americans' determination to resist. "Let the people see what they did to my boy," Mamie Till Bradley said. No one must look away. "Let the people see...."[17]

ACKNOWLEDGMENTS

THIS HAS been a difficult book to write. Any decent work of history is hard, requiring at least five years to complete, usually more like ten. But this one added an emotionally painful story to the usual rigors of research and writing. Worse still, I finished at a time when the forces of racism, hatred, and ethnic fear were on the rise once again. If one job of the historian is to bear witness to the past's cruelty, then at least we can be sure there will be no lack of work in the future.

One of my old teachers, Lawrence Levine, used to warn his students that writing books put family and friends through an ordeal. There certainly were times that I was not present to those who deserved better from me. For that I am deeply sorry. In the words of Bruce Springsteen, "I've got debts no honest man could pay."

Yet I've been blessed with nothing but kind support for this project. Many great institutions and their staffs helped me do my research, among them the Carter Woodson Library in Chicago; Special Collections, Delta State University Library, Cleveland Mississippi; Library of Congress, Manuscripts, Folk Life, and Prints and Photographs, Audio Recordings, and Moving Image Research Center; the Mississippi Department of Archives and History, Jackson Mississippi; the National Archives and Records Administration, Silver Spring, Maryland; the University of Chicago Library Special Collections; the Eisenhower Presidential Library, Abilene Kansas; the Newberry Library, Chicago; the Chicago History Museum Research Center; New York's Schomburg Center for Research in Black Culture; Ohio State University Library Special Collections, Columbus, Ohio; the Summit, Illinois, Public Library; Special Collections, University of Mississippi Library, Oxford Mississippi (special thanks to Leigh McWhite); the Leflore County Public Library, Greenwood Mississippi; and the Federal Bureau of Investigation.

My employer, Loyola University of Chicago, has been generous with time and resources, allowing me to finish this work. And my colleagues at Loyola are nothing but excellent. It has been a pleasure to work with—in no particular order—Tony Cardoza, Kyle Roberts, Suzanne Kaufman, Michael

Khodarkovsky, Ted Karamanski, Ellie Shermer, Ben Johnson, Michelle Nickerson, John Donoghue, John McManamon, Pat Mooney-Melvin, Elizabeth Fraterrigo, Tanya Stabler, Robert Bucholz, Stephen Schloesser, Tom Regan, and especially my good friend Timothy Gilfoyle. Several fine graduate students at Loyola have assisted my research, doing everything from running down documents to proofreading footnotes. Thanks to Adam Carston, Jeffrey Wing, Ruby Orem, Sebastian Wuepper, Chelsea Denault, and Christopher Ramsey.

Two friends gave the manuscript a close reading and offered me important criticisms and suggestions, Lynn Dumenil and Robert Self; it is much improved by their editing and friendship. Early in the project, conversations with two men—Bob Howard and Wheeler Parker—helped me imagine Emmett Till's early life and the trauma of that night in Mississippi. James Cobb, who knows the Mississippi Delta as well as anyone, helped me think through some of the early conceptual problems. My earliest conversations about Emmett Till were with Francoise Hamlin, colleague, friend, and author of her own fine book on the freedom struggle in the Delta.

Timothy Bent at Oxford University Press took the project in hand and helped straighten many crooked places. Through two books now, Tim has tried to keep my prose clean and my thinking orderly. It is a tall order, but he does it well. Others at Oxford did stellar work: Amy Whitmer kept the line moving and always with good grace; Mariah White helped with countless details, small and large; and Mary Sutherland copyedited the manuscript masterfully. Donald Lamm and Christy Fletcher found a good home for this book. Cecilia Cancellaro of Word Creative Literary Services helped tighten and clean up the manuscript at a critical time in its life. And John Bealle provided a fine index. Thanks to Angela Ford at the *Chicago Defender*, Melissa Lindberg at Library of Congress, as well as Vicki Perez and Nicholas Beyelia for help with photographs. Others who constantly helped smooth the way included Mary Beth Bryson, Julissa Bautista, Patricia Clemente, Myles Ostrowski, David Hays, and Timothy Libaris.

Let me single out two special friends, Art Casciato and John Powell, sterling men, I don't care what anyone says. Nicole Brodsky miraculously appeared at just the right moment. Others have helped me think about this project, have told me jokes, or otherwise kept me from going crazy: Thomas Jundt and Meg Myette, Sheyda Jahanbani and Jonathan Hegel, Charles Eagles, Derek Seidman, Will Brucher, Chris Lamberti and Milena Sjekloca, Sean Dinces, Chris and Karen Elzey, Tom Silfen, Charlotte Kirchgaesser, Kristen Mercado, Robert Orsi, Blair Davison, Frank Travisano, Patrick

Miller, Genai Powell, Jim Diedrick and LeeAnne Richardson, Anne Flannery, Tim Spears, Susan Schulten, Steve Smith, Ashley Dodge, John Schulian, Robert Warde, Gary Ogimachi, Mike and Christine Gorn, Lonnie Bunch, Gerry Gorn, Ed and Loraine Gorn, Joe and Gay Scarpa, Larry and Maggie Malley, Danny Greene and Lisa Meyerwitz, Bruce Levine and Ruth Hoffman, Randy Roberts, Kaiulani Lee, Wiley Prewitt, Mikko Saikku, Markku Henriksson, Heather Lee, Ken Sacks, Maud Mandel, Kevin Boyle, David Schwartz.

This book is dedicated to my daughter Jade and her husband, Farid. If only we could leave our children a world that banished stories like this one.

NOTES

ABBREVIATIONS

ACLU	American Civil Liberties Union
CHM	Chicago History Museum
DSU Till	Delta State University, Special Collections, Emmett Till Collection
EPL	Eisenhower Presidential Library
LC	Library of Congress
MDAH	Mississippi Department of Archives and History
NAACP	National Association for the Advancement of Colored People
NARA	National Archives and Records Administration
NYPL	New York Public Library
OSU Huie	Ohio State University, Huie Papers
SERS	Southern Education Reporting Service Collection
UM DASC	University of Mississippi, Department of Archives and Special Collections

INTRODUCTION

1 "The Most Influential Images of All Time," *Time*, Nov. 28, 2016, 74–75.
2 David Halberstam, *The Fifties* (New York, Ballantine Books, 1994), 437.
3 LC, Motion Picture Reading Room, Vanderbilt Television News Archive, CNN, "A Mother's Fight," Jan. 7, 2003.

CHAPTER ONE

1 The Till trial transcript disappeared shortly after 1955 and reappeared only when the FBI opened a new investigation fifty years later. The copy they found was in such bad shape they had to have it retyped. The retyped transcript is available as "Appendix A—Transcript," of the *Federal Bureau of Investigation, Prosecutive Report of Investigation Concerning Roy Bryant, et al., Transcript—Emmett Till Trial Sept 1955*. In the Circuit Court Second District of Tallahatchie County, Seventeenth Judicial District, State of Mississippi, State of Mississippi vs. J. W. Milam and Roy Bryant, Indictment-Murder, Proceedings of Trial at September Term, 1955 in Sumner Mississippi. Document number 4 4A-JN-30112, 62D-30045-FD302. Available online at: https://vault.fbi.gov/Emmett%20Till%20/Emmett%20Till%20Part%2002%20of%2002/view

Each typed page of the transcript has two different page numbers, one at the top right, one at the bottom right. When I give page numbers, I am using the latter number, which is the number from the original 1955 transcript. The 1955 transcript was produced by the official court reporter, James T. O'Day, one month after the trial ended, and signed by O'Day on October 28, 1955. The "Court Reporter's Certificate" at the end of the transcript declares that "the above and forgoing pages of typewritten matter contain a true and correct copy of my shorthand notes, properly transcribed, as taken down by me during the trial . . .," 351.

For clarity's sake, I have altered passages from the transcript slightly: In the original, each witness is introduced, the attorney doing the questioning is named, and then the testimony follows:

Q   What is your name, please?
A   Robert Hodges.
Q   Where do you live, Robert?
A   Down in Philipp, Mississippi.

Instead, I include the name of the attorney and witness before each question and answer, thus,

Smith: What is your name, please?
Hodges: Robert Hodges.
Smith: Where do you live, Robert?
Hodges: Down in Philipp, Mississippi.

Till Trial Transcript, Robert Hodges, 100–104.

2 Ibid., 105–6.
3 Ibid., 106–9.
4 *Till Trial Transcript*, B. L. Mims, 110–15.

CHAPTER TWO

1 James Grossman, *Land of Hope: Chicago, Black Southerners, and the Great Migration* (Chicago: University of Chicago Press, 1989), 13–37; James N.

Gregory, *The Southern Diaspora: How the Great Migration of Black and White Southerners Transformed America* (Chapel Hill: University of North Carolina Press, 2005), 11–27.

2 See maps in Grossman, *Land of Hope*, 124–25; Gregory, *Southern Diaspora*, 23–24.

3 Simeon Wright with Herb Boyd, *Simeon's Story: An Eyewitness Account of the Kidnapping of Emmett Till* (Chicago: Lawrence Hill Books, 2010), 15–24; Mamie Till-Mobley, *The Death of Innocence: The Story of the Hate Crime That Changed America*, ed. Christopher Benson (New York: Ballantine, 2005), 19–21. Emmett's mother, Mamie, changed her last name a few times: Mamie Carthan became Mamie Till, Mamie Till Bradley, Mamie Till-Mobley. By 1955 she used the name Mamie Till Bradley, and for clarity's sake, this is the way I refer to her throughout this book for the years after 1955. Her autobiography, *Death of Innocence*, was written under the name Mamie Till-Mobley, and it is cited as such.

4 Grossman, *Land of Hope*, remains the authoritative work on the Great Migration and Chicago. On the 1919 riot, see William M. Tuttle, *Race Riot: Chicago in the Red Summer of 1919* (Urbana: University of Illinois Press, 1919); Christopher Lamberti, "Riot Zone, Chicago, 1919" (PhD diss., Department of History, Brown University, 2013). For Chicago in the post–World War II era, see Arnold Hirsch, *Making the Second Ghetto: Race and Housing in Chicago, 1940–1960* (Chicago: University of Chicago Press, 1998).

5 Grossman, *Land of Hope*, 259–65.

6 Till-Mobley, *Death of Innocence*, 18–25.

7 Robert Kott, *Summit (Images of America)* (Charleston, SC: Arcadia Publishing, 2009), 23–32.

8 William Cronon, *Nature's Metropolis: Chicago and the Great West* (New York: Norton, 1991), 23–25.

9 Ibid., chaps. 2, 3; Kott, *Summit*, 33, 57. Just two months after Till's death, the *Des Plaines Valley News* lamented that the local history of Summit was not better known; "Hidden in the Weeds," *Des Plaines Valley News*, Oct. 20, 1955, 4.

10 Kott, *Summit*, 69, 83. Summit's population started a slow decline in the 1960s, and by 1986, almost a third of the town was over the age of sixty-five; Gary S. Meyers, "Enterprise-zone Benefits, Diversity Enliven Summit," *Chicago Sun Times*, Sept. 12, 1986, n.p., in Chicago History Museum vertical file, "Towns, Summit"; Kott, *Summit*, 83.

11 Kott, *Summit*, 83.

12 For a fine description of the factory, see Gerald V. Stokes, *A White Hat in Argo: Family Secrets* (Lincoln, NE: iUniverse, 2004), 19–23. The local paper covered union/company relations; see, for example, "Corn Products Co. C.I.O. Union Report Agreement on Issues," *Des Plaines Valley News*, Sept. 22, 1955, 1. Walter Sutherland, "Argo-Summit Community Enjoys Boom," *Chicago American*, July 3, 1953.

13 On Argo's isolation, see "Future Is Brighter for Argo and Summit," *Chicago Daily News*, Sept. 12, 1925, 14.

14 Till-Mobley, *Death of Innocence*, 21–23; Stokes, *White Hat in Argo*, 39–45.

15 Till-Mobley, *Death of Innocence*, 18–23; Stokes, *White Hat in Argo*, 4–18. For the Carthan family in the Federal Census, see Cook County, Illinois, Village of Summit, 1930, sheets 16A–18A; 1940, sheets 16A–B.

16 Kott, *Summit*, 114–15; Till-Mobley, *Death of Innocence*, 18–22. Special thanks to Bob Howard, who lived in Argo in the early 1960s and knew the community as a mail carrier. He recalled, for example, that gangs were not yet a problem for Argo's youth and that the police force had an African American officer who handled problems on the black side of town: if someone got drunk and unruly, a call would go out and the offender would be driven home.

17 Till-Mobley, *Death of Innocence*, 46–49.

18 Ibid.

19 Ibid., 14–16.

20 Till-Mobley, *Death of Innocence*, Apparently, Louis Till was orphaned at a young age; Lt.Col. James G. Chestnutt to William Bradford Huie, Nov. 9, 1956, in OSU Huie, 15–16, 96–97.

21 Ibid., 16–17.

22 Ibid.

23 Ibid., 37–40, 103.

24 Ibid., 26, 81.

25 Ibid., 26–30, 99.

26 Ibid., 28–31.

27 Ibid.

28 Chicago remained residentially rigidly segregated in these years; see Hirsch, *Second Ghetto*; Beryl Satter, *Family Properties, How the Struggle Over Race and Real Estate Transformed Chicago and Urban America* (New York: Picador, 2010).

29 Till-Mobley, *Death of Innocence*, 69, 80–81; LC, American Folklife Center, "The Civil Rights History Project," Southern Oral History Program, interview with Wheeler Parker Jr., by Joseph Mosnier, May 23, 2011, 12–14; LC, American Folklife Center, "Civil Rights History Project," Southern Oral History Program, interview with Simeon Wright by Joseph Mosnier, May 23, 2011, 5–7.

30 Parker, Civil Rights History Project Interview, 12–14.

31 Till-Mobley, *Death of Innocence*, 46–60, 91. A year or two later, Emmett still worried that men might abuse his mother, and initially he urged her not to marry her fiancé Gene for that reason.

32 Till-Mobley, *Death of Innocence*, 69–72; John Barrow, "Emmett Till Remembered as Quiet, Well-Mannered Boy," *Norfolk Journal-Guide*, Sept. 24, 1955, 11; Murray Kempton, "The Future," *New York Post*, Sept. 23, 1955, 3; interview with Mamie Till-Mobley, conducted Dec. 3, 1996, by Devery S. Anderson, at www.emmetttillmurder.com, 1.

33 Till-Mobley, *Death of Innocence*, 83–95; Borrow, "Emmett Till Remembered," 11; Devery S. Anderson, *Emmett Till: The Murder That Shocked the World and Propelled the Civil Rights Movement* (Oxford: University Press of Mississippi, 2015), 75–77.

34 Till-Mobley, *Death of Innocence*, 80–83, 94–95.

35 Ibid., 98.

36 Ibid., 99–103; Simeon Wright, Civil Rights History Project Interview, 5–7.

37 Till-Mobley, *Death of Innocence*, 103–5.

CHAPTER THREE

1 Wright, *Simeon's Story*, 4–5.

2 On southern agriculture in this era, see Jack Temple Kirby, *Rural Worlds Lost: The American South, 1920–1960* (Baton Rouge: Louisiana State University Press, 1987), chap. 2; Neil R. McMillen, *Dark Journey: Black Mississippi in the Age of Jim Crow* (Urbana: University of Illinois Press, 1989) chap. 4; Edward L. Ayers, *The Promise of the New South: Life after Reconstruction* (New York: Oxford University Press, 1992), chap. 8. On the daily life of sharecropping, see Theodore Rosengarten, *All God's Dangers: The Life of Nate Shaw* (New York: Knopf, 1974).

3 Wright, *Simeon's Story*, 5–7; Parker, Civil Rights History Project Interview, 15; Wright, Civil Rights History Project Interview, 26; Arthur Everett, "Till Nearly Missed His Fatal Journey to Land of Cotton," *Jackson Clarion-Ledger*, Sept. 18, 1955, 1.

4 Parker, Civil Rights History Project Interview, 3; Wright, *Simeon's Story*, 11–12. Lee was killed by a shotgun blast; the sheriff refused to investigate.

5 Calvin White Jr., *The Rise to Respectability: Race, Religion, and the Church of God in Christ* (Fayetteville: University of Arkansas Press, 2012), 75–76, 102–12; Anthea D. Butler, Women in the Church of God in Christ (Chapel Hill: University of North Carolina Press, 2007).

6 Wright, *Simeon's Story*, 15–24.

7 Ibid.; Parker, Civil Rights History Project Interview, 6; Wright, Civil Rights History Project Interview, 2.

8 Wright, *Simeon's Story*, 25–36.

9 Ibid.

10 Ibid., 34–39.

11 Ibid., 41–45.

12 Ibid., 45–47; Wright, Civil Rights History Project Interview, 5.

13 Wright, *Simeon's Story*, 48–49; Wright, Civil Rights History Project Interview, 8–12. I rely on Simeon Wright's memoir here. It is uncertain but perfectly reasonable to surmise from other sources, as Devery Anderson does, that two more people were in the car: Roosevelt Crawford's sister Ruth, and Wheeler Parker's cousin Thelton Parker; Anderson, *Emmett Till*, 27.

14 Hallie Eggleston, "Responsibility to Country His Guide," *Carrollton Conservative*, Apr. 11, 1968, n.p., in the Vertical File, Cities and Towns files, Leflore Public Library. In the same location, also see the pamphlet, "Leflore County Communities and Their History," 1962, "Money," 2. Senator Money, incidentally, became a prominent advocate for the war with Spain in 1898, but he was against acquiring overseas territories. See Leonard Schlup, "Hernando De Soto Money: War Advocate and Anti-Imperialist, 1898–1900," *Journal of Mississippi History* 60 (Winter 1998): 315–39.

15 Wright, *Simeon's Story*, 50–51; Wright, Civil Rights History Project Interview, 8–12. My account is based on the testimony of Wheeler Parker and Simeon Wright. I give their words priority because unlike other "witnesses" interviewed over the years, they were certainly present at Bryant's Grocery Store that night.

16 Parker, Civil Rights History Project Interview, 9–10.

17 Ibid.; Wright, *Simeon's Story*, 50–51. The most thorough parsing of the story is Anderson, *Emmett Till*, 361–63.

18 Wright, quoted in Civil Rights History Project Interview, 8–12; Parker, Civil Rights History Project Interview, 9–10; Wright, *Simeon's Story*, 50.

19 Wright, quoted in *Simeon's Story*, 51; Wright, Civil Rights History Project Interview, 13–15; Parker, Civil Rights History Project Interview, 9–15.

20 Wright, *Simeon's Story*, 51–55.

21 Again, Anderson does a good job of bringing the conflicting stories together and comparing them; no single version is fully convincing; Anderson, *Emmett Till*, 363–67.

22 Parker, Civil Rights History Project Interview, 11–12.

23 Wright, Civil Rights History Project Interview, 15; Wright, *Simeon's Story*, 53–57.

CHAPTER FOUR

1 All from *Greenwood Commonwealth*, Aug. 29, 1955; "Delegates Discuss Disarmament Plan," 1; "Controversial Truce Teams Reduced in Korea," 1; "Still Watching Hurricane Edith," 1; "Major Leagues," 4; "'Plantation Barbecue' Is Enjoyed Honoring Two Popular Couples," 3; "Bridal Luncheon Is Given in Greenville," 3; "Dinner Party Honors Three GHS Graduates," 3; "Klan Holds Meet and Burns Cross," 2.

2 "Chicago Negro Youth Abducted by Three White Men at Money," *Greenwood Commonwealth*, Aug. 29, 1955, 1. For more detail, see John N. Popham, "Racial Issues Stirred by Mississippi Killing," *New York Times*, Sept. 18, 1955, E7.

3 "Two White Men Charged with Kidnapping Negro," *Delta Democrat-Times*, Aug. 30, 1955, 1; "'Kidnaped' Negro Boy Still Missing; Fear Foul Play," *Jackson Daily News*, Aug. 30, 1955, 1.

4 "Find Missing Boy's Bullet-Torn Body," *Jackson State Times*, Aug. 31, 1955, 1; "Missing Chicago Negro Youth Found in Tallahatchie River," *Greenwood Commonwealth*, Aug. 31, 1955, 1.

5 "Negro Boy, 14, Is Slain, 2 Men Held as Lynchers," *New York Herald Tribune*, Sept. 1, 1955, 4; "Kidnaped Negro's Body Found in Mississippi," *Louisville (KY) Courier-Journal*, Sept. 1, 1955, 9; "Find Kidnaped Chicago Boy's Body in River," *Chicago Tribune*, Sept. 1, 1955, 1.

6 "River Yields Body of Negro, 14, After Insult to White Woman," *Montgomery Advertiser*, Sept. 1, 1955, 7; "Kidnap-slaying of Negro Boy Stirs Mississippi Delta," *Birmingham News*, Sept. 2, 1955, 3; "Muddy River Gives Up Body of Brutally Slain Negro Boy," *Memphis Commercial Appeal*, Sept. 1, 1955, 1.

7 "Kidnap-slaying of Negro Boy Stirs Mississippi Delta," *Birmingham News*, AP, Sept. 2, 1955, 3.

8 "Officials Abandon Search for Woman in Negro's Slaying," unidentified newspaper clipping in Ed King Papers, Mississippi Department of Archives and History (MDAH), box 1, "Miscellaneous" file. Harry Marsh, writing in the *Delta Democrat-Times*, was one of the few reporters to ask questions about the investigation: Why was Bryant's store not searched, why didn't officers question Mrs. Bryant or, for that matter, Milam's family? Did police ever locate the kidnap vehicle, did they do proper ballistics work to determine what kind of gun and ammunition ended Till's life? Harry Marsh, "Unanswered Questions Nag Newsmen at Trial," *Delta Democrat-Times*, Sept. 20, 1955, 1.

9 Till-Mobley, *Death of Innocence*, 37–41, 65–66.

10 Ibid., 100–102. Mayor Richard J. Daley wrote to President Eisenhower, urging him to intervene; *Delta Democrat-Times*, "White Demands Full Probe into Murder; Mom Stands by Sons," and "Dead Lad's Mother Joins Mayor in Asking Ike to Act" both, Sept. 2, 1955, 1; "Kidnap-Murder Case Will Be Transferred to Tallahatchie," *Greenwood Commonwealth*, Sept. 1, 1955, 1; "Slain Boy's Kinfolk Tell of Begging White Men to Let Him off with Whipping," *Jackson Daily News*, Sept. 3, 1955, 1; "Appeal to Ike in Dixie Slaying," *Edwardsville Intelligencer*, Sept. 2, 1955, 1.

11 "'Were Never into Meanness' Says Accused Men's Mother," *Memphis Commercial Appeal*, Sept. 2, 1955, 1 (the story was cited and reprinted in other papers by the United Press, for example, in "White Demands Full Probe into Murder; Mom Stands by Sons," *Delta Democrat-Times*, Sept. 2, 1955, 1; also see "Milam Is Pictured a War Hero and Also Snatched Negro from Drowning," DSU Till Delta State Scrapbook, no date or page number.

12 "'Were Never into Meanness,'" 1.

13 "'Mississippi to Pay for This...,'" *Jackson Daily News*, Aug. 31, 1955, 1; for an example of the *Daily News* article showing up in other papers, see "Chicago Negro Boy Kidnapped by 4 in South Found Shot to Death in River," *Washington Post and Herald*, Sept. 1, 1955, 1.

14 "'Mississippi to Pay for This,'" 1.

15 Hugh Stephen Whitaker argues that Mamie Till Bradley was misquoted; "A Case Study in Southern Justice: The Emmett Till Case" (master's thesis, Florida State University, 1963), 122.

16 Gene Roberts and Hank Klibanoff, *The Race Beat: The Press, The Civil Rights Struggle, and the Awakening of a Nation* (New York: Vintage, 2006), 82.

17 "Find Kidnaped Chicago Boy's Body in River," 1.

CHAPTER FIVE

1 Hannah Rosen, *Terror in the Heart of Dixie: Citizenship, Sexual Violence, and the Meaning of Race in the Post-Emancipation South* (Chapel Hill: University of North Carolina Press, 2009); Grace Elizabeth Hale, *Making Whiteness: The Culture of Segregation in the South, 1890–1940*

(New York: Vintage, 1998); Neil R. McMillen, *Dark Journey*. There were, of course, challenges to the regime, but they were not yet existential threats; see, for example, Glenda Elizabeth Gilmore, *Defying Dixie: The Radical Roots of Civil Rights* (New York: Norton, 2008); and John Egerton, *Speak Now Against the Day, The Generation Before the Civil Rights Movement in the South* (Chapel Hill: University of North Carolina Press, 1994).

2 Jules Tygiel, *Baseball's Great Experiment: Jackie Robinson and His Legacy* (New York: Oxford University Press, 2008); Taylor Branch, *Parting the Waters: America in the King Years, 1954–63* (New York: Simon & Schuster, 1988); David A. Nichols, *A Matter of Justice: Eisenhower and the Beginning of the Civil Rights Revolution* (New York: Simon & Schuster, 2007).

3 There is an enormous amount of literature, but see Mary L. Dudziak, *Cold War Civil Rights: Race and the Image of American Democracy* (Princeton: Princeton University Press, 2000); and Penny von Eschen, *Race Against Empire: Black Americans and Anticolonialism, 1937–1957* (Ithaca, NY: Cornell University Press, 1997).

4 Ida B. Wells, *Southern Horrors and Other Writings*, ed. Jacqueline Jones Royster (Boston: Bedford Books, 1996); Christopher Waldrep, *African Americans Confront Lynching: Strategies of Resistance from the Civil War to the Civil Rights Era* (Lanham, MD: Rowman and Littlefield, 2009); Ashraf H. A. Rushdy, *The End of American Lynching* (New Brunswick, NJ: Rutgers University Press, 2012); Michael J. Pfeifer, *Rough Justice: Lynching and American Society, 1874–1947* (Urbana: University of Illinois Press, 2004); Jacqueline Goldsby, *A Spectacular Secret: Lynching in American Life and Literature* (Chicago: University of Chicago Press, 2006); Philip Dray, *At the Hands of Persons Unknown: The Lynching of Black America* (New York: Modern Library, 2002). For an excellent discussion of lynching after it had gone underground during the 1930s through the 1950s, see the interview with Jay W. Driskell, "Documenting Lynching and Its Influence," in the *Metropole Blog*, June 26, 2017. Driskell's research suggests that lynching not only became more furtive but also that police killings of black men replaced it in many situations.

5 Amy Louise Wood, *Lynching and Spectacle: Witnessing Racial Violence in America, 1890–1940* (Chapel Hill: University of North Carolina Press, 2009).

6 Pfeifer, *Rough Justice*, 139–47; Rushdy, *End of American Lynching*, 95–127.

7 Rushdy, *End of American Lynching*, 95–127.

8 This "things are getting better" perspective was the dominant theme of northern editors who toured the Deep South for a few weeks in the mid-1950s. See "Report to the People; A Summary of Articles Written by New England Editors after Their Tour of Mississippi," a compendium of editorials appearing in northern newspapers, in Race Relations Collection, 76-15, box 2, folder 7, UM, DASC.

9 "The U.S. Negro," *Time*, May 11, 1953, 57–66.

10 Alan Paton, "The Negro in America Today," *Collier's*, Oct. 15, 1954, 52–66, quoted on 55; the second part of the series, "The Negro in the

North," *Collier's*, Oct. 29, 1954, 70–80, painted a darker picture of deepening racial violence and especially housing discrimination, even as progressive forces sometimes pushed back.

11 Timothy B. Tyson, *The Blood of Emmett Till* (New York: Simon & Schuster, 2017), 110–21.

12 Howard quoted in "Lynching of Youth to Be Investigated," *St Louis Argus*, Sept. 2, 1955; Roy Wilkins quoted in article "River Gives up Body of Slain Negro Boy; White Men Accused," *Memphis Commercial Appeal*, Sept. 1, 1955, 1.

13 Governor White quoted in "Chicago Negro Boy Kidnapped by 4 in South Found Shot to Death in River," *Washington Post*, Sept. 1, 1955, 1; "'Murder,' White Says; Promises Prosecution," *Chicago Defender*, Sept. 10, 1955, 1; "Boy, 14, Victim of Race Hate," *Pittsburgh Courier*, Sept. 10, 1955, 1. Southern papers gave considerable space to the controversy; see, for example, "Murder Indictments to Be Asked in Case of Slain Negro Boy," *Memphis Commercial Appeal*, Sept. 2, 1955, 1; "White 'Deplores' Slaying in Note to NAACP Which Is Creating National Issue," *Jackson Daily News*, Sept. 1, 1955, 1; "No New Developments in Negro Slaying," *Greenwood Commonwealth*, Sept. 2, 1955, 2; James Kilgallen, "Wolf Whistle Murder Trial Opens Tomorrow," *Lowell Sun*, Sept. 18, 1955, 50. The *Jackson Daily News* ran a full-page, page-one story but under a very odd headline implying that the coverage of Till's murder happened only because of the NAACP; James Featherston, "White 'Deplores' Slaying in Note to NAACP Which Is Creating National Issue," *Jackson Daily News*, Sept. 1, 1955, 1.

14 "State Papers Hit Slaying of Negro," *Jackson Clarion-Ledger*, Sept. 3, 1955, 1.

15 "A Brutal Slaying," *Delta Democrat-Times*, Sept. 2, 1955, 4.

16 "Brutal Crime and Stupid Slander," *Raleigh News and Observer*, Sept. 2, 1955, in Chicago History Museum (CHM), Claude Barnett papers, Till file, no page or date; "This Killing No Lynching," *Atlanta Journal*, Sept. 2, 1955, 14; "Bryant, Milam Trial Date Set by Judge September 19," *Greenwood Commonwealth*, Sept. 9, 1955, 1; "Clean Up Chicago First," *Greenwood Morning Star*, Sept. 11, 1955, 6; The *Montgomery Advertiser* took a similar position, "Murder in Mississippi," Sept. 4, 1955, 2-B.

17 Egerton, *Speak Now Against the Day*, esp. 398–409.

18 "Boy's Slaying Is Classified as Lynching," *Atlanta Constitution*, Sept. 7, 1955, 5; "Urban League Calls Murder of Till Racial 'Lynching,'" *Delta Democrat-Times*, Sept. 6, 1955, 1; "Killing of Till Listed as Lynch in Records," *Greenwood Morning Star*, Sept. 7, 1955, 1.

19 "Negro Boy, 14, Is Slain, 2 Men Held as Lynchers," 13; "Disgrace in Mississippi," *New York Herald Tribune*, Sept. 3, 1955, 6.

20 "A Just Appraisal," *Greenwood Commonwealth*, Sept. 2, 1955, 1.

21 "Claims Negroes Not Permitted to Vote," *Greenwood Commonwealth*, Sept. 2, 1955, 1.

22 Ibid.; "Fiery Cross Is Burned in Jackson," *Greenwood Commonwealth*, Sept. 1, 1. For a more detailed story, see, "Mississippi Will Resist Any Federal Probe on Elections," *Delta Democrat-Times*, Sept. 2, 1955, 1.

23 Telegrams and letters regarding Till can be found in the Eisenhower
Presidential Library (EPL), White House Central Files, Alphabetical
file, box 3112, 3113. See especially F. L. Price to Mr. Rosen, Aug. 29
and Sept. 2, 1955, EPL, Office of the Special Assistant for National
Security Affairs, 1952–1961, FBI Series, box 3, Office Memoranda;
"Ike Asked to Act in Negro Lad's Death," *New York World Telegram and
Sun*, Sept. 2, 1955, 5.

24 The assistant Attorney General Warren Olney met with Roy Wilkins,
Thurgood Marshall, Clarence Mitchell, Ruby Hurley, and Medgar
Evers for nearly two hours to discuss the Till case as well as voter
intimidation in Mississippi. Olney repeated that the Feds could do
nothing about Till, but he said that voter intimidation was under
investigation. Ethel L. Payne, "U.S. Can't Enter Till Case," *Chicago
Defender*, Sept. 17, 1955, 1; Louis Lautier, "Official Is Cautious on
Lynch-Murder Commitment," *Atlanta Daily World*, Sept. 9, 1955, 1.

25 J. Edgar Hoover to Dillon Anderson, "Emmett Till, Personal and
Confidential," Sept. 6, 1955, and Sept. 13, 1955, EPL, Office of the
Special Assistant for National Security Affairs: Records, 1952–1961,
series, box 3; "CP Urges Federal Intervention Against Mississippi
Lynchers," *Daily Worker*, Sept. 9, 1955, 2.

26 In a presentation to the President's Cabinet, Hoover declared, "Mayor
Richard J. Daley of Chicago on September 2, 1955, wired the President
urging intervention. I hasten to say that Mayor Daley is not a
Communist, but pressures engineered by the Communists were
brought to bear on him." J. Edgar Hoover to the Secretary of the
Cabinet Max Rabb, "Racial Tensions and Civil Rights," Mar. 1, 1956,
11, Eisenhower Archives.Gov/Research/Digital_Documents/Civil_
Rights_Emmett_Till_Case. Also see United Press coverage, "Ike Asked
to Act in Negro Lad's Death," *New York World-Telegram and Sun*, Sept. 2,
1955, 5.

CHAPTER SIX

1 On the history of antimiscegenation laws, see Charles F. Robinson II,
Dangerous Liaisons: Sex and Love in the Segregated South (Fayetteville:
University of Arkansas Press, 2003); Wood, *Lynching and Spectacle*,
19–68; McMillen, *Dark Journey*, 224–53; Egerton, *Speak Now Against
the Day*, 345–611.

2 "Kidnap-Murder Case Will Be Transferred to Tallahatchie" *Greenwood
Commonwealth*, Sept. 1, 1955, p. 1.

3 James T. Patterson, *Brown v. Board of Education: A Civil Rights Milestone
and Its Troubled Legacy* (New York: Oxford University Press, 2001),
1–85; Egerton, *Speak Now Against the Day*, 586–611. Medgar Evers, the
NAACP field secretary for Mississippi, estimated that 95 percent of
the Mississippi press was openly hostile to *Brown*; "Report, Mississippi
State Conference," typescript dated Feb. 1955, in Evers papers, box 2,
file 39, MDAH.

4 Tom Pickens Brady, *Black Monday* (Winona, MS: Associations of
Citizens' Councils, 1955).

5 On nativism, racism, and immigration restriction, see John Higham, *Strangers in the Land: Patterns of American Nativism, 1860–1925* (New York: Atheneum, 1975); Mae M. Ngai, *Impossible Subjects: Illegal Aliens and the Making of Modern America* (Princeton, NJ: Princeton University Press, 2014); Lynn Dumenil, *The Modern Temper: American Culture and Society in the 1920s* (New York: Hill and Wang, 1995), 201–49.

6 Linda Gordon, *The Second Coming of the KKK: The Ku Klux Klan of the 1920s and the American Political Tradition* (New York: Liveright, 2017), 25–61; Nancy MacLean, *Behind the Mask of Chivalry: The Making of the Second Ku Klux Klan* (New York: Oxford University Press, 1994), 132–35, 177–88. James Q. Whitman argues that the southern Jim Crow regime profoundly influenced the Nazi's Nuremberg Laws; see *Hitler's American Model: The United States and the Making of Nazi Race Laws* (Princeton, NJ: Princeton University Press, 2017).

7 Brady, *Black Monday*, 3–5. Note that from here on, *Black Monday* refers to the book, not the speech.

8 Ibid., 2, 11–12.

9 Ibid., 45.

10 For classic sociological writings on miscegenation, see Gunnar Myrdal, *An American Dilemma*, vol. 2 (New Brunswick, NJ: Transaction Publishers, 2009), 587–92, 1355–56; John Dollard, *Caste and Class in a Southern Town*, rev. ed. (1937; repr., New York: Doubleday, 1957), 134–72; Wilbur J. Cash, *The Mind of the South*, rev. ed. (1991, repr., New York: Vintage, 1941,), 83–87.

11 Brady, *Black Monday*, 92–93.

12 Ibid., 62. In a speech to the US Senate delivered just a month before Till's murder, Senator James O. Eastland described to his colleagues "the methods and techniques that were adopted in 'brainwashing' the Supreme Court" and pointed out the individuals, groups, and organizations that were "responsible for this deliberate destruction of our Constitution and established law." Seventeen social scientists—collaborators with Dr. Gunnar Myrdal on his book *The American Dilemma*—poisoned the mind of the court. For each of these scholars, Eastland presented evidence that they were "identified with the Communist conspiracy, Communist-front organizations, and alien ideologies." James Eastland papers, UM, ASC, series 2, subseries 9, box 1, folder 1–95, "Press Release." Eastland gave this same speech over and over again; see "The Supreme Court's 'Modern Scientific Authorities' in the Segregation Cases" speech of Hon. James O. Eastland of Mississippi in the Senate of the United States, May 26, 1955, repr. from the Congressional Record, in UM, ASC, Race Relations Collection, 00-342, box 2, folder 1.

13 Brady, *Black Monday*, 66–70.

14 Neil R. McMillen, *The Citizens' Council: Organized Resistance to the Second Reconstruction, 1954–1964* (Urbana: University of Illinois Press, 1994), 15–40.

15 Tom Brady, *Review of Black Monday* (Winona, MS: Associations of Citizens' Councils of Mississippi, 1954), 14; Will D. Campbell, *Brother to a Dragonfly* (New York: Continuum, 1977), 111.

16 Campbell, *Brother,* 110–11; Hoover, March 1, 1956, "Racial Tension and Civil Rights," EPL, presentation to Eisenhower's cabinet, 16–18.

17 J. Edgar Hoover was quite explicit in his talk to Eisenhower's cabinet, March 1, 1956, "Racial Tension and Civil Rights," EPL, 16–18; *Jackson Clarion-Ledger,* Sept. 14, 1954, 1.

18 Dan Wakefield, "Respectable Racism: Dixie's Citizens' Councils," *Nation,* Oct. 22, 1955, 339–41.

19 Robert Patterson to University of Mississippi Library, Dec. 9, 1954, Citizens' Council Collection, UM, ASC, box 1. Citizens' Councils pamphlets are scattered throughout folders 17–24.

20 Pamphlet, "The Citizens' Council," Greenwood, Mississippi, Nov. 1954, 1–4, Citizens' Council Collection, UM, ASC, box 1.

21 McMillen, *Citizens' Council,* 18–19, 357–63.

22 A mimeographed sheet from the "Citizens' Protective Association" echoed Brady's fears, stripped of his high-toned niceties—Negro blood destroyed Egypt and India, Greece and Rome; integration is Russia's strongest weapon against the United States; discrimination enforces God's natural law—including an illustration of an ape about to kiss a white woman with the title "The Kiss of Death," n.d., UM, ASC, Citizens' Council Collection, box 1. Also see the collection of segregationist newspapers in the James Eastland papers, UM, ASC, Series 2, subseries 9, box 1, file labeled "Communism, 1955."

23 Patterson quoted in Dan Wakefield, "Respectable Racism: Dixie's Citizens' Councils," *Nation,* Oct. 22, 1955, 339.

24 "Says NAACP Pressured Government into Meddling with Local Problems," *Greenwood Commonwealth,* Sept. 13, 1955, 1.

25 Eastland quoted in "The South versus the Supreme Court," *Look,* Apr. 3, 1956, vol. 30, no. 7, 24. See also Petition to the School Board of Hinds County, July 25, 1955, Medgar Evers papers, MDAH.

26 Eastland gave the same basic speech to Citizens' Councils meetings across the South: "Address to Mississippi Citizens' Councils," Dec. 1, 1955, 6–9; "Address to South Carolina Association of White Citizens' Councils," Jan. 26, 1956; "Joint Statement of United States Senator James O. Eastland, Judge Tom P. Brady and Congressman John Bell Williams," Dec. 12, 1955, all in Eastland papers, UM, ASC, "Speeches" file.

27 Dan Wakefield, "Respectable Racism: Dixie's Citizens' Councils," 339.

28 Hodding Carter, "A Wave of Terror Threatens the South," *Look,* Mar. 22, 1955, 34–35.

29 "White Castle Drops Its Bias after Picketing," *St. Louis Argus,* Sept. 2, 1955, 1.

30 Simeon Booker with Carol McCabe Booker, *Shocking the Conscience: A Reporter's Account of the Civil Rights Movement* (Jackson: University of Mississippi Press, 2013), 46–47.

31 Ibid., 3–4, 14–15, 48.

32 David T. Beito and Linda Royster Beito, *Black Maverick: T.R.M. Howard's Fight for Civil Rights and Economic Power* (Urbana: University of Illinois Press, 2009), 106–14.

33 Booker, *Shocking the Conscience,* 18–25, 49–50.

34 Beito and Beito, *Black Maverick*, 108–12; Tyson, *Blood of Emmett Till*, 110–20.

35 Booker, *Shocking the Conscience*, 3–17. Part 1 of H. S. Whitaker, "A Case Study in Southern Justice" does an excellent job of setting the scene for Mississippi, especially in Tallahatchie County.

CHAPTER SEVEN

1 Till-Mobley, *Death of Innocence*, 117–20.

2 Ibid., 119–27; Christopher Manning, *William L. Dawson and the Limits of Black Electoral Leadership* (Dekalb: Northern Illinois University Press, 2009), 138–39.

3 Till-Mobley, *Death of Innocence*, 129.

4 "40,000 at Till Youth's Funeral," *St Louis Argus*, Sept. 9, 1955, 1; Till-Mobley and Benson, *Death of Innocence*, 129–31. A copy of the death certificate is reproduced in *Death of Innocence*, 134–35.

5 Till-Mobley, *Death of Innocence*, 129–41; "40,000 at Till Youth's Funeral," *St. Louis Argus*, 1. For more on Dawson, see Ethel Payne, "Mrs. Bradley Bares Dawson Aid: Says Ike Ignored Pleas for Help," *Chicago Defender*, Oct. 22, 1956, 3; Ethel Payne, "Dawson Tells Reason for Aiding Till's Mother," *Daily Defender*, Oct. 30, 1956, 1; Ethel Payne, "Aid in Till Case Just Human Thing to Do—Dawson," *Daily Defender*, Oct. 31, 1956, 5; Manning, *William L. Dawson*, 138–39.

6 Till-Mobley, *Death of Innocence*, 130.

7 Ibid., 130–32; Mattie Smith Colon, "Mother's Tears Greet Son Who Died a Martyr," *Chicago Defender*, Sept. 10, 1955, 1.

8 Colon, "Mother's Tears," 1; Till-Mobley, *Death of Innocence*, 130–31; *Life*, Sept. 12, 1955, 47.

9 Till-Mobley, *Death of Innocence*, 131–33.

10 Ibid., 132–37.

11 Both the AP and UP quoted Mamie Till-Bradley's, "Let the people see what they did to my boy," so her words were carried in newspapers all over America, often on page one. For example, see "Slain Boy's Mother Exhibits his Body," *Republican-Courier (Findlay, OH)*, Sept. 7, 1955, 2; "10,000 View Body as Funeral Rites Held in Chicago," *Delta Democrat-Times*, Sept. 4, 1955, 1. Some versions quoted Mrs. Bradley saying, "Let the people see what I have seen," not "Let the people see what they did to my boy." In her autobiography, *Death of Innocence*, 139, written almost fifty years after Emmett's funeral, the phrase is, "Let the world see what I've seen."

12 Beito and Beito, *Black Maverick*, 118; Till-Mobley, *Death of Innocence*, 138–40.

13 Till-Mobley, *Death of Innocence*, 139–40.

14 Ibid.

15 Mamie Till Bradley also credited William Dawson with helping her keep Emmett's body on view for several days; "Till's Mother Says Ike Ignored Pleas for Help," *Chicago Defender*, SERS collection, Till file, dated Nov. 3, 1956, 1. The estimate of fifty thousand mourners

apparently came from A. A. Rayner; it was reported by the UP and by the *Defender*. Police refused to guess a number, saying merely that "thousands" showed up.

16 David Smothers, "50,000 Chicago Area Negroes Jam Funeral Parlor to See Dead Boy," *Lowell Sun*, Sept. 3, 1955, 1. Smothers's article was widely reprinted, but note how a headline could give virtually the same UP story a different inflection—In Holland, Michigan, the front-page headline over Smothers's story read, "Negro Mob Jams Funeral Parlor; Left a 'Shambles.'" *Holland Evening Sentinel*, Sept. 2, 1955,1; Robert Elliott, "Thousands at Rites for Till," *Chicago Defender*, Sept. 10, 1955, 1.

17 Smothers, "50,000 Chicago Area Negroes Jam Funeral Parlor," 1; "Thousands Honor Slain Negro Boy," *New York Herald Tribune*, Sept. 4, 1955, 22; White Jr., *Rise to Respectability*, 113–22.

18 On the history of the Roberts Temple, see City of Chicago, Commission on Landmarks, "Roberts Temple Church of God in Christ," Preliminary Landmark Designation Report, Nov. 3, 2005, 12–20; White Jr., *Rise to Respectability*, 113–22. On Holiness worship, see Lawrence Levine, *Black Culture and Black Consciousness, Afro-American Folk Thought from Slavery to Freedom* (New York: Oxford University Press, 1977), 179–89.

19 These stories differed in detail but were substantially similar. For an example from the Independent News Service, see "10,000 at Funeral Services for Slain Boy," *Lowell Sunday Sun*, Sept. 4, 1955, 1; "50,000 View Body of 14-Year-Old Boy Found Slain in Mississippi," *Birmingham World*, Nov. 6, 1955, 1; for UP, see "Thousands View Body of Murdered Negro Youth," *Provo Daily Herald*, Sept. 4, 1955, 2; for the AP coverage, see "Thousands View Body of Slain Boy," *Waterloo Sunday Courier*, Sept. 4, 1955, 1; "Argo Residents Attend Funeral of Till Boy," *Des Plaines Valley News*, Sept. 8, 1955, 1.

20 "Thousands Honor Slain Negro Boy," *New York Herald Tribune*, Sept. 4, 1955, 22. *Newsweek* reported that mourners contributed $3,100 to a fund for Mrs. Bradley, and that another $1,000 came stuffed in letters to her. "Mississippi: The Accused," *Newsweek*, Sept. 19, 1955, in SERs collection, n.p.

21 "50,000 View Body of 14-Year-Old Boy Found Slain in Mississippi" *Atlanta Daily World*, Sept. 4, 1955, 1.

22 "50,000 View Body," *Atlanta Daily World*, 1; "Thousands of Mourning Negroes Jam Church in Chicago to View Slain Boy," *Louisville (KY) Courier Journal*, Sept. 4, 1955, 2.

23 "'Tens of Thousands' Saw Body of Lynching Victim," *Norfolk Journal and Guide*, Sept. 24, 1955, 11; "3d Lynching of the Year Shocks Nation," *Baltimore Afro-American*, Sept. 10, 1955, 1.

24 "Bury Chicago Boy, 14, Slain in Mississippi," *Chicago Tribune*, Sept. 7, 1955, 1; "Mother Faints; 100,000 View Body," *Chicago Tribune*, Sept. 7, 1955, 1; "Southern Jury Indicts Two in Till Slaying," *Chicago Tribune*, Sept. 7, 1955, 5; "Roberts Temple," Landmark Designation Report, 12–20.

25 Booker, *Shocking the Conscience*, 59–62.

26 Till-Mobley, *Death of Innocence,* 139; Roberts and Klibanoff, *Race Beat,* 88; Shaila Dewan, "How Photos Became Icon of Civil Rights Movement," *New York Times,* Apr. 28, 2005, http://www.nytimes.com/2005/08/28/us/how-photos-became-icon-of-civil-rights-movement.html.

27 A penetrating analysis of the funeral can be found in Adam Green, *Selling the Race: Culture, Community, and Black Chicago, 1940–1955* (Chicago: University of Chicago Press, 2009), 179–210.

CHAPTER EIGHT

1 "Mississippi's Infamy," *Chicago Defender,* Sept. 17, 1955, 9; also see "Boy, 14, Victim of Race Hate," *Pittsburgh Courier,* Sept. 10, 1955, 1; The newspaper coverage of the Till case has received excellent scholarly treatment. See Davis W. Houck and Matthew A. Grindy, *Emmett Till and the Mississippi Press* (Jackson: University of Mississippi Press, 2010); Gene Roberts and Hank Klibanoff, *Race Beat,* 86–108, and most recently Darryl Mace, *In Remembrance of Emmett Till: Regional Stories and Media Responses to the Black Freedom Struggle* (Lexington: University of Kentucky Press, 2014).

2 "Savagery, Southern Style," *Chicago Defender,* Sept. 17, 1955, 9. An editorial in the African American *Norfolk Journal and Guide* was even more pointed; it laid Till's death at the feet of the Citizens' Councils in general and Judge Tom P. Brady in particular, whose famous "Black Monday" speech was distributed by the Councils throughout the South. "Mississippi's Latest Crime," *Norfolk Journal and Guide,* Sept. 10, 1955, 10.

3 "On the Emmett Louis Till Incident," *Jackson Advocate,* Sept. 10, 1955, 4.

4 "Lynching Post-Facto" *Delta Democrat-Times,* Sept. 6, 1955, 4. The Associated Press ran a summary of southern editorial opinion condemning the NAACP for exploiting the tragedy, but it also insisted on stern justice: "Slaying, NAACP Methods Rapped by Newspapers," *Biloxi Daily Herald,* Sept. 3, 1955, 8. The *New York Times* reporter John N. Popham, himself a southerner, agonized over the dilemma; for example, see Popham, "Racial Issues Stirred by Mississippi Killing," E7.

5 "Meddling in Local Case Creates Problem," *Greenwood Morning Star,* Sept. 6, 1955, 4; "Why Didn't They Get the Same Publicity," *Greenwood Morning Star,* Sept. 7, 1955, 4; "Nation Shocked, Vow Action in Lynching of Chicago Youth," *Chicago Defender,* Sept. 10, 1955, 1. Even John Popham, who had reported the story with subtlety, accepted the self-congratulatory narrative of progressive southerners who were appalled by the murder, ready to do the right thing, until outsiders took up Till's cause; Popham, "Racial Issues Stirred," E7.

6 "For a Few Extra Nickels," *Greenwood Commonwealth,* Sept. 13, 1955, 6; "This State Owes Nobody an Apology," *Tupelo-Lee County Tribune,* Sept. 8, 1955, n.p., in UM ASC, Eastland Papers, series 3, subseries 1, box 35, "Correspondence, 1956."

7 All newspapers quoted in the Ed King Paper, box 1, miscellaneous file, MDAH. Also see "Slaying, NAACP Methods Rapped by Newspapers," *Biloxi Daily Herald*, Sept. 3, 1955, 8.

8 "Indictment in Mississippi," *New York Times*, Sept. 7, 1955, 30.

9 Albert Barnett, "Till's Murderers Didn't Know That a Drowned Body Floats to the Surface," *Chicago Defender*, Sept. 17, 1955, 9. Claude Barnett published under his middle name, Albert.

10 "Blood on Their Hands," *Chicago Defender*, Sept. 10, 1955, 1.

11 For the struggle ahead, see especially John Dittmer, *Local People: The Struggle for Civil Rights in Mississippi* (Urbana: University of Illinois Press, 1995).

CHAPTER NINE

1 On the history of the Delta in the early twentieth century, see James Cobb, *The Most Southern Place on Earth: The Mississippi Delta and the Roots of Regional Identity* (New York: Oxford University Press, 1993), 98–183.

2 On the topography and environment of the Delta, see Mikko Saikku, *This Delta, This Land: An Environmental History of the Yazoo-Mississippi Floodplain* (Athens: University of Georgia Press, 2005) 87–219.

3 "Mississippi Grand Jury Recesses without Verdict in Slaying of Negro," *Louisville (KY) Courier Journal*, Sept. 6, 1955, 1; "Two White Men Go on Trial in Negro's Death Tomorrow," *Memphis Commercial Appeal*, Sept. 18, 1955, 1.

4 "Trouble Shooters," *Memphis Commercial Appeal*, Sept. 6, 1955, 1; "National Guard Called to Protect Accused Men after Outside Threats," *Greenwood Commonwealth*, Sept. 6, 1955, 1; "Suspects in Negro Slaying Threatened," *Los Angeles Times*, Sept. 5, 1955, 22; "Grand Jury Calls Several Witnesses in Till Murder Case; More Due to Testify; Guards at Courthouse," *Greenwood Morning Star*, Sept. 6, 1955, 1; "Two White Men," *Memphis Commercial Appeal*, 1.

5 "Mississippi Sheriff Voices Doubt Body Was That of Till," *Greenwood Morning Star*, Sept. 4, 1955, 1. Sheriff George Smith also received ugly letters; "New Threats Irk Sheriff in Money," *Chicago Defender*, Sept. 17, 1955, 3; "Threats on 2 Suspects Cause Vigil," *Cedar Rapids Gazette*, Sept. 5, 1955, 1; "2 Guarded in Lynch Rumor," *Oakland Tribune*, Sept. 5, 1955, 2. On Sunday night, just before the grand jury met in Sumner, Leflore County officials released a statement that the brothers had been moved to Vicksburg. In fact, this was a diversion; Milam and Bryant were still in Greenwood as National Guardsmen patrolled the courthouse.

6 "Mississippi Sheriff Voices Doubt Body Was That of Till," 1; "Wolf-Whistle Murder Evidence Called 'Slim,'" *Birmingham Post-Herald*, Sept. 5, 1955, 16; "Grand Jury to Call 5 More Witnesses in Kidnap-Slaying Case," *Delta Democrat-Times*, Sept. 6, 1955, 1; "Grand Jury Calls Several Witnesses in Till Murder Case," 1; James McBroom, "Question Is Again Raised If Dead Body Was That of Till as Jury Probes Killing," *Jackson Daily News*, Sept. 6, 1955, 1.

7 Strider told his doubts about the body's identity to the press before he testified to the grand jury; the *Delta Democrat-Times*'s page one headline on Sept. 4 read, "Sheriff Says Body Thousands Viewed May Not be Till's." In Chicago, that same day, the *Chicago Sun Times* led its coverage with a headline that read, "Rites Held for Slain Boy; Blast Wrong Identity Claim," in which Mamie Till Bradley offered a point-by-point description of how she knew that the body was Emmett's, see p. 4. The wire service stories on the indictments often made the front page; see, for example, the UP story, "'Whistle' Death Indictment Asked," *Nevada State Journal*, Sept. 6, 1955, 1, and the AP version, "2 White Men Face Negro Slaying Counts," *Anderson (IN) Herald*, Sept. 8, 1955, 16.

8 State of Mississippi, Tallahatchie County, Second Circuit Court District, Sept. 1955 term, "True Bill" against Roy Bryant and J. W. Milam for the murder of Emmett Till, Sumner County Courthouse, Sept. 5, 1955, Gerald Chatham, District Attorney. Both the UP and the AP covered these events. See, for examples, "Early Trial Due in Kidnap-Killing" *Lima (OH) News*, Sept. 7, 1955, 14; "Indict Two in Murder of Boy," *New Castle (PA) News*, Sept. 7, 1955, 8; also see "Trial Date Is Debated," *Kannapolis (NC) Daily Independent*, Sept. 7, 1955, 1, 6; "Sets Date for Murder Trial," *Traverse City (MI) Record Eagle*, Sept. 9, 1955, 19; "Justice Department Promises Action If Civil Rights Violated," *Delta Democrat-Times*, Sept. 8, 1955, 1; Robert M. Ratcliffe, "Eyes of Nation Focused on Monday Trial in Miss.," *Pittsburgh Courier*, Sept. 17, 1955, 1; "Southern Jury Indicts Two in Till Slaying," 5.

9 MDAH, Attorney General J. P. Coleman Papers, box 8, folder 33, Coleman to Robert B. Smith, Sept. 10, 1955; "Till Case Gets New Prosecutor," *Waukesha Daily Freeman*, Sept. 9, 1955, 25; "Jury Drawing Is Started in Mississippi," *Danville (VA) Bee*, Sept. 12, 1955, 3.

10 Hugh Stephen Whitaker, a native of Tallahatchie County, interviewed many of the locals just a few years after the Sumner trial. See his "A Case Study in Southern Justice: The Emmett Till Case," 120–29. Whitaker argues that Breland and Whitten initially turned down the case by asking an exorbitant fee. But see n. 11 below.

11 "Two Go on Trial in Kidnap Death," *Philadelphia Inquirer*, Sept. 20, 1955, 8; "Two White for Murder," *Birmingham World*, Sept. 20, 1955, 1; Petitions from Humphreys County, Mississippi to Breland and Whitten, Sept. 9, 1955, in Ohio State University, Special Collections, William Bradford Huie Papers (hereafter OSU Huie), box 85, folder 346; William Bradford Huie to Roy Wilkins, Oct. 12, 1955, OSU Huie, box 39, file 353c. Breland and Whitten were on the case shortly after Till's body was found. The attorneys' interviews in the Huie Papers with the defendants and with Carolyn Bryant are dated Friday, Sept. 2, 1955; Emmett's body was found the previous Wednesday.

12 Letter from J. J. Breland to Mr. C. L. Puckett, Belzoni Mississippi, Sept. 13, 1955; Thomas R. Miller, Florence, South Carolina, Sept.

12, 1955, to Gerald Chapman (Chapman forwarded the letter to Breland and Whitten); J. J. Breland to Thomas R. Miller, Sept. 15, 1955; and J. J. Breland to Bob Wright, Gulfport, Mississippi, Sept. 15, 1955, all in OSU Huie, box 85, folder 346. Clark Porteous, writing in the *Memphis Press-Scimitar*, put the total collected at $5,000: "New Angle in Till Case Claimed," *Memphis Press-Scimitar*, Sept. 20, 1955, 5. Also see Virgil Adams, "State Granted Recess to Produce New Witnesses in Till Case; Defense to Testify Attack Tried," *Greenwood Morning Star*, Sept. 2, 1955, 1. Note that southern newspapers often did not capitalize "negro" while northern papers did.

13 "Defense Anxious for Early Trial of Men Charged with Kidnap, Murder," *Greenwood Morning Star*, Sept. 8, 1955, 1.

14 Clark Porteous, "Till Trial Opens at Sumner Today," *Memphis Press-Scimitar*, Sept. 19, 1955, 1. "Raising Fund for Bryant, Milam," *Hattiesburg American*, Sept. 13, 1955, 1; Whitaker, "A Case Study in Southern Justice," 147; "Set Murder Case for Sept. 19," *Kansas City Call*, Sept. 16, 1955, 1; "Jury Drawing Is Started in Mississippi," *Danville (VA) Bee*, Sept. 12, 1955, 3.

15 "Mississippi Sheriff Voices Doubt Body Was That of Till," 1; John N. Popham, "Trial Tomorrow in Boy's Murder," *New York Times*, Sept. 18, 1955, 50; Arthur Everett, "Prosecutor in Till Case Points Out Legal Flaws," *Montgomery Advertiser*, Sept. 20, 1955, 2; "Men Plead Innocent in Negro's Death," *Danville (VA) Bee*, Sept. 7, 1955, 5; "Abandon Search for Mrs. Bryant," *Hattiesburg American*, Sept. 3, 1955, 13; "Defense Predicts State Cannot Prove Murder; Till Trial Opens Monday," *Greenville Morning Star*, Sept. 18, 1955, 1; "Grand Jury Indicts White Men with Kidnaping, Murder," *Greenwood Commonwealth*, Sept. 6, 1955, 1. Again, the attorney's notes found in the Huie Papers indicate that Carolyn Bryant spoke to Breland and Whitten as early as Sept. 2. "Mrs. Roy Bryant" in OSU Huie, box 85, folder 356. None of the press reports had Breland and Whitten representing Milam and Bryant at that early date.

16 Three criminal subpoenas for Tallahatchie County's Second District Circuit Court remain extant, all signed by Charles Cox, clerk of the court. They're difficult to read. The first was issued Sept. 6, right after the grand jury handed down indictments. It asks several Leflore County individuals to appear in Sumner on Sept. 9 even though the trial didn't begin until the 19th. A second subpoena was issued by Cox on Sept. 20. Record-keeping during the trial and in the years that followed was haphazard; not only was the trial transcript lost for fifty years but there is no official record of the attorneys' closing arguments. Also see "Mother to Testify at Trial; May Set Date Today," *Greenwood Morning Star*, Sept. 9, 1955, 1; "Mother of Till to Testify at Murder Trial," *Greenwood Morning Star*, Sept. 11, 1955, 1; "Plan to Invite Slain Negro's Mom to Trial," *Chicago Tribune*, Sept. 8, 1955, 8; Robert M. Ratcliffe, "Eyes of Nation Focussed [*sic*] On Monday Trial in Miss.," *Pittsburgh Courier*, Sept. 17, 1955, 1; "$100,000 Civil Suit Planned," *Memphis Press-Scimitar*, Aug. 23, 1955, 8.

CHAPTER TEN

1 Jay Milner, "Negro's Funeral at Sumner Takes Spotlight from Trial," *Jackson Clarion-Ledger*, Sept. 18, 1955, 1.

2 William Street, "Murder Trial Publicity Irks Placid Town," *Memphis Commercial Appeal*, Sept.18, 1955, n.p., in DSU Till, Newspaper Scrapbook. Also see Kirby, *Rural Worlds Lost*, "Black and White, Distance and Propinquity," 232–271.

3 To be precise, Hicks counted five white women, four men, and three children; James L. Hicks, "Hicks Says Key Witnesses in Jail During Till Case Hearing," *Birmingham World*, Oct. 4, 1955, 6. Hicks noted in an earlier report that Townsend—here he calls him "Townsler"—was beloved in Sumner, though one white reporter, anticipating the coming trial, quipped, "He sure picked a convenient time to die." James L. Hicks, "Mother Arrives with Her Pastor," *Baltimore Afro-American*, Sept. 4, 1955, 1.

4 Hicks, "Hicks Says Key Witnesses in Jail," 6; Hicks, "Mother Arrives," 1.

5 Ray Brennan, "2 On Trial Monday in Till Slaying; Defense Questions Body Identity," *Chicago Sun-Times*, Sept. 18, 1955, 3; "Trial Opens Tomorrow in 'Wolf-Whistle' Murder," *Washington (DC) Star*, Sept. 18, 1955, 14-A; James Gunter, "Little Sumner Quiet on Eve of Big Trial," *Memphis Commercial Appeal*, Sept. 18, 1955, n.p., DSU Till, Scrapbook; Steve Duncan, "Dixie Town is Unusually Calm in 'Heat,'" *St. Louis Argus*, Sept. 23, 1955, 11.

6 Robert H. Denley, "Sumner, Cotton Town of 700 Inhabitants," *Kansas City Call*, Sept. 23, 1955, 1. The story of cotton and capitalism is once again a major topic for historians; see Sven Beckert, *Empire of Cotton: A Global History* (New York: Vintage, 2015); Edward E. Baptist, *The Half Has Never Been Told: Slavery and the Making of American Capitalism* (New York: Basic Books, 2016); Walter Johnson, *River of Dark Dreams: Slavery and Empire in the Cotton Kingdom* (Cambridge, MA: Belknap Press of Harvard University Press, 2013).

7 Denley, "Sumner," 1; Porteous, "Till Trial Opens," 1. On Civil War memorialization in the early twentieth century, see David Blight's fine analysis in *Race and Reunion: The Civil War in Memory* (Cambridge, MA: Belknap Press of Harvard University Press, 2001) esp. 338–97.

8 Denley, "Sumner," 1; Porteous, "Till Trial Opens," 1.

9 Denley, "Sumner," 1; Duncan, "Dixie Town" 11; Arthur Everett, "Till Nearly Missed His Fatal Journey to Land of Cotton," 1.

10 Denley, "Sumner," 1. On change in the Delta, see James N. Gregory, *The Southern Diaspora: How the Great Migrations of Black and White Southerners Transformed America* (Chapel Hill: University of North Carolina Press, 2005) 11–79; Cobb, *Most Southern Place on Earth*, 253–76; Kirby, *Rural Worlds Lost*, 275–360; Ditmer, *Local People*, 19–69; McMillen, *Dark Journey*, 257–281; Cobb, *Most Southern Place on Earth*, 209–229.

11 L. Alex Wilson, "Don't Want Mess Here, They Say," *Chicago Defender*, Sept. 24, 1955, 2; "Till Lynching Displaces Cotton, Jim Crow as Top Topic in Delta," *Chicago Defender*, Sept. 14, 1955, 5; "2 White Men Go

on Trial Monday in Negro's Death," *Odessa (TX) American*, Sept. 18, 1955, 6; Clark Porteous, "Till Trial," 1.

12 John N. Popham, "Racial Issues Stirred by Mississippi Killing," E7; see also Popham, "Trial Tomorrow in Boy's Murder," *New York Times*, Sept. 18, 1955, 50.

13 Popham, "Racial Issues," E7; Kilgallen, "Wolf Whistle Murder Trial Opens Tomorrow," 50.

14 Paul Holmes, "A Way of Life Going on Trial in Mississippi," *Chicago Sunday Tribune*, Sept. 18, 1955, pt. 1, 6.

15 James Edmond Boyack, "Men's Souls Are Torn by Hatred, Violence, Fear," *Pittsburgh Courier*, Sept. 24, 1955, 1.

16 Robert H. Denley, "Southern Accent at Trial Stumps Northern Newsmen," *Memphis Commercial Appeal*, Sept. 25, 1955, 7.

17 W. C. Shoemaker, "Sumner Citizens Turn Public Relations Experts while Spotlight Beams at Them," *Chicago Daily News*, Sept. 21, 1955 n.p., DSU Till, Scrapbook; James Gunter, "Early Crowd Fills Courtroom, Unrest Mounts at Late Start," *Memphis Commercial Appeal*, Sept. 22, 1955, 1; Virgil Adams, "10 Jurors Accepted as Milam and Bryant Go on Trial at Sumner," *Greenwood Morning Star*, Sept. 20, 1955, 1; William Street, "Murder Trial Publicity Irks Placid Town," *Memphis Commercial Appeal*, Sept. 18, 1955, n.p., in DSU Till, Scrapbook.

CHAPTER ELEVEN

1 "Mississippi: The Place, The Acquittal," *Newsweek*, Oct. 3, 1955, 24, 29, 30; "Find 4 New Witnesses in Till Slaying," *Chicago American*, Sept. 21, 1955, 1; "Newsmen and Photographers Are Frisked for Weapons," *Memphis Commercial Appeal*, Sept. 20, 1955, 1, DSU Till, Scrapbook; Gunter, "Jokes, Threats Are Blended," 8; Harry Marsh, "Anonymous Telephone Calls Kept Sheriff Strider Awake All Night," *Delta Democrat-Times*, Sept. 20, 1956, 1; James L. Kilgallen, "Spectators Searched at 'Whistle' Death Trial," *Los Angeles Herald and Express*, Sept. 19, 1955, A-3; "Search Spectators at Mississippi Murder Trial," *El Paso Herald Post*, Sept. 19, 1955, 1.

2 "Find 4 New Witnesses," 1.

3 David Halberstam, *The Fifties*, 437; "Newsmen and Photographers Are Frisked for Weapons," 7; Gunter, "Jokes, Threats Are Blended," 8; Harry Marsh, "Communist Writer at Trial Lauds Citizens," *Delta Times-Democrat*, Sept. 22, 1955, 1.

4 Harry Marsh, "Hundred Newsmen Jam Scene of Till Trial," *Delta Democrat-Times*, Sept. 19, 1955, 1; Marsh, "Unanswered Questions Nag Newsmen at Trial," *Delta Democrat-Times*, Sept. 20, 1955, 1; Clark Porteous, "Big Names in Nation's Press Are at Trial," *Memphis Press-Scimitar*, n.p., n.d., DSU Till, Scrapbook; W. C. Shoemaker, "Reporter For Commies Relates How He Shifted to 'Left'—Says Trial 'Fair,'" *Chicago Daily News*, n.p., n.d., DSU Till, Scrapbook; Harry Marsh, "Communist Writer at Trial," 1; "Newsmen and

Photographers Are Frisked," 7. For an excellent study of news reporting and the Till case, see Davis W. Houck and Matthew A. Grindy, *Emmett Till and the Mississippi Press*. Also excellent is Gene Roberts and Hank Klibanoff, *Race Beat*, esp. chap. 7.

5 Roberts and Klibanoff, *Race Beat*, 86–87, 93–94.

6 James Kilgallen, "Wolf Whistle Murder Trial Opens Tomorrow," 50; Paul Holmes, "2 Go on Trial in South for Till Murder," *Chicago Daily Tribune*, Sept. 20, 1955, 1; Holmes, "A Way of Life," pt. 1, 6; David A. Shostak, "Crosby Smith: Forgotten Witness to a Mississippi Nightmare," *Negro History Bulletin* 39, no. 8 (1974–75): 328; "Mississippi Slaying Trial Opens," *Raleigh News and Observer*, Sept. 20, 1955, 1; Baker Marsh, "Trial Opens Monday in Boy Slaying," *Miami Herald*, Sept. 18, 1955, 10a; Charles G. Hamilton, "Delta Perturbed by Till Verdict," *Christian Century* 72, no. 52 (Dec. 28, 1955): 1531–32; "Cast in Impelling Court Drama Match the Movies," no source, n.p., n.d., DSU Till, Scrapbook.

7 "Judge in Mississippi Case Has Long Service Record," *Memphis Commercial Appeal*, Sept. 18, 1955, n.p., DSU Till, Scrapbook; "Cast in Impelling Court Drama," DSU Till, Scrapbook, n.p., n.d.; "Informality of Till Trial Belies Its Seriousness," an Associated Negro Press Story dated Sept. 28, 1955, CHM, Bennett Papers, box 374, "Emmett Till" file; Holmes, "2 Go on Trial," 1; Harry Marsh, "Judge Swango is Good Promoter for South," *Delta Democrat-Times*, Sept. 21, 1955, 1.

8 Patrick Chura, "Prolepsis and Anachronism: Emmet [*sic*] Till and the Historicity of *To Kill a Mockingbird*," *Southern Literary Journal* 32, no. 2 (Spring 2000): 8–10. Chatham's son Gerald Chatham Jr., a Mississippi attorney, discussed some of the parallels between Chatham Sr. and Finch in an oral history—Gerald Chatham Jr., interviewed by Dr. Henry Outlaw, Jan. 19, 2005, oral history #293, DSU Till.

9 "Cast in Impelling Court Drama," DSU Till, Scrapbook; "Judge in Mississippi Case," DSU Till, Scrapbook; Holmes, "2 Go on Trial," 1.

10 James Gunter, "Wives Serious, Children Romp as Trial Begins," *Memphis Commercial Appeal*, Sept. 20, 1955, 1; James Kilgallen, "'Wolf Whistle Murder Trial Jury Being Completed,'" *Elyria (OH) Chronicle Telegram*, Sept. 20, 1955, 13.

11 "Cast in Impelling Court Drama," DSU Till, Scrapbook; Kilgallen, "Wolf Whistle Murder Trial," 50.

12 "Milam Is Pictured a War Hero and Also Snatched Negro from Drowning," DSU Till, Scrapbook; "Milam Saved Lives of Two Other Negroes," *Biloxi and Gulfport Daily Herald*, Sept. 21, 1955, 9.

13 John N. Popham, "Slain Boy's Uncle Ready to Testify," *New York Times*, Sept. 19, 1955, 50; Clark Porteous, "At Sumner Today," *Memphis Press-Scimitar*, Sept. 19, 1955, 1; Holmes, "A Way of Life," pt. 1, 6; Kilgallen, "Wolf Whistle Murder Trial," 50; Roy Bryant later corrected the story about the black soldier for reporters—Roy was the sergeant, the other man was a corporal serving under Bryant, but yes, they understood each other.

14 Gunter, "Wives Serious," 1; John Herbers, "Testimony Opens Today in Till 'Wolf-Whistle' Murder Trial," *Delta Democrat-Times*, Sept. 20, 1955,

1–2. Although they generally praised Judge Swango's courtroom, members of the black press corps found the presence of the children undignified, even demeaning to the case.

15 "13 Witnesses Called in Trial," *Salina (KS) Journal*, Sept. 20, 1955, 1.

16 "Mother of Till Still in Chicago as Trial Begins," *Jackson Clarion-Ledger*, n.d., n.p., DSU Till, Scrapbook. According to Mamie Till-Mobley's autobiography, she arrived in Memphis on Friday and in Mound Bayou on Saturday, two days before the trial, and she was in court on Monday morning but secluded from the jury selection process. Newspapers, however, reported her first public appearance on Tuesday morning. Her Cleveland speech, according to the press, took place on Sunday; "Lynch Victim's Mother Opens NAACP Campaign," *Atlanta Daily World*, Sept. 28, 1955, 1; Till-Mobley, *Death of Innocence*, 152–53.

17 John Spence, "Till's Mother Pauses in Memphis on Way to Trial," *Memphis Press-Scimitar*, Sept. 20, 1955, 1.

18 "'Wolf Whistle' Murder Trial Opens," *Austin (MN) Daily Herald*, Sept. 19, 1955, 3; "Begin Racial Murder Trial," *Saint Joseph (MI) Herald Press*, Sept. 19, 1955, 1; James Featherston, "Uncle Points out Milam, Bryant as Two White Men Who Hauled off Slain Boy," *Jackson Clarion-Ledger*, Sept. 21, 1, 14.

19 Gunter, "Jokes, Threats Are Blended," 8; "All-White Jury Picked for Case in Mississippi," *Manitowoc Herald-Times*, Sept. 20, 1955, 1; Steve Duncan, "Dixie Town Is Unusually Calm in 'Heat,'" *St. Louis Argus*, Sept. 23, 1955, 1; "Mother of Till Still in Chicago as Trial Begins," DSU Till, Scrapbook.

20 Christopher Manning, *William L. Dawson and the Limits of Black Electoral Leadership* (Dekalb: Northern Illinois University Press, 2009), 137–39; "All White Jury Picked for Case in Mississippi," 1; Gunter, "Jokes, Threats Are Blended," DSU Till, Scrapbook; Herbers, "Testimony Opens Today," 1–2.

21 Porteous, "At Sumner Today," 1; "Jury Selection Begins in 'Wolf-Whistle' Murder Trial," *Big Spring Texas Daily Herald*, Sept. 19, 1955, 1; John Herbers, "Till Trial Bogs Down in Jury-Picking Job," *Delta Democrat-Times*, Sept. 19, 2015, 1.

22 Paul Holmes, "2 Go to Trial in South for Till's Murder," *Chicago Daily Tribune*, Sept. 20, 1955, 1; Clark Porteous, "New Angle in Till Case Claimed," *Memphis Press-Scimitar*, Sept. 20, 1955, 1; "Mississippi Slaying Trial Opens," *Raleigh News and Observer*, Sept. 20, 1955, 3.

23 William Sorrels, "10 Jurymen Are Selected for Trial of 2 White Men in Slaying of Negro Youth," *Memphis Commercial Appeal*, Sept. 19, 1955, 1.

24 Sorrels, "10 Jurymen Are Selected," 1; Holmes, "2 Go on Trial," 1; Sam Johnson, "State Will Not Ask Death Penalty in Trial of White Men at Sumner," *Greenwood Commonwealth*, Sept. 19, 1955, 1; Clark Porteous, "Till Trial Opens at Sumner Today," *Memphis Press-Scimitar*, Sept. 19, 1955, 1; "'Wolf Call' Case Trial Is Started," *Galveston Daily News*, Sept. 20, 1955, 1; "May Complete Jury for Till Murder Case Today," *Brownsville (TX) Herald*, Sept. 20, 1955, 9. Journalist Art Everett hedged his bet and wrote "Rarely if ever has a white man been executed in a Mississippi case involving a Negro slaying"; in

"10 Jurors Seated in Murder Trial at Sumner, Miss.," *Joplin (MO) Globe*, Sept. 20, 1955, 1.

25 Sorrels, "10 Jurymen Are Selected," 1; "Select Jury for Murder Trial in Mississippi," *Mt. Pleasant (IA) News*, Sept. 20, 1955, 8. Clark Porteous description of the jury was slightly different—see "New Angle in Till Case Claimed," *Memphis Press-Scimitar*, Sept. 20, 1955, 1.

26 James Featherston, "Startling Developments Predicted in Till Trial," *Jackson Clarion-Ledger*, Sept. 20, 1955, 1; Sam Johnson, "Complete Till Murder Case Jury," *Hattiesburg American*, Sept. 20, 1955, 1; "Prosecution in 'Wolf-Whistle' Trial Wins Recess for 'New Witnesses,'" *Atlanta Constitution*, Sept. 21, 1955, 2; John Herbers, "State Granted Recess to Produce New Witnesses in Till Case; Defense to Testify Attack Tried," *Greenwood Morning Star*, Sept. 21, 1955, 1; Harry Marsh, "Judge Swango Is Good Promoter for South," *Delta Democrat-Times*, Sept. 21, 1955, 1.

27 "'Wolf Whistle' Trial Is Recessed; Judge Warns of Crowded Courtroom," *Albuquerque Journal*, Sept. 21, 1955, 17.

CHAPTER TWELVE

1 David Bready, "Sidelights of Trial at Sumner," *Greenwood Commonwealth*, Sept. 21, 1955, 1; Herbers, "Testimony Opens Today," 1; Sam Johnston, "Uncle of Till Identifies Pair as Men Who Abducted Chicago Negro," *Greenwood Commonwealth*, Sept. 21, 1955, 1; *Daily Worker* quoted in John Herbers, "Cross-Burning at Sumner Went Almost Un-Noticed Yesterday," *Delta Democrat-Times*, Sept. 22, 1955, 1.

2 Bready, "Sidelights of Trial," 1; Murray Kempton quoted in Tom Brennan, "World Watched Drama Unfold in Rural County Courtroom," *Jackson Clarion-Ledger*, Aug. 25, 1985, 2H. Kempton's comments on Swango were not merely those of a reporter; Kempton was also a board member of the American Civil Liberties Union (ACLU), which quietly asked him to serve as an observer in Sumner to make sure the case was handled fairly. Letters from Kenneth Douty, Director, Illinois ACLU to Pat Malin (Sept. 16, 1955), Murray Kempton (Sept. 20, 1955), and Mamie Bradley (Oct. 6, 1955), all in ACLU Papers, Illinois Division, box 430, folder 1 "Emmett Till," University of Chicago Special Collections.

3 Holmes, "2 Go on Trial," 1; "'Wolf Whistle' Trial Opened in Mississippi," *Centralia (WA) Daily Chronicle*, Sept. 19, 1955, 1; Arthur Everett, "Defendants Admit Kidnapping Till Boy but Deny 'Murder,'" *Jackson Clarion-Ledger*, Sept. 22, 1955, 1, 13.

4 "10 Jurors Accepted as Milam and Bryant Go on Trial at Sumner," "Sumner Enjoying the Spotlight," and "Bitterest Statements from Chicago," *Greenwood Morning Star*, Sept. 20, 1955, 1, 6; Herbers, "Cross-Burning at Sumner," 1.

5 James L Hicks, "Mother Arrives with her Pastor," *Baltimore Afro-American*, Sept. 24, 1955, 1.

6 "Latest News on Till Trial," *Mississippi Sun*, Sept. 22, 1955, 1; Johnston, "Uncle of Till's Identifies Pair," 1; John N Popham, "Brothers Admitted Till Abduction, Sheriff Says," *Atlanta Constitution*, Sept. 22, 1955, 8; Everett, "Defendants Admit Kidnapping Till Boy," 1; James L. Kilgallen, "Slain Boy's Uncle Identifies 2 Men Who Abducted Youth," *Atlanta Daily World*, Sept. 22, 1955, 1; W. F. Minor, "Statements Let into Testimony," *New Orleans Times-Picayune*, Sept. 22, 1955, 1. For the rest of the "Trial" section, I rely heavily on the trial transcript. The transcript had been lost for many years, but FBI agents found a copy in 2005, had it retyped and digitized. The transcript does not include courtroom ambiance, for which I rely on newspaper reports. On the rediscovery of the transcript, see Shaila Dewan and Ariel Hart, "F.B.I. Discovers Trial Transcript in Emmett Till Case," *New York Times*, May 18, 2005, online edition: http://www.nytimes.com/2005/05/18/us/ fbi-discovers-trial-transcript-in-emmett-till-case.html.

7 Everett, "Till Nearly Missed His Fatal Journey to Land of Cotton," 1.

8 Moses Newson, "Emmett's Kin Hang on in Miss. to Harvest Crop," *Chicago Defender*, Sept. 17, 1955, 36; Steve Duncan, "Rev. Mose Wright Says He'll Leave Miss. as Soon as Crop Is Harvested," *St. Louis Argus*, Sept. 23, 1955, 1; Till-Mobley, *Death of Innocence*, 140.

9 "Appendix A–Transcript," of the *Federal Bureau of Investigation, Prosecutive Report of Investigation Concerning Roy Bryant, et al., Transcript—Emmett Till Trial Sept. 1955*, In the Circuit Court Second District of Tallahatchie County Seventeenth Judicial District, State of Mississippi, State of Mississippi vs. J. W. Milam and Roy Bryant, Indictment-Murder, Proceedings of Trial, September Term, 1955 in Sumner Mississippi. Document number 4 4A-JN-30112, 62D-30045-FD302, Mose Wright testimony, 4–7, available online at: https://vault.fbi.gov/Emmett%20Till%20/Emmett%20Till%20 Part%2002%20of%2002/view. Throughout, the abbreviated citation is *Till Trial Transcript*, Mose Wright testimony, 4–7 (note that I cite names as they are written in the trial transcript). The reporter John N. Popham noted that the prosecution called him "Uncle Mose," the defense simply "Mose." Popham noted, "In turn, Wright answered the prosecution with 'yes sir,' and the defense examiners with 'that's right, that's right.'" In his column, James Kilgallen referred to him as "Wright" but also as "Old Uncle Mose" and "Preacher Mose Wright"; Kilgallen, "Wright Tells Story of Negro Kidnapping," n.p., n.d. DSU Till, Scrapbook.

10 *Till Trial Transcript*, Wright, 7–8. My account of the trial follows the official transcript chronology—witnesses, testimony, cross examination are given mostly in order they were recorded, and in the exact words of the transcript. In order to keep the narrative clear and the flow going, I've compacted testimony, cut some detail, and rearranged a few things for clarity.

11 Ibid., 8–9.

12 Ibid., 9. For representative newspaper accounts, see "Witness Tags Milam, Bryant as Abductors," *Burlington (IA) Hawk Eye Gazette*, Sept. 21, 1955, 1; Kilgallen, "Slain Boy's Uncle Identifies 2 Men," 1.

13 An AP story described Wright's testimony this way: "The little Negro rose from the big chair and pointed at the defendant, 'There he is,' he said"; in "Witness Says Accused Men Abducted Till," *Thomasville (GA) Times-Enterprise*, Sept. 21, 1955, 1. Also see William Sorrels, "Uncle of Slain Boy Points Out Milam, Says Body Was Till," *Memphis Commercial Appeal*, Sept. 22, 1955, 1. *Life* magazine, incidentally, quoted Wright as saying not "There he is," as he pointed to Milam, but "Thar he." For years afterwards that phrase "Thar he" was repeated in accounts of the trial, and it became a source of irritation to Wright's family because, they said, he did not speak in such "negro dialect"; he was always clear and proper. Many newspapers reprinted a photo of Wright, standing and pointing, taken surreptitiously against the judge's orders, by the *Chicago Defender* photographer Ernest Withers, seated at the black press table. Till-Mobley, *Death of Innocence*, 174–76.
14 *Till Trial Transcript*, Wright, 12.
15 Ibid., 15–18.
16 Ibid., 19–20.
17 Ibid., 21.
18 Ibid., 23.
19 Ibid., 28–29.
20 Ibid., 10–11, 14, 19, 26; John N. Popham, "Brothers Admitted Till Abduction," 8.
21 *Till Trial Transcript*, Wright, 30–35.
22 Ibid., 36.
23 Ibid., 39–44.
24 Ibid., 45–46.
25 Ibid., 47–52.
26 Ibid., 35, 60–62.
27 Ibid., 62.
28 "State Asks Mississippi Trial Delay," *New York Herald Tribune*, Sept. 23, 1955, 1; Murray Kempton, "He Went All the Way," *New York Post*, Sept. 22, 1955, quoted in Christopher Metress, *The Lynching of Emmett Till: A Documentary Narrative* (Charlottesville: University of Virginia Press, 2002), 66.

CHAPTER THIRTEEN

1 *Till Trial Transcript*, 63–64.
2 *Till Trial Transcript*, Chester A. Miller testimony, 64–65.
3 Ibid., 64–67. The very fact that Sheriff Smith called on a black undertaker indicates his belief that the corpse was Emmett Till.
4 Ibid., 65–70.
5 Ibid., 67–72.
6 Ibid., 78.
7 *Till Trial Transcript*, C. A. Strickland testimony, 80–84.
8 *Till Trial Transcript*, Breland, Chatham, and Swango discussion, 90–93.

9 *Till Trial Transcript*, George Smith testimony, 85–93.

10 *Till Trial Transcript*, Miller, 76, 79–80.

11 Ibid., 76, 94–98.

12 Ibid., 99.

13 Ibid., 75–84, 99.

14 *Till Trial Transcript*, Robert Hodges, B. L. Mims testimony, 100–115.

CHAPTER FOURTEEN

1 "State Asks Mississippi Trial Delay," 1. For a newspaper account of Smith and Cothran's testimony, see W. F. Minor, "Statements Let into Testimony," *New Orleans Times-Picayune*, Sept. 22, 1955, 1, and Everett, "Defendants Admit Kidnapping Till Boy," 1, 18.

2 *Till Trial Transcript*, Smith testimony, 116–20.

3 Ibid., 120. Both Sheriff Smith and, later, Carolyn Bryant used the word "nigger" for Emmett Till, according to the trial transcript, but newspapers routinely quoted them saying "Negro"; see for example, "Sheriff Says 2 Admitted Kidnapping," *Anderson (IN) Herald*, Sept. 22, 1955, 2.

4 *Till Trial Transcript*, Smith, 121–26.

5 Ibid., 126–28.

6 Ibid., 130. Eleven years later, in the famous Miranda decision of 1966, the US Supreme Court held that defendants must be advised of their right to remain silent and to seek legal counsel during interrogation. Incidentally, page 133, the last page of Sheriff Smith's testimony and the first page of Deputy John Ed Cothran's is missing from the trial transcript.

7 *Till Trial Transcript*, Cothran testimony, 134–41.

8 Ibid., 141.

9 Ibid., 135–36, 141–46.

10 Ibid., 146–53.

11 Ibid., 153–59.

12 Ibid., 155–62.

13 Ibid., 162–69.

14 Ibid., 170–73.

15 Ibid.

16 Ibid., 175.

CHAPTER FIFTEEN

1 *Till Trial Transcript*, C. F. "Chick" Nelson testimony, 177–79.

2 Clark Porteous, "Jury May Get Till Murder Case Today," *Memphis Press-Scimitar*, Sept. 23, 1955, 1–2, 7–8; "Till Boy Carried into Barn by 4 Men, Witness States," *Long Beach [CA] Press-Telegram*, Sept. 22, 1955, 3; "Molested by 'Wolf-Whistler,' Defendant's Wife Testifies," *Bridgeport (CT) Telegram*, Sept. 23, 1955, 14.

3 Till-Mobley, *Death of Innocence*, 178–79.

4 *Till Trial Transcript*, Mamie Till Bradley testimony, 180–83; Till-Mobley, *Death of Innocence*, 180–81.

5 *Till Trial Transcript*, Bradley, 183–86; Till-Mobley, *Death of Innocence*, 180–81. Newspaper columns routinely noted that Emmett Till's father was a veteran; see for example, James Kilgallen, "Two Till Witnesses May Present Dramatic Accounts," *Lowell Sun*, Sept. 21, 1955, 51; Minor, "Statements Let into Testimony," 1.

6 *Till Trial Transcript*, Bradley, 186–87; Till-Mobley, *Death of Innocence*, 178–79; John Herbers, "He Saw Milam Take Lad into Barn; Heard Screams," *Delta Democrat-Times*, Sept. 22, 1955, 1. James L. Kilgallen, "Jury, Mostly Farmers, Deliberates One Hour for 'Not Guilty' Verdict," *Birmingham World*, Sept. 27, 1955, 1; "Till Boy Carried into Barn by 4 Men," 3; "Victim's Mother Takes Stand at Murder Trial," *Big Spring (TX) Daily Herald*, Sept 22, 1955, 1; John Herbers, "Jury Absent as Mrs. Bryant Tells of Struggle with Till; Expect to Complete Case Today," *Greenwood Morning Star*, Sept. 23, 1955, 1; Murray Kempton, "The Future," 3.

7 *Till Trial Transcript*, Bradley, 187–88; Kempton, "The Future," 3; Dan Wakefield, "Justice in Sumner," *Nation*, Oct. 1, 1955, repr. in Metress, *Lynching of Emmett Till*, 122.

8 *Till Trial Transcript*, Bradley, 190–91; Clark Porteous, "Jury May Get Till Murder Case," 8.

9 *Till Trial Transcript*, Bradley, 192–93.

10 For a history of the *Chicago Defender*, see Ethan Michaeli, *The Defender: How the Legendary Black Newspaper Changed America* (Boston: Houghton Mifflin, 2016). On the *Defender*'s distribution in the South, especially the Delta, see Gregory, *Southern Diaspora*, 49–54; and for the centrality of the newspaper early in the twentieth century, James R. Grossman, *Land of Hope*, chap. 3.

11 *Till Trial Transcript*, Bradley, 193–94.

12 Ibid., 195–200; Roberts and Klibanoff, *Race Beat*, 92–93.

13 *Till Trial Transcript*, Bradley, 200–202; Kempton, "The Future," 3.

14 *Till Trial Transcript*, Bradley, 202–4.

15 Ibid., 204–5.

16 Ibid., 205.

17 Ibid., 205–6.

18 Ibid., 206.

19 Ibid., 207–9.

CHAPTER SIXTEEN

1 The story comes from several sources, and while they differ in detail, the broad outlines are fairly consistent. James Hicks's reporting in the African American press is the single most important source. Several of his articles are conveniently reprinted in Metress, *Lynching of Emmett Till*, 154–77. See also Devery Anderson's version of the story in *Emmett Till*, 94–95; 102–6.

2 Simeon Booker, *Shocking the Conscience*, 68–73; Simeon Booker, "A Negro Reporter at the Till Trial," *Nieman Reports*, Jan. 1956, 13–15.

3 "Hicks Says Key Witnesses in Jail During Till Case Hearing," *Atlanta Daily World*, Oct. 4, 1955, 1, 4. Hicks began as a reporter in Cleveland, Ohio, in the mid-1930s, moved to the *Baltimore Afro-American* as an investigative reporter and served as the Washington bureau chief of the National Negro Press Association before the *New York Amsterdam News* named him as its director.

4 Hicks, "Hicks Says," 4. Hicks also wrote about it in an open letter to Attorney General Brownell and FBI chief J. Edgar Hoover, "New Till Evidence Disclosed in Letter," *Baltimore Afro-American*, Nov. 26, 1955, 2. Hicks loved noir flourishes, casting himself as the beleaguered private eye. He emphasized for his mostly black readership the dangers of his situation, how he took care to rent a car fast enough to outrun trouble, to treat deputy sheriff's warily, to spend his nights in safe havens. He warned that sometimes his coverage would read like "a cheap and fantastic Hollywood movie script," but he swore to the veracity of his stories. Hicks published a four-part series of articles after the trial ended, syndicated in dozens of African American papers. James L. Hicks, "Hicks Lays Careful Plans for Rapid Travel in Mississippi," *Baltimore Afro-American*, Sept. 24, 1955, 2.

5 Hicks, "Hicks Says," 4.

6 David T. Beito and Linda Royster Beito, *Black Maverick*, 120–21; James Hicks, "Unbelievable!: Jimmy Hicks Inside Story of Lynch Trial," *Baltimore Afro-American*, Oct. 15, 1955, pt. 2 of 4, 1–2. Hicks was not always careful with his details; at one point he referred to Emmett Till as "Willie Till," and he mentions filing copy on Mose Wright and Mamie Till Bradley's testimony on Monday, even though they didn't take the stand until days later.

7 Beito and Beito, *Black Maverick*, 120–21; Hicks, "Unbelievable," pt. 2, 1–4.

8 Hicks, "Unbelievable!," pt. 2,1–2.

9 Ibid.

10 Booker, *Shocking the Conscience*, 70–74; Beito and Beito, *Black Maverick*, 123–25.

11 Booker, *Shocking the Conscience*, 70–74; Beito and Beito, *Black Maverick*, 123–25; James Featherston, "Uncle Points Out Milam, Bryant," 1; Hicks, "Unbelievable!" (pt. 3 of 4), *Baltimore Afro-American*, Oct. 22, 1955, 2; John Herbers, "Uncle Tells How Lad Was Seized," *New York World Telegram and Sun*, Sept. 21, 1955, 1. Also see the UP story, "Courtroom Bristles with New Tenseness," *Kannapolis (NC) Daily Independent*, Sept. 21, 1955, 1; for the AP story by Arthur Everett, see "Defendants Admit Kidnapping Till Boy but Deny 'Murder,'" *Jackson Clarion-Ledger*, Sept. 22, 1955, 1.

12 Booker, *Shocking the Conscience*, 70–73; James Hicks, "Reporters with Hicks in Darkest Hour of Till Trial," *Houston Informer*, Oct. 22, 1955, 1, 3; Featherston, "Uncle Points Out Milam, Bryant," 1; Clark Porteous, "Three Slated as Till Witnesses Now Missing," *Memphis Press-Scimitar*, Sept. 22, 1955, 1. Booker more than Hicks

credits Mississippi sheriffs' officers from Leflore and Sunflower Counties with making it possible for the witnesses to actually appear at court. There was considerable speculation about a change of venue because the events Willie Reed described took place in Sunflower County. Prosecutors in all counties consistently rejected that possibility simply because there was no single logical place to try the case; see, for example, "'Whistle' Murder Trial Shift May Be Necessary," *Elyria Chronicle Telegram* (OH), Sept. 22, 1955, 25; William Sorrels, "New Trial Evidence Disclosed by State in a Dramatic Fashion," *Memphis Commercial Appeal*, Sept. 21, 1955, 1.

13 Sorrels, "New Trial Evidence Disclosed," 1; Booker, *Shocking the Conscience*, 70–73; Porteous, "Three Slated," 1; Hicks, "Reporters with Hicks," 3.

14 James Hicks, "Hicks Tells of Strange Night Calls in Last Till Trial Story," *Atlanta Daily World*, Oct. 22, 1955, 6.

CHAPTER SEVENTEEN

1 Exactly who owned the land is a little unclear. Clark Porteous wrote, "Mr. Sheridan, who enjoys a good reputation among the negroes, said he wanted it clear that the beating of Till about which the 'surprise' witnesses testified, did not take place on his plantation, which adjoins Leslie Milam's place"; "Kidnap Trial Delay Sure," *Memphis Press Scimitar*, Sept. 22, 1955, 1; *Till Trial Transcript*, Willie Reed testimony, 210–11.

2 John Herbers, "Tells of Screams in 'Whistle' Trial," *New York World Telegram and Sun*, Sept. 22, 1955, 1, 2; John Herbers, "Jury Absent as Mrs. Bryant Tells of Struggle with Till; Expect to Complete Case Today," *Greenwood Morning Star*, Sept. 23, 1955, 1. Arthur Everett described Reed as a "gangling Negro youth"; "Mother Testifies He Sought Date," *Montgomery Advertiser*, Sept. 23, 1955, 2A. Herbers referred to Willie Reed as "Mr. Reed," a departure from the southern press's custom of using first names for African Americans.

3 Herbers, "Jury Absent," 1; Porteous, "Jury May Get Till Murder Case," 1.

4 *Till Trial Transcript*, Willie Reed testimony, 210–13.

5 Ibid., 214–16.

6 Ibid., 216–19.

7 Ibid., 219–21.

8 Ibid., 222.

9 Ibid., 222–24.

10 Ibid., 224–25.

11 Ibid., 226–32.

12 Ibid., 233–35.

13 Ibid., 233–40.

14 Ibid., 238.

15 Ibid., 241–43.

16 Ibid., 243–45.

17 James Featherston, "Trial Nears Jury," *Jackson Daily News*, Sept. 23, 1955, 1; Herbers, "Witness Says He Saw Milam Take Lad into Barn; Heard Screams," *Delta Democrat-Times*, Sept. 22, 1955, 1, 11; Clark Porteous, "Jury May Get Till Murder Case," 1–2, 7–8.

18 Herbers, "Jury Absent," 1; "Whistle Killing May Go to Jury Today; 2d Negro Accuses Two Defendants," *New York Post*, Sept. 23, 1955, 3.

19 *Till Trial Transcript*, Amandy Bradley testimony, 245–55; "Victim's Mother Takes Stand at Murder Trial," *Big Spring (TX) Daily Herald*, Sept. 22, 1955, 1.

20 *Till Trial Transcript*, 256–57.

CHAPTER EIGHTEEN

1 James T. Patterson, *Brown v. Board of Education: A Civil Rights Milestone and Its Troubled Legacy*, 70–90.

2 Wilbur J. Cash refers to the southern "rape complex." See Cash, *The Mind of the South*, 17. For historical perspective, see Winthrop D. Jordan, *White Over Black: American Attitudes Toward the Negro, 1550–1812* (Chapel Hill, NC: Omohundro Institute, 2012), pt. 2, "Fruits of Passion: The Dynamics of Interracial Sex."

3 William F. Minor, "Court Refuses to Let Jurors Hear Testimony," *New Orleans Times-Picayune*, Sept. 23, 1955, 1; "Mrs. Bryant Tells How Northern Negro Grabbed Her, 'Wolf-Whistled' in Store," *Jackson Daily News*, Sept. 23, 1955, 1 (this story, incidentally, tried to capture Carolyn Bryant's full testimony verbatim); Porteous, "Jury May Get Till Murder Case," 1; Tom Yarbrough, "Three Say Body Identified as Negro Boy Was in River Long before He Vanished," *St. Louis Post Dispatch*, Sept. 23, 1955, 1; William Sorrels, "Till Case May Reach Sumner Jury Today; State's Side Is Over," *Memphis Commercial Appeal*, Sept. 23, 1955, 1; Herbers, "Jury Absent," 1; "Molested by 'Wolf-whistler,' Defendant's Wife Testifies," *Bridgeport (CT) Telegram*, Sept. 23, 1955, 14; "Verdict Likely Today in Trial of 2 as Killers of Negro Boy 14," *St. Louis Post Dispatch*, Sept. 23, 1955, 1.

4 *Till Trial Transcript*, Mrs. Roy Bryant testimony, 258–59.

5 Ibid., 259–60.

6 Ibid., 260–61.

7 Ibid., 261–62.

8 Ibid., 262.

9 Ibid., 263.

10 Ibid., 263.

11 Ibid., 263–64.

12 Ibid., 264–65.

13 *Till Trial Transcript*, Bryant, 264–65; Sam Johnson, "Jury Hears Defense and Prosecution Arguments as Testimony Ends in Kidnap-Slaying Case," *Greenwood Commonwealth*, Sept. 23, 1955, 1.

14 *Till Trial Transcript*, Bryant, 265–72. Note that most newspapers reprinted the exchange as "I've been with white women before," but the trial transcript reads as follows: Carlton: Did he say anything after that one unprintable word? Bryant: Yes. Carlton: And what was that? Bryant: Well, he said...well..."With white women before." [272]. See Herbers, "Jury Absent," 1. William F. Minor's version in "Court Refuses to Let Jurors Hear Testimony" 1, suggested a more vulgar version of the exchange.
15 *Till Trial Transcript*, Bryant, 272–73.
16 Simeon Wright, *Simeon's Story*, 273–74. Wright wrote in his memoir that he heard nothing untoward, and that the two cousins simply walked out of the store together. Note that normally, an African American adult male was referred to as "boy" in the Jim Crow South, but that derogatory term didn't work well here since the defense attorneys needed to make Emmett Till a credible sexual threat—a man, not a boy.
17 *Till Trial Transcript*, Bryant, 275–76.
18 Ibid., 276–77.
19 Ibid., 277.
20 *Till Trial Transcript*, Bryant, 277; Yarbrough, "Three Say Body Identified," 1.

CHAPTER NINETEEN

1 *Till Trial Transcript*, Mrs. J. W. Milam testimony, 277–81.
2 The death certificate Strider signed is reproduced in Till-Mobley, *Death of Innocence*, 134 and 135.
3 "Mississippi Sheriff Voices Doubt," 1; "Question Is Again Raised if Dead Body Was That of Till," 1; *Till Trial Transcript*, H. C. Strider testimony, 281; "Wolf-Whistle Murder Evidence Called 'Slim,'" 16.
4 *Till Trial Transcript*, Strider, 281–85.
5 Ibid., 286–87.
6 Ibid., 287–88.
7 Ibid., 288–89.
8 Ibid., 289–90.
9 Ibid., 290–91.
10 Ibid., 288–91.
11 Ibid., 304–5.

CHAPTER TWENTY

1 *Till Trial Transcript*, Dr. L. B. Otken testimony, 293–94.
2 Ibid., 296–98.
3 Ibid., 298–301.

4 Ibid., 302–3.
5 *Till Trial Transcript*, H. D. Malone testimony, 306–9.
6 Ibid., 309–11.
7 Ibid., 311–15.
8 Ibid., 315–17.
9 Ibid., 317–18.
10 Ibid., 319–20.
11 Ibid., 320.

CHAPTER TWENTY-ONE

1 Till-Mobley, *Death of Innocence*, 188.
2 *Till Trial Transcript*, Lee Russell Allison testimony, 322–27.
3 *Till Trial Transcript*, Harold Terry testimony, 337–40.
4 *Till Trial Transcript*, 347. Each side submitted their suggestions for jury
   instructions to the judge, but the trial transcript did not record them
   nor what the judge did or did not approve. We simply do not know
   what instructions the jurors took to the jury room. A few of the
   suggestions by the defense survive in the Sumner County courthouse,
   but they were all marked rejected by Judge Swango.
5 The trial transcript does not reproduce the closing arguments; it
   merely mentions the order of the presentations. Most newspapers
   wrote that the prosecution presented first, followed by the defense.
   The trial transcript, however, indicates that District Attorney
   Chatham spoke first, followed by defense attorneys Henderson,
   Carlton, and Kellum, then a two-hour break for lunch, then final
   summations by defense attorney Whitten followed by prosecutor
   Smith. I base my account of the closing arguments on the newspaper
   reports, but I present them in the order indicated by the trial
   transcript.
6 Coverage by reporters in Sumner often was picked up by the wire
   services, but local newsmen writing for Mississippi papers tended to
   publish the longest accounts.
7 As Gerald Chatham Jr. recalled the story fifty years later, he found
   Shep on Highway 51, carried him home, and buried him; there was
   no mention of Shep missing for days then being found in a ravine;
   DSU Till, transcription of interview by Dr. Henry Outlaw with Gerald
   Chatham Jr., Jan. 19, 2005, 10.
8 Hicks, "Miss. DA Pleads in Vain for Lynching Conviction," 10.
9 James W. Silver, *Mississippi: The Closed Society* (1964; repr., Jackson:
   University Press of Mississippi, 2012). My reconstruction of the
   closing arguments is based on the reports of journalists who were
   present in Sumner. The most detailed stories appeared in the *Jackson
   Clarion-Ledger*, Sept. 24, 1955, 1, one by Jay Milner, the other by
   Arthur Everett, under a single banner headline "Till Case Defendants
   Freed by Jury on Third Ballot Because of Doubt Concerning
   Identification of Body." Other good stories include John Herbers, "Not
   Guilty Verdict in Wolf Whistle Murder Trial," *Greenwood Morning Star*,
   Sept. 24, 1955, 1; Johnson, "Jury Hears Defense," 1; John N.

Popham, "Mississippi Jury Acquits 2 Accused in Youth's Killing," *New York Times*, Sept. 24, 1955, 1; W. F. Minor, "Accused Slayers Found Not Guilty," *New Orleans Times-Picayune*, Sept. 24, 1955, 5. James Hicks wrote an admiring and very detailed account of Chatham's closing arguments, widely syndicated in African American newspapers—see "Miss. DA Pleads in Vain for Lynching Conviction," *Houston Informer*, Oct. 1, 1955, 1. Other details and quotations are from "Defendants Found Not Guilty in Mississippi Slaying Trial," *Raleigh News and Observer*, Sept. 24, 1955, 1–2; "Trial of 2 in Boy's Murder Nears Close," *Oakland Tribune*, Sept. 23, 1955, 2; "D.A. Asserts Negro Slaying Was 'Cowardly Act' in Final Argument," *Wisconsin Rapids Tribune*, Sept. 23, 1955, 1.

CHAPTER TWENTY-TWO

1 *Till Trial Transcript*, 348–49.
2 Ibid.
3 Ibid., 349–50; Clark Porteous, "Next: 2 Face Till Kidnap Charges," *Memphis Press-Scimitar*, Sept. 24, 1955, 1; "Verdict Due Today on Pair Charged with Boy's Death," *Chester (PA) Times*, Sept. 23, 1955, 2.
4 Arthur Everett, "Trial in Leflore Must Await Action by Next Grand Jury," *Jackson Clarion-Ledger*, Sept. 24, 1955, 1.
5 Porteous, "Next: 2 Face Till Kidnap Charges," 1.
6 Porteous, "Next: 2 Face Till Kidnap Charges," 1; William Sorrels, "Two Mississippians Acquitted in Slaying of Chicago Negro; Jurors Out Only 67 Minutes," *Memphis Commercial Appeal*, Sept. 24, 1955, 1; John N. Popham, "Mississippi Jury Acquits 2 Accused in Youth's Killing," 1; Everett, "Trial in Leflore," 1; Jay Milner, "Attorneys Outline Case in Summaries before Jury Verdict," *Jackson Clarion-Ledger*, Sept. 24, 1955, 1. Most United States newspapers included a photo of Milam and Bryant with their wives; a Canadian newspaper, on the other hand, the *Lethbridge (AB) Herald* ran the AP story with a photo of Mamie Till Bradley leaning her head on her father's chest under the heading, "Picture of Sorrow," Sept. 24, 1955, 1.
7 Popham, "Mississippi Jury Acquits," 1; Sam Johnson, "Mississippians Acquitted in Death of Negro; Held for Kidnapping," *Dover (OH) Daily Reporter*, Sept. 24, 1955, 1.
8 Till-Mobley, *Death of Innocence*, 188–90.
9 Till-Mobley, *Death of Innocence*, 189; "Mother of Till Expected Verdict," *Jackson Clarion-Ledger*, Sept. 24, 1955, 1; Porteous, "Next: 2 Face Till Kidnap Charges," 1.
10 Till-Mobley, *Death of Innocence*, 190.
11 John Popham, "Mississippi Seeks Kidnapping Count," *New York Times*, Sept. 25, 1955, 61; "Mississippi Pair Freed on Murder Charge Still Jailed for Kidnapping," *Mississippi Daily Chronicle*, Sept. 24, 1955, 1; John Herbers, "State to Try Men for Kidnap in Leflore Co.," *Greenwood Morning Star*, Sept. 24, 1955, 1; Porteous, "Next: 2 Face Till Kidnap Charges," 1; "Mississippi Pair Freed," 1.
12 Whitaker, "A Case Study in Southern Justice," 154–55.

13 "Bryant and Milam Released on $10,000 Bonds for Appearance before Grand Jury November 7," *Greenwood Commonwealth*, Sept. 30, 2016, 1.

14 William Middlebrooks, "Milam and Bryant Freed on $10,000 Bond at Hearing," *Northwest Mississippi Morning Sun*, Oct. 1, 1955, 1; "Two White Men Accused of Kidnapping Emmett Till Freed on $10,000 Bond," *Waco (TX) News Tribune*, Oct. 1, 1955, 2; "Bryant and Milam Released," 1.

15 Helen Shearon, "Bryant and Milam Freed under Bond," *Memphis Commercial Appeal*, Oct. 1, 1955, 1.

16 "Rumors on Till Case Sweep State," *Delta Democrat-Times*, Oct. 2, 1955, 21; "Strider Believes Till Is Still Alive," *Greenwood Commonwealth*, Sept. 29, 1955, 1; Middlebrooks, "Milam and Bryant Freed on $10,000," 1; "Emmett Till Still Alive, Says Sheriff," *Biloxi Daily Herald*, Sept. 29, 1955, 1; "Negro Youth May Still Be Alive, Rumor," *Frederick (MD) News*, Sept. 30, 1955, 9; "Wild Rumors," *Greenwood Morning Star*, Sept. 30, 1955, 4. Also see the anti-Semitic broadside "Is Emmett Till Alive?," put out in early 1956 by the American Anti-Communist Militia, Chicago Division, in University of Mississippi, Special Collections, Race Relations Collection, box 3, folder 32. Hodding Carter's *Delta Democrat-Times* rebuked the *Memphis Press-Scimitar* for publishing a demonstrably false Till sighting, in "Irresponsible Journalism," *Delta Democrat-Times*, Oct. 2, 1955, 4.

17 Ted Poston, "NAACP Fears Bloodshed as Till Trial Aftermath," *New York Post*, Oct. 5, 1955, 52; "Willie Reed Won't Go Back to Miss," *Baltimore Afro-American*, Oct. 22, 1955, 2.

18 "2 Lynch Trial Witnesses Leave Miss. for the North," *Houston Informer*, Oct. 1, 1955, 1.

19 Ted Poston, "Mose Wright Left Everything to Flee for Life," *New York Post*, Oct. 3, 1955, 5; details changed a bit, but Poston's story was adapted and widely distributed by the AP. Devery Anderson does an excellent job of bringing together multiple versions of this story, and whether Mose's home was ransacked before he left Mississippi, after he left the state, or if it happened at all is in question; see *Emmett Till*, 438.

20 "Bryant, Milam Seek Bond as Rumors Fly," *Memphis Commercial Appeal*, Sept. 30, 1955, 17; "Aftermath of 'Wolf Whistle' Trial Finds Key Witnesses in Move North," *Huronite and Daily Plainsman* (Huron, SD), Sept. 25, 1955, 1; George F. Brown, "Willie's Up North but He's Scared," *Pittsburgh Courier*, Oct. 8, 1955, 1; "Willie Reed Won't Go Back to Mississippi," *Baltimore Afro-American*, Oct. 22, 1955, 2; Chester M. Hampton, "World Shocked by Till Trial; Old, Young Leave Mississippi," *Birmingham World*, Sept. 30, 1955, 6; Till-Mobley, *Death of Innocence*, 196–97.

21 "Till Witness Guarded in Chicago Due to Illinois Racial Tension," *Jackson Daily News*, Sept. 30, 1955, 1; Bill Spell, "State Negroes Held 'Captive' in Chicago," *Jackson Daily News*, Oct. 5, 1955, 1; Bill Spell and W. C. Shoemaker, "'Missing' Negro Is Found, Refutes NAACP Propaganda," *Jackson Daily News*, Oct. 6, 1955, 1; Bill Spell, "Woman Witness Told to Keep Silent," *Jackson Daily News*, Oct. 6, 1955, 1.

22 Bill Spell, "How the NAACP Network Operates," *Jackson Daily News*, Oct. 7, 1955, 1.

23 Ibid.

24 "Paper Charges NAACP Holds 3 Witnesses," *Anderson (IN) Herald Bulletin*, Oct. 7, 1955, 13; "Tale about Negro Captives Is Disputed by Paper in Chicago," *Lawrence (KS) Journal World*, Oct. 7, 1955, 1; "Denies Negroes Are Held Captive," *Joplin (MO) Globe*, Oct. 8, 1955, 1; "Negro Paper Says Witnesses Free," *Charleston News and Courier*, Oct. 8, 1955, n.p. The *Chicago Defender* noted that Spell was in the city for a mere twenty-four hours; "Dixie Newsman Probes Till Case," *Chicago Defender*, Oct. 15, 1955, 2; Green, *Selling the Race*, 202–4.

25 "2 Negro 'Whistle Killing' Witnesses Still Missing and Are Feared Slain," *New York Post*, Sept. 29, 1955, 5; Ted Poston, "FBI Asked to Hunt for 'Missing' Till Witnesses," *New York Post*, Sept. 30, 1955, 5; Ted Poston, "NAACP Fears Bloodshed as Till Trial Aftermath," *New York Post*, Oct. 5, 1955, 57; "2 Negroes Taken from Mississippi," *Joplin (MO) Globe*, Oct. 2, 1955, 1.

26 Transcript of Collins's interview from the *Memphis Tri-State Defender*, Oct. 8, 1955, included in memo from J. Edgar Hoover to Warren Olney III, Oct. 14, 1955, NARA, Department of Justice, RG 60, section 30, container 956, folder 144-40-116. The AP report cited the *Defender* as its source: "Collins Disclaims Knowledge of Till," *Memphis Commercial Appeal*, Oct. 10, 1955, 28. Ruby Hurley noted that often in her organizing work in the Deep South, she heard stories about one or more blacks who betrayed others out of fear or for special favors; she put those who aided Milam and Bryant in that category. See interview with Ruby Hurley, director, Southeastern Regional office, NAACP, interviewed by John H. Britton, Jan. 26, 1968, Civil Rights Documentation Project, Moreland-Spingarn Manuscript Research Center, Howard University.

27 Collins interview, *Tri-State Defender*, Oct. 8, 1955, see n. 26; "Collins Disclaims Knowledge," 28.

28 James A. Haught, "Negro Said Unjustly Jailed to Stifle Truth of Till Death," *Charleston (WV) Gazette*, Mar. 11, 1956, 1; Louis Lomax, "Ask FBI to Open Probe," *Washington Afro-American*, Apr. 8, 1958, in NARA, RG 60, sec. 30, container 956, folder 144-40-116.

29 Lomax, "Ask FBI"; Adam Clayton Powell to Lawrence E Walsh, Deputy Attorney General, and W. Wilson White, Assistant Attorney General, Civil Rights Division, filed Apr. 28, 1958, W. Wilson White's reply, also filed Apr. 28, and "Additional Evidence in Connection with the Emmett Till Case," marked "Highly Confidential," all in NARA, RG 60, section 30, container 956, folder 144-40-116.

CHAPTER TWENTY-THREE

1 "Mississippi's Shame," Oklahoma City *Black Dispatch*, Sept. 29, 1955, 10.

2 The authority on the Mississippi press in the immediate aftermath of the Till case is the carefully researched book by Davis W. Houck and

Matthew A. Grindy, *Emmett Till and the Mississippi Press*, 107–25; "Justice," *Kingsport (TN) News*, Sept. 26, 1955, 4; "Justice Was Done," *Kannapolis (NC) Daily Independent*, Oct. 7, 1955, 4; "Make It a Two-Way Inquiry," *Memphis Commercial Appeal*, Sept. 27, 1955, n.p., DSU Till, Scrapbook; "It Was a Fair Trial," *Greenwood Commonwealth*, Sept. 24, 1955, 4; "Fair Trial Was Credit to Mississippi," *Greenwood Morning Star*, Sept. 23, 1955, 4, "A New Wrinkle in the Vilification of Mississippi," *Greenwood Morning Star*, Sept. 27, 1955, 6, and "Challenge to the Sensational News Hunters," *Greenwood Morning Star*, Oct. 9, 1955, 2.

3 "Mississippi 'Prejudice' Verdict Calls for Calmness in Both Races," *Charleston (WVA) Gazette*, Sept. 24, 1955, p. 4; "Jury Trial in Mississippi," *Winston-Salem Journal*, n.d., in CHM, Claude Bennett Papers, box 374, Till file; "The State of Mississippi Still Carries the Burden," *Atlanta Constitution*, Sept. 26, 1955, 4; "Mississippi Shames the South," *Raleigh News and Observer*, Sept. 25, 1955; "Acquittal," *Delta Democrat-Times*, Sept. 25, 1955, 4; Whitaker, "A Case Study in Southern Justice," 170.

4 "We Weep for Mississippi," *Chicago Defender*, Oct. 8, 1955, 9; "Mississippi Decision Nothing New," *Baltimore Afro-American*, Oct. 1, 1955, 4; "Mississippi's Shame," 10; "White Supremacy Wins Again," *Kansas City Call*, Sept. 30, 1955, 18; "State Negroes See Verdict in Keeping with Southern Tradition," and "The Till Case Verdict," *Jackson Advocate*, Oct. 1, 1955, 1; Roi Ottley, "Southern Style," *Chicago Defender*, Oct. 8, 1955, in Metress, *Lynching of Emmett Till*, 133.

5 "A Mockery of Justice in Mississippi," *Chicago Sun-Times*, Sept. 27, 1955, n.p., in CHM, Barnett Papers, box 374, Till file (accompanying the *Sun-Times* editorial was a cartoon titled "Another Victim in Mississippi" depicting Justice sinking, her hands and feet bound, a weight around her neck labeled "Till Murder Acquittal"); "Predictable Victory," *St. Louis Post-Dispatch*, repr. in *Idaho Falls Post Register*, Oct. 2, 1955, 4; "As We See it," repr. of *Detroit Free Press* editorial, n.p., n.d., in CHM, Barnett Papers, box 374, Till file; "Mississippi Nightmare," *New York Post*, Sept. 30, 1955, n.p., in CHM, Barnett Papers, box 374, Till file; "Reds Seize Chance to Exploit Murder," *Journal-Times* (Racine, WI) Oct. 11, 1955, 32.

6 "Double Murder in Mississippi," *Christian Century*, Oct. 5, 1955, n.p. SERS (SERS is a newspaper clipping file on southern stories from the Civil Rights era); Murray Kempton, "The Future," 3.

7 "The Murder of Emmett Till" originally appeared Oct. 3, 1955, *I. F. Stone's Weekly*, repr. as "The South Is Sick" *Baltimore Afro-American*, Oct. 22, 1955, 8, most readily available in Karl Weber, ed., *The Best of I. F. Stone* (New York: Public Affairs Press, 2006), 168–170.

8 Bobby Parkins, "Negro Is Not Key to Our Existence"; "Observer," "Emmett Till Would Be Alive Today If He'd Respected South's Customs"; Mrs. Willis P. Newman, "Reds, NAACP Were Real Killers; Till Was Only Means to an End," all from the *Memphis Commercial Appeal*, in DSU Till Scrapbook, n.p. n.d.

9 Letters to Breland and Whitten are in OSU Huie, box 38, file 353a, "Emmett Till Story, Related Correspondence," letters from Mrs. Frank E. Moore, W. W. Malone, and Westbrook Pegler.

10 On Gerald Chatham's life, see transcription of interview by Dr. Henry Outlaw with Gerald Chatham Jr., Jan. 19, 2005, DSU Till, Scrapbook Archive; "Till Case Prosecutor Is Dead," *Hattiesburg American*, Oct. 10, 1956, 1.

11 David Brown, "Sumner Revisited: How Several Lives Altered by Till Trial," *Delta Democrat-Times*, Aug. 19, 1956, 7.

12 All of these letters are housed in the DSU Till, Scrapbook Archive. They've been scanned and placed in digital files labeled "positive and negative mail," and "extremist mail." Note that I do not give each correspondent's full name, just his or her initials. See R.S.H to Chatham, Los Angeles, Sept. 22, 1955; J.N.H. to Chatham, n.p., Sept. 6, 1955; E.E. to Chatham, New York City, Sept. 2, 1955, all in positive and negative mail file. Also worth noting are letters from A.D. St. A., H.B., and M.A.H.

13 Unsigned letter to Chatham, Chicago, Sept. 24, 1955, extremist file; unsigned letter to Chatham, Chicago, Sept. 22, 1955, extremist file.

14 Unsigned letter to Chatham, Chicago, Sept. 5, 1955, extremist file; unsigned letter to Chatham, Cleveland, Sept. 20[?], 1955, extremist file.

15 Unsigned letter to Chatham, New York City, Sept. 24, 1955, extremist file; unsigned letter to Chatham, New York City, Oct. 4, 1955, extremist file.

16 J.S.C. to Chatham, Morehouse, MO, Sept. 11, 1955, extremist file; P.J.S. to Chatham, Philadelphia, MS, Sept. 12, 1955, extremist file.

17 No name, date or place to Chatham, extremist file; unsigned to Chatham, Chicago, Sept. 7, 1955, extremist file; unsigned to Chatham, Chicago, Sept. 4, 1955, extremist file.

18 Mrs. R.B. to Chatham, New York City, Sept. 23, 1955, extremist file; no name or date, from New York City to "County Attorney," extremist file; unsigned to Gerald Chatham, Sept. 9, 1955, in extremist file; unsigned to Gov. Hugh White and Gerald Chatham, Frederick, MD, Sept. 12, 1955, extremist file.

19 Unsigned letter to Chatham, Jamaica, NY, Sept. 20, 1955, positive and negative file.

20 Unsigned letter to Chatham from Manhattan, KS, Sept. 29, 1955, extremist file; R.T.H. to Chatham, Tacoma, WA, Sept. 29, 1955, extremist file; L.H., Ysleta, TX, to Chatham, Sept. 24, 1955, positive and negative file, J.B. to Chatham, Glens Falls, NY, Sept. 20, 1955, positive and negative file.

21 E.H.J. to Governor White, Chatham, and several others, Fort Worth, TX, Sept. 26, 1955, positive and negative file; M.C.M. to Chatham, Ardsley, PA, n.d., positive and negative file; unsigned to Chatham, Jamaica, NY, Sept. 20, 1955, positive and negative file; C.S. to Chatham, Ashton, MD, Sept. 27, 1955, positive and negative file; M.A.P. to Chatham, Grants Pass, OR, Sept. 23, 1955, positive and negative file.

22 S.P. and B.F. to Chatham, San Jose, CA, Sept. 20, 1955, positive and negative file; "A Minister," to Chatham, Detroit, Sept. 20, 1955,

positive and negative file; C.J. to Chatham, Springfield, OH, Sept. 22, 1955, positive and negative file; M.G., Hutchinson, KS, Sept. 23, 1955, positive and negative file; E.H.J. to Governor White, Chatham, and others, Fort Worth, TX, n.d., extreme file.

23 Mrs. M.G. to Chatham, Los Angeles, Sept. 26, 1955, positive and negative file; R.T.H. to Chatham, Tacoma, WA, Sept. 29, 1955, positive and negative file; unsigned to Chatham, Manhattan, KS, Sept. 23, 1955, extremist file; J.A.B. to Chatham, Glens Falls, NY, Sept. 20, 1955, positive and negative file; C.L. to Chatham, n.p., Sept. 19, 1955, positive and negative file.

24 M.A.P. to Chatham, Grants Pass, OR, Sept. 23, 1955, positive and negative file; R.T.H. to Chatham, Tacoma, WA, Sept. 29, 1955, positive and negative file; unsigned to Chatham, Manhattan, KS, Sept. 23, 1955, extremist file.

25 Dr. Henry Outlaw interview with Gerald Chatham Jr., Delta State Archives, Till Collection, Jan. 19, 2005, 6.

CHAPTER TWENTY-FOUR

1 "Mississippi Jury Denounced Here," *New York Times*, Sept. 25, 1955, 1; "10,000 in Harlem Protest Verdict," *New York Times*, Sept. 26, 1955, 10.

2 "Mississippi Jury Denounced," 1.

3 "10,000 in Harlem Protest Verdict,"10.

4 Ted Poston, "My Son Didn't Die in Vain, Till's Mother Tells Rally," *New York Post*, Sept. 26, 1955, 5; "Rally Protests Mississippi Killing," *New York Herald Tribune*, Sept. 26, 1955, 1. The *Post* estimated the crowd at 8,000, the *Times* at 10,000, and the *Herald Tribune* at 15,000. A. Philip Randolph to Roy Wilkins, Sept. 22, 1955, LC, NAACP papers, group 2, box A424, file 1, correspondence.

5 Handbill, "NAACP Mass Meeting," UM DASC Race Relations Collection, box 6, file 16; "Diggs Gives Far Different Appraisal of Trial at Detroit Than at Sumner," unidentified newspaper clipping, CHM, Barnett Papers, box 374, "Till" file. The $14,000 figure comes from a Sept. 29, 1955, memo from Mr. Moon to Mr. Current, LC, NAACP papers, group 2, box A424, "Relief Fund" file.

6 Yvonne Ryan, *Roy Wilkins: The Quiet Revolutionary and the NAACP* (Lexington: University Press of Kentucky, 1914), 53–80.

7 Ibid.

8 "NAACP Ad Asks End of Tyranny," unidentified newspaper, DSU Till, Newspaper Scrapbook; Ruby Hurley to Branch Officers, Sept. 27,1955, in MDAH, Medgar Evers Papers, box 2, file 19; Alfred Baker Lewis to Roy Wilkins, Sept. 27, 1955, LC, NAACP Papers, group 2, box A424, "Relief Fund" file; letters addressed to "Christian Friends," "Youth Leader," and "Honorable Dwight D. Eisenhower," all dated Sept. 1955, and signed by Camille Carter, in LC, NAACP papers, group 2, box A424, "Rallies and Meetings–Youth" file.

9 Mr. Moon to Mr. Current, Sept. 29, 1955, LC, NAACP papers, group 2, box A424, "Relief Fund" file; "Mr. Diggs' Timely Suggestion,"

Baltimore Afro-American, Oct. 8, 1955, 4; "Urges U.S. to Act in Mississippi," *New York Daily News*, Oct. 7, 1955, n.p., in ACLU, Illinois Branch Papers, University of Chicago, Special Collections, Till file; "Congressman Asks Boycott of Mississippi's Products," *Memphis Clarion-Ledger*, Oct. 11, 1955, 1; "Will Introduce Move in 1957," *Racine (WI) Journal Times*, Oct. 11, 1955, 1; "Would Take $77,880,783.51 to Haul All Our Good Negroes to the Nawth," *Jackson Daily News*, Sept. 28, 1955, 4; "On Internal Security," *St. Louis Argus*, Oct. 28, 1955, 14, repr. from the *Baltimore Afro-American*.

10 "Church Council Rips Mississippi Justice," *Racine (WI) Journal Times*, Nov. 30, 1955, 30; "Demonstrate at White House in Till Case," *Chicago Daily Tribune*, Oct. 25, 1955, 10; "Pickets Threaten March on Capital," *Baltimore Afro-American*, Nov. 5, 1955, 22; "Dr. Harry Emerson Fosdick Chairman at Meeting Protesting Till Boy's Death," *Nashville Globe and Independent*, Nov. 11, 1955, 1; letter and program from Harry Emerson Fosdick, Nov. 3, 1955, LC NAACP Papers, group 1, box A424, file 1; handbill, "Who Murdered Emmett Till?," in LC, NAACP Papers, group 2, box A425, file 1.

11 "20,000 Attend Till Rally in New York," *Kansas City Call*, Oct. 21, 1955, 1. The Law Office Workers Union in New York City demanded that the justice department intervene, Oakland's local of the International Longshoreman's Union wrote directly to President Eisenhower, and Seattle's International Woodworkers telegraphed Attorney General Brownell. Chicago's postal employees and Jersey City's Beauty Culturists added their voices, while New York's Laundry Workers resolved that Milam and Bryant's wanton crime against a child and their subsequent acquittal, "reads the state of Mississippi out of the family of civilized communities and shames America before the rest of the world." News release, "Crisis Urges Nationwide Interracial Protest Meetings on Till Lynching," in LC, NAACP Papers, group 2, box A424, file 1; letter from Fraternal, Trade Union and Law Office Workers, Oct. 18, 1955; Roy Wilkins to Warehouse Union, Local 6, Oct. 13, 1955; Local 23–90 of the International Woodworkers to James E. McIver, Nov. 18, 1955; Chicago Branch National Alliance of Postal Employees, "Petition for Justice," Sept. 9, 1955; National Beauty Culturist's League to Rev. Louis Ford, Sept. 26, 1955; Laundry Workers Joint Board to Roy Wilkins, Oct. 5, 1955; all in LC, NAACP Papers, group 2, box A 425, file 1, "Correspondence—Organizations." Also see "Intervention by Eisenhower Urged by CIO," *St. Louis Argus*, Sept. 23, 1955, 1.

12 Letter from Walter Reuther to all UAW-CIO Local Union Presidents, Oct. 27, 1955, in LC, NAACP Papers, group 2, box A425, file 1, "Correspondence–Organizations." The NAACP journal, *Crisis*, noted the rarity of integrated events and urged more of them be held; Press Release, "Crisis Urges Nationwide Interracial Protest Meetings on Till Lynching," NAACP Papers, group 2, box A424, file 1; Franklin H. Williams to Staff, Nov. 4, 1955, NAACP Papers, group 2, box A424, file 3. The Los Angeles NAACP Branch seemed to be a constant source of headaches for the national office, stemming from an alleged unwillingness to work with labor unions or Jewish community

groups; see Tara Pittman to Gloster Current, Oct. 14, 1955, LC, NAACP Papers, group 2, box A424, file 3. Union locals kept up a steady stream of letters to various government agencies. See, for example, the telegram from the president of Chicago's Warehouse Distribution Union Local 208 to the Attorney General, Sept. 1, 1955, the letter from the Human Relations director of the New Jersey State Council of the CIO to Attorney General Brownell, Oct. 3, 1955, or the note to him from the secretary of the UAW Aircraft Workers of America, Jan. 20, 1956, all in NARA, RG 60, DOJ, section 30, container 956, 144-40-116.

13 "33 Cities Slate Till Murder Protest Meetings," *Los Angeles Tribune*, Sept. 30, 1955, 3; "Negro Rally Hits Acquittal in Till Case," *Chicago Daily Tribune*, Sept. 30, 1955, 4; "Till's Mom Here Thursday," unnamed Detroit paper, Oct. 1, 1955, 1, in CHM, Barnett Papers, box 374, Till file; "Public Protest Mounts Over Nation on Emmett Till Case," *Little Rock State Press*, Oct. 7, 1955, 1; "Mother of Murder Victim Speaks Here," *St. Louis Post Dispatch*, Oct. 10, 1955, n.p. in SERS.

14 "Mrs. Bradley Addresses Wash. Throng," *St. Louis Argus*, Oct. 28, 1955, 4; "Emmett Till's Mother Tells 6,100 of Killing," *Washington Evening Star*, Oct. 17, 1955, 14A; "5,000 Donate to Till Rally," *Atlanta Daily World*, Oct. 16, 1955, 1; "Mrs. Bradley Makes Plea 'For Us to Wake Up; Been Asleep a Long Time,'" *Des Moines Bystander*, Oct. 27, 1955, 1; "Till's Death Turning Point, Mother States," *Biloxi Daily Herald*, Oct. 25, 1955, 1.

15 "Mrs. Bradley Addresses Wash. Throng," 4; "Emmett Till's Mother Tells 6,100," 14A; "5,000 Donate to Till Rally," 1; "Mrs. Bradley Makes Plea," 1; "Till's Death Turning Point, Mother States," 1.

16 Ruth Feldstein makes this argument with great detail and subtlety in *Motherhood in Black and White: Race and Sex in American Liberalism, 1930–1965* (Ithaca, NY: Cornell University Press, 2000), 86–110.

CHAPTER TWENTY-FIVE

1 Eleanor Roosevelt, "I Think the Till Jury Will Have Uneasy Conscience," *Memphis Press-Scimitar*, Oct. 11, 1955, 6, Delta State Newspaper Scrapbook. See also Metress, *Lynching of Emmett Till*, 136–37.

2 Thomas J. Sugrue, *Sweet Land of Liberty: The Forgotten Struggle for Civil Rights in the North* (New York: Random House, 2008), chaps. 2–4, esp. 57–112.

3 Historians have long been uncomfortable with the popular notion that the Civil Rights Movement began with *Brown* and ended with the Civil Rights Act of 1964, or even the death of Martin Luther King Jr. in 1968. The early radical roots of the movement are the subject of Penny M. Von Eschen's, *Race Against Empire: Black Americans and Anticolonialism, 1937–1957* (Ithaca, NY: Cornell University Press, 1997). An important article is Jacquelyn Dowd

Hall, "The Long Civil Rights Movement and the Political Uses of the Past," *Journal of American History* 91, no. 4 (March 2005): 1233–63. On the radical tradition in the South, see Glenda Elizabeth Gilmore, *Defying Dixie: The Radical Roots of Civil Rights, 1919–1950* (New York: Norton, 2008). And for the early movement in the North, see Sugrue, *Sweet Land of Liberty*, 3–162.

4 The historical literature is strong on this subject. See Von Eschen, *Race Against Empire;* Mary L. Dudziak, *Cold War Civil Rights: Race and the Image of American Democracy;* Thomas Borstelmann, *The Cold War and the Color Line: American Race Relations in the Global Arena* (Cambridge, MA: Harvard University Press, 2001); Carol Anderson, *Eyes Off the Prize: The United Nations and the African American Struggle for Human Rights, 1944–1955* (Cambridge: Cambridge University Press, 2003).

5 "Infoguide: An Act of Anti-Negro Violence," NARA, RG 360, USIA, Records Relating to Labor and Minorities, 1948–1968, box 41, "Till and Mississippi" file.

6 "Soviet Orbit Propaganda," Sept. 3–7, Sept. 14–16, Oct. 5–7, Oct. 12–14, 1955; "New 'Racial Atrocities' Occur in U.S." Moscow, Soviet Home Service; telegram dated Sept. 9, 1955, from London to USIA; all in NARA RG 360, USIA, box 41, Till file.

7 USIA, "Soviet Orbit Propaganda," Sept. 3–7, Sept. 14–16, Oct. 5–7, Oct. 12–14, 1955, "New 'Racial Atrocities' Occur in U.S." Moscow, Soviet Home Service; telegram dated Sept. 9, 1955, from London to USIA; message from Department of the Army, Melbourne to Department of the Army, Washington, DC; Foreign Service Dispatch, Sept. 9, 1955, from American embassy, Caracas to Department of State, Washington; USIA "Daily Summary," Oct. 11, 1955, 2; telegram dated Sept. 29, 1955 from Leopoldville to USIA; all in NARA RG 360, USIA, box 41, Till file; "Protest Verdict," *Biloxi Daily Herald*, Sept. 29, 1955, 13; Roger Baldwin to Roy Wilkins, in LC, NAACP Papers, group 2, box A424, file 1.

8 William H. Stoneman, "Sumner Acquittal Makes Europe Front Pages," *Memphis Commercial Appeal*, n.p., n.d., in Delta State Newspaper Scrapbook.

9 Powell's office released a full text of his speech under the title "Congressman Powell Speaks at Labor Rally Held at 7th Avenue and 37th Street," Oct. 11, 1955, LC, NAACP Papers, group 2, box A424, file 1. Powell's speech was widely covered by the wire services—see *Racine (WI) Journal-Times*, Oct. 11, 1955, 1; "Powell Hits Mississippi," *Kannapolis (NC) Daily Independent*, Oct. 11, 1955, 1; "Till Affair Hurt American Prestige, Says Powell," in CHM, Barnett Papers, box 374, Till file; telegrams from AP on the Powell speech, NARA, RG 360, USIA, box 41, Till file.

10 Memo, American Jewish Committee, Paris Office to National Office, New York, "European Reaction to Emmett Till Case in Sumner, Mississippi, Oct. 7, 1955," LC, NAACP Papers, group 2, box A425, file 1, Till Correspondence.

11 Ibid.

12 "Strengthen Justice Department's Civil Rights Powers..." For release Saturday, Oct. 22, 1955, LC, NAACP Papers, group 2, box A425, file 1, Till Correspondence.

13 AJC, "European Reaction to Emmett Till Case."
14 In addition to the AJC report, see "Note to City Editors," Oct. 22, 1955, "Strengthen Justice Department's Civil Rights Powers," Oct. 22, 1955, and "Resolution on the Till Case," Oct. 16, 1955, all in LC, NAACP group 2, box A425, file 1, Till Correspondence.
15 Francis M. Hammond to Mr. Streibert, Oct. 26, 1955, and Theodore Streibert to Edward Bernays, Nov. 1, 1955, both in NARA, RG 306, USIA, box 41, Till file; E. Frederic Morrow, *Black Man in the White House* (New York: Coward-McCann, 1963), 266–68.

CHAPTER TWENTY-SIX

1 "Editorial: In Memoriam, Emmett Till," *Life*, Oct. 10, 1955, 48.
2 "Till's Father Had Been Billed 'War Hero' During Fund Raising Drives," *Jackson Daily News*, Oct. 15, 1955, n.p., SERS.
3 "About Till's Father," *Jackson Daily News*, Oct. 16, 1955, n.p., SERS.
4 Till-Mobley, *Death of Innocence*, 103, 202–3.
5 More precisely, Louis Till served in the 177th Port Company, 379th Port Battalion, Transportation Corps. See Lt. Col. James G. Chesnutt to William Bradford Huie, Nov. 9, 1956, OSU, Huie, box 38, file 349; Headquarters, Mediterranean Theater of Operations, US Army APO 512, General Court-Martial Orders Number 89, June 13, 1945, signed by Colonel C. W. Christenberry, in OSU, Huie, box 24, file 349.
6 General Court-martial, Orders Number 89, June 13, 1945, OSU Huie, box 24, file 349. For the original trial transcript and related documents, see *Record of Trial of Private Fred A. McMurray, 38184335, and Private Louis NMI Till, 36392273, 177 Port Company, 379 Port Battalion, T.C. by General Court Martial, appointed by the Commanding General, Peninsular Base Section, Tried at Leghorn, Italy, 17 February 1945*; Hereafter, *Record of Trial*. Professor Robert Lilly owned a full transcript of pretrial proceedings, the trial itself with ancillary materials, and the review, which he was kind enough to share with me.
7 *Record of Trial*, testimony of Benni Lucretzia, 11–18, Frieda Mari, 19–29.
8 *Record of Trial*, Prosecution exhibit 1, n.p. After the court-martial trial came the review: *Report of Branch Office of the Judge Advocate General, Board of Review, MTO 6866, APO 512, U.S. Army, 13 June 1945, United States Versus Privates Fred A. McMurray and Louis Till, Review of the General Court-Martial Trial convened at Leghorn, Italy, 17 February 1945*, in Huie Papers, OSU, box 38, file 349, 3–5. Hereafter *Review of the General Court-Martial*.
9 *Record of Trial*, Prosecution exhibit #4, n.p. (McMurray's confession). See also the introductions to the exhibit, 68–80.
10 Ibid.; *Review of the General Court-Martial*, 7–11.
11 *Record of Trial*, testimony of James Thomas Jr., 33–52, and exhibits 1–4, n.p.; *Review of the General Court-Martial*, 6–7.

12 In a pretrial statement, John Masi, a friend of the Zanchi family visiting their home when the murder of Anna Zanchi took place, said of the taller assailant, "From his actions and manner of speech I am of the opinion that he was white. Both men were armed, the taller with a large pistol which looked like the U.S. Army .45. . . ." Yet in a supplemental pretrial statement, and then in his testimony before the court-martial, Masi claimed he was mistaken, that he had lived in the United States for twelve years, could distinguish black from white speech, that what he heard from both assailants on the night of the murder was black American English. Pretrial Investigating Officer's Report, submitted Nov. 30, 1944, including the statement of John Masi, dated June 30, 1944, an "additional statement" dated Oct. 27, 1944, and Proceedings of a General Court-Martial, Leghorn, Italy, Special Orders Number 16, Jan. 16, 1945, 58–62; *Record of Trial*, 52–64. Also see, *Review of the General Court-Martial*, 3–11.
13 See J. Robert Lilly's important book, *Taken by Force: Rape and American GIs in Europe During World War II* (New York: Palgrave, 2007).
14 *Record of Trial*, 11–69; *Review of the General Court-Martial*, 4, 11–15.
15 Two "News Flashes" can be found in UM, DASC, Citizens' Council Collection (95–20), box 1, folder 3; *Right: A Monthly Newsletter of, by and for the American Right Wing*, no. 2 (Nov. 1955): 3–4. Six months later, William Bradford Huie "Why the Army Hanged Emmett Till's Father," *Confidential* 4, no. 2 (May 1956): 52.
16 James Eastland to Fred L. Boon, Nov. 30, 1955, Eastland Papers, series 3, subseries 1, box 5, "Civil Rights, 1955" file; Flora M. Cole to Senator James Eastland, Oct. 25, 1955, and Eastland to Cole, Oct. 31, 1955, in Eastland Papers, series 3, subseries 1, box 35, "Correspondence, Civil Rights file," both in UM, DASC; Ethyl L. Payne, "Army Gave Till Facts to Eastland," and "Mississippi Solons Bare Hanging of Till's Father," both in *Chicago Defender*, Oct. 29, 1955, 1. Accusations of sexual assault by black troops was nothing new for Senator Eastland. During World War II, he traveled to Europe and reported back for the Military-Naval Affairs Committee that African American soldiers were prone to laziness, desertion, and criminally assaulting white civilian women; Mary Louise Roberts, *What Soldiers Do: Sex and the American GI in World War II France* (Chicago: University of Chicago Press, 2013), 235.
17 Huff's words were covered only by the African American press— "Huff Fears Plot to Free Accused," *Chicago Defender*, Oct. 22, 1955, 1; "Rap at Till's Dad Hit by Atty. Huff," *Pittsburgh Courier*, Oct. 29, 1955, 3; "Attorney in Till Case Says Newspaper Story Is Attempt to Condone Slaying of Youth," *Oklahoma City Black Dispatch*, Oct. 20, 1955, 1; "Mrs. Bradley's Lawyer Raps 'Expose' on Till's Father," *St. Louis Argus*, Oct. 21, 1955, 1.
18 "Huff Fears," 1; "Rap at Till's Dad," 3; "Attorney in Till Case," 1; "Mrs. Bradley's Lawyer," 1; W. D. Ferguson, Santa Rosa, to unidentified newspaper, LC, NAACP Papers, group 2, box A424, "Rallies and Meetings, Youth" file; "The Till Case Backfire," *Danville (VA) Bee*, Oct. 19, 1955, 6.
19 *Till Trial Transcript*, Mamie Till Bradley, 180–86.

20 Tobias letter is quoted in Morris Cunningham, "Till's GI Dad Hanged in Italy for Women Attacks in 1944," *Memphis Commercial Appeal*, Oct. 16, 1955, 4; Lt. Col. James G. Chesnutt to William Bradford Huie, Oct. 18, 1956, in OSU, Huie Papers, box 38, file 349.

21 "The Till Case Backfire," *Danville (VA) Bee*, Oct. 19, 1955, 6; "In Memoriam, Life," *Delta Democrat-Times*, Oct. 18, 1955, 4; "Tour Canceled," *Montgomery Advertiser*, Nov. 9, 1955, 4a.

22 "On the Wrong Scent," *Baltimore Afro-American*, Oct. 29, 1955, 4; "Upon Their Conscience," *St. Louis Argus*, Oct. 21, 1955, 14; "Notes on the Till Case," *Chicago Defender*, Oct. 29, 1955, 2.

23 *Record of Trial*, 74–80; *Review of the General Court-Martial*, 14. Of course, McMurray also had the burden of the letter with his name on it, found near the murder scene.

24 "Notes on the Till Case," 2.

25 Alice Kaplan, *The Interpreter* (Chicago: University of Chicago Press, 2005), 151–55; Lilly, *Taken by Force*, 11–12.

26 J. Robert Lilly and Michael Thomson point out in their paper "Death Penalty Cases in WWII Military Courts: Lessons Learned from North Africa and Italy" that in the European Theater, 1,608 capital courts-martial resulted in 1,056 guilty verdicts, with 443 death sentences, of which 70 were carried out. Paper presented at the Forty-first Meeting of the Academy of Criminal Justice Sciences, Las Vegas, March 10–13, 2004, 7–8, 16–33. Lilly further observes that arrests for crimes like going AWOL were close to proportionate between blacks and whites whereas sex offenses skewed much more heavily black; Lilly, *Taken by Force*, 35–36. Also see Kaplan, *Interpreter*, 155–56.

27 Kaplan, *Interpreter*, 155–57; Lilly, *Taken by Force*, 7–9; Roberts, *What Soldiers Do*, 195–202, 207–11, 218.

28 Lilly, *Taken by Force*, 83, 90–94, 107–8.

29 Roberts, *What Soldiers Do*, 217–29; 243–48; 257–60.

30 For less a history than a thoughtful and, at times, moving meditation on the fate of Louis Till, see John Edgar Wideman, *Writing to Save a Life: The Louis Till File* (New York: Scribner, 2016).

CHAPTER TWENTY SEVEN

1 Till-Mobley, *Death of Innocence*, 205–9; "Mother of Till out of Hospital," *Lumberton (NC) Robesonian*, Nov. 4, 1955, 7.

2 Roy Wilkins to W. Dale Phillips, Nov. 16, 1955, in LC, NAACP Papers, group 2, box A424, file 2, Meetings and Rallies.

3 Bradley later claimed that the $5,000 idea came from Franklin Williams and the Reverend Sylvester Odum during a television conversation—"NAACP Drops Mrs. Bradley," *Kansas City Call*, Nov. 18, 1955, 4; "Mrs. Bradley Says Fee NAACP Idea," *Chicago Defender*, Nov. 19, 1955, 1.

4 Roy Wilkins memo to Gloster Current, Nov. 7, 1955; Report on Mamie Bradley Mass Meetings Sponsored by NAACP Branches; Roy Wilkins telegram to branches, Nov. 9, all in LC, NAACP Papers, group 2, box A424, file 2, "Rallies and Meetings, Nov.–Dec. 1955."

As it turned out, the West Coast tour grossed $22,000 with expenses just over $5,000; "West Coast Regional Office NAACP Financial Report," Nov. 9–22, 1955, NAACP Papers, group 2, box A424, file 3.

5 Roy Wilkins to branch officers, Oct. 7, 1955, in LC, NAACP Papers, group 2, box A424, file 7, "Correspondence."

6 Steve Duncan, "Mother Won't Wind Up in Communist 'Hot Bed.'" *St. Louis Argus*, Oct. 14, 1955, 1; "Movie Exposes Reds' Methods," *Racine (WI) Journal-Times*, Nov. 22, 1955, 17.

7 Till- Mobley, *Death of Innocence*, 202–4.

8 Telegram, Roy Wilkins to J. C. Austin, Sept. 24, in LC, NAACP Papers, group 2, box A424, file 7, "Correspondence."

9 Henderson's letter was originally sent to Dr. T. R. M. Howard, who passed it to Roy Wilkins. Memo to Dr. Howard from Dr. Henderson, no date; Roy Wilkins to J. Raymond Henderson, n.d., LC, NAACP Papers, group 2, box A424, file 3, Rallies and Protests, West Coast; American Civil Liberties Union Papers, Illinois Division, box 430, folder 1, "Emmett Till," University of Chicago Special Collections.

10 Wilkins to Henderson.

11 Ibid.

12 Ibid. Also see in the same file a later and less angry version of this letter, presumably the one that went out to Henderson, dated Oct. 26,1955. In the earlier letter Wilkins wrote, "We do not wish to misrepresent ourselves to the public by appealing for funds with the chance that many donors will believe they are giving money to help specifically in the Till case. We are considering launching an appeal with a clear explanation that the funds will be used to tackle the whole complex southern pattern of oppression so that in the future we will have no more Till cases"; Wilkins to Julius R. Primus, Sept. 21, 1955, LC, NAACP Papers, group 2, box A424, file 8, Correspondence. Thurgood Marshall offered similar advice—focus on changing federal law—to a rally at Holy Rosary Church in Brooklyn; James L. Hicks, "'Forget Emmett Till,' Marshall Tells 500; Bares Plan for Action," *Baltimore Afro-American*, Oct. 8, 1955, 15. Also see "Till Rally Demands Negro Vote Probe," *European Stars and Stripes*, Oct. 5, 1955, 7; "7 Point Program Planned to Curb Miss. Terror Reign," *St. Louis Argus*, Oct. 28, 1955, 3.

13 Roy Wilkins to NAACP Officers, Oct. 7, 1955, LC, NAACP Papers, group 2, box A424, file 3; "Quotes from the Negro Press," *Virginian*, Dec. 1955, 2, in MDAH, Ed King Papers, box 1.

14 Bradley's and Wilkins's letters are reprinted in a long article by James L. Hicks, "Why Emmett Till's Mother and NAACP Couldn't Agree," *Baltimore Afro-American*, Dec. 31, 1955, 2.

15 Ibid. The NAACP-sponsored Till rallies continued into 1956.

16 "Deeply Hurt by NAACP Rebuke," *Chicago Defender*, Nov. 26, 1955, 2; "Mrs. Bradley and the NAACP," *St. Louis Argus*, Nov. 18, 1955, 14.

17 "Mother of Till Bitter!" *Pittsburgh Courier*, Dec. 24, 1955, 3; "Huff Quits, Mrs. Bradley NAACP Cancels Tour," *Chicago Defender*, Nov. 12, 1955, 1; "Mamie's 'Little Problem,'" *Chicago Defender*, Jan. 21, 1956, n.p., in CHM, Barnett Papers, box 374, Till file.

18 Ryan, *Roy Wilkins: The Quiet Revolutionary,* 1–2, 54–55.
19 Ibid. Roy Wilkins's biographer expresses this well: "Wilkins lacked the oratorical skills that could lift an audience, in part because he appeared to lack the passion to paint a vision of freedom. Instead, he often appeared aloof, patrician, and urbane: more like a sophisticated chief executive of a multinational corporation than of an organization dedicated to righting a set of fundamental injustices." It was this very detachment, she argues, that allowed him "to serve as the conduit between civil rights activists demonstrating on the streets of Selma, for example, and the white power structure."
20 Feldstein, *Motherhood in Black and White,* 102–10; Till-Mobley, *Death of Innocence,* 202–9.
21 David Halberstam describes this dualism well in *The Children* (New York: Random House, 1998), 216–17, 449.

CHAPTER TWENTY-EIGHT

1 "Till's Uncle to Visit Friends in Chicago," *Memphis Commercial Appeal,* Sept. 26, 1955, n.p., DSU Till, Newspaper Scrapbook.
2 John Popham, "Kidnapping Case Revived in South," *New York Times,* Oct. 30, 1955, 87. Also see slightly different syndicated versions of this same article, "Till Case Rocked by Many Factors," *Chattanooga Times,* Oct. 30, 1955, n.p., SERS; and "Conflicts and Tensions Strong as Till Case Nears Second Jury," *Atlanta Journal and Constitution,* Oct. 30, 1955, 16A.
3 Popham, "Kidnapping Case Revived in South," 87.
4 Ibid.
5 "Grand Jury to Hear Till Case Kidnaping Charges," *Lebanon (PA) Daily News,* Nov. 7, 1955, 2; Sam Johnson, "Two Negroes to Give Testimony in Till Case," *Rocky Mountain (NC) Evening Telegram,* Nov. 8, 1955, 1; "Grand Jury Ready to Hear Wolf Whistle Kidnap Case," *Miami Herald,* Nov. 9, 1955, 27a.
6 "Grand Jury to Hear Till Kidnap Evidence," *Birmingham News,* Nov. 6, 1955, 1; Sam Johnson, "Till Kidnap Hearing Postponed," *New Orleans Times-Picayune,* Nov. 8, 1955, 18; W. F. Minor, "Jury Spends Three Hours Hearing Till Witnesses," *New Orleans Times-Picayune,* Nov. 9, 1955, 26.
7 Sam Johnson, "Jury to Decide on Kidnap Count," *New Orleans Times-Picayune,* Nov. 6, 1955, 28; "Grand Jury to Hear Till Charges," 2; "Grand Jury to Hear Till Kidnap Evidence," 1; "World Eyes Mississippi Grand Jury," *Chicago Defender,* Nov. 12, 1955, 1.
8 Sam Johnson, "Grand Jury Empaneled Today, Expect Action in Kidnapping," *Greenwood Commonwealth,* Nov. 7, 1955, 1; "Mississippi Grand Jurors Hear Till Case Witnesses," *Raleigh News and Observer,* Nov. 9, 1955, 1; Sam Johnson, "Till Kidnap Hearing Postponed," *New Orleans Times-Picayune,* Nov. 8, 1955, 18; "Grand Jury Quizzes Till Case Witnesses," unidentified newspaper, n.p., n.d., DSU Till, Newspaper Scrapbook; Minor, "Jury Spends Three Hours," 26.

9 Sam Johnson, "Bryant and Milam Not Indicted for Kidnapping Emmett Louis Till," *Greenwood Commonwealth*, Nov. 9, 1955, 1; "End of Kidnapping Case Where Leflore Concerned," *Greenwood Commonwealth*, Nov. 10, 1955, 1; "Brother Pair is Not Billed in Till Kidnap," *Atlanta Constitution*, Nov. 10, 1955, 1; "2 Free in Till Kidnapping; Case Declared Closed," *Washington Evening Star*, Nov. 10, 1955, 38A; "Till Grand Jury Refuses to Act," *New York Times*, Nov. 10, 1955, n.p., SERS; "No Indictment Returned in 'Wolf Whistle' Case," *Logansport (IN) Tribune*, Nov. 10, 1955, 7; "The Final Verdict," *Baltimore Afro-American*, Jan. 28, 1956, 3.

10 *Greenwood Morning Star* quoted in "Till Case Justice Brings on Storm," *Miami Herald*, Nov. 11, 1955, 5b; "Critics of the South Are Hurting the Negro Race," *Jackson Daily News*, Dec. 14, 1955, in CHM, Barnett Papers, box 374, Till file.

11 "The Real Loser," *Mississippi State Times*, Nov. 11, 1955, 4A; "—and Found Wanting," *Memphis Commercial Appeal*, Nov. 11, 1955, n.p., MDAH, King Papers, box 1, file 13; "Till Case Black Eye for Entire South," *Florence (SC) Morning News*, Nov. 11, 1955, 4; "Kidnaping Goes Unpunished," from the *Milwaukee Journal*, repr. in *Wisconsin Rapids Daily Tribune*, Nov. 16, 1955, 6; "Till Case Reaction," *Baltimore Afro-American*, Nov. 17, 1955, 5; "Congress Urged to Investigate Mississippi," *Houston Informer*, Nov. 12, 1955, 1; "The Final Verdict," 3. Also see Hodding Carter quoted in "Sheriff Claims Negroes Didn't Want Indictment," *Raleigh News and Observer*, Nov. 11, 1955, 1; "U.S. Investigation of Till Murder Asked," *Galveston (TX) Daily News*, Nov. 11, 1955, 13; "Are All Men Created Equal in Mississippi?" *Oelwein (IA) Daily Register*, Nov. 11, 1955, 2.

12 Carter, "Sheriff Claims Negroes Didn't Want Indictment," 1.

13 No record was kept of the proceedings, and since no reporters were in the jury room, we don't know what the jurors discussed or how they made their decision. Nonetheless, the editor of one of the Greenwood papers made it quite explicit to a fellow editor from Oklahoma that by November, a white grand jury was in no mood for a new trial: "The Mississippi Case," *Ada (OK) Evening News*, Nov. 11, 1955, 4. Also see "The Final Verdict," 3.

14 "Mississippi Grand Jury Fails to Indict in Till Outrage," *Lowell (MA) Sun*, Nov. 10, 1955, 32; Till-Mobley, *Death of Innocence*, 197–98.

15 "NAACP Rally Urges Anti-Lynching Law," *Greenwood Commonwealth*, Nov. 14, 1955, 1—but note that the *Commonwealth* headline got the story wrong; the rally was sponsored by the United Auto Workers, not the NAACP.

CHAPTER TWENTY-NINE

1 Ethel Payne, "Mrs. Bradley Bares Dawson Aid: Says Ike Ignored Pleas for Help," *Chicago Defender*, Oct. 22, 1956, 3. Ethel Payne's story appeared a year after Emmett's murder, but the story was important enough that cabinet secretary Maxwell Rabb wrote a memo to James Hagerty, Eisenhower's press secretary, stating that a courteous reply

to Mamie Till Bradley was inadvisable because—and this was confidential—"the FBI had definite knowledge that Mrs. Bradley permitted herself to be the instrument of the Communist party [*sic*], which seized upon the case as a cause celebre and upon her as the means of making the race question a burning issue. Mrs. Bradley was taken around the United States by Communists as a prize exhibit and they pulled all the stops in their exploitation." Rabb, who handled minority affairs for the administration, added that Bradley's ex-husband was executed by the army for rape, that she used her son's death to make a living, and that she was a "phoney." Max Rabb to Jim Hagerty, Oct. 23, 1956, Eisenhower Presidential Library (hereafter EPL), Office of Special Assistant for National Security Affairs, FBI Series, box 3, Till file.

2 F. L. Price to Mr. Rosen, Aug. 29 and Sept. 2, 1955, EPL, Office of the Special Assistant for National Security Affairs, 1952–1961, FBI Series, box 3, Office Memoranda file; "Ike Asked to Act in Negro Lad's Death," *New York World Telegram and Sun*, Sept. 2, 5; J. Edgar Hoover to Dillon Anderson, "Emmett Till, Personal and Confidential," Sept. 6, 1955, and Sept. 13, 1955, EPL, Office of the Special Assistant for National Security Affairs: Records, 1952–1961, FBI series, box 3, Till file.

3 Memo from National Administrative Committee (CP USA) to All Districts, "Emmett Louis Till Lynching," EPL, Office of the Special Assistant for National Security Affairs, FBI series, box 3, Till file. See also Hoover's memos to Attorney General Brownell, both dated Oct. 17, 1955, "Communist Party, USA, Negro Question," NARA, RG60, DOJ, section 30, container 956, folder 144-10-116.

4 Edward E. Strong, "The Till Case and the Negro Liberation Movement," *Political Affairs*, Dec. 1955, 35–51.

5 The literature on Communism and anti-Communism is enormous, but see Ellen Schrecker, *Many Are the Crimes: McCarthyism in America* (Princeton, NJ: Princeton University Press, 1999); Martha Biondi, *To Stand and Fight: The Struggle for Civil Rights in Postwar New York City* (Cambridge, MA: Harvard University Press, 2009); Sugrue, *Sweet Land of Liberty*, 102–11.

6 Howard University's Spingarn Research Center holds half a dozen mimeographed CP USA items in the Edward E. Strong Papers, "Till, Emmett Case," 167.7, file 13. Also see "CP Calls for New Policy by Govt. on Negro Rights," *Daily Worker*, Oct. 5, 1955, 4.

7 FBI, "Current Intelligence Summary," Sept.–Jan., 1955/56, EPL, White House Office of the Special Assistant for National Affairs, Records, 1952–1961, box 6.

8 J. Edgar Hoover, FBI, "Racial Tension and Civil Rights," Mar. 1, 1956, EPL, Office of the Special Assistant for National Security, box 3.

9 An FBI report "The Communist Party and the Negro, 1953–1956" emphasized how the Party's ambitions to organize the black proletariat and gain support by advocating for civil rights had largely failed—not only had the party declined in numbers, but African American participation fell even further. EPL, Office of the Special Assistant for National Security, FBI Series, box 3. Almost every week

from September 1955 to January 1956, the FBI's two page "Current Intelligence Summary" devoted a paragraph to Till and the Communists; EPL, Office of Special Assistant for National Security Affairs, box 6. Little escaped Hoover's watchful eye. On October 19, 1955, he wrote a memo to Attorney General Brownell warning that Cleveland's Labor Youth League staged a play about Emmett Till, and nearly one hundred people attended it—NARA RG 60, DOJ, section 30, container 956, folder 144-40-116.

10 There are several obituaries tracing Perry's life in the Pettis Perry Papers, NYPL, Schomburg Center for Research in Black Culture, MG 354, box 1, Correspondence from Prison, Jan.–Dec., 1955: See "Pettis Perry, 68, A U.S. Communist," *New York Times*, July 28, 1965, n.p.; "Pettis Perry, Communist Leader, Dies," *People's World*, July 31, 1965, n.p.; "Pettis Perry, CP Leader, Dies in Moscow at 68," no source, n.d., n.p. The literature on J. Edgar Hoover and the FBI is enormous, but see Tim Weiner, *Enemies: A History of the FBI* (New York: Random House, 2012), 131–238.

11 Pettis Perry to Rose Perry, Sept. 22, Oct. 9, Oct. 12, Oct. 27, Oct. 30, Nov. 9, Nov. 20, 1955, all in NYPL, Schomburg Center, Perry Collection, box 1, Prison correspondence file. For a left analysis tying violence like the Till murder to the South's antilabor campaigns, see Leonard Myers, "The Death of Emmett Till," *Party Voice*, vol. 9, 1955, 3–5.

12 Pettis Perry to Rose Perry, Correspondence from Prison, Nov. 9, 20, in Perry Papers.

13 W. Beverly Carter to E. Frederick Morrow, Sept. 29, 1955, EPL, Office of Special Assistant for National Security Affairs, FBI Series, box 3.

14 E. Frederick Morrow, "Memorandum for the Record," Nov. 22, 1955, in EPL, Files of Administrative Officer—Special Projects (Morrow), Civil Rights Clippings and Data (3), box 10, "Official Memoranda" file. Morrow sent a copy of his memorandum to Roy Wilkins, who agreed that "an ugly racial conflict" impended, and he asked why was the administration "for free elections everywhere in the world except in the southern states of America?" Roy Wilkins to E. Frederic Morrow, Dec. 2, 1955, in Special Projects (Morrow), box 10, Official Memoranda.

15 E. Frederick Morrow, memo to Mr. Maxwell Rabb, Nov. 29, 1955, in EPL, Civil Rights Clippings and Data (3), box 10.

16 Ibid.

17 E. Frederick Morrow to Governor Adams, Dec. 16, 1955, EPL, Special Projects (Morrow) box 10, Official Memoranda file.

18 "Department of Justice Decides That Murder of Boy Is Not Federal Case," *De Moines Bystander*, Sept. 15, 1955, 6; "United States Department of Justice Official Tells NAACP Group Federal Govt. Has No Jurisdiction in Till Kidnap Murder Case," *Jackson Advocate*, Sept. 15, 1955, 1; Roy Wilkins to Dwight D. Eisenhower, Sept. 16, 1955, in EPL, Maxwell Rabb Papers, box 52, NAACP file 2; EPL, White House Central Files, Alphabetical Files, box 3113, "Till, Emmett Louis."

19 "Group Asks U.S. to Act in Till Case," *Washington Post*, Oct. 25, 1955, 10; "No Intervention Planned in Case," *New Orleans Times-Picayune*, Oct.

26, 1955, 45; "Hennings' Subcommittee May Hear Mrs. Bradley," *St. Louis Argus*, Oct. 28, 1955, 1; "Mississippi Civil Rights Investigation," *Hattiesburg American*, Oct. 29, 1955, 1; "On Internal Security'" *St. Louis Argus*, Oct. 28, 1955, 14, reprinted from the Baltimore Afro-American; NARA, RG60, DOJ, Class 144, Civil Rights, 1936–1997, container 956, folder 144-40-116.

20 Herbert Brownell to William G Stratton, Nov. 23, 1955, NARA RG 60, DOJ, section 30, container 956, folder 144-40-116; "NAACP Asks Clarification of FBI Policy in Kidnap Cases," *Houston Informer*, Nov. 12, 1955, 1; "Brownell Will 'Consider' Till Case; Protests Up," *St. Louis Argus*, Nov. 18, 1955, 1; "That's News," *Petersburg (VA) Progress-Index*, Nov. 22, 1955, 4; "Fear U.S. Move in Mississippi Shooting Case," *Chicago Tribune*, Nov. 29, 1955, 1; "Deputy Attorney General Gives Till Case Views," *Biloxi Daily Herald*, Nov. 21, 1955, 1; "Shooting of Negro Leader Provokes Uproar in South," *Nevada State Journal*, Nov. 29, 1955, 1; "Turn Down Request for Till Probe," *Indiana Evening Gazette*, Dec. 7, 1955, 2; "Govt. Unable to Act in Till Slay Case," *European Stars and Stripes*, Dec. 8, 1955, 6; "Emmett Till Case Termed Black Mark," *Albuquerque Tribune*, Jan. 5, 1956, 1; "Department Finds No Basis to Intervene," *Aiken (SC) Standard-Review*, Feb. 10, 1956, 1; "Brownell Says He Will 'Consider' Till Probe," *Kansas City Call*, Nov. 25, 1955, 1; "Brownell Rejects Till Case Pleas," *Chicago Defender*, Dec. 17, 1955, 3.

21 "Says Probe FBI Indifference to Miss. Murders," *Atlanta Daily World*, Sept. 27, 1955, 1.

22 John Edgar Hoover to Dr. T. R. M. Howard, no date, LC, NAACP records, group III, box A230, file 1, "Mississippi Pressures, Howard, T. R. M. 1956"; "Dr. Howard Accused by FBI Head," DSU Till, Newspaper Scrapbook, no source, n.p., n.d. Hoover first tested out his response in a letter to Thurgood Marshall, dated Sept. 30, 1955, in which he complained that Howard had maligned the bureau; he also rehearsed his argument that the FBI made war on the Klan and on lynching. Then in a letter dated Dec. 13, Hoover warned Attorney General Brownell that Dr. Howard had insulted the entire Justice Department. Both in NARA, RG 30, DOJ, section 30, container 956, folder 114-40-116.

23 Dr. T. R. M. Howard to Mr. J. Edgar Hoover, Jan. 19, 1956, LC, NAACP records, group III, box A230, file 1, "Mississippi Pressures, Howard, T.R.M.," 1956.

24 "FBI Chief 'Floored for Count' by Dr. T.R.M. Howard," *Los Angeles Tribune*, Jan. 27, 1956, 6; "J. Edgar Hoover Disappoints Us," *Kansas City Call*, Jan. 27, 1956, 18; "The FBI and Mississippi," *Philadelphia Tribune*, Jan. 24, 1956, 4; "Mr. Hoover Is Wrong," *California Eagle*, Jan. 26, 1956,4.

25 "Message Drafted on Discrimination," *San Antonio Express*, Jan. 13, 1956, 3; Drew Pearson, "Brownell's 'Hot Potato,'" *Portsmouth (NH) Herald*, Feb. 6, 1956, 4; Thomas L. Stokes, "President's Program on Civil Rights Issue Doesn't Go Very Far," *Berkshire Eagle* (Pittsfield, MA), Apr. 12, 1956, 17; Edmond Lebreton, "House Group Meets

Again to Discuss Civil Rights Legislation," *Blytheville (AR) Courier-News*, June 26, 1956, 12; Interview with Herbert Brownell, #4 of 5, by Ed Edwin, Jan. 31, 1968, Columbia University Oral History Project, deposited at EPL. For an example of how Southern politicians approached the new legislation, see the testimony of Congressman Jamie Whitten (cousin of Attorney John Whitten), who argued that Negroes were not being mistreated in the South, that all right-thinking people deplored what happened to Emmett Till, that the sheriff of Tallahatchie County was a fine citizen who did good work on the case, and that no one kept blacks from voting in Mississippi; UM DASC, Race Relations Collection, Box 2, Folder 10, "Congressional Testimony by Jamie Whitten."

26 Morrow, *Black Man in the White House*, 163–65, 179.
27 Ibid., 184.
28 Earl Warren, *The Memoirs of Earl Warren* (New York: Doubleday, 1977), 290–93.
29 Political Scientist Heather Pool's article "Mourning Emmett Till," in *Law Culture and the Humanities* 11, no. 3 (2015), argues that the public ritual of mourning created the conditions for the passage of the 1957 Civil Rights Act. Certainly, the Till murder and the lobbying accompanying it mattered, but Pool's article is entirely too triumphant. To the extent that the "politics of mourning" was decisive during the civil rights struggles, many more years and corpses would pile up before substantial change took place. They are still piling up today.

CHAPTER THIRTY

1 An insightful piece on Huie appeared in the *Atlanta Journal and Constitution* magazine section, May 4, 1975, 9–10, 49–50.
2 Ibid. Also see "The Press," *Time*, Sept. 13, 1968, 47; Edward Linn, "The Last of the Great Reporters," *SAGA*, 15(1), Oct. 1957, 16–19; Roberts and Klibanoff, *Race Beat*, 101–8. Also see online *Encyclopedia of Alabama*, "William Bradford Huie," http://www. encyclopediaofalabama.org/article/h-1547; "Eyes on the Prize," interview with William Bradford Huie, http://digital.wustl.edu/cgi/t/text/text-idx?c=eop;cc=eop;rgn=main;view=text;idno= hui0015.1034.050.
3 William Huie to Roy Wilkins, Oct. 12, 1955, OSU, Huie papers, box 39, file 353c.
4 Ibid.
5 Ibid.
6 Ibid.
7 Ibid.
8 Ibid.
9 Davis W. Houck and Matthew A. Grindy, *Emmett Till and the Mississippi Press*, 2008), 149–52; Roberts and Klibanoff, *Race Beat*, 101–6; Anderson, *Emmett Till*, 220–51.

10 William Huie to Mr. Walters, Oct. 18, 1955; William Huie to Dan
   Mich, Oct. 17, 1955, both in OSU, Huie Papers, box 39, file 353c.
   Daniel D. Mich was editorial director for *Look*.

11 William Huie to Mr. Walters, Oct. 18, 1955; William Huie to Dan
   Mich, Oct. 17, 1955; William Huie to Dan Mich, Oct. 21, 1955, all in
   OSU, Huie Papers, box 39, file 353c.

12 William Huie to Mr. Walters, Oct. 18, 1955; William Huie to Roy
   Wilkins, Oct. 12, 1955; William Huie to Dan Mich, Oct. 27, 1955, all
   in OSU, Huie Papers, box 39, file 353c.

13 William Huie to John Whitten, Oct. 30, 1956, OSU, Huie Papers, box
   39, file 353c.

14 William Huie to Mr. Walters, Oct. 18, 1955, William Huie to Dan
   Mich, Oct. 17, 1955, William Huie to Dan Mich, Oct. 21, 1955, all in
   OSU, Huie Papers, box 39, file 353c.

15 For example, see "Consent and Release," Oct. 28, 1955, Sumner
   Mississippi, signed by John W. Milam, OSU, Huie Papers, box 85, file
   353; William Huie to Dan Mich, Oct. 23, 1955, in OSU, Huie Papers,
   box 85, file 353c.

16 Ibid.

17 William Huie to Dan Mich, Oct. 17, 1955, William Huie to Dan Mich
   Oct. 23, 1955, both in OSU, Huie Papers, box 39, file 353c; United
   Artists contract, re: The Emmett Till Story, Feb. 9, 1956, in OSU, Huie
   Papers, box 85, file 353; publishing agreement with Simon &
   Schuster, in OSU, Huie Papers, box 85, file 353. While many have
   claimed that Huie's payment to Milam and Bryant was the first time a
   writer had practiced "checkbook journalism," it clearly was not. See
   Jeremy W. Peters, "Paying for News? It's Nothing New," *New York
   Times*, Aug. 6, 2011, SR4. Checkbook journalism remains ethically
   controversial; see, for example, Robert Boynton, "Checkbook
   Journalism Revisited," *Columbia Journalism Review*, Jan./Feb. 2008,
   on-line at: https://archives.cjr.org/essay/checkbook_journalism_
   revisited htt.

18 William Bradford Huie, "The Shocking Story of Approved Killing in
   Mississippi," *Look*, Jan. 24, 1956, 46.

19 Ibid.

20 Ibid., 49.

21 Ibid., Huie, "Approved Killing," 46–47. Years later, Carolyn
   Bryant told the FBI that they owned a television but not a
   telephone.

22 Ibid., 46–47.

23 Ibid., 47.

24 Ibid., 47–48.

25 Wright, *Simeon's Story*, 133–36.

26 Huie, "Approved Killing," 49–50.

27 Ibid.

28 Huie, "Approved Killing," 50.

29 Ibid.

30 The ad took up nearly a quarter page in the *Oakland Tribune*, Jan. 11,
   1955, 9. Telegram, Larry Grossman to Roy Wilkins, Jan. 5, 1956;

Letter, Roy Wilkins to NAACP Branch Officers, Jan. 6, 1956; telegram, Roy Wilkins to J. P. Coleman, Attorney General of Mississippi, Jan. 9, 1956, all in LC, NAACP Papers, part 3, box A229, file 6, "Till, Emmett," 1956–57. For newspaper reactions to "Approved Killing," see "Federal Government Must Act Now," *Kansas City Call,* Jan. 20, 1956, 18; "Diggs Puts *Look* Yarn on Till Case into Congressional Record," *Delta Democrat-Times,* Jan. 13, 1956, 1; "Article Libels Mississippi, Carolina Lawmakers Say," *Birmingham Post and Herald,* Jan. 18, 1956, 4; "*Look*'s Article on Till Case Reviewed," *Kannapolis (NC) Daily Independent,* Jan. 13, 1956, 1. Sam Yorty, the future mayor of Los Angeles, requested that the federal government intervene; Yorty to AG Herbert Brownell, Jan. 15, 1956, and Brownell to Yorty, Jan. 24, 1956, in NARA, RG 60, DOJ, section 30, container 956, folder 144-40-116. Yorty, incidentally, wrote on House of Representatives stationary, though he was no longer a member of Congress.

31 The *Little Rock (AK) State Press,* for example, simply reported "factually" on the *Look* story, but it led with Till's taunting of Milam and Bryant, the most incendiary yet dubious part of the story: "Emmett Till's Bravado Led to Killing, It Is Disclosed in 'Look,'" Jan. 13, 1956, 1; "Man Acquitted in Till Slaying Termed Guilty," *Hayward (CA) Daily Review,* Jan. 13, 1956, 12; "Milam Shot Everett Till Says Magazine Writer," *Washington Post and Times-Herald,* Jan. 14, 1956, 3; "Look Says Till's Boastful Defiance Spelled His Death," *Jackson State Times,* Jan. 9, 1956, 1; "Baseless Reporting," *Jackson State Times,* Jan. 11, 1956, 4a; "New Angle to Till Case," *Greenwood Morning Star,* Jan. 11, 1956, 4. In an interesting sidelight, Huie's old newspaper, the *Birmingham Post-Herald* published a column by staff writer John Temple Graves calling the *Look* article "fantasy . . . the false imaginings of a sensationalist." Graves accused Huie of making the story up and inciting hatred against the South. The article was widely reprinted. Huie wrote letters to Graves and to the *Post-Herald*'s editor James Mills demanding a retraction. Huie threatened to sue (for a million dollars) Graves, Scripps-Howard, and any source that reprinted the Graves article. When Huie revealed his signed releases from Milam and Bryant, Graves signed a retraction. William Huie to James Mills, Jan. 21, 1956; William Huie to John Temple Graves, Jan. 21, 1955; William Huie to Jean Franklin, Feb. 1 and Feb. 4, 1955; Graves retraction, dated Feb 23; all in OSU, Huie Papers, box 39, file 353D. Also see Huie's version of the story in William Bradford Huie, *Wolf Whistle and Other Stories* (New York: New American Library, 1959), 44.

32 "Mississippi Urged by NAACP to Reopen Till Case," *Kansas City Call,* Jan. 26, 1956, 4; "Coleman Denies He Made Quotes about Guilt of Pair," *Delta Democrat-Times,* Jan. 13, 1956, 1; "No New Trial for Milam, Bryant," *Chicago Defender,* Jan. 28, 1956, 1; "Civil Liberties Group Seeks Review Till Case," *Jackson Advocate,* Jan. 21, 1956, 1; "Article on Till Case Goes into Congressional Record Touching Off Disputes," *Jackson Daily News,* Jan. 13, 1956, n.p., in SERS; "Magazine Story

Claims New Till Killing Angle," *Lowell (MA) Sun*, Jan. 13, 1956, 20; "Coleman Quoted on Till Killing," *Charleston (WV) Daily Mail*, Jan. 13, 1956, 3.

33 Roy Wilkins telegram to J. P Coleman, January 9, 1956, in NAACP Papers; "Judge Says He Will Not Reopen Till Kidnap Case, press release, Jan. 16, 1956, Associated Negro Press, CHM, Barnett Papers, box 374, Till file; William Bradford Huie, "The Shocking Story of Approved Killing," *Reader's Digest*, April 1956, 57–62.

34 "Milam Denies *Look* Article Quotes; May Sue Magazine," *Delta Democrat-Times*, Jan. 10, 1956, 1; "Denies Magazine's Report That He Admitted Till Slaying," *Racine (WI) Journal-Times*, Jan. 13, 1956, 5; "Acquitted Man May Sue *Look*," *Elyria (OH) Chronicle-Telegram*, Mar. 31, 1956, 27; "Milam, Bryant Deny 'Look' Story, 'Terrible Lies' Says Mrs. Bradley," *New Orleans Weekly*, Jan. 21, 1956, 3.

35 Jay Milner, "Milam Says He's 'Not Sure' If He Has Grounds for Libel Suit," *Delta Democrat-Times*, Jan. 15, 1956, 1; "Bryant and Milam Deny *Look* Story," *Greenwood Commonwealth*, Jan. 13, 1956, 1; "Milam, Bryant Sign for Till Case Movie," *Baltimore Afro-American*, Jan. 28, 1956, 1.

36 "Milam and Bryant Deny 'Look' Story," 3; "Milam, Bryant Sign," 1; "Son No Braggart, Says Mrs. Bradley," *Chicago Defender*, Jan. 21, 1956, 1; "Mother of Till Blasts Article," *Norfolk (VA) Journal and Guide*, Jan. 27, 1956, 13. Roy Wilkins pointed out in an open letter to the editors of *Look* that Huie merely repeated Carolyn Bryant's testimony from the trial, the very testimony that Judge Swango had refused to let the jury hear. Wilkins also noted that the murderers had no direct knowledge of Emmett's behavior at the grocery store.

37 "Mother of Till Blasts Article," 13; Till-Mobley, *Death of Innocence*, 212–16.

38 Manuscript of "Wolf Whistle," a screenplay by William Bradford Huie, "To be produced by Louis De Rochemont for United Artists," copyright 1960, in OSU, Huie Papers, box 38, file 353b. Mamie Till Bradley also signed on for the movie around the first of the year, but she told reporters she had the right to reject the script, which she would do if it was like the *Look* magazine article; "Milam, Bryant Sign" 1.

39 William Huie to Dan Mich, Oct. 25, 1955, OSU, Huie Papers, box 39, file 353c; Roi Ottley, "Race Neurosis," manuscript in CHM, Bennett Papers, repr. in the *Chicago Defender*, Saturday, Jan. 28, 1956.

40 Huie, "Approved Killing," 46; "Mrs. Roy Bryant, 9-2-55," manuscript notes in OSU, Huie Papers, box 85, file 346; "'I Told the Truth,' Huie Tells Courier," *Pittsburgh Courier*, Jan. 21, 1956, 3.

41 Huie, "Approved Killing," 50; "Milam, Bryant Deny *Look* Story," 3.

42 "Barrage of Segregation Bills Await Action of Legislature," *Greenwood Commonwealth*, Jan. 13, 1956, 1; Huie, "Approved Killing," 50.

43 Huie, "Approved Killing," 50. On the issue of white resentment during this era, see Jason Sokol, *There Goes My Everything: White Southerners in the Age of Civil Rights, 1945–1975* (New York: Vintage Books, 2007), esp. 19–113.

44 While I think Dave Tell makes too much of the fact that "Approved Killing" is not truly a confession, two of his articles on the Till case are filled with insight: "The 'Shocking Story' of Emmett Till and the Politics of Public Confession," *Quarterly Journal of Speech* 94, no. 2 (May 2008): 156–78, and "Confession and Race: Civil Rights, Segregation, and the Murder of Emmett Till," chap. 3 of David Tell, *Confessional Crisis and Cultural Politics in Twentieth-Century America*, (State College: Pennsylvania State University Press, 2012), 66–90.

CHAPTER THIRTY-ONE

1 History and memory is an enormous topic, and an elusive one at that. Three books that I have found particularly useful because they emphasize the political nature of memory are David Blight, *Race and Reunion: The Civil War in American Memory* (Cambridge, MA: Harvard University Press, 2002); and Peter Novick, *The Holocaust in American Life* (Boston: Mariner Books, 2000); and Ari Kelman, *A Misplaced Massacre: Struggling Over the Memory of Sand Creek* (Cambridge, MA: Harvard University Press, 2013). On the Civil Rights Movement, try Renee C. Romano and Leigh Raiford, eds., *The Civil Rights Movement in American Memory* (Athens: University of Georgia Press, 2006), W. Fitzhugh Brundage, *The Southern Past: A Clash of Race and Memory* (Cambridge, MA: Belknap Press of Harvard University Press, 2005), 227–315; and Scott A. Sandage, "A Marble House Divided: The Lincoln Memorial, the Civil Rights Movement, and the Politics of Memory, 1939–1963," *Journal of American History* 80, no. 1 (June, 1993), 135–67. For a sociological perspective, see Larry J. Griffin and Kenneth A. Bollen, "What Do These Memories Do? Civil Rights Remembrance and Racial Attitudes," *American Sociological Review* 74, no. 4 (August 2009): 594–614.
2 These databases change over time, and I did this informal search early in 2017. The numbers come from entering the name Emmett Till into Newspaperarchive.com and into Google Ngram Viewer. The former database is often used by genealogists, and contains hundreds of newspapers, with new ones added every year. The latter tracks book publications. Proquest reveals a similar trend based on the *New York Times, Los Angeles Times*, and *Chicago Tribune*.
3 Newsletter of the South Deering Improvement Association, Sept. 10, 1955, 2 (my thanks to Christopher Ramsey for calling my attention to this source.)
4 Two of the best works on segregation on Chicago's South and West Sides are Beryl Satter, *Family Properties;* and Arnold Hirsch, *Making the Second Ghetto*.
5 *Westport (CT) Town-Crier*, Sept. 29, 1955, retyped as a press release, Oct. 6, 1955, NARA, RG 306, United States Information Agency, box 41, Till file.
6 "Whites Demand Full Justice," *Holland (MI) Evening Sentinel*, Dec. 8, 1955, 10; "Defendant in Till Case in Spotlight Again," *Biloxi (MS) Daily Herald*, Dec. 9, 1955, 1; "White Man Denied Bond in Slaying of

Negro," *Joplin (MO) Globe*, Dec. 29, 1955, 15; "Till Case Judge Denies Bond to Accused Slayer," *Baltimore Afro-American*, Jan. 21, 1956, 2; "Till Case Court Again to Try White Man in Slaying of Negro," *Charleston (WV) Gazette*, Mar. 9, 1956, 13; Warner Ragsdale, "Selecting Jury in Slaying of Glendora Negro," *Hattiesburg (MS) American*, Mar. 12, 1956, 1; "Sumner Trial of White Man Nearing Jury," *Laurel (MS) Leader Call*, Mar. 13, 1956, 1; "Jury Acquits Negro's Slayer in Mississippi," *Mt. Vernon (IL) Register News*, Mar. 14, 1956, 1.

7 "Sumner Revisited," *Delta Democrat-Times*, Mar. 16, 1956, 3.

8 David Halberstam, "Tallahatchie County Acquits a Peckerwood," *Reporter*, Apr. 19, 1956, 26–30.

9 William Faulkner, "Faulkner Sees Grim Lesson in Mississippi Slaying Case," *Galveston Daily News*, Sept. 10, 1955, 2; "Faulkner Says World Freedom at Stake in US Segregation Issue," *Delta Democrat-Times*, Nov. 11, 1955, 1, repr. in *Christian Century*, Nov. 30,1955, 1395–96; Faulkner in the *Memphis Commercial Appeal*, retyped as a "Press Release, June 30, 1955" in Ed King Papers, Mississippi Department of Archives and History, box 1; William Faulkner, "A Letter to the North," *Life*, Mar. 9, 1956, 51–52.

10 William Faulkner, "On Fear: The South in Labor," *Harper's Magazine*, 29–34, quote on 32. For a rejoinder arguing that privilege surrenders nothing voluntarily, that going slow is a way of avoiding change, see Albert E. Barnett, "A Southerner Answers," *Christian Century*, May 30, 1956, 1–4.

11 Interview with William Faulkner, *The Tex and Jinx McCreary Show*, NBC radio, Feb. 24, 1956, in Library of Congress, NAACP collection, Sound Recordings Division, Preservation tape #RWC9541.

12 Tony Albaralla, "Noon on Doomsday," in *Beyond the Zone*, at https://www.rodserling.com/beyond_the_zone/slow_fade_to_black.htm http://www.rodserling.com/beyond_the_zone/noon_on_doomsday.html.

13 Jack Gould, "TV: 'Noon on Doomsday'" *New York Times*, Apr. 26, 1956, 67. A week before "Noon on Doomsday" aired, Margaret Buhrman's syndicated column described it as "based on the Emmett Till Murder Case in Mississippi;" Buhrman, "TV-Radio Highlights," *Kokomo (IN) Tribune*, Apr. 18, 1956, 15. Richard Davidson, poet, playwright, and Communist Party member wrote a play titled *Mississippi* based on the Till murder. It was given a dramatic reading in a Lower East Side theater. A reviewer for the United Press called it "uninspired," "more propaganda than art," and "a heavy and at times inept drama." Frederick M. Winship, "Few See 'Heavy' Play Based on Till Case," *Jackson (MS) State Times*, Jan. 21, 1956, 1.

14 Jack Gould, "TV: Prejudice Dissected," *New York Times*, June 20, 1958, 47; Jon Miller, "Fifty Years Later, Rod Serling's Play Is Performed," NPR, *Weekend Edition Sunday*, Mar. 30, 2008; William Kates, "Uncensored: 'Twilight Zone' Creator's Script on Emmett Till Case," *Washington Post*, Mar. 27, 2008, 11. Incidentally, Serling's reputation soared at the end of the decade with the TV series *The Twilight Zone*, and with teleplays like *Requiem for a Heavyweight*.

15 William Bradford Huie to John Whitten, Oct. 30, 1956, OSU, Huie Papers, box 39, file 353d.

16 William Bradford Huie, "What's Happened to the Emmett Till Killers?" *Look*, Jan. 22, 1957, 63–64. As his memo of Oct. 30 indicated, Huie stayed in close touch with Attorney John Whitten, eliciting photos and details for this new *Look* article and asking Whitten to act as a go-between with J. W. Milam.

17 Huie, "What's Happened to the Emmett Till Killers," 65.

18 Ibid., 66–67.

19 Ibid.

20 Again, Huie claims that Emmett Till's friends in Chicago told him of his sexual exploits, but Till's cousins denied ever talking to him; Simeon Wright, *Simeon's Story*, 133–35. By the time *Wolf Whistle*, the book version of Huie's story appeared, Huie described Emmett Till as heavily muscled and easily mistaken for an eighteen-year-old, a description that would have perplexed Till's friends and family; William Bradford Huie, *Wolf Whistle: And Other Stories* (New York: Signet, 1959), 38–43. For the advertisement for the *Look* article, see *Washington Post and Times Herald*, Jan. 9, 1957, 8; for African American press coverage of the *Look* story, see, for examples, "Accused in Emmett Till Case Bare Death Threats," *Baltimore Afro-American*, Jan. 1, 1957, 10; and "Acquitted Till Killers Tell of Death Threats," *Pittsburg Courier*, Jan. 12, 1957, 6. For the UP version of the story, see "Emmett Till Defendant Threatened," *Chicago Daily News*, Jan. 8, 1957, 5. At least one other movie was proposed that never got made; see Thomas M. Pryor, "Integration Issue to Be Pinpointed in Movie, 'The Till Murder Case,'" *New York Times*, June 14, 1956, n.p., in SERS.

21 Al Kuettner, "After Two Years, Few Talk about Till Case," *Jackson State Times*, Aug. 28, 1957, n.p., in Mississippi State Sovereignty Commission Papers, filed Nov. 17, 1958; "In the Circuit Court of Cook County, Illinois, Mamie Bradley, Plaintiff, vs. Cowles Magazines incorporated, filed by Attorney Joseph M. Tobias, January 1958," in OSU, Huie Papers, box 85, file 347; "Mom of Slain Negro Boy Sues Look," *Chicago Daily News*, Jan. 22, 1958, n.p., in SERS; "Emmett Till's Mother Loses Libel Lawsuit," *Jackson Daily News*, June 24, 1959, n.p., State Sovereignty Commission Papers.

22 William Minor, who covered the Till trial for the *New Orleans Times-Picayune*, wrote forty years later, "If you have seen the 1960s movie *To Kill a Mockingbird* based on the 1960 Pulitzer Prize–winning novel by Harper Lee set in a rural Alabama courtroom, you can vividly imagine the Till Trial setting;" Minor, "After 40 Years, Trial in Emmett Till's Murder Remains Vivid, Significant," *Jackson Clarion-Ledger*, Sept. 28, 1995, 9A; Jay Milner, *Incident at Ashton* (Fort Worth: TCU Press, 1961; Bob Dylan, "The Death of Emmett Till" (1962), repr. in Metress, *Lynching of Emmett Till*, 318–19.

23 Susan Brownmiller, *Against Our Will: Men, Women and Rape* (New York: Random House, 1975).

24 Ibid., 245–47.

25 Ibid., 247.

26 Ibid., 247–55.

27 Angela Y. Davis, *Women Race and Class* (New York: Random House, 1981), 178–83, 196–201; see also Alison Edwards, *Rape, Racism, and the White Women's Movement* (Chicago: Sojourner Truth Organization, 1975; 1979) online repr. at http://www.sojournertruth.net/rrwwm.pdf, 15–17.

CHAPTER THIRTY-TWO

1 Louis Burnham, *Behind the Lynching of Emmett Louis Till* (New York: Freedom Associates, 1955); Ernest Withers, *Complete Photo Story of Till Murder Case* (Memphis: Wither's Photographers, 1955); "Emmett Till Kidnap-Murder Case Photos Now on Sale in Pamphlet Form," *Pittsburgh Courier*, Oct. 8, 1955, 4; James Hicks, "Inside Story," a series of four articles published on successive weeks in Oct. 1955 in the *Cleveland Call and Post*, the *Baltimore Afro-American*, and the *Atlanta Daily World*, repr. in Metress, *Lynching of Emmett Till*, 154–77. Langston Hughes, "Mississippi—1955," was first published in the *Chicago Defender*, repr. in Metress, *Lynching of Emmett Till*, 293–94. Metress reprints several other poems, many from the left-wing press, 289–349.

2 The full five-part *California Eagle* series is available on the excellent website, emmetttillmurder.com: http://www.emmetttillmurder.com/california-eagle-january-february-1956/; Olive Arnold Adams, *Time Bomb: Mississippi Exposed and the Full Story of Emmett Till* (Mound Bayou, MS: Mississippi Regional Council of Negro Leadership, 1956).

3 Ethel Payne, "Mamie Bradley's Untold Story," *Chicago Defender*, April–June, 1956, excerpted in Metress, *Lynching of Emmett Till*, 226–35; "A Little Child Shall Lead Them," *Baltimore Afro-American*, Sept. 8, 1956, 17. On T. R. M. Howard and the writing of both *Time Bomb* and the *California Eagle* series, see the excellent biography by David T. Beito and Linda Royster Beito, *Black Maverick*, 148–51.

4 Jacquelyn Dowd Hall, "The Long Civil Rights Movement," 1233–63.

5 Joyce Ladner in Charles M. Payne, *I've Got the Light of Freedom: The Organizing Tradition and the Mississippi Freedom Struggle* (Berkeley: University of California Press, 2007), 54–55; and in Fredrick C. Harris, "It Takes a Tragedy to Arouse Them: Collective Memory and Collective Action during the Civil Rights Movement," *Social Movement Studies* 5, no. 1 (May 2006): 36.

6 Harris, "It Takes a Tragedy to Arouse Them," 9–43; Maurice Berger, For All the World to See: Visual Culture and the Struggle for Civil Rights (New Haven, CT: Yale University Press, 2010), 108–9.

7 John Lewis and Michael D'Orso, *Walking with the Wind: A Memoir of the Movement* (New York: Simon & Schuster, 1998), 46–48.

8 Ibid.

9 Anne Moody, *Coming of Age in Mississippi* (New York: Doubleday, 1968),11. The historian John Dittmer found that many of the young

people he interviewed for his book *Local People: The Struggle for Civil Rights in Mississippi* identified personally with Emmett Till (Urbana: University of Illinois Press, 1995), 57–58.

10 Moody, *Coming of Age*, 121–26.

11 Ibid., 126–38.

12 Muhammad Ali, with Richard Durham, *The Greatest: My Own Story* (New York: Random House, 1975), 34–35; Gerald Early notes that *The Greatest* was ghostwritten and should be taken metaphorically; see Early, "Some Preposterous Propositions from the Heroic Life of Muhammad Ali: A Reading of *The Greatest: My Own Story*" in *Muhammad Ali, The People's Champ*, ed. Elliott Gorn (Urbana: University of Illinois Press, 1995), 70–87.

13 Thomas Hauser, *Muhammad Ali: His Life and Times* (New York: Simon & Schuster, 1991), 89; Mike Marqusee, *Redemption Song: Muhammad Ali and the Spirit of the Sixties* (London: Verso, 1999), 215.

14 Sellers, Evers, and Abdul-Jabbar are excerpted in Metress, *Lynching of Emmett Till*, 263–64, 247–50, 276–77; see also the website www. emmetttillmurder.com.

15 Clenora Hudson-Weems, *Emmett Till: The Sacrificial Lamb of the Civil Rights Movement* (Troy, MI: Bedford Publishers, 1994), 95–96.

16 Shelby Steele, "On Being Black and Middle Class," *Commentary*, Jan. 1, 1988, https://www.commentarymagazine.com/articles/on-being-black-and-middle-class/.

17 Ibid.; Stephen J. Whitfield, *A Death in the Delta: The Story of Emmett Till* (1991; repr., Baltimore: Johns Hopkins University Press), 104–5.

18 James Baldwin, *Blues for Mr. Charlie* (New York: Vintage, 1992, originally the Dial Press, 1964), 25.

19 Eldridge Cleaver, *Soul on Ice* (New York: Dell, 1968), 22–23.

20 Cleaver, *Soul on Ice*, 24–27.

21 Gwendolyn Brooks, "A Bronzeville Mother Loiters in Mississippi. Meanwhile, a Mississippi Mother Burns Bacon," *Blacks* (Chicago: Third World Press, 1991, repr. from *The Bean Eaters*, 1960), 333–36.

22 Ibid., 334–35.

23 Ibid., 337–39.

24 Ibid., 338–39.

25 Ibid.

26 As always, Devery Anderson does a fine job of digging out the sources and telling the story in *Emmett Till*, 217–19; also see Beito and Beito, *Black Maverick*, 138–39.

27 Rosa Parks with Jim Haskins, *Rosa Parks, My Story* (New York: Puffin Books, 1992), 116–17; Anderson, *Emmett Till*, 217–19; Beito and Beito, *Black Maverick*, 138–39.

CHAPTER THIRTY-THREE

1 The literature on the Civil Rights Movement is vast, but for a concise overview try Bruce J. Dierenfield, *The Civil Rights Movement* (New York: Routledge, 2008); Juan Williams, *Eyes on the Prize:*

America's Civil Rights Years, 1954–1965 (New York: Penguin Books, 2013); Harvard Sitkoff, *The Struggle for Black Equality* (New York: Hill and Wang, 2008); and Sugrue, *Sweet Land of Liberty*.

2 Wesley Morris, "Last Taboo," *New York Times Magazine*, Oct. 27, 2016, online edition, https://www.nytimes.com/interactive/2016/10/30/magazine/black-male-sexuality-last-taboo.html.

3 Jonathan Scott Holloway, *Jim Crow Wisdom: Memory and Identity in Black America Since 1940* (Chapel Hill: University of North Carolina Press, 2013),66.

4 As noted above, newspaper databases such as newspaperarchive.com and indexes to publications like the *Chicago Defender* reveal remarkably few anniversary stories.

5 Clenora Hudson-Weems, *Emmett Till: The Sacrificial Lamb of the Civil Rights Movement* (Troy, MI: Bedford Books, 1994), 4–5, 22–24, 84–95; Parker, The Civil Rights History Project, 27–29; Parker quoted in John Kass, "59 Years Later, Cousins of Emmett Till Recall Murder," *Chicago Tribune*, Aug. 29, 2014, 2. A quick check of the first histories of the Civil Rights Movement bear out Hudson-Weems's point. For example, David Garrow's *Bearing the Cross: Martin Luther King, Jr. and the Southern Christian Leadership Conference* (New York: William Morrow, 1986) begins with Montgomery but has nothing on Till; Sitkoff's *The Struggle for Black Equality* mentions Till on p. 49 but gives few details; and Simeon Booker's informal history, *Black Man's America* (New York: Prentice Hall, 1964) gives the Till story just two pages, even though Booker covered the case in Sumner, Mississippi.

6 Holloway, *Jim Crow Wisdom*, 174–76. Black history was also in the vanguard of academic studies inspired by "the new social history," which emphasized not elites but average people, workers, women, ethnic minorities.

7 Williams, *Eyes on the Prize*; Sitkoff, *Struggle for Black Equality*.

8 Samuels tells the story on his website. See www.richsamuels.com/nbcmm/till/till.html. Also see www.imbd.com/title/tt2295736/

9 See www.richsamuels.com/nbcmm/till/till.html.

10 See www.pbs.org/wgbh/ames/eyesontheprize/ Thirteen years later, Blackside released eight more episodes covering the period from 1965 to 1985.

11 www.pbs.org/wgbh/amex/eyesontheprize/about/pt/html

12 For an excellent essay on the complexities of media, public memory, and civil rights, see Edward P. Morgan, "The Good, the Bad, and the Forgotten: Media Culture and Public Memory of the Civil Rights Movement," in Romano and Raiford, *The Civil Rights Movement in American Memory*, 137–66. On the proliferation of civil rights history in the South, see Brundage, *The Southern Past: A Clash of Race and Memory*, 270–315.

13 Simeon Booker, "How Emmett Till's Lynching Launched the Civil Rights Drive," *Jet* , June 17, 1985, vol. 68, no. 14, 12.

14 Clotye Murdock Larsson, "Land of the Till Murder Revisited," *Ebony*, Mar. 1986, vol. 41, 53–58.

15 Joe Atkins, "Slain Chicago Youth was a 'Sacrificial Lamb'"; Eric Stringfellow, "Memories Sketch Varied Portraits of Emmett Till"; Atkins and Tom Brennan, "Bryant Wants the Past to 'Stay Dead'"; Brennan, "World Watched Drama Unfold in Rural County Courtroom"; Atkins, "Poor Economy, Past Haunt Delta Towns"; Billy Skelton, "Mississippi Has Come a Long Way Since Those Dispirited Days of 1955," all in *Jackson Clarion-Ledger*, Aug. 25, 1985, Section H, 1–3. The transformation was remarkable, given the picture Houck and Grindy paint in *Emmett Till and the Mississippi Press*.

16 Whitfield, *A Death in the Delta*; Ruth Feldstein, "'I Wanted the Whole World to See': Race, Gender and Constructions of Motherhood in the Death of Emmett Till," in Joanne Meyerowitz, *Not June Cleaver: Women and Gender in Postwar America, 1945–1960* (Philadelphia: Temple University Press, 1994), 263–301. For Mamie Till Bradley, see George E. Curry, "Killed for Whistling at a White Woman," *Emerge* magazine, July/Aug. 1995, 24–32; Dan Sewell, "40 Years After Brutal Killing, Emmett Till Still Not Forgotten," *Nashville Tennessean*, Sept. 27, 1995, 1; and Mamie Till-Mobley, *Death of Innocence*.

17 Louis Nordan, *Wolf Whistle* (Chapel Hill, NC: Algonquin Books, 1993); Nordan, "Growing Up White in the South: An Essay," in Metress, *Lynching of Emmett Till*, 270–75; Sam Staggs, "Lewis Nordan," *Publisher's Weekly*, Oct. 18, 1993, 50–51; Bebe Moore Campbell, *Your Blues Ain't Like Mine* (New York: Ballantine, 1993); Elizabeth Spencer, *Landscapes of the Heart: A Memoir* (Baton Rouge: LSU Press, 2003), 313, 286–91; Anthony Walton, *Mississippi: An American Journey* (New York: Vintage, 1996), 267. Spencer's memoir was first published by Random House in 1998. The southern literary scholar Fred Hobson convincingly interprets Spencer's book within the context of what he calls the southern antiracist conversion narrative, books by post–World War II authors like Will Campbell, Willie Morris, Lillian Smith, Kathrine Du Pre Lumpkin, and many others renouncing racism; Fred C. Hobson, *But Now I See: The White Southern Racial Conversion Narrative* (Baton Rouge: LSU Press, 1999). For essays on Till in fiction, see Harriet Pollack and Christopher Metress, *Emmett Till in Literary Memory and Imagination* (Baton Rouge: LSU Press, 2008).

18 Bill Minor, "Saga of Till Slaying Will Live on Despite Death of 2nd Killer," *Jackson Clarion-Ledger*, Sept. 25, 1994, C3.

19 Paul Hendrickson, "Mississippi Haunting," *Washington Post Magazine*, Feb. 27, 2000, 13–18, 26–27.

20 Richard Rubin, "The Ghosts of Emmett Till," *New York Times Magazine*, July 31, 2005, http://www.nytimes.com/2005/07/31/magazine/the-ghosts-of-emmett-till.html.

21 Brundage, *Southern Past*, 270–74, 290–94, 301–15.

22 Romano and Raiford, *Civil Rights Movement*, esp. Jennifer Fuller's "Debating the Present Through the Past," 167–96.

23 "Chicago Park Name Sought for Slain Negro," *Anderson (IN) Herald-Bulletin*, Oct. 6, 1955, 9; "Would Name Park for Murdered Boy," *Logansport (IN) Press*, Oct. 6, 1955, 4.

24 Jerry Mitchell, "Trash or Treasure? Fate of Historic Till Site Unsure,"
Jackson Clarion-Ledger, Feb. 29, 2004, 8a; Emily Wagster Pettus,
"Store in Till Case May Get Marker," *Jackson Clarion-Ledger*, Mar. 23,
2006, 1b; "Plans Discussed for Restoring Old Bryant's Grocery,
Linked to Till Case," *Jackson Clarion-Ledger*, Apr. 7, 2007, 2b;
"Activists Hope to Turn Till Church into Landmark," *Jackson Clarion-
Ledger*, Nov. 20, 2005, 5a; "Mayor Hopes to Create Till Tourist
Center," *Delta Democrat-Times*, Sept. 27, 2005, A1; Timothy R. Brown,
"Emmett Till Park to Open in Glendora," *Jackson Clarion-Ledger*, Sept. 17,
2008, 2b; "Memorable Photos from the Ebony Files," *Ebony*, July
2004, 186. For Delta State's Till exhibit and archive, see http://www.
deltastate.edu/academics/libraries/university-archives-museum/
traveling-exhibit/emmett-till-traveling-exhibit-host-site-assistance.
The story about the sign on the Tallahatchie River being shot up
went viral on the web in October 2016; see for example, http://
www.cnn.com/2016/10/22/us/mississippi-emmett-till-sign-bullets/
index.html.
25 Network coverage from CNN, ABC, and NBC is readily available in
the Vanderbilt Television News Archive, Motion Picture Reading
Room, LC; Timothy R. Brown, "Till Slaying Focus of Documentary,"
Jackson Clarion-Ledger, Jan. 12, 2003, 1a; Tommie Jackson, "Upcoming
PBS Documentary Recounts Saga of Emmett Till," *Clarksdale Press
Register*, n.p., n.d., in SERS.
26 *The Murder of Emmett Till*, Stanley Nelson, dir., Firelight Media, 2003.
See also, "The Ghost of Emmett Till," Mar. 22, 2004, and "What
Happened to Emmett Till," May 12, 2004, both in *New York Times*, at
http://www.nyt.com; Jerry Mitchell, "Filmmaker to Show Movie on
Emmett Till," *Jackson Clarion-Ledger*, Feb. 7, 2004, 1.
27 *The Untold Story of Emmett Louis Till*, Keith Beauchamp, dir., Till
Freedom Come Productions, 2005.
28 Maria Newman, "U.S. to Reopen Investigation of Emmett Till's
Murder in 1955," *New York Times*, May 10, 2004; "Till Kin Pleased
about Reopening of Case," *New York Times*, May 11, 2004; Eric
Lichtblau and Andrew Jacobs, "U.S. Reopens '55 Murder Case,
Flashpoint of Civil Rights Era," *New York Times*, May 11, 2004;
Andrew Jacobs, "In Mississippi Delta Town, an Unwelcome Past
Calls," *New York Times*, May 12, 2004; Robin Finn, "Putting History on
Film and a Crime in Court," *New York Times*, May 21, 2004, all at
www.nyt.com.
29 In addition to the *New York Times* articles cited in n. 28, see "Emmett
Till: Blacks React to Reopening of Tragic Case," *Jet*, May 31, 2004,
7–10, 60–62; David Van Biema, "Revisiting a Martyrdom," *Time*, May
24, 2004, 57; Jerry Mitchell, "Probe of Till Slaying to Reopen," *Jackson
Clarion-Ledger*, May 11, 2004, 1; Jerry Mitchell, "Group Seeks to
Exhume Till Body," *Jackson Clarion-Ledger*, Oct. 31, 2004, 1; Ana
Radelat, "Lawmaker Says He'll Press AG over Till Probe," *Jackson
Clarion-Ledger*, Nov. 20, 2004, 1; Laura Parker, "DA Has Tough, Final
Call in Till Case," *USA Today*, Mar. 27, 2006, 3-a; Gary Younge, "US
Reopens Murder Case That Lit Civil Rights Fuse," *Guardian Online*,

May 11, 2004; Younge, "Justice At Last?" *Guardian Online*, June 6, 2005. The popular CBS news program *60 Minutes* covered the story with a segment called "Justice, Delayed but Not Denied," which aired on Oct. 21, 2004., https://johnsville.blogspot.com/2004/05/murder-of-emmett-till.html.

CHAPTER THIRTY-FOUR

1 The FBI's Prosecutive Report of Investigation (hereafter Prosecutive Report), which includes the 1955 trial transcript from Sumner, can be found at https://vault.fbi.gov/Emmett%20Till%20/Emmett%20 Till%20Part%2001%20of%2002/view. The names of most informants and even the number identifying the agent who signed the report were redacted; it is dated Feb. 9, 2006. The full raw Till case on which the summary report is based is about ten-thousand pages long. Through an FOIA request to the FBI, I was able to obtain some of the raw documents, several hundred pages in total. Much of the testimony is heavily redacted. FBI Records Management Division, FOIPA #1216596. The case was assigned two numbers, 44A-JN-30112, and 62D-JN-30045-SF302 (for reference, I use the former). The full FBI Till case file is not yet available to the public. I received the selected and redacted documents on CDs in Aug. 2015. Far from clarifying every question about the case, these documents leave many unanswered and raise some new ones. But certain things are clear, above all that William Bradford Huie's account of the hours between 2:00 a.m. and dawn on Aug. 28, 1955, was hopelessly flawed.

2 This information is available in the FBI summary of the case: https:// vault.fbi.gov/Emmett%20Till%20.

3 FBI, 44A-JN-30112.94, u.i., 9/9/2004, n.l., 21–23; 44A-JN-30112.496, u.i., 8/16/04, Drew, MS, 55 (these notations refer to the raw FBI files obtained through my FOIA request; after the Till file number—44A-JN-30112—comes the interview number, then the informant's name or the letters u.i. meaning unidentified informant, next the day of the interview or n.d. where no date was indicated, the place where the interview took place or the letters n.l. if no location was given, and the page numbers of the interview transcription). Stephen Whitaker writes that when he interviewed Tallahatchie residents in 1962, he found that they mostly disliked Milam and Bryant, were afraid of them, and referred to them as "white trash" and "peckerwoods"; "A Case Study in Southern Justice," 144. On race and the small grocery stores, see James W. Loewen's insightful discussion in *The Mississippi Chinese: Between Black and White* (Long Grove, IL: Waveland Press, 2nd ed., 1988), 46–53.

4 Prosecutive Report, 26–28. One of the FBI's informants was Bonnie Blue, a Chicagoan who became interested in Till while in college in the late 1970s. Ms. Blue published her research in *Emmett Till's Secret Witness: FBI Confidential Source Speaks* (Park Forest, IL: B. L. Richey

Publishing, 2013). Ms. Blue describes having four telephone conversations with J. W. Milam, the tapes of which no longer exist. Her book is a difficult source to evaluate, and she calls it a "non-fictional novel." Some dialogue clearly is made up, and there are things she gets wrong, such as the condition of Emmett's body and the presence of an audience sitting in bleachers to watch his torture and murder; the physical evidence uncovered in the FBI contradicts this part of her account. But many of her details about who participated, where, when, and how are confirmed by other sources.

5 Prosecutive Report, 26–27, 92–93; the name of Leslie Milam's confessor was redacted in the FBI files.

6 Ibid., 28–30.

7 Ibid.

8 Ibid., 106–7.

9 Ibid., 108–9. J. W. Milam's son Horace made the claim about shooting bumblebees; 44A-JN-30112.512, Ocean Springs, MS, Aug. 25, 2004, 4.

10 Prosecutive Report, 110–12; 44-A-JN-30112.101, u.i., Aug. 31, 2005, Warwick, RI; 44A-JN-30112.94, u.i., 9/9/2004, n.l., 20–21; 44A-JN-30112.518, u.i., June 20, 2005, Chicago. This last witness appears to be Bonnie Blue, author of *Emmett Till's Secret Witness*.

11 On trauma and history, see Dominick LaCapra, *Writing History, Writing Trauma* (Baltimore: Johns Hopkins University Press, repr. 2014); Anthony S. Parent and Ulrike Wiethaus, eds., *Trauma and Resilience in American Indian and African American Southern History* (New York: Peter Lang, 2013); Steven High, ed., *Beyond Testimony and Trauma: Oral History in the Aftermath of Mass Violence* (Vancouver: University of British Columbia Press, repr. ed., 2015).

12 44-A-JN-30112.483, u.i., Mar. 31, 2005, Chicago, 1–18; 44A-JN-30112.484, u.i., n.l., n.d., 1–6; 44A-JN-30112.56, u.i., 5/17/2004, Tallahatchie County.

13 44-A-JN-30112.496, u.i., Aug. 16, 2004, Drew, MS, 41–56.

14 44-A-JN-30112.497, u.i., Sept. 2, 2004, Detroit, 3–34.

15 44-A-JN-30112.57, u.i., May 11, 2004, Oxford, MS, 1–2. The same informant was interviewed again, but the file number was garbled in the original. The precise file number is between 546 and 552, u.i., Sept. 1, 2004, Detroit, 15–26.

16 44-A-JN-30112.482, Feb. 12, probably 2005, probably Dayton, OH, 7–11, 14–22, 36–37, 41–43.

17 This theme weaves in and out of Sokol, *There Goes My Everything*, 3–113, and Cobb, *The Most Southern Place on Earth*, 209–29.

18 Deputy John Ed Cothran was unaware that there was a warrant for Carolyn Bryant written by his boss, but the agents who interviewed Cothran knew about the warrant from old FBI files; 44-A-JN-30112.499, John Ed Cothran, Aug. 12, 2004, Moorhead, MS. For Carolyn Bryant, see 44A-JN-30112.513, July 16, 2004, Greenville, MS, and 44A-JN-30112.533, June 9, 2005, Greenville, MS. For Juanita Milam, see 44A-JN-30112.498, Ocean Springs, MS, Aug. 25, 2004. After she divorced and remarried, Carolyn Bryant changed her name to Carolyn Donham. However, for clarity's sake I refer to her as Carolyn Bryant. The interviews with Carolyn Bryant and Juanita

Milam were redacted, their names blacked out, but their identities are unmistakable.

19 44-A-JN-30112.533, June 9, 2005, Greenville, MS, 2–22, 36–42.

20 Ibid., 16–30, 52, 67, 137. The agents even asked her to consider hypnosis; Carolyn was willing, she said, but her children feared it might raise traumatic memories.

21 44-A-JN-30112.498, Aug. 25, 2004, Ocean Springs, MS, 10, 22–34, 42–52.

22 Ibid.

23 Ibid.

24 Ibid., 53–54. A truncated and redacted version appears in Prosecutive Report, 42.

25 Wright, *Simeon's Story*, 50–51; FBI Prosecutive Report, 42–45. In Huie's "Approved Killing," J. W. Milam claimed that Till had a photo of a white girl in his wallet, and that he bragged that she was his girlfriend back in Chicago. Emmett's cousin Curtis Jones repeated the story and told others that some of Emmett's friends egged him on to proposition Carolyn Bryant. Emmett's cousins Wheeler Parker and Simeon Wright have consistently denied these stories; during the entire time they were with him in Mississippi, Emmett never showed such a photo or made such boasts, and no one egged him on to say anything to Carolyn Bryant; LC, Parker, Civil Rights History Project interview, 9–15; Wright, Civil Rights History Project interview, 10–11.

26 Prosecutive report, 30; Tyson, *The Blood of Emmett Till*, 1–7, 51–55.

27 Prosecutive Report, 30; Tyson, *Blood of Emmett Till*, 35–59, gives by far the fullest account of the Milam-Bryant clan.

28 44-A-JN-30112.533, June 9, 205, Greenville, MS.

29 44-A-JN-30112.512, 8/25/2004, Ocean Springs, MS.

30 Joe Atkins and Tom Brennan, "Emmett Till: More than a Murder," *Jackson Clarion-Ledger*, Aug. 25, 1985, 1H, available online at http://www.emmetttillmurder.com/new-page-12/.

31 Prosecutive Report, 91–92.

32 Laura Parker, "DA Has Tough Final Call in Till Case," *USA Today*, Mar. 27, 2006, 3; Jerry Mitchell, "Grand Jury Issues No Indictment in Till Killing," *Jackson Clarion-Ledger*, Feb. 27, 2007, 1; William Browning, "Till Jury Talks: Grand Jurors Say Evidence Wasn't There to Indict," *Greenwood Commonwealth*, Sept. 30, 2007, 1.

EPILOGUE

1 Anderson, *Emmett Till*, summarizes many of these developments, 352–55. Also see Houck and Grindy's thoughtful assessment in *Emmett Till and the Mississippi Press*, 4, 153–65. *Southern Quarterly* published a special memorial issue, edited by Philip C. Kolin, "The Legacy of Emmett Till," *Southern Quarterly* 45, no. 4 (Summer 2008). There are far too many new Till references to include here, but for

some examples see "Local Leaders Officially Apologize for Till's Murder Trial," Oct. 2, 2007, http://www.meridianstar.com/local-leaders-officially-apologize-for-till-s-murder-trial/article_e8a87c4e-698b-5b72-8c25-42bd4ae9e79c.html; "Emmett Till Unsolved Civil Rights Crime Act of 2007," Public Law 110-344-Oct. 7, 2008, H.R. 923, https://www.congress.gov/110/plaws/publ344/PLAW-110publ344.pdf.

2 On historic preservation efforts, see Charles Sheehan, "Till Rites Site Could Become a Landmark," *Chicago Tribune*, Nov. 1, 2005, 2C; Jay Koziarz, "Preservationists Seek Landmark Protection for Emmett Till's Chicago Home," Nov. 14, 2017, in Curbed Chicago, a website at Chicago.curbed.com; Jerry Mitchell, "Another Emmett Till Sign Attacked—and This Time Erased," blog post at www.clarionledger.com/blog/journeytojustice/ June 26, 2017; Peter Holley, "An Emmett Till Historical Marker in Mississippi Was Destroyed by Vandals—Again," *Washington Post*, June 26, 2017, https://www.washingtonpost.com/news/post-nation/wp/2017/06/26/an-emmett-till-historical-marker-in-mississippi-was-destroyed-by-vandals-again/?utm_term=.3c487f96071a.

3 Anderson, *Emmett Till*; John Edgar Wideman, *Writing to Save a Life*; Tyson, *Blood of Emmett Till*; David Holmberg, "In Era of Black Lives Matter, Films Focus on Emmett Till Lynching," *New York Times* online, Aug. 30, 2016; *My Nephew Emmett*, 2017, directed by Kevin Wilson Jr., http://www.imdb.com/title/tt6598290/. Anderson, *Emmett Till*, 361–80, includes a brief appendix to sort out the conflicting evidence of what Emmett did or did not do in Bryant's Grocery Store, who was in the barn beating him, and so forth.

4 Krissah Thompson, "Emmett Till's Casket a 'Sacred Object' at the African American Museum," *Chicago Tribune*, Aug. 19, 2016, *Tribune* online, originally from the *Washington Post*; Rebekah Barber, "The Living Legacy of Emmett Till's Casket," @Facing South, Aug. 26, 2016; Erika Blount Danois, "The National Museum of African American History and Culture Opens, Housing 'Sacred' Objects," *The Root* (online), Sept. 24, 2016; Judith Weisenfeld, "Religion on Display at the National Museum of African American History and Culture," *Sacred Matters, Religious Currents in Culture* (online) Jan. 3, 2017; "Oprah: There's a New Emmett Till Every Day Now," TMZ Online, Sept. 23, 2016, http://www.tmz.com/2016/09/23/oprah-emmett-till-african-american-museum/.

5 "Oprah: There's a New Emmett Till,"; official release from the office of Representative John Lewis, http://www.lexisnexis.com.flagship.luc.edu/hottopics/lnacademic/.

6 The comparison of Emmett Till and Trayvon Martin was ubiquitous, as evidenced in the compendium in *Reader's Almanac*, "Linking the Deaths of Emmett Till and Travon Martin: Meaningful or Misleading?" Mar. 26, 2012, http://blog.loa.org/2012/03/deaths-of-emmett-till-and-trayvon.html. Also see Peter Dreier, "Will the Killing of Trayvon Martin Catalyze a Movement Like Emmett Till Did?" *Huffington Post* blog, Sept. 19, 2013. http://www.huffingtonpost.com/

peter-dreier/will-the-murder-of-trayvo_b_3628274.html; "Beyoncé Compares Trayvon Martin to Emmett Till," *History News Network,* originally from BBC News, July 22, 2013, http://historynewsnetwork. org/article/152728. There were several side-by-side versions of the photo of Emmett and Trayvon revealed by a web search of their names.

7 See, for examples, Isabel Wilkerson, "Emmett Till and Tamir Rice, Sons of the Great Migration," *New York Times,* Feb. 12, 2016, https:// www.nytimes.com/2016/02/14/opinion/sunday/emmett-till-and-tamir-rice-sons-of-the-great-migration.html; Allyson Hobbs, "The Power of Looking, From Emmett Till to Philando Castile," *New Yorker,* Aug. 5, 2016, https://www.newyorker.com/news/news-desk/the-power-of-looking-from-emmett-till-to-philando-castile; Holmberg, "Era of Black Lives Matter," Aug. 30, 2016; "The Photo That Proved a Black Life Matters," *Time,* 74–75; Jamelle Bouie, "White Won," *Slate,* Nov. 9, 2016, https://www.nytimes.com/2016/11/11/books/review-they-cant-kill-us-all-tallies-the-unarmed-black-men-shot-by-police. html.

8 On the Black Lives Matter movement and its origins, try Jelani Cobb, "The Matter of Black Lives," *New Yorker,* Mar. 14, 2016, http://www. newyorker.com/magazine/2016/03/14/where-is-black-lives-matter-headed.

9 For a fine discussion of institutional racism, planted deep in society and culture, using Birmingham, Alabama, in 1963 as an example, see Diane McWhorter's "Good and Evil in Birmingham," *New York Times,* Jan. 21, 2013, A21.

10 Jonathan Chait, "Donald Trump's Race War," *New York* magazine, Apr. 4, 2017, http://nymag.com/daily/intelligencer/2017/04/trump-is-failing-at-policy-but-winning-his-race-wars.html; Michelle Alexander, *The New Jim Crow: Mass Incarceration in the Age of Colorblindness* (New York: New Press, 2010).

11 Bryan Stevenson, *Just Mercy: A Story of Justice and Redemption* (New York: Spiegel and Grau, 2014); Ta-Nehisi Coates, *Between the World and Me* (New York: Spiegel and Grau, 2015).

12 For example, the *Chicago Sun-Times* carried a front-page headline, "Why No Justice for Emmett Till," Sept. 18, 2017. Some of the best recent reporting on Till has been done by Jerry Mitchell. See, for example, his "Justice Department May Reopen Emmett Till Case," *Jackson Clarion-Ledger,* Apr. 5, 2017, http://www.clarionledger.com/story/news/local/journeytojustice/2017/04/04/justice-department-may-reopen-emmett-till-case/100039882/.

13 Scott Cacciola and Jonah Engel Bromwich, "Act of Vandalism Puts James in Pensive Place," *New York Times,* June 1, 2017, B12; Jerry Brewer, "Racist Vandals Didn't Demean LeBron James; They Gave Him a Platform for Dialogue," *Washington Post,* June 1, 2017, online edition.

14 Dave Chappelle, *Equanimity,* 2017, directed by Stan Lathan, https:// www.netflix.com/title/80230402.

15 The controversy over the Schutz painting was covered in the newspapers and on television. See, for example, Randy Kennedy,

"Painting of Emmett Till Draws Protests," *New York Times*, Mar. 22, 2017, C1; Oliver Basciano, "Whitney Biennial: Emmett Till Casket Painting by White Artist Sparks Anger," *Guardian* online edition, Mar. 21, 2017. Some of the best commentary was to be found in the online journal of the arts, *Hyperallergic*, for example. Anya Garemko-Greenwold, "Protesters Block, Demand Removal of a Painting of Emmett Till at Whitney Biennial," *Hyperallergic*, Mar. 22, 2017, https://hyperallergic.com/367012/protesters-block-demand-removal-of-a-painting-of-emmett-till-at-the-whitney-biennial/?utm_source=twitter&utm_campaign=wt&utm_medium=link

16 *Hyperallergic* also covered the criticism directed at Schutz's critics, especially this long article by the artist Coco Fusco: "Censorship, Not the Painting, Must Go: Dana Schutz's Image of Emmett Till," Mar. 27, 2017, https://hyperallergic.com/368290/censorship-not-the-painting-must-go-on-dana-schutzs-image-of-emmett-till/ c.

17 Adam Green focuses on the photographs in his discussion of simultaneity at Emmett's funeral in *Selling the Race*, 179–210. Also see Shaila Dewan, "How Photos Became Icon of Civil Rights Movement."

INDEX

Page numbers in italics refer to illustrations.

Leflore kidnapping trial
arraignment, 176–77
grand jury testimony and verdict,
219–21, 229
Loggins and Collins disappearance and, 180
Louis Till rape story and, 206
Moses Wright as witness, 218
murder trial handling of, 75, 174
Lewis, Alfred Baker, 192
Lewis, John, 261–62
Licorish, David, 190
life insurance policies, 122
Life magazine, 58, 84, 201, 218
Lightfoot, Claude, 43
Lilly, J. Robert, 208
Loggins, Henry Lee, 129–32, 180–81, 277,
280–81
Look magazine, 237–48, 252, 254–55
Loretha (cousin of Emmett), 17
Los Angeles Tribune, 230
lynching
alleged FBI actions against, 229–30
black improvement narrative and, 38–39
federal anti-lynching initiative, 42–43, 190,
214, 217, 230–31, 243–44
history of racial lynching, 37, 45
Jim Crow deterrent-to-lynching argument,
45–46, 65
Mississippi associatiion with, 15, 24
Till murder as, 3–6, 31, 81
Till murder effect on, 274
Tuskegee files on, 41
verdict as endorsment of, 178
See also Jim Crow segregation

Malcolm X, 264
Malone, H. D. (embalmer), 158–61
March on Washington, 261
Marquette, Jacques, 12
Marshall, Thurgood, 51–52, 214, 228
Martin, Trayvon, 292
Matthews, Bishop (juror), 90–91
McCarthy, Joseph, 224
McDonald, Laquan, 292
Meany, George, 192
media
black history movement, 275–76
black press trial coverage, 18, 64–65, 84–85,
128, 175
black response to "Approved Killing" (Huie),
259–60
black response to verdicts, 183–84
decline of interest in Till, 249–50,
255–56, 270
historical tracking of publications, 249–50
Huie "Approved Killing" and, 235–40,
243–45, 252, 257–58, 280

international Till coverage, 197–200
kidnapping trial coverage, 220–21
literary and fictional accounts,
255–56, 274
local coverage of funeral, 65–67
local coverage of Till disappearance, 30–32
Louis Till rape story, 201–10, 213,
218, 222
national media treatment at trial, 82, 83–85
South as "real victim" in, 41–42, 66
southern response to verdicts, 179–80,
182–83
Till photo in, 1–2, 62–63
trial as civil rights media event, 83–85
white media response to murders, 39–40,
54–55
See also photos; television
Melnick, Curtis (school principal), 19
Melton, Clinton, 251–52, 280
Melton, Garland (deputy sheriff), 9, 103–4
Memphis Clarion-Ledger, 184
Memphis Commercial Appeal, 198, 207, 221
Memphis Press-Scimitar, 84, 90, 124, 220–21
Milam, Juanita, 26, 86, 146, 149, 151, 175,
284–87, 290
Milam, J. W. "Big"
arrest and arraignment, 73, 113
Clinton Melton murder and, 251
comments after verdict, 175, 177
confession by, 242–47, 254
decision not to testify, 151
Huie interview, 240–45
jail conditions, 72
"Judas Nigger" incitement rumor, 28
liquor and gambling business, 85
as local character, 86–87
media treatment of, 33–34
as peckerwood, 279–80
post-trial life, 219, 254–55
testimony about, 96–99
Willie Reed sighting of, 135–41
Milam, Leslie, 130–31, 133, 178, 279–80
Miller, Chester A. (undertaker), 97–98, 103–8,
117–18
Milner, Jay, 245, 256
Milwaukee Journal, 221
Mims, B. L. (Till family landlord), 9, 10,
103–4, 109
Minor, Bill, 84, 273–75
Minoso, Minnie, 17–18
Mississippi Council of Negro Leadership, 39
Mitchell, Clarence, 228
Mitchell-Turner, Nannie, 84
Mobley, Gene (husband of Mamie), 19, 56
Money, Mississippi, 24–29, 31, 276–77,
290–91
Montgomery Advertiser, 207